W9-BYK-657

ULTIMATE ADVENTURES

A ROUGH GUIDE TO ADVENTURE TRAVEL

by Greg Witt

PORTER COUNTY PUBLIC LIBRARY

Portage Public Library
2665 Irving Street
Portage, IN 46368

NF   910.202 WIT   POR
Witt, Greg, 1952-
Ultimate adventures : a rough
33410010160887   JAN 2 0 2009

ROUGH GUIDES

LONDON • NEW YORK • DELHI
www.roughguides.com

PUBLISHING INFORMATION

This 1st edition published August 2008 by
Rough Guides Ltd, 80 Strand, London WC2R 0RL
345 Hudson St, 4th Floor, New York, NY 10014, USA
14 Local Shopping Centre, Panchsheel Park, New Delhi 110017, India
Distributed by the Penguin Group
Penguin Books Ltd, 80 Strand, London WC2R 0RL
Penguin Group (USA) 375 Hudson Street, NY 10014, USA
Penguin Group (Australia) 250 Camberwell Road, Camberwell, Victoria 3124, Australia
Penguin Books Canada Ltd, 10 Alcorn Avenue, Toronto, Ontario, Canada M4V 1E4
Penguin Group (NZ) 67 Apollo Drive, Mairangi Bay, Auckland 1310, New Zealand
Typeset in Egyptienne and Berthold Akzidenz Grotesque to an original design by Diana Jarvis
Printed and bound in China
© Greg Witt 2008
No part of this book may be reproduced in any form without permission from the publisher
except for the quotation of brief passages in reviews.
376pp includes index
A catalogue record for this book is available from the British Library
ISBN: 978-1-85828-199-5
The publishers and authors have done their best to ensure the accuracy and currency of all the
information in **Ultimate Adventures**, however, they can accept no responsibility
for any loss, injury, or inconvenience sustained by any traveler as a result of information or advice contained in the guide.

1   3   5   7   9   8   6   4   2

CREDITS

Editors: Steven Horak, Andrew Rosenberg **Picture editor**: Nicole Newman **Design and layout**: Diana Jarvis **Cartography**: Katie Lloyd-Jones
Cover design: Chloë Roberts **Production**: Rebecca Short **Proofreaders**: Anna Leggett, Susannah Wight
Additional design input: Michelle Bhatia, Sarah Cummins, Scott Stickland, Emily Taylor, Mark Thomas
Contributing editors: Stephen Timblin, Seph Petta, Natasha Foges, Paula Neudorf
Contributing writers: Victor Borg, Roger Norum, James Smart, Keith Drew,
Polly Evans, Scott Stickland, Rob Coates, Rosalba O'Brien, Mike Leung, Sara Humphreys

AUTHOR ACKNOWLEDGMENTS

I appreciate the hundreds of guides, outfitters, mountaineers, explorers, divemasters, cavers, rangers, and naturalists whose expertise and passion enliven and
inform these pages. Thanks to Serene Leavitt, Travis Austin, Ty Campbell, Dawnee Burson, and Kent West for research and editorial assistance.
And to my wife Elain, thank you for your inspiration, diligence, and support.

PUBLISHER'S NOTE

Realizing the double-edged impact of travel, we've tried to encourage responsible travel throughout this book and the need to limit your environmental
impact and to be respectful and sensitive to local cultures. In all of the accounts we've listed guides, outfitters, or tour operators who can assist you in
having a great experience. These operators have been identified as reputable, experienced, reliable and environmentally responsible service providers
whose expertise and on-site capabilities can be invaluable.

CONTACT US

If you think you've got an experience worthy of consideration as an ultimate adventure – or want to give your own take on one of the adventures included
– we'd love to hear from you. If you want to submit photos of your experience, all the better.

Send in suggestions to ©ultimateavdentures@roughguides.com.

Contents

We do not live to eat and make money. We eat and make money in order to be able to enjoy life. This is what life means and what life is for.

George Leigh Mallory

Think of this book as a field guide for living. Its purpose: to expand your world, rattle your cage, enlarge your soul, and inspire you to undertake some of the greatest outdoor experiences on earth. These are uncommon adventures for the common man. This book shows that you can do anything, given the right planning, information and, most importantly, the desire.

Ultimate Adventures contains an adventurer's life list – as much as they'll fire the imagination, these are, ultimately suggestions for travel. Every continent is covered, all kinds of activities are included: you'll explore canyons and mountains, deserts and oceans, bike on rutted roads, and charge down foamy rivers. And you'll never run out of ideas for more.

Each adventure included is designed to help you to escape, at least momentarily, the manmade world and to bring you face to face with the power of nature. You may be thrust into an unfamiliar environment with challenges and risks you won't find at home. You may squirm, sweat, shake, or do all three simultaneously. At some point along the way you may ask yourself: "What on earth was I thinking?" Consider that moment a rite of passage.

The completion of a great outdoor adventure is a physical achievement and a personal triumph – it's much more than just wind in your face or an adrenaline rush. It's doing what you love to do, and finding unexpected results. What you take from it goes well beyond the satisfaction of pushing your limits or becoming part of a select group. Adventure changes who you are from the inside out. First the mountains move you, and then you move mountains. So go, explore, discover, and get your heart pumping and your mind aroused. It may be the most rewarding thing you've ever done.

making the most of Ultimate Adventures

Ultimate Adventures contains the best and most achievable adventures on earth. We've organized the guide geographically, each section starting off with a map keying the locations for each adventure. The main accounts follow and are full of authoritative, evocative detail on what the adventure is like and what it takes to do it – in essence what makes it "ultimate". The **Is this for me?** box rates the adventure on a 1 to 5 scale for the following factors: **PHYSICAL** (the physical demands), **PSYCH** (the risk and emotional demands), **SKILL** (technical skills required) and **WOW!** (the enjoyment and excitement delivered). The **need to know** section gives you essential information to get started and tells you when to go, how to get there, and what you might want to read or view to gain a fuller picture. Each region concludes with a **best of the rest**, shorter capsules of adventures well worth your time and attention, followed by **miscellany**, which brings together all sorts of fun facts about the great outdoors. At the back is an **adventure calendar** followed by an **index** that organizes the adventures both by country and type of activity.

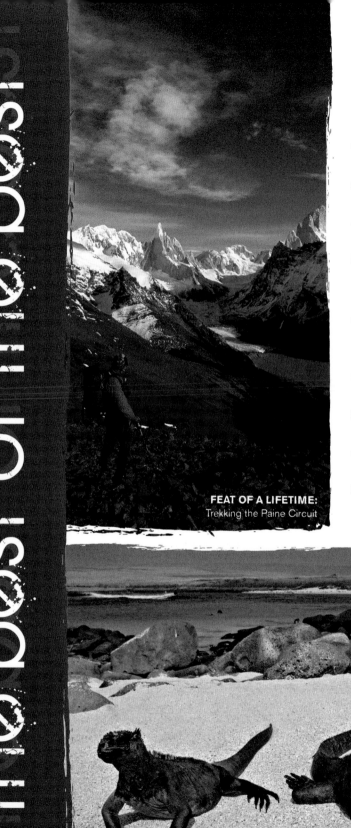

The best of the best

FEAT OF A LIFETIME:
Trekking the Paine Circuit

FAMILY ADVENTURE:
Wildlife viewing in the Galápagos

PHOTO OP:
Safari in the Okavango Delta

PHOTO OPS

ENERGY AND ENDURANCE

ENERGY AND ENDURANCE:
Trekking the GR20

MENTAL TOUGHNESS

MENTAL TOUGHNESS:
Expedition to the North Pole

USA & CANADA

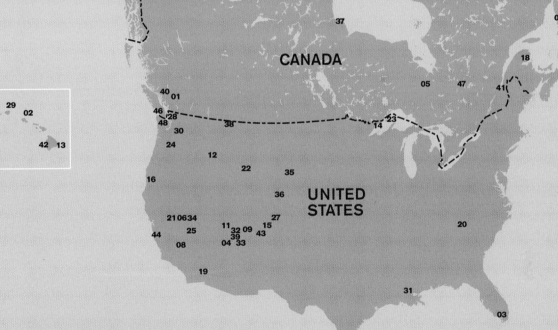

01 Heliskiing in British Columbia **02** Surfing Oahu's North Shore **03** Paddling the Everglades **04** Hiking the Grand Canyon rim to rim **05** Canoeing the Missinaibi River **06** Climbing El Capitan **07** Exploring Gros Morne **08** Kayaking the Kern River **09** Mountain biking the Slickrock Trail **10** Climbing Denali **11** Hiking the Zion Narrows **12** Rafting the Middle Fork of the Salmon River **13** Climbing Mauna Loa **14** Canoeing in the Boundary Waters **15** Skiing hut to hut in the Rockies **16** Hiking the Pacific Crest Trail **17** Sea kayaking the Kenai Fjords **18** Canoeing the Bonaventure River **19** Rock climbing in Joshua Tree **20** Hiking the Appalachian Trail **21** Rafting Cherry Creek **22** Climbing the Grand Teton **23** Exploring Isle Royale **24** Windsurfing in the Columbia River Gorge **25** Hiking the John Muir Trail **26** Dogsledding in the Yukon **27** Climbing Colorado's Fourteeners **28** Sea kayaking in the San Juan Islands **29** Hiking the Na Pali Coast **30** Climbing Mount Rainier **31** Paddling the Atchafalaya Basin **32** Exploring the Escalante Canyons **33** Running the Grand Canyon in a dory **34** Hiking Half Dome **35** Climbing Devils Tower **36** Hiking the Continental Divide Trail **37** Tracking polar bears in the tundra **38** Hiking in Glacier National Park **39** Canyoneering in Paria River and Buckskin Gulch **40** Rafting the Klinaklini River **41** Ice-climbing in Québec **42** Diving with manta rays in Kona **43** Mountain biking on the Kokopelli Trail **44** Bodysurfing Steamer Lane **45** Paddling Tatshenshini-Alsek Park **46** Hiking the West Coast Trail **47** Magpie river rafting **48** Hiking the Hoh Rainforest

Heliskiing in British Columbia

01

CANADA

VANCOUVER

>> Plunge into a sea of bottomless powder

As you step onto an icy summit, the whipped-up spindrift flicks in your face and settles in your collar. The clap of rotors quickly fades into the distance as you survey a panorama of sawtooth peaks, exposed cliffs, and – most importantly – slopes coated in layers of untracked snow. This is your moment, and you breathe in the chilled air before leaning forward to plunge into a sea of bottomless powder. Within seconds you're whooshing through wide-open bowls, blasting your way down small valleys, and braiding though stands of spruce.

the world's most dangerous sport?

What's the first thing that comes to mind when you see a 78-meter cliff? Jumping off it is probably way down on the list, but that was skier Jamie Pierre's plan in 2006 when he skied off of towering bluff just outside of Wyoming's Grand Targhee ski resort. Pierre shattered the previous world record for "hucking" a cliff, but amazingly shattered no bones after landing headfirst in a deep snowbank. But not everyone who slides down a mountain is as lucky as Pierre. Statistically speaking, skiing and snowboarding rank right near the top as the most dangerous sports. One recent study based on data from the US's National Safety Council calculated that there are an average of 34 deaths a year between skiers and snowboarders in the US alone, along with a whopping 135,000 injuries requiring medical attention. There's an ever-increasing list of more esoteric pursuits ranging from cave diving to bullriding that also top the list for danger, but for more mainstream adventures, alpine skiing and snowboarding are both a crippler and widow-maker.

It would be easy to call this the best run of your life, if the previous seven that day weren't just as good – you never even skied the same slope twice. You'd be lucky to get one or two runs like this in a week spent at a top resort, but with a helicopter as your chairlift and entire mountain ranges to explore, you've quickly become spoiled.

Heliskiing was conceived and developed in British Columbia in the 1960s as a new form of alpine ski touring. Today approximately ninety percent of all commercial heliskiing takes place in Canada's westernmost province, and the reasons for this are clear: abundant quantities of high-quality snow combined with massive amounts of exceptional backcountry terrain. Add sunny skies and fair temperatures to the mix and the result is paradise for avid skiers and snowboarders.

While heliskiing trips are run on mountain ranges throughout western Canada, the overall experience on any given tour is generally the same. Over breakfast in a cozy timbered lodge you discuss the awaiting terrain and potential runs with your guide. Maybe your idea of the perfect run is a steep alpine drop laced with a handful of small cliffs to jump along the way, or perhaps you'd rather go for the natural slalom of tree skiing. Difficult, if enviable, decisions having been made, it's time to head out to the helicopter for the day's first run. The breathtaking ride up to the drop-off point supplies the first thrills as you survey pristine mountains below, with no other souls in sight, then spend the rest of the morning carving laps through virgin snow. After a calorie-loaded lunch by the shores of a hidden lake, it's time for more before returning to the lodge by dusk. On a good day you might complete seven to ten runs, knocking off 4500 to 6000 vertical meters of terrain.

If your skiing or snowboarding experience is built around resorts, then the idea of bottomless snow may be new to you. With no groomed base underneath the freshly fallen snow, you'll discover that when you push your pole down it keeps on going. The weightlessness felt in floating through bottomless snow for the first time – puffs of powder blasting you in the face

British Columbia has over 114,000 square kilometers of parks and protected areas, an area three times the size of Switzerland.

need to know

Most packages are based out of a single lodge and serve a particular mountain range, and typically include transportation, accommodation, meals, and even a guarantee of vertical meters per day. HeliCat Canada (Ⓦ www.helicatcanada.com) is an industry association with information about heliskiing, safety, environmental concerns, and links to operators.

guides and gear Most skiers and snowboarders bring their own gear, with operators providing only avalanche safety equipment; rentals of deep powder skis and boards are sometimes available. TLH Heliskiing (Ⓣ 250/558-5379 or 1-800/667-4854, Ⓦ www.tlhheliskiing.com) offers two-to seven-day heliskiing packages at various lodges throughout British Columbia.

when to go Heliskiing trips are run from mid-December through mid-April, with some variation on either end based on weather conditions.

getting there Most heliskiing operators offer transport from Vancouver or Calgary airports to lodges in the region; the prime heliski areas are around Golden and Revelstoke, in the BC interior.

and with an arching rooster tail of snow in your wake – is enough to make you positively giddy. Wider, specially designed powder skis and snowboards should be used in such conditions as they make cutting through deep powder less of a struggle to stay afloat; they also make it easier to dig out after falling into the deep stuff – always a sweat-inducing chore.

Unlike resorts, the remote reaches of British Columbia's rugged mountains never see a ski patrol or avalanche control operations. Instead, you must place your faith in your guide to get you down the mountain safely. Skiing in the backcountry – whether heliskiing or under your own steam – always comes with avalanche risks, and having an expert on hand familiar with the current conditions is essential. Before the first day out, you'll take part in an intensive avalanche safety and rescue briefing. Each skier or boarder should be equipped with a small beacon used to transmit location in case they're caught in an avalanche. Top heliskiing operators also offer a new life-saving technology – avalanche airbags. If the worst occurs and you get caught in an avalanche, a quick pull of the cord attached to a small backpack causes a pair of large inflated wings to burst out, greatly increasing your chances of survival.

The risks involved in heliskiing are real, and even the best guides and equipment can't guarantee your safety. But that doesn't mean you need to be a world-class skier or snowboarder; strong intermediate skiers and snowboarders with some experience in powder are more than capable of joining in. That said, the better your overall conditioning, the more you'll be able to accomplish and the more enjoyable the experience will be. If you're not already in top shape, start getting there now; the majesty and serenity of the British Columbia backcountry is definitely worth it.

is this for me?

PHYSICAL ✦✦✦✦✦
Challenging conditions and extended runs

PSYCH ✦✦✦✦
Steep descents on unmarked slopes

SKILL ✦✦✦✦✦
Strong skiing skills essential

WOW! ✦✦✦✦
Spectacular scenery, exceptional skiing

Surfing Oahu's North Shore

02

>> Get out, get up, and ride

Since the arrival of Captain Cook in 1778, *haoles* – the Hawaiian term for foreigners – have been fascinated with the traditional Hawaiian sport of surfing. Long a preserve of ancient Hawaii's *ali'i* royalty, who proved their sovereignty by riding waves on giant planks of koa wood, the "sport of kings" entered a period of near extinction in the nineteenth century. Calvinist missionaries, who filled the vacuum left after the dismantling of Hawaii's caste system, preached that it was an affront to modesty and industry. The sport managed to grimly hang on, and Mark Twain couldn't resist trying when he visited the islands in 1866, as described in *Roughing It*: "I got the board placed right and at the right moment, too; but missed the connection myself. The board struck the shore in three-quarters of a second, without any cargo, and I struck the bottom about the same time, with a couple of barrels of water in me."

How would you like to stand like a god before the crest of a monster billow, always rushing to the bottom of a hill and never reaching its base, and to come rushing in for a half mile at express speed, in graceful attitude, until you reach the beach and step easily from the wave?

Duke Kahanamoku

The sport's fortunes changed thanks to Duke Kahanamoku, who started surfing in his home-waters of Oahu's Waikiki Beach. Kahanamoku gained world fame as an Olympic swimmer in the early 1900s and traveled the globe giving surfing shows from California to Australia. While "the father of surfing" created an international following, the sport was hamstrung by cumbersome, hundred-pound solid-wood boards. The creations of lighter boards – utilizing balsawood and polyurethane cores reinforced by fiberglass – fuelled the surf boom that swept the US in the 1960s. And while the popularity of surfing has since spread far beyond Hawaiian shores, the island of Oahu, and especially the legendary North Shore, remains the spiritual home of surfing.

As swells roll unobstructed across the Pacific from Japan and Alaska, they build strength to deliver their full impact on the fabled North Shore. During the winter months, when storm surges are at their peak, thirty-foot waves draw top surfers from around the world. But even when the monster waves are attracting competitors and spectators at places like Sunset Beach and the Banzai Pipeline, there are more tranquil beaches nearby where you can learn to surf in preparation for larger waves.

It looks so easy, so effortless, as a surfer catches a wave and gracefully rides it to shore. Don't be fooled; that kind of skill, especially on big waves, comes only with years of experience. Surfing requires upper body strength for paddling and swimming, good overall balance, and cardiovascular conditioning. Still, with the right equipment and good instruction, you should be able to stand up and ride a small wave on your first day out.

The most important surfing preparation happens before even entering the water. Take time to watch the surf, studying the swells and pinpointing where they are breaking. To get out to that point, look for a channel or slow rolling waves that will allow you to paddle out with the fewest hazards. Once beyond the shorebreak, center yourself on the board and paddle with long, elbow-deep strokes. Now for the part where it all comes together: when you've reached the break line, begin paddling on the swollen wave before it breaks. Once you feel caught in the momentum of the wave, it's time to stand up. Slide your dominant foot to the front of the board and pop up. Keep equal weight on both feet, a slight bend in your knees, and a low center of gravity – you're surfing!

monster waves

What was the biggest wave ever surfed? It's a question that many a surfer has mulled over, and nowadays there are surfers making big money trying to be the title-holder. No one knows the definitive answer, as not only is getting accurate wave measurements difficult, but not having a camera crew on call to confirm the size of the wave nullifies any claims. Starting in 1957, surfing icon Greg Noll used to consistently paddle into 25- to 30-foot waves on Waimea Bay at a time when the North Shore was unexplored territory for most surfers. In what's considered a seminal event for big-wave surfers, Noll arrived at Makaha on Oahu's west side on December 4, 1969, as a giant storm washed waves across the road. As these monstrous waves, estimated between forty and sixty feet high, pounded the shore and the radio began broadcasting evacuation orders for the homes in the area, Noll rode an estimated fifty-foot wave to shore on what he nonchalantly described as a "sea of glass."

But there comes a point where waves are so big and fast moving that its impossible for a paddle into them by hand – hence the invention of tow-in surfing. Originated in the mid-1990s, surfers are towed into giant waves by a jet-ski or helicopter with an attached towline. While purists argue that tow-in surfing is both polluting and cheating, it has allowed daring surfers to shatter big wave barriers. The legendary Laird Hamilton has been filmed riding waves upwards of 90ft, while wave warrior Ken Bradshaw is credited with an 85-foot encounter in 1998. With the tow-in technology pushing daredevils to search for ever-bigger waves, the hundred-foot ride can't be far off.

need to know

With an abundance of beaches and surf shops dotting a ten-mile stretch of coastline, Oahu's North Shore is the perfect spot to develop your surfing skills. The island's compact size and accessibility make finding a piece of paradise a snap. Beaches are public and parking, though not always ample, is available. Accommodations in either buzzing Honolulu or the laid-back North Shore are plentiful.

guides and gear Beginners should start with a board longer than 9ft as it will be more stable than shorter boards preferred by today's top riders. Located in Haleiwa, Surf Hawaii Surf School offers good private and group surfing instruction (☎ 808/295-1241, Ⓦ www. surfhawaii4u.com).

when to go Oahu's weather and water temperatures allow for year-round surfing, although November to February brings potential for storm surges and hazardous conditions at some of the prime spots. Local conditions should be checked daily.

getting there In good traffic, Oahu's North Shore beaches are a 45-minute drive from Honolulu.

suggested reading Bruce Jenkins, *North Shore Chronicles: Big-Wave Surfing in Hawaii* (Frog Books). A look at the surfing elite who have conquered Hawaii's deadliest waves. Guy Motil, *Surfboards* (Falcon Guides). Explores the history, technology, lore, and art of the surfboard. Matt Warshaw, *The Encyclopedia of Surfing* (Harvest Books). A pro surfer provides a comprehensive guide to all things surfing.

is this for me?

PHYSICAL ✦ ✦ ✦ ✦ ✦

Requires balance, coordination, paddling strength

PSYCH ✦ ✦ ✦ ✦ ✦

Big waves can be intimidating

SKILL ✦ ✦ ✦ ✦ ✦

Strong swimming skills and solid judgment

WOW! ✦ ✦ ✦ ✦ ✦

Exhilarating experience with exceptional conditions

On a good day, the North Shore delivers ideal conditions for surfers of all skills. Top spots for new riders include Puaena Point, Haleiwa, Chun's Reef, or Laniakea where the waves tend to be mellow. Even though you won't be facing huge waves, you'll still have long rides since the takeoff zone on some of these beaches is an impressive three to four hundred yards from shore. These breaks also have the advantages of being easy to read and having a safe bottom, mostly free from sharp coral and nasty rocks.

Once your riding reaches a more advanced level, it's time to take a dip with the legends at Waimea Bay or Sunset Beach, the former most likely to have the largest waves of any North Shore beach. On a good day Waimea Bay is home to ten- to twelve-foot waves, while on great day fifteen- to twenty-foot waves come crashing in. Sunset Beach is the widest white sand beach in Oahu with some of the island's longest wave breaks and an ever-lively beach scene. Another hot spot for experts is Ehukai Beach Park, where the legendary Banzai Pipeline forms a giant glistening tube in waves as they break onto a coral reef. It's a beautiful sight, and watching the best thread it can be alluring to surfers with intermediate skills. But beware, as the sheer power and water weight of a ten- to fifteen-foot wave can be deadly.

If you're going to surf with the big boys, be prepared to play by their rules. There's no one in uniform to direct traffic, so while paddling out remember that the surfer on the wave has the right of way – it's your job to get out of the way. When it comes to catching a wave, the best surfers get the best waves; don't try horning in on a wave that's clearly beyond your ability. Once on the wave, the right of way goes to the surfer closest to the peak; if that's not you, get out of the way. But the ultimate rule of surfing is that the surfer who rides the most waves wins. So get out, get up, and ride. Even on small waves the challenge and exhilaration of surfing is irresistible, and each day on the North Shore there are thousands of opportunities to come out a winner.

03 Paddling the Everglades

>> Catch the flip of a gator's tail

USA

EVERGLADES
NATIONAL PARK

The sight of an alligator several feet off the bow of your canoe is enough to get anyone's blood racing. Whether you find it exhilarating or frightening will likely be determined by the size of the gator and what it does next. If it's sunning itself on a bank, alarm will quickly turn to wonder, as your eyes meet and you hold the gaze of a creature that has changed little in the last few million years. Catching the lightning-fast flip of a gator's tail and a splash of water as it dives out of view can be a little more unsettling, however. Still, you're in the Everglades after all, and it's moments like this that drew you here.

restoration of the Everglades

The water in the Everglades once flowed from Lake Okeechobee to Florida Bay in a "river of grass" 120 miles long, fifty miles wide, and only a foot deep. As canals and levees built in the 1930s diverted the flow for agricultural and other human needs, the normal water levels were changed, turning marsh to dry ground. Hundreds of species' natural habitats and cycles of feeding and nesting were disturbed or destroyed entirely.

After years of dispute and stalled efforts, the plan to save the greatest wetland in North America was finally approved in 2000 under the Comprehensive Everglades Restoration Program (CERP). Paramount to restoring the wetland to its prior glory is to permit significantly more water – about twenty percent – to reach the Everglades. Dikes, dams, and levees once used for agricultural purposes are now being removed to increase the flow of water into the wetlands, and various government and conservation organizations are helping to see the plan through. It will take an estimated thirty years for enough water to enter the Everglades area to promote the return of plant and animal life to levels it was at before the waters were funneled out.

The Everglades, on the southern tip of Florida, is an expanse of sawgrass prairies, mangrove swamps, pinelands, coastal islands, and marine environments. It's both temperate and tropical, with a complex mix of fragile ecosystems found in a labyrinth of freshwater lakes and rivers, saltwater coastline, and brackish swamps. It's not a region bursting with breathtaking grandeur, majestic landforms and photogenic panoramas, but rather one with an understated and enduring beauty. In part, it's the lack of obvious individual scenic wonders that makes a trip here so rewarding. To really appreciate just how unique the Everglades is, you need to think in terms of days rather than hours, to arrive knowing that there will be no instant gratification. And if you really want to know this languid land, you'll need a canoe and arms ready to row.

The reserve is the flattest area in the United States, over a million acres where the landscape never exceeds 8ft above sea level, with a gradient of just an inch or two per mile and water that may only travel 100ft in a day – a paddler's paradise, to be sure. On multi-day loop trips you can explore mangrove swamps, grassy inlets and coastal islands and glimpse wildlife found nowhere else in North America. Some of the large wading birds at home in the Everglades include the roseate spoonbill, great blue heron, wood stork, and egrets. West Indian manatees, bottle-nosed dolphins, and even bull sharks can be seen in the deeper coastal waters. American crocodiles live here too, but are found only in the southern Flamingo area of the park; you can expect to see alligators throughout the Everglades, however. One Everglades species you're not like likely to see is the Florida panther, one of the rarest mammals on the planet, with less than fifty currently living in the wild.

It is a river of grass.
Marjorie S. Douglas

Before entering the Everglades, particularly on independent trips, you should be competent with map and compass navigation and have ample sunscreen, insect repellent, raingear, and a tent with insect netting. For an overnight stay in Everglades National Park, you'll need to obtain a permit at the Gulf Coast ranger station in Everglades City no more than 24 hours before you enter the water. Backcountry campsites can be found on beaches, ground sites, or on *chickees*, elevated wooden platforms built over water, which come with a roof and a self-contained toilet.

guides and gear If it's your first time in the Everglades backcountry, consider going with a guide. In Everglades City, Ivey House Eco Adventures (☎ 239/695-3299 or 1-877/567-0679, Ⓦ www.evergladesadventures.com) provides outfitting services for guided and independent trips. They rent canoes, kayaks, dry bags, cooking gear, water containers, and tents suitable for use on chickees. Food, nautical charts, fuel, and other supplies are also sold.

when to go Cooler temperatures from December through May make this the most enjoyable time to paddle through the Everglades.

getting there To access the Gulf side of the Everglades, fly into Fort Myers and drive seventy miles to Everglades City. Miami International Airport provides convenient access to the Everglades National Park main entrance and Flamingo.

suggested reading Michael Grunwald, *The Swamp: The Everglades, Florida, and the Politics of Paradise* (Simon & Schuster). Environmental journalism at its best in an examination of the spoiling and reclamation of the Everglades. Johnny Mollow, *A Paddler's Guide to Everglades National Park* (University of Florida Press). A detailed guided to the Everglades' 53 designated paddling routes.

The ultimate Everglades adventure can be had along the Wilderness Waterway, a 99-mile route that connects Everglades City on the Gulf side with Flamingo on the south. Departing from the park's Gulf Coast Visitor Center, you'll follow a chain of bays, rivers, channels, and open water that lead past white-sand fantasy islands, sawgrass prairies, mangrove forests, and even conifer woodlands. Numbered markers guide you through narrow channels made into tunnels with overhanging vegetation. Through quiet inland stretches the water is normally shallow enough for you to touch the bottom with your paddle, and even in the open water you can see the sandy bottom. Allow at least eight days for the trip in either direction, and remember that you'll need to carry all of your water with you, at least a gallon per person per day. Don't plan too many miles per day, know your limits, and remember that even in winter the sun can take its toll on you. Expect to be hot, tired, and sweaty at the end of the day.

If the prevailing wind, tides, and weather has worked in your favor, you'll arrive at the park's Flamingo Visitor Center eight or nine days after your put-in. Your skin will be encrusted with salt, pricked with mosquitoes, and roughed and reddened by hours in the sun and wind. You will have witnessed the delicate balance of life unfolding daily, but like everything in the Everglades, changes are subtle and often imperceptible. What will be noticeable, however, is that a shower is long overdue – hopefully you've rationed your water so you can wash up a bit before catching a shuttle back.

is this for me?

PHYSICAL ✦ ✦ ✦ ✦ ✦
Prolonged paddling

PSYCH ✦ ✦ ✦ ✦ ✦
In the land of alligators

SKILL ✦ ✦ ✦ ✦ ✦
Navigational skills required

WOW! ✦ ✦ ✦ ✦ ✦
Surprising encounters, unique environment

Hiking the Grand Canyon rim to rim

>> Crossing the chasm on foot

USA

● GRAND CANYON

Every year nearly five million people travel to the Grand Canyon, making it the western United States' most visited national park. They stand at designated viewpoints and admire what from these distances is a rather flat, one-dimensional display of geologic majesty. But the view from the rim doesn't give a hint at the variety of wonders that await those who drop below and actually come face-to-face with the canyon's inner sanctum at the Colorado River, nearly a vertical mile below.

Grand Canyon National Park receives about 50,000 requests for 13,000 available backcountry permits each year. If you're not one of the lucky few who receives a permit, but you'd still like to delve deeply into the canyon you are left with one daunting prospect: a one-day rim-to-rim crossing of the Grand Canyon. With this option there will be no campsite available below the rim, important to note if you run out of steam before making it out of the canyon. There is no easy way out, no simple Plan B if things go south at the Colorado River.

no easy feat

Although park officials publish warnings on the potential dangers and difficulty of one-day rim-to-rim hikes, they estimate that some 20,000 people per year perform this feat. Park rangers rescue about five hundred debilitated hikers annually, most of whom enter the canyon unprepared for the challenge. The ascent out of the canyon at the end of the hike is particularly brutal, and portions of it may be in the blistering heat of mid-afternoon. Even in the spring and fall, temperatures in excess of 100°F are common near the canyon floor. Consequently, timing plays an important part in a successful rim-to-rim. Many hikers leave the rim in the near-freezing temperatures of pre-dawn to avoid the midday heat.

Both heatstroke and heat exhaustion are very real risks, so be sure to carry at least a liter of water and drink and refill at every opportunity. Because you can sweat a liter per hour walking in the heat, there is also the risk of hyponatremia from drinking too much water and depleting the body's stores of electrolytes. Combat this deadly threat by maintaining your caloric intake, particularly with salty foods like pretzels and peanuts.

need to know

The majority of hikers completing a rim-to-rim route do it in one day, and either camp or reserve accommodation at both ends. If you don't have a shuttle vehicle, TransCanyon Shuttle (☎928/638-2820) provides daily shuttle service between the North and South Rim from mid-May to mid-Oct.

guides and gear If you want to make your rim-to-rim experience a longer backpacking trip, contact Grand Canyon National Park Backcountry Office (☎928/638-7875, ⓦ www.nps.gov/grca/planyourvisit/backcountry.htm), where backcountry permit forms and application procedures are available online. Grand Canyon Hikes (☎928/779-1614 or 1-877/506-6233, ⓦ www.grandcanyonhikes.com) offers a wide variety of single and multi-day hikes in the Grand Canyon on a year-round basis for hikers of all experience and skill levels. They provide gear, food, permits, and medically-trained guides.

when to go From May through June and from September through October you have services available at the North Rim, yet avoid the sweltering and potentially deadly heat of summer in the depth of the Grand Canyon.

getting there For a trek starting at the South Rim, fly into Flagstaff, Arizona, with shuttle services available to the South Rim. For North Rim departures, fly into Page, Arizona or Kanab, Utah. Shuttle services are available to the South or North Rim.

suggested reading Thomas M. Myers and Michael P. Ghiglieri, *Over the Edge: Death in Grand Canyon* (Puma Press). A medical doctor and a river guide compile a fascinating account of death and disaster in the Grand Canyon. Ron Adkison, *Hiking Grand Canyon National Park* (Falcon). A comprehensive guide to all of the park's developed trails.

is this for me?

PHYSICAL ✦ ✦ ✦
Long hike in extreme heat

PSYCH ✦ ✦
Toughest stretch is at the end

SKILL ✦
Well-maintained trail

WOW! ✦ ✦ ✦ ✦
Solid challenge, breathtaking scenery

Begin your trek at the North Rim, which stands about one thousand feet higher than the South Rim – a more inviting, but still grueling ascent at the day's end. From here, the North Kaibab Trail is your only option for a descent and crossing of the Colorado River. The trail, a well-crafted route that drops quickly from the plateau forests of ponderosa pine and Douglas-fir, offers a spectacular study of canyon geology with layers of unexpected beauty. After dropping below the rim, you enter forests of spruce and twisted piñon. The trail passes through Supai Tunnel, carved though a cliff of ruddy Navajo Sandstone, before crossing a bridge and descending the lip of a side canyon to Roaring Springs, a waterfall that gushes from the canyon wall. Below Roaring Springs, the trail follows Bright Angel Creek through cottonwood stands and beaver burrows; be sure to take the short side trail to Ribbon Falls for a refreshing rest in its fern-lined grotto. After passing through the Box, a narrow chasm surrounded by dark walls of two-billion-year-old Vishnu Schist, you'll arrive at Phantom Ranch with a ranger station, campground, cantina, and a rustic lodge near the river. Depending on your timing, this may be either a brief stop before pressing on or a good place to rest a few hours during the hottest part of the day. At this point you will have hiked 14.5 miles and descended 5800ft.

Continuing on, the trail parallels the river for about a mile before arriving at Pipe Creek. Here the Bright Angel Trail begins its 4500-foot, eight-mile ascent to the South Rim along an ancient Havasupai footpath. Frequent shaded rest areas with drinking water make this final steep ascent achievable, particularly if done in the shadows of the late afternoon. If you've stayed well hydrated and kept a steady pace, you'll crest the lip of the South Rim by sunset as the western panorama reddens. Pat yourself on the back, survey the immensity behind you, and take a long shower before trying to be seated at one of the South Rim restaurants.

Canoeing the Missinaibi River

>> **A land of snowmelt lakes and boreal forest**

CANADA

MISSINAIBI RIVER

During the last ice age, the vast continental glaciers that covered North America scraped and scoured their way across the horseshoe-shaped landform surrounding Hudson Bay. Left in their wake was the Canadian Shield, the largest mass of exposed Precambrian rock on the face of the earth. Covering most of eastern and central Canada, it's a land of snowmelt lakes and dense boreal forest concealing a web of unbridled rivers flowing north to the Arctic. None of these wild rivers are longer, lonelier or more perfectly suited for a journey by canoe than the Missinaibi.

There is no life so happy as a voyageur's life; none so independent; no place where a man enjoys so much variety and freedom as in the Indian country. Huzza, huzza pour le pays sauvage!

Anonymous *coureur-de-bois*

hypothermia

In the northwoods of the Missinaibi, comfortable temperatures can turn to freezing quickly, and if your clothes are already wet from a few splashes of water, hypothermia is a real risk. You've heard the stories, but do you really know when it's the right time to strip down to your bare skin with a freezing buddy and wrap up in a sleeping bag to reverse hypothermia? That knowledge could be the difference between saving a life and a rather awkward state of affairs.

At the first signs of hypothermia, the first step is to get the victim – or yourself – out of the cold as gently as possible, replacing wet clothes with dry clothes. Insulation (such as blankets, sleeping pads, and spare clothes) should be placed beneath and around the body and head, making sure the victim stays dry while lying in a horizontal position. Shivering, pale blue-grey skin, and fumbling about characterize mild hypothermia. If a companion has mild hypothermia, don't stop the shivering with external heat (like a body or heating pads); shivering in a dry and insulated setting generates internal heat and is the most effective method of re-warming. Give a person with mild hypothermia warm, sugary liquids to hydrate and add energy. A person with severe hypothermia, however, will stop shivering completely. Such a person may become unresponsive, have an irregular pulse, or go into a coma; indeed, it may be hard to tell if the victim is dead or alive. When someone is past the point of shivering, they need help with generating heat. Cover the victim's head with a wool cap, and heat the victim's trunk with any available means. If using hot water bottles, hot rocks, or heating pads, place clothing between the heat source and the skin to avoid burning. After making sure everyone in the group is sheltered, either gently evacuate the victim or send the most competent members of the group for help.

Lined with massive granite outcroppings and coniferous forests, the Missinaibi River courses untamed from Lake Missinaibi in southern Ontario, gathering strength as dozens of other rivers join it before it eventually forms the Moose River and lumbers into James Bay, the southern thumb of Hudson Bay. Not a single damn restrains it along its 560-kilometer length. So isolated is the river that it's only crossed in four places by roads or railroads.

Recognized as a Canadian Heritage River for its exceptional natural and historical significance, the Missinaibi, with its overland links to Lake Superior and its flow into James Bay, has been a vital trade route for over one thousand years. For the native Ojibwa and Cree, the Missinaibi was a lifeline for hunting and fishing. And for European fur traders, the river was one of their earliest access routes into Canada from the Hudson Bay Company's settlement at Moose Factory on James Bay.

In canoeing the length of the Missinaibi, you become a participant in its rich history, passing ancient pictographs, remains of old fur trading posts, and occasional lumber camps abandoned over a century ago. You'll also camp at riverside clearings that were used by Native Americans for hundreds of years. The Missinaibi's main appeal, however, lies in the almost-forgotten journey through a beautiful and largely uninhabited wilderness; it's likely you'll paddle along its mix of flat water and rapids for days without encountering another group. From June through September it's estimated that as few as 75 canoeists run the river's length.

It takes around three weeks to canoe the Missinaibi, a trip that's most easily broken into two parts. Both sections offer a challenging test of skills and endurance in a blend of flat water and Class I–II rapids that are thrilling in an open canoe. How you tackle the river depends on your judgement: Are your skills sufficient to navigate a fully loaded canoe through the whitewater, or should you unload your canoe and make a time-consuming portage? Shooting the rapids may be the more rousing option, but there's no replacement waiting around the bend should you lose a canoe in this remote wilderness.

The Upper Missinaibi starts from the village of Missinaibie, flows through Missinaibi Lake and then on to the tiny town of Mattice. The 236-kilometer route requires nearly thirty portages – you're guaranteed a few each day – and is lined with boreal forest dotted with long-forgotten logging camps and voyageur outposts that invite exploration. Here you'll paddle through the Chapleau Game Preserve, the world's largest, where it's possible to spot moose, black bear, lynx, fox and even an occasional wolf. You might row past a native, permitted to hunt and trap the preserve, with a prize beaver or marten slung over his shoulder.

Paddle for days without encountering another group

need to know

Canoeing the length of the Missinaibi is a journey best suited for those with plenty of canoeing and camping experience. The Missinaibi Provincial Park, which surrounds Lake Missinaibi, can provide information on permits and regulations (☏ 705/864-1710, ⓦ www.ontarioparks.com).

guides and gear Missinaibi Headwaters Outfitters in Chapleau offer guided tours along with equipment rentals and shuttle services for self-guided trips on the Missinaibi (☏ 705/444-7804, ⓦ www.missinaibi.com).

when to go The river can be run from mid-May through early September. Water levels are highest and provide the best challenge for experienced whitewater canoeists around mid-June, but that's also black fly and mosquito season. Late summer sees a lower water level and additional campsites on exposed riverbanks and sandbars, but also rocky shallows where canoes must be emptied for another tiresome portage.

getting there To start from Lake Missinaibi, take an 88-kilometer gravel road north from Chapleau, Ontario. An alternate headwaters start point is from the village of Missinaibie, paddling along Crooked Lake with a portage to Lake Missinaibi. Either way, your primary logistical concern will come at the end of the trip as you choose between leaving a personal vehicle, reserving a private shuttle, or planning a return by train.

suggested reading Hap Wilson, *Missinaibi: Journey to the Northern Sky* (Canadian Recreational Canoeing Association). The definitive canoeing guide to this historic trade route between Lake Superior and James Bay.

The Lower Missinaibi flows for 324km from Mattice to the confluence with the Mattagami River, where the waterway widens considerably before reaching the Moose River rail crossing (a possible exit point). Here, as on the Upper Missinaibi, you'll encounter abandoned fur trading posts, marked by foundations of long-ruined cabins and gravestones of trappers who worked and died in this remote wilderness. You sense the river gaining momentum long before you reach Thunderhouse Fall – a chain of small falls along the northern rim of the Canadian Shield. As you pass from lake to rapids to waterfalls, the width of the river widens from 30m to literally kilometers across at its mouth. Approaching James Bay (and the take-out point at the town of Moosonee), seals can be spotted playing alongside your canoe and beluga whales sightings in the estuary are common. A highly social Arctic species, with a bulbous head and a strangely human smile, a full quarter of the planet's belugas live in Hudson Bay.

For today's voyages an average day's travel includes six to eight hours of paddling and a few rugged portages, which with a thirty-kilogram canoe and a fully loaded expedition become double carries. Just remind yourself that such days are truly a vacation when compared to those for whom this river was their livelihood and who packed a ton of cargo into a 140-kilogram canoe and paddled fifteen hours at a time.

is this for me?

PHYSICAL ✦ ✦ ✦ ✦ ✦
Strength for paddling and portages

PSYCH ✦ ✦ ✦ ✦ ✦
A challenging remote wilderness expedition

SKILL ✦ ✦ ✦ ✦ ✦
Prior canoeing experience recommended

WOW! ✦ ✦ ✦ ✦ ✦
Exceptional scenery on a great wild river

Climbing El Capitan

YOSEMITE
NATIONAL
PARK

USA

>> **Not the least bit scripted**

It was, quite simply, the most magnificent moment in rock climbing. At dawn on November 12, 1958, Warren Harding drilled his last bolt and scrambled atop the final summit overhang to complete a 45-day siege on Yosemite's El Capitan. The night before, Harding and his teammates, Wayne Merry and George Whitmore, had climbed to a ledge so yearningly close to the summit that Harding worked through the night, hand-drilling holes, placing bolts, and setting line. Behind him were 675 pitons, 125 bolts and 2900 feet of manila rope leading down The Nose, a prow on the most intimidating of Yosemite's granite faces. While some critics branded Harding's climb as "rope tricks" or a "stunt", his feat smashed the existing boundaries for physical and technical achievement and set in motion a generation of climbing successes.

The Nose was climbed next in 1960 by Royal Robbins, Joe Fitschen, Chuck Pratt, and Tom Frost, who made the first continuous climb of the route in seven days without using Harding's "siege" tactics that required fixed ropes on the length of the route and re-supplied base camps along the way. In 1969, the first solo climb of The Nose was accomplished by Tom Bauman. As climbers realized that any rock face could be conquered with enough bolts and tenacity, the new goal moved on to "free climbing" El Cap, relying on climbing hardware and rope as protection only. Lynn Hill took fours days in 1993 to become the first person to free climb The Nose. One year later, she returned to free The Nose in an astonishing 23 hours of continuous climbing.

sleeping on a portaledge

If you've ever wondered what it feels like to live like a spider, try spending the night on a portaledge. A cot-like piece of gear that's attached to a cliff and suspended high off the ground, a portaledge allows climbers to take part in multi-day quests. Hanging a portaledge correctly is a tricky affair, so be familiar with the equipment before it's time to perform. Climbing normally takes longer than expected, especially when hauling all of the gear needed to top out on a big wall, and in some cases you may be setting camp up in the dark.

Along with reliable anchors or bolts to hang it from, you'll also need a knowledge of weight ratios, physics, and even geology. Some rock is more fragile than others, so know your medium. Overloading a bolt could lead to a redeye flight to the ground. The number one rule is to never take off your harness, the only piece of equipment connecting your body to the portaledge. While this can get tiresome, just keep reminding yourself you'd rather see the top next than the bottom. Sleeping on a portaledge is not for the faint of heart or those who suffer from claustrophobia, but once the sun rises, the views from your skybox are worth the work. Just remember not to jump out of bed in the morning.

As I hammered in the last bolt and staggered over the rim, it was not at all clear to me who was the conqueror and who was the conquered. I do recall that El Cap seemed to be in much better condition than I was.

Warren Harding

need to know

Yosemite National Park (☏ 209/372-0200, Ⓦ www.nps.gov/yose) requires no permits for climbing El Capitan other than the standard park entrance fee. The traditional hangout for Yosemite climbers is Camp 4, a walk-in campground near El Cap and at the base of the Yosemite Falls Trail.

guides and gear
The Yosemite Mountaineering School and Guide Service (☏ 209/372-8344, Ⓦ www.yosemitepark.com) has operated in Yosemite since 1969 and is the only authorized service to guide big wall climbs within the park. They can supply all necessary climbing equipment including racks, ropes, haulbags, and a portaledge.

when to go
With low elevations and mild weather, El Capitan can be climbed most of the year, although warm summer temperatures and long days make spring and fall climbs most desirable.

getting there
Yosemite National Park is located four to five hours from San Francisco. Take I-580 east to I-205 east to Highway 120 east (Manteca) into Yosemite National Park.

suggested reading
Chris McNamara and Erik Sloan, *Yosemite Big Walls* (Supertopo). The bible of Yosemite big wall climbing. Highly detailed, with historical write-ups, quick overviews of gear needed and pitch-by-pitch ratings. Steve Roper, *Camp 4, Recollections of a Yosemite Climber* (The Mountaineers). Memoirs from the Golden Age of Yosemite climbing.

suggested viewing
Vertical Frontier (2002). The character-driven story of the art, sport and philosophy of climbing the legendary big walls of Yosemite.

is this for me?

PHYSICAL ✦ ✦ ✦ ✦
Exceptional stamina, strength, and coordination

PSYCH ✦ ✦ ✦ ✦ ✦
Mentally challenging, and often frightening

SKILL ✦ ✦ ✦ ✦ ✦
Have solid climbing skills in place

WOW! ✦ ✦ ✦ ✦ ✦
A climber's ultimate achievement

It's not too bold to say that rock climbing as we know it today – and particularly big wall climbing – was invented in Yosemite. Even with the development of locations across the globe, an ascent of El Cap is still the capstone on many a climber's career. There are now over seventy routes up, and not a single one is easy. The Nose, however, is still the most popular and one that remains on every great climber's "to do" list.

Climbing El Capitan is hard work; it's intimidating and not the least bit scripted. An ascent is typically the culmination of years of practice. But climbers with a year or more of disciplined experience can consider a guided climb of El Capitan. Such a climb shortcuts the amount of preparation required, but it doesn't eliminate the need for good judgment, physical strength, and all around climbing experience. Prospective clients are screened carefully, with at least a full day of climbing elsewhere with the guide as a prerequisite. Guides have no desire to push clients into a potentially dangerous situation, and won't start up the wall if they think they're not going to make it. Once you've completed the screening and a day of mandatory training with a focus on rope-team responsibilities, plan on four days on the rock for the climb, plus the final strain of a long hike down carrying your gear.

On the first morning of a guided climb you'll be standing on a pile of talus looking straight up a granite cliff so tall that you won't be able to immediately make out the climbers already halfway up. The guide will be carrying a hefty climbing rack with forty to fifty carabiners and plenty of cams, nuts, chalks and stoppers, with an occasional hook and possibly some pitons. You'll be climbing light, with just a water bottle and snacks, followed by a 150-pound haulbag, or "pig", holding all the water, food, and gear. You'll climb primarily with ascenders, though even that can be tough, as well as doing all of the essential cleaning on the route. The Nose has 31 pitches – almost all crack climbing – and you'll be expected to climb ten to twelve pitches per day, each 100–150ft long.

When it comes to accommodations, every room on El Cap has a view. Though these "rooms" can't be seen from the ground, The Nose has natural ledges perfect for sleeping overnight. By climbing fast – twelve pitches a day – it's possible to pace a climb to spread out on a natural ledge on each of the three evenings. The first night's ledge is fairly level, about four feet wide and fifteen feet long, and has room for three people. Failing to make it to a natural ledge, or having another party beat you to one, means spending the night on a portaledge.

When you clean the final cam and stagger over the rim at the top of El Capitan, there won't be a crowd of reporters at the top to greet you as there was for Harding in 1958. After high-fives and hugs, it's back to work as you load up one hundred pounds of gear for the grueling four-mile descent on foot.

Exploring Gros Morne

>> Where moose and caribou roam

CANADA

GROS MORNE
NATIONAL PARK

You've just stepped off the grid of predictable travel. Standing on the small dock at the head of a giant inland fjord and adjusting the hip belt on your backpack, the shuttle boat pulls away to begin the trip back to the coast. If all goes well, you'll be descending a trail back to a small fishing village on Newfoundland's Great Northern Peninsula in five days. If not, you'll be lost in a confusing maze of caribou trails that wind endlessly through thickets of tuckamore – a dense growth of wind-stunted spruce and fir that coats much of the uplands in the Long Range Mountains, a slump-shouldered high plateau that is twenty times older than the Rocky Mountains.

a glacial pace

Gros Morne National Park sheds great light on the geological evolution of ancient mountain belts. Somewhere within the Precambrian era 1.2 billion years ago, the core of what is now North America's Atlantic seaboard slowly collided with another continent to form a vast mountain range. The eroded granites and gneisses of the Long Range Mountains are the remains of that collision. In the late Precambrian period, the supercontinent began to break apart. As it split, fractures formed and were filled with molten rock from below. This cooled magma can be seen today in the dykes on the cliffs of Western Brook Pond and Ten Mile Pond.

The continental collisions continued for another 100 million years. As the Appalachian Mountains grew, the rocks of Gros Morne were uplifted, folded, and faulted by movements in the Earth's crust. The most scenic features of Gros Morne, the inland fjords known as "ponds," are actually some of the most recent formations – occurring only in the last two million years – and are the result of repeated glaciation and associated sea-level changes. A basic knowledge of geology and the park's geologic history will make your tablelands traverse all the more interesting, as you identify formations, observe up-thrusts, and see the effects of glacial scouring.

As a reminder of how easy it is to get desperately disoriented in the tuckamore, the wardens at Gros Morne National Park's visitor center require anyone attempting the Long Range traverse to undergo a briefing to establish their backcountry navigation prowess. Once completed, hikers are given a radio transmitter to carry in the top of their backpack, an aid used to rescue backpackers who never complete the 35-kilometer traverse and end up returning back to the boat dock.

The classic Long Range traverse begins with a mild 45-minute walk across a coastal plain to the boat dock at the mouth of Western Brook Pond, a 16-kilometer long freshwater fjord. The ride across the "pond" treats you to all the scenic splendor found in the more famous fjords of Norway or Alaska, with steep-sided cliffs fronted by waterfalls spilling furiously into midnight-blue water. At the head of the fjord is a trailhead without an actual trail beyond it – just undefined routes through woods of birch, giving way to boreal forests of spruce and fir. Most of the first day is spent gaining 600m of elevation to reach this upper plateau, following a route that changes yearly as avalanches, blowdowns, and boulders tumbling from the lip above into the gorge open new routes and alter previously established routes.

The undulating plateau above the fjord is an arctic alpine ecosystem, with a diverse landscape of wide stone barrens, tuckamore, mossy bogs, and toughened tundra. Viewed from the fjords, the uplands look deceptively flat, but once on top the rolling terrain studded with deep valleys becomes a frustrating navigational snag, demanding first-rate map and compass skills. On the traverse, you'll spend two or three nights camping on a windswept plateau where snowfields often stick around year-round. The views are dramatic, with cresting hills offering spectacular overlooks into Ten Mile Pond, Bakers Brook Pond and other deep glacial fjords and valleys. A constellation of lakes large and small cover the plateau, forming the headwaters of the brooks and rivers that fill the fjords. The traverse requires several shallow stream crossings, some spanning 30-meters, where your ability to bound from one rock to the next will determine if you arrive at the other side wet and cold or ready to continue on unshaken.

Routefinding on the traverse is a necessary skill

need to know

Gros Morne National Park (☎ 709/458-2417, Ⓦ www.pc.gc.ca/pn-np/nl/grosmorne) is open year-round and offers exceptional autumn hiking, along with cross-country skiing and snowshoeing in winter. Advanced reservations are required for boat service. The Gros Morne Co-operating Association (☎ 709/458-3610) is a good resource for information on the park.

guides and gear Gros Morne Adventures (☎ 709/458-2722 or 1-800/685-4624, Ⓦ www.grosmorneadventures.com) offers small group hiking and sea kayaking, and multi-sport adventure vacations in Newfoundland, including guided four- and five-day trips into the Long Range.

when to go The mid- to late summer, from July through the middle of September, offers the best weather. Even then, however, you need to be prepared for windy, wet, and cool conditions.

getting there Newfoundland's Deer Lake Airport has regularly scheduled services and is thirty minutes from the Gros Morne National Park entrance.

suggested reading Michael Burzynski, *Gros Morne National Park* (Breakwater Books). The authoritative park guidebook, written by a long-time resident and staff member.

With no marked trails, it's easy to step onto a caribou track and within minutes find yourself far off your bearing. The ultimate test of routefinding skills comes as severe weather – particularly rain and fog – rolls in, even in the middle of summer. At times like these, a local guide who knows the "sweet routes" within the rugged terrain, and the location of the best overlooks and campsites, becomes especially valuable.

A highlight of hiking through Gros Morne National Park is the rare opportunity to explore a region filled with arctic wildlife in a relatively southerly setting – further south than London, in fact – that's just a three-hour flight from New York City. Along the traverse you'll spot small herds of up to forty woodland caribou warming in the sun on the late snowbeds of August. Moose are also commonly seen in wooded areas and browsing on wetland vegetation. A non-native species introduced in 1904 as a food source for local hunters, moose populations have flourished and now number well over 100,000 on the island of Newfoundland. Within Gros Morne National Park, where hunting is not permitted, they have become a serious threat to native flora, with a 680-kilogram moose able to devour 130kg of tender birch, balsam fir and other forest vegetation in a week. Other arctic species include rock ptarmigan and arctic hare, while black bear, red fox, mink, beaver, ermine, and other northern woodland species also thrive. One relatively new arrival is the ever-adaptive coyote, first confirmed as a resident in 1986. They likely came across the Gulf of St Lawrence from Cape Breton on ice floes, feeding on whelping seals before making their landfall.

Picking the right routes, the traverse makes a southwesterly swing to Gros Morne Mountain, where the last few miles descend along a day-use trail where you'll likely see other people for the first time after several days in the wild. In top conditions, the trip across this arctic landscape is a challenging hike, and with a few wrong turns and the onset of bad weather you're in for a serious undertaking. Either way, you'll be immersed in the majesty of one of the few remaining expanses of wilderness on North America's eastern coast.

is this for me?

PHYSICAL ✦ ✦ ✦
Backpacking in rugged terrain

PSYCH ✦ ✦ ✦
Wilderness and rough weather

SKILL ✦ ✦ ✦
Routefinding and wild camping

WOW! ✦ ✦ ✦
Dramatic scenery, solid challenge

Kayaking the Kern River

>> Plan on getting dumped

USA

● KERN RIVER

Scrambling from the stalled traffic and high-rise buildings of Los Angeles, you head north on I-5 toward the Kern River. Thoughts of an invigorating ride down this well-loved waterway tucked into the foothills of the Sierra Nevada are keeping your spirits high. Then, with the flatlands of California's Central Valley in your rear-view mirror, you're met with a sign at the mouth of Kern Canyon that gives you pause: it reads *Danger. Stay Out. Stay Alive*, and tallies the deaths on the Kern River since 1968, now over 250. Continuing up Highway 178 along the river's roaring throat to Kernville, you pass mile after mile of boulder-choked Class V rapids. You left your comfort zone back in Bakersfield and you're starting to question your sanity. Maybe a spot in the Whitewater Hall of Fame isn't all it's cracked up to be.

Without question, the Kern River is intimidating. Fed by snowmelt on the western flanks of Mount Whitney, the highest peak in the lower 48, and strengthened by forks flowing from Sequoia National Park in the southern Sierra Nevada, the frothy torrent runs for 155 miles to Bakersfield where it nourishes one of the most productive agricultural regions in the world. The river was named for Edward Kern, one of explorer John C. Fremont's men, who almost drowned in the turbulent waters – a historical tidbit that will do little to build your confidence as an aspiring whitewater kayaker.

The Kern River is the only river in the Sierra Nevada that runs in a southerly direction

Whatever your kayaking skills, the Kern is a daunting challenge. Just below the headwaters is a wilderness run so difficult it has only been descended a few times by experts; you can save that for later. For now, set your sights on the four distinctive sections that make up what's known as the Wild and Scenic Kern River. Below the expert-only wilderness run is a twenty-mile stretch north of the Johnsondale Bridge known as the Forks of the Kern. The Forks contain some of the most spectacular, accessible whitewater kayaking runs in the world. Here you'll find the Seven Teacups, a polished granite chain of drops in the Dry Meadow Creek tributary, which was only discovered as boatable in the 1990s. The next section, from the Johnsondale Bridge down to Kernville, is known as the Upper Kern. It's a popular section of Class II–V spring snowmelt, where the explosive nine-mile, Class IV–V Thunder Run gets rave reviews.

Lake Isabella, a popular reservoir for recreational boating and fishing, separates the Upper Kern from the Lower Kern. This 24-mile section is great for intermediate kayakers along with one- and two-day raft trips. Dotted with Class II–IV rapids, the Lower Kern is fed by releases from Lake Isabella's dam down to Democrat Beach throughout the summer. Finally,

the hunter's boat

History indicates that the Inuit were the first to solve the challenge of building a boat suitable for arctic conditions. They needed a seaworthy vessel that could be easily maneuvered in frigid waters while keeping the occupant dry. It had to be sturdy enough to handle hunting large mammals and hauling in huge fish. And it had to be constructed with simple tools and made with sparsely available materials such as driftwood, whale bones, and animal skins.

The kayak, or "hunter's boat," is still used by natives within northern Canada, Alaska, and Greenland and can be traced back more than 2000 years. Originally constructed from salvaged wood and sealskins, this almost tubular watercraft, propelled by a double-ended paddle, has served as the most dependable form of transportation through the icy inland waters and coastal waterways of the far north. Once outsiders understood the genius of its design, it evolved into a fiberglass version in the 1950s. Molded plastic, inflatable and lightweight collapsible styles followed, and the kayak has now proven itself in almost every water environment.

need to know

A kayaking adventure on the Kern River normally begins with instruction on some of the tamer sections before graduating to the Class II-plus runs. Kernville is the hub for lessons, rentals, and guided trips. It's an easy day-trip for many California residents, but if planning on staying the night come with reservations as campgrounds and accommodations here and in nearby Lake Isabella are heavily booked on summer weekends.

guides and gear Local outfitters can provide all the gear and protective equipment needed for the section of the river you want to run. Sierra South (☎ 760/376-3745 or 1-800/457-2082, Ⓦ www.sierrasouth.com), with a large retail store in Kernville, offers equipment rentals, instruction, and guided kayaking and rafting trips. Mountain & River Adventures (☎ 760/376-6553 or 1-800/861-6553, Ⓦ www.mtnriver.com), also in Kernville, offers much the same.

when to go Most companies run guided trips from April through September. In spring, the ideal conditions are on the Upper Kern, shifting to the Lower Kern in summer.

getting there There are plenty of great kayaking rivers in the Sierra Nevada, but none are as accessible as the Kern, only three hours north of Los Angeles by car. The closest airport of size is in Bakersfield, fifty miles southwest of Kernville.

suggested reading Lars Holbeck & Chuck Stanley, *The Best Whitewater in California, The Guide to 180 Runs* (Watershed Books). An insiders guide to great whitewater with mile-by-mile descriptions.

is this for me?

PHYSICAL ◆ ◆ ◆ ◆ ◆
Requires speed, balance, torso strength

PSYCH ◆ ◆ ◆ ◆
Rapids from tame to potentially deadly

SKILL ◆ ◆ ◆ ◆
Challenging runs require expert skill levels

WOW! ◆ ◆ ◆ ◆
A scenic, wild, exciting river

the Kern ends with a bang of boulders and runnable pockets known as the Cataracts of the Kern. This section delivers excellent technical Class V action later in the season.

The early spring snowmelt in the southern Sierra Nevada makes the Kern one of the first boatable whitewater rivers in the US each year, with plenty of activity even in March when most other Sierra and northern rivers are unrunnable. The water warms quickly in summer, and kayakers are normally out of their wetsuits by late June. Additional releases from the Isabella Dam into the Lower Kern extend the whitewater action into late September. Diehards, undeterred by ice-cold water, will tell you that in the mild southern California climate, sections of the Kern are runnable year round; technically they're right, but don't expect to find commercially guided trips operating in winter.

Both rafts and kayaks run many of the same sections on the Kern, but the accessibility and a variety of easy-to-shuttle runs make the Kern especially attractive to kayakers. Whitewater kayaking is a rollercoaster without the tracks, and since you're covered in water you'll never notice that your palms are sweating. Less experienced paddlers should spend their initial training on flatwater, practicing a wet exit, and developing the control to make their boat move responsively. In the process, you'll begin to sense an essential difference between whitewater kayaking and any other paddle sports – while you sit in a canoe, you wear a kayak. It becomes a playful prosthesis that responds to the tilt of your hips, twist of your torso, and shift of your shoulders.

Then there's the mental game. Kayaking demands every bit as much mental agility as physical as you learn to read currents, waves, and eddies and respond almost intuitively. Plan on getting dumped – "taking a swim," as kayakers say. Even the best kayakers pop their sprayskirt, make a wet exit, and drag their kayak to shore every now and again. Eventually you'll progress to running Class II–III rapids with control and confidence. Soon, getting slapped in the face with cold water even becomes exhilarating.

Mountain biking the Slickrock Trail!

>> **The ride of your life**

What to do with miles of sculpted desert plateau rising above the Colorado River in southeastern Utah? It's no good for grazing cattle and it certainly can't be farmed. The ranchers who settled in the valley below around the town of Moab called this Navajo sandstone plateau "slickrock" as it didn't provide much traction for a shod horse or leather cowboy boots. But eventually motorcyclists and mountain bikers arrived with their fat rubber tires, discovering that the slickrock's sandpaper-like finish grips a bike tire at gravity-defying angles. Soon recreational riders mapped out their favorite section and created a sinuous course on the golden sandstone, taking advantage of its natural bowls, dips, and hills. With a few hundred white dotted lines to formalize the route, the resulting Slickrock Trail has put Moab on the adventure map with a mountain-biking experience that that delivers an exhilarating mix of physical demands, technical challenge and raw scenic beauty.

mountain bike central

When *Mountain Bike* magazine featured the Slickrock Trail as the cover story in its inaugural 1987 issue, a boom was born. Riding the Slickrock Trail is still the headliner for mountain-biking aficionados, but the Moab area offers many other trails well worth exploring. Indeed, the town has staked claim to the title of "home of the greatest mountain biking on the planet." Here are three perennial favorites:

Sovereign Singletrack: A good mix of rocky stretches, technical sections, and flowing slickrock over a sixteen-mile point-to-point.

Hurrah Pass Trail: This trail has it all: petroglyphs, a scenic canyon, towering cottonwood, sinuous switchbacks, and views of the Colorado River along with a paved and graded dirt road. Best done as a 33-mile out-and-back from the heart of town.

Porcupine Rim: Best completed as a sixteen-mile run with a shuttle ride back, this ride begins with a sweat-inducing 800f-footelevation gain before the technical tricks kick in. The real stomach-churner is the downhill ride with dozens of hairy drop-offs.

For all its fame, the Slickrock Trail is less then thirteen miles long. But within that short distance, the solid sandstone trail winds through a wind-carved, juniper-dotted frenzy of fins, domes and gullies and hugs unnerving cliffs and precipitous slopes. If you're an advanced rider or even a well-conditioned intermediate rider, you're in for the ride of your life. For that matter, even beginners will find that the trail has a forgiving side. If you don't like the way you handled a particular hill or turn, you can always turn around and try it again until you pull it off right. And there's no shame in hopping off the bike to walk the sections that are beyond your skill level; you'll have lots of company.

The trail starts with a two-mile section billed as a "practice loop." An alleged preparatory stretch, it dishes out enough tight twists, exposed drop-offs and scary descents to be better called a "warning loop." It's certainly a good test of both your skills and bike, and if you find it beyond your comfort level, it's best to make a 180 back to the trailhead rather than risk what lies ahead.

With over 100,000 riders per year, the Slickrock Trail is the world's most popular mountain-bike trail

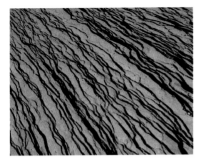

The next section is a lead-in – also called a lollipop stick – to the main loop. This demanding segment traverses some steep mounds where, with a good head of steam and strong legs, you'll be able to keep your pedals rotating to the top without having to hop of. On the downhill side, it's a question of whether you want to break all the way down, or risk flying over your handlebars. As you conquer this tough section prior to hitting the loop, remember that you'll be facing it again in reverse at the end of the trail, so save your energy and your water.

The heart of the trail is a seven-mile loop that roughly follows the plateau's perimeter with some great views of Moab below to the west and the snow-capped La Sal Mountains to the east. Along this stretch there are free-flowing sections like "Baby Bottom Bowl," where you'll sail effortlessly along the rim of a 45 degree banked bowl. Then you'll be beaten into submission on thrill hills like "Thrust or Bust" and "Steep Creep," where even the sturdiest riders in the lowest gear will pump so hard their eyes bulge out. Even a long, rolling stretch known as "Swiss Cheese Ridge" will test your suspension and seat with its bumps. Although the Slickrock Trail isn't known for its flying jumps, you'll find several small points where you can catch for some big air. Over a three-mile stretch along the back of the loop you'll have repeated and dramatic views of the cinnamon cliffs and bending flow of the Colorado River 1000 feet below.

The Slickrock Trail's route is well marked with white dashes every five to ten feet and painted warnings for some of the hazardous sections and abrupt drop-offs. There are no signs announcing slopes angled over 45 degrees, however. The only way to descend such steep passages without flying over the bars is to shift your body weight back behind the seat and lower your center of gravity. Don't attempt to level out the slope by taking it sideways; you'll end up slipping and doing some major damage to you and your bike. You'll also find plenty of twists, narrow bridges and off-camber turns to test your technical expertise. Although the terrain can be tough, the trail itself is generally smooth and free of rubble or protruding rocks. The only flat spots are several short sand pits that may force you to dismount and take a well-deserved breather. One final hazard is 4x4s and ATVs at points where the bike trail intersects with an OHV (off-highway vehicle) trail, but thankfully their numbers don't severely diminish the thrill of the ride.

Along with common mountain-biking nicks and bruises, the Slickrock Trail delivers some distinctive injuries. Falling on slickrock results in more fractures and makes mincemeat of flesh faster than a wooded trail, but the greatest risks come from the harsh desert environment and the lack of water. Mountain biking in the heat of the day, with no shade, can take its toll, and even in the mild temperatures of spring and fall, desert weather can change quickly and unpredictably. Be prepared with plenty of water, snacks, proper clothing, gloves, and, especially, a helmet.

need to know

Moab is also the gateway to two national parks – Arches and Canyonlands – as well as further mountain biking and Colorado River rafting adventures, so you'll find a good variety of accommodations in this bustling bend in the road.

guides and gear Moab's Rim Tours offer guided rides on both the Slickrock Trail and other routes in the area (☎ 435/259-5223 or 1-800/626-7335, ⓦ www.rimtours.com). Plenty of local shops, including Poison Spider Bicycles (☎ 435/259-7882, ⓦ www.poisonspiderbicycles.com), rent full suspension bicycles, the vehicle of choice for this trail.

when to go The trail is open year-round, but two chunks of the year – February through May and September through November – offer the most comfortable temperatures for biking.

getting there The closest airport of size to Moab is Grand Junction, Colorado, located about two hours away by car. The trailhead's parking area is three miles east of Moab in the Sand Flats Recreation Area. You can ride to the trailhead from Moab, though most arrive by car to avoid the steep ascent to the higher plateau.

suggested reading Bob Ward, *Moab, Utah: A Travelguide to Slickrock Bike Trail and Mountain Biking Adventures* (Mountain N'Air Books). Details for arranging a mountain-biking trip both on and off the trail in Moab. Lee Bridgers, *Mountain Biking Moab, 2nd Edition: A Guide to Moab, Utah's Greatest Off-Road Bicycle Rides* (Falcon). Trail details and tips from a knowledgeable local guide.

is this for me?

PHYSICAL ✦ ✦ ✦ ✦ ✦
Aerobic workout requiring leg strength

PSYCH ✦ ✦ ✦ ✦ ✦
Precipitous descents with exposed drop-offs

SKILL ✦ ✦ ✦ ✦ ✦
Experience riding trails helps

WOW! ✦ ✦ ✦ ✦ ✦
Mountain biking as it was meant to be

Climbing Denali 10

>> The Great One indeed

Mount McKinley, the tallest mountain in North America, is a ferocious snowy mass flanked by five giant glaciers. It rises from a base of just 2000ft to a summit elevation of 20,320ft, creating one of the earth's steepest vertical rises and boasting an overall bulk that's larger than Mount Everest. Officially named after William McKinley, the former governor of Ohio and soon-to-be US president during a 1896 survey, the hulking mass is more commonly known as Denali – an apt name that translates as "The Great One" in the native Dena'ina language.

The towering centerpiece of Denali National Park, the peak is the classic proving ground for climbers on their way to Everest. Similarities include harsh weather, high elevation, and the demands of an expedition climbing style, with multiple carries from a base to successively higher camps. Denali was first climbed from the north side in 1913, but Bradford Washburn pioneered the most popular route up the mountain – the West Buttress – in 1951. It's considered a technically straightforward climb as there are no steep faces requiring ice climbing or fixed protection. Don't be fooled, however, into thinking it's an easy one. Severe weather, fierce winds, high altitude, and the sheer scale of the mountain all add up to make climbing Denali an epic undertaking and a demanding feat of physical endurance and mental strength.

In recent years, an average of 1200 climbers attempt to reach the summit: around half will make it – and two will die. Obviously, climbing Denali is not an excursion taken lightly. Following months of physical conditioning, planning and provisioning, climbs begin on an airstrip in tiny Talkeetna, a two-hour drive north of Anchorage. A 45-minute flight on a ski-equipped Cessna leads to Base Camp (7100ft) on the southeast fork of the 36-mile long Kahiltna Glacier, skidding down on a patch of snow nicknamed the "Kahiltna International Airport."

Denali's climbing season runs from mid-April until mid-July, but the best time to go is the short window from mid-May to early June before the snow becomes unstable from extended hours of sunlight. Even in this prime season, the weather is fierce and unpredictable. The typical plan is to allow three weeks for the climb, with a full week of that time spent huddled in a tent waiting for the weather to clear. Every experienced guide on Denali has stories of sixty-mile-per-hour winds whipping through at a painful minus 40°F, and supposedly bombproof tents imploding or flying off the mountain.

the father of Mount McKinley

A Mount McKinley legend, Bradford Washburn (1910–2007) was the first man to map Alaska's highest mountain. He was described by friends as a very exact person – a man who wanted to know down to the foot the height of a mountain – so any information supplied by him could be trusted. This was especially true of his maps, and Washburn created some of the most accurate mountain maps in the world, including Mount Everest and New Hampshire's Presidential Range closer to his home state of Massachusetts. He also pioneered the use of aerial photography, at points strapping himself in so he could lean out of open plane doors to snap photos of peaks. In over seventy trips to Alaska, Washburn captured some of the most indelible views of Mount McKinley ever photographed and pioneered major climbing routes to the top, establishing the main route used today. Washburn's wife even climbed McKinley with him in 1947, becoming the first woman to ever reach the summit. In addition to his mountaineering exploits, Washburn, armed with a Masters degree in geology and geography from Harvard, took the helm of Boston's Museum of Natural History at the age of 29. Through his aggressive fund-raising and expansion efforts, it became today's Boston Museum of Science. He held the position of museum director for 41 years, finally retiring in 1980. In 1999, at the age of 87, he even organized an expedition to Mount Everest to more accurately measure the summit at 29,035ft, adding seven feet to the top of the world.

need to know

Denali National Park (℡ 907/683-2294, Ⓦ www.
nps.gov/dena) operates the Talkeetna Ranger
Station and issues permits for climbing Mount
McKinley. The park has imposed a cap of 1500
climbers per year on Denali and has a sixty-day
pre-registration requirement. The most important
prerequisites for climbing Denali include patience,
excellent physical conditioning, winter camping
skills in survival conditions, and solid climbing
experience at high altitude, with proven ability in
climbing steep, exposed slopes while carrying
heavy equipment.

guides and gear
With headquarters in
Talkeetna, the Alaska Mountaineering School
(℡ 907/733-1016, Ⓦ www.climbalaska.org)
teaches instructional courses and leads guided
climbs on Mount McKinley and throughout the
Alaska Range, Talkeetna Mountains, and Chugach
Mountains.

when to go
Denali's climbing season runs from
mid-April until mid-July; the period from mid-May to
early June is considered the best time to go.

getting there
After flying into Anchorage, take
continuing air service to Talkeetna Airport. From
here, Talkeetna Air Taxi (℡ 907/733-2218, Ⓦ www.
talkeetnaair.com) provides flights to the Kahiltna
Glacier base camp.

suggested reading
Colby Coombs and
Bradford Washburn, *Denali's West Buttress: A
Climber's Guide to Mount McKinley's Classic
Route* (Mountaineers). An excellent historical
overview along with step-by-step instructions for
climbing the standard route. Jonathan Waterman,
*In the Shadow of Denali: Life and Death on
Alaska's Mt. McKinley* (The Lyons Press). Essays
of triumph and tragedy on Mount McKinley.

is this for me?

PHYSICAL ✦ ✦ ✦ ✦ ✦
Requires strength, endurance and conditioning

PSYCH ✦ ✦ ✦ ✦ ✦
Extreme weather at high elevation

SKILL ✦ ✦ ✦ ✦ ✦
Advanced mountaineering and winter survival skills

WOW! ✦ ✦ ✦ ✦ ✦
An epic climb testing your fortitude and endurance

Whether climbing Mount McKinley independently or as part of a guided
expedition, you're still faced with the daunting task of moving three
weeks' worth of gear and provisions up the mountain. The expedition-
style ascent requires carrying 150 pounds of gear and provisions in a
backpack and towed sled. From Base Camp, the first four days are spent
ascending to the top of the glacier, gaining only 4000ft of vertical elevation
while establishing camps and caches on the mountain. Once above the
bergschrund – the point on any glaciated peak where the moving glacier
separates from the mass of the mountain – the typical camps are Windy
Corner (13,500ft), Basin Camp (14,200ft), and High Camp (17,200ft). This
staging of camps is a tedious process, but along with moving gear up
the mountain in an efficient manner it also enables climbers to slowly
acclimatize to the altitude.

From High Camp, summit bids hinge on good weather. There's nothing
hospitable about the cold, windy High Camp plateau, but parties must be
prepared to spend several days waiting for a clear weather window. Once
a break occurs, it's a ten- to fourteen-hour round-trip climb to the summit;
with 24 hours of daylight in summer, departure times are somewhat
flexible. After traversing a steep, snowy face to the saddle of Denali Pass
(18,000ft), the West Buttress route continues for another two hours past
the rocky outcropping of Archdeacons Tower to a large plateau dubbed the
Football Field (19,400ft).

From here it's time to ascend a headwall to the Summit Ridge, where a
vertical ascent along an exposed, narrow cornice dishes out magnificent
views of nearby Ruth Glacier and the adjacent peaks of Foraker to the
west and Huntington and Hunter to the south. Anticipation builds in every
panoramic step on the Summit Ridge, which finally culminates on Denali's
small summit dome. The view from the top is an overpowering visual
experience, summed up succinctly by Robert Tatum, a member of the team
that first summited it: "The view from the top of Mount McKinley is like
looking out the windows of Heaven!"

USA

ZION
NATIONAL
PARK

11 Hiking the Zion Narrows

>> **In the shadows of sheer-walled canyons**

Conceived by wind and water, slot canyons are rare in number and intricate in form. Deeper than they are wide, they are mysterious and inviting, providing a refreshing escape from scorching desert heat along with wavy overhangs, sculpted hollows, and cold-water pools. They also can be deadly, laced with climbing obstacles and capable of swallowing hikers in explosive flash floods. Once down inside them there's often no easy way out. Still, don't let that stop you – slot canyons can change your perspective of the earth in a way few landscapes can..

technical canyoneering gear

The Narrows is one of the few non-technical slot canyons in Zion National Park, meaning that no ropes or other climbing and protective hardware are required. But once you've hiked through a slot canyon it's likely you'll next want to descend or climb up one. Here is but a sampling of the basic gear needed on a typical technical canyoneering trip; considering the level of gear available, you can easily run out of money long before you run out of new gear to buy.

Ascenders: Looking like something Batman might carry, these handles grab onto rope so you can climb without slipping downwards.

Carabiner: This multi-purpose link is nothing more than a metal loop with a spring-loaded gate that allows you to quickly connect one rope, harness or piece of equipment to another.

Harness: Like a diaper made of nylon webbing; a loop in the front with a carabiner securely connects you with a rope.

Helmet: Protecting your head is essential in any deep canyon; tree limbs, rocks, and suspended debris can shift and fall at any moment.

Rope: A 200-foot length will typically suffice, but you may need to double up for longer descents in large, deep canyons.

The world's largest concentration of slot canyons can be found on the sandstone terraces of southern Utah's Colorado Plateau. The Zion Narrows, located within Zion National Park, is the best known of the bunch, and hiking along – and often in – the North Fork of the Virgin River through its length is the only way to experience its grandeur. The most memorable stretches of the sixteen-mile hike occur where the canyon walls rise in vertical splendor above the river, constricting the waterway into intimate and spectacular gorges dressed with hanging gardens, spraying waterfalls, and sandstone grottoes.

It's virtually impossible to get lost on this adventure as the river is the route; you'll spend more than half of the hike walking, wading, and occasionally swimming in it. You can day-hike a portion of the Narrows upstream from the park's Temple of Sinawava, the point along the Virgin River where the larger Zion Canyon constricts into the lower Narrows, but doing so misses out on many of the best sights. The only way to see the entire Narrows is from top to bottom, either as a tough one-day slog or a more enjoyable overnight adventure.

The hike downstream begins within Chamberlain's Ranch, a private property bordering Zion National Park. The trail first cuts through an idyllic setting of rolling hills and grassy fields, but about three miles in, the Virgin River starts carving through the sandstone, causing canyon walls to gradually rise. The path peters out to nothing as it drops from the meadows into a rocky wash, and the flow of the Virgin points the rest of the way. Near the boundary of Zion National Park, the canyon walls rise 800ft as the river slices through the first of the classic narrows. These towering walls are often just twenty feet apart, meaning direct sunlight is rare and the cooling effect can be wonderful. Keep your wits about you, though, as walking in cool water with wet clothes can lead to hypothermia, even when the ambient temps are above 80°F.

Throughout the Narrows, both wet and dry side canyons feed in from both sides. Around five miles into the canyon, a large and unnamed waterfall begs to be climbed and jumped; it frequently is, but the pool beneath is lined with large boulders and is too shallow for a guaranteed safe landing. Beyond the falls, the canyon opens up briefly before you arrive at the confluence of Deep Creek and the Virgin River. Immediately the volume of water in the river triples, filling the chasm from side to side and forming deeper channels in the stream ahead.

Without mile-markers as a guide, a chain of numbered campsites, the mouth of Kolob Creek and Big Springs charts your progress, before the canyon constricts again, darkening and leading into an especially beautiful stretch of deeper narrows. Here red, black and gold cliffs rise up almost 2000ft, while the canyon squeezes down to only 22ft. Even the shallowest channels in the water can be waist-deep, and it's a struggle to stay standing as the powerful currents shove you about. You'll need to carry your backpack over your head in the deepest section, but in this top-heavy pose, move steadily as the current can easily send you underwater. With an absence of high ground, this tight two-mile corridor presents the greatest flash flood risk. If there is any threat of rain, remain upstream of Big Springs until things look clear.

Although no ropes are required on the hike, it's far from easy. Hiking on the algae-coated rocks in the river is no simple feat; doing so is commonly described as walking on greased bowling balls. The best approach is to wear high-traction rubber-soled shoes and hike with two alpine style ski poles

Hiking in the river is no simple feat...

need to know

To hike the length of the canyon, you'll need a backcountry permit plus a camping permit if using one of the twelve numbered campsites located in the midsection. As one-way hike, you'll need to arrange for a shuttle to the trailhead; be sure to get an early start and remember to allow 1.5 hours for the trip from the town of Springdale to the trailhead. Zion National Park's Backcountry Desk is a prime source for information on the Narrows (☎ 435/772-0170, Ⓦ www.nps.gov/zion).

guides and gear Zion Adventure Company (☎ 435/772-0990, Ⓦ www.zionadventures. com) offers shuttle transportation and outfits trips through the Narrows and other nearby canyons. Several outfitters in Springdale rent or sell canyoneering equipment, hiking poles, and wetsuits. With the potential for hypothermia, even in summer, bring a fleece or other wicking fabric for added warmth once you're out of the water.

when to go The hike is most popular from May to September. From October to April you'll want a wet- or drysuit to help combat the icy water. All trips are cancelled when heavy spring runoff or late-summer thunderstorms in the canyon or upstream cause the river to rise to dangerous levels.

getting there Fly into St George, Utah and drive about 45 minutes west to the town of Springdale and the park entrance.

suggested reading Erik Molvar and Tamara Martin, *Hiking Zion and Bryce Canyon National Parks* (Falcon). Detailed guide with 56 hikes in two nearby national parks.

that you don't mind losing or bending. Under good conditions, the trip takes ten to fourteen hours, and all that wading makes for a strenuous day.

As you approach the mouth of the Narrows and the Temple of Sinawava, you'll encounter an upstream surge of day hikers signaling that the end of the hike is near. The canyon exit is along the Riverside Walk, the most heavily used trail in Zion National Park, but your pack and sopping wet shoes will distinguish you from the other visitorswho have never known the depths of the Narrows and its extraordinary sheer-walled beauty.

is this for me?

PHYSICAL ✦ ✦ ✦ ✦ ✦
Good balance in current is essential

PSYCH ✦ ✦ ✦ ✦ ✦
Potentially treacherous currents and flood danger

SKILL ✦ ✦ ✦ ✦ ✦
No technical canyoneering skills required

WOW! ✦ ✦ ✦ ✦ ✦
Dramatic setting and a fun challenge

Rafting the Middle Fork of the Salmon River

>> Into the wet and wild

● SALMON RIVER

USA

No one would ever dream of calling Lewis and Clark quitters. In their epic exploration of the western US, there was no obstruction or obstacle, no mountain or river, that kept them from reaching the Pacific Coast – but the Salmon River came close. On arriving at it, Captain William Clark wrote "the river…is almost one continued rapid," and concluded that "the passage . . . with canoes is entirely impossible," before taking a northern detour on horseback. Much of the Salmon River remains as wild today as it was in 1805, dotted with the same rapids that convinced Lewis and Clark that the river was too dangerous to canoe.

The Salmon is a sturdy branch of the huge Columbia River system that drains parts of seven western states and Canada. From the Continental Divide headwaters in eastern Idaho, creeks gurgle into the Salmon's various forks, which in turn tumble into the Snake, which then rumbles its way to the Columbia before rolling into the Pacific. Of the Salmon's eight principle tributaries, it's the Middle Fork that has it all – clear water, hot springs, great fishing, ancient pictographs, and magnificent scenery. It also delivers the best whitewater adventure, as along its descent the waterway is fed by an incredible 240 tributaries, increasing its size five fold and creating a hundred named rapids.

traveling in style

With no re-supply options along the way, you'll be starting a trip by loading your raft with all the essentials – and then some. A six-day trip on the Middle Fork of the Salmon includes ice-packed coolers loaded with beers, fresh fruit and vegetables, not to mention steaks and salmon for waterside grilling parties. Tents and sleeping bags are kept dry in waterproof bags, while a propane-fueled camp kitchen compacts neatly in the center of the raft. You eat like a lumberjack and no one ever goes hungry.

Lewis and Clark could never have imagined the comfort. Before leaving St Louis, Meriwether Lewis made meticulously planned purchases for his two-year, 33-man dinner party using a $2500 appropriation from Congress. Even though most of their food was hunted or acquired by trade with Indians, a mention of some of their provision helps catch a glimpse of the enormity of the expedition: six-hundred pounds of grease, fifty kegs of pork, one hundred gallons of whiskey, thirty gallons of wine, nearly 4000 pounds of flour, and seven barrels of salt. When game was available, each man consumed nine pounds of meat daily, which required killing a full-grown buffalo, elk, bear or four deer every day. They also packed trading goods, including eleven pounds of beads, 2800 fishhooks, and 4600 sewing needles. Even though food was scarce at times and they faced some periods of starvation along with dysentery, boils, exhaustion, and gunshot wounds, only one man was lost – Sgt. Charles Floyd – and he most likely died of a ruptured appendix.

The water runs with great violence… foaming and roaring through rocks in every direction, so as to render the passage of anything impossible.

Captain William Clark

need to know

If you want to run the river on your own, be advised that permits (☎ 208-879-4101, Ⓦ www.fs.fed.us/r4/sc/) to run the river are required all year. During the control season (late May to early Sept) permits are allocated through a computerized lottery and applications must be submitted by January 31.

guides and gear A number of commercial operators are permitted to guide the Middle Fork of the Salmon. ECHO River Trips (☎ 1-800/652-3246, Ⓦ www.echotrips.com) has guided and outfitted trips on the Middle Fork since 1971, and offers two trips per week throughout the season, including trips with an array of watercraft.

when to go Boats run the river May to September. For an active whitewater experience, don a wetsuit and go when water levels peak in late May to early June. For the best combination of weather and water, look to mid-June through July. If great fishing is a priority, or if you want a trip better suited to young children, consider going in the calmer month of August. Be aware, however, that later in the season (usually from late July on), the upper 25 miles of the river are too low to run, and you'll begin your trip by flying into an airstrip near Indian Creek.

getting there From Boise, Idaho, fly or drive 130 miles northeast to Stanley, where the trip begins. Outfitters provide car-shuttle service to Salmon, Idaho near the trip's end.

suggested reading Stephen Stuebner and Mark W. Lisk, *Salmon River Country* (Caxton Press). The natural and human history of the river, with dramatic photography.

is this for me?

PHYSICAL ✦ ✦ ✦
Coordination and upper body strength

PSYCH ✦ ✦ ✦
Class III rapids and days spent in the wild

SKILL ✦ ✦
All skills can be learned on site

WOW! ✦ ✦ ✦ ✦ ✦
A classic trip on a legendary, wild river

What makes a six-day trip down the Middle Fork of the Salmon so irresistible is that it flows through the Frank Church/River of No Return Wilderness, the largest federally protected wilderness area in the lower 48. No motorized craft are permitted; in fact, even battery operated pumps are prohibited. Without modern obtrusions, you'll find a pristine region – completely uninhabited, undeveloped, and unpaved – that's bound to stay that way.

Most commercial trips cast off with a flotilla of various vessels. The most popular craft is a 14-foot paddle-boat with a guide providing direction from the stern. The longer oar boat is a more leisurely option, best for those who want to spend more time relaxing or fishing. The guide provides the oar-power from the center of the boat, while two or three passengers enjoy the scenery. The one- or two-man inflatable kayak, or duckie, is the high adventure option, and puts you close to the water and in full control on some of the river's most energetic rapids. Over the course of a five- or six-day trip, you'll have the opportunity to rotate among the various boats and enjoy the distinct experience that each offers. Initially you may be hesitant to take on a Class III rapid in a duckie, but after a few days it may become your ride of choice. Since the remnants of an old pack trail follow the bank of the river for the first 80 miles, you can even get out and stretch your legs by hiking sections of the trail during the day.

The river's commercially rafted stretch covers 100 miles. From the put-in at Boundary Creek, the Middle Fork starts small and fast in a tight boulder-strewn canyon lined with spruce, fir and lodgepole pine. For the first two days, rapids with names like Ram's Horn, Velvet Falls, and Pistol Creek are telling tributes to the energy of the upper river. This section is also dotted with hot springs, some right on the water and others within short hiking distance. You'll have opportunities to stop for a mid-day soak, or even camp near these springs for a little therapeutic attention to those overworked paddling muscles.

The middle section of the Middle Fork opens up to broad canyons dotted with sagebrush and pink granite. The sweeping views make it easier to spot wildlife from the water. Bighorn sheep are virtually always spotted, while sightings of elk, bear, and river otter are common. Recently introduced to the area, wolves are more elusive, though you might hear them howling while grouped around the campfire. You'll also find your best opportunities for fly-fishing for cutthroat and rainbow trout, both from the raft and at camp later in the day. Throughout this middle section of the river, you can hike to waterfalls and the cabins of early settlers, and see pictographs and hunting blinds left by the Mountain Shoshone or Sheepeater Indians who called these river-cut mountains home.

In the final two days of the trip descend through Impassable Canyon, a chasm of vertical granite barely capable of containing the swollen river. Some of the Middle Fork's most intense rapids, including Devil's Tooth and House Rock, await. As you near the end of the trip, you've dropped 3000 vertical feet and the Middle Fork joins with the Main Salmon River. The last three miles take place on the Main Salmon River and features the trip's biggest and newest rapid at Cramer Creek, often referred to as De-rigger Rapid. In August 2003 a flash flood caused a landslide just above the take-out at Cache Bar, creating a thrilling Class III–IV hole that delivers an almost impossibly perfect climax to an epic river trip.

HAWAII

MAUNA LOA

13 Climbing Mauna Loa

>> Peer into a deceptively somnolent caldera

Rising over 30,000 feet from the floor of the Pacific Ocean, Mauna Loa (Long Mountain in Hawaiian) is the most massive mountain in the world. Taking up half of the island of Hawaii, the volcano is more than one hundred times the size of Mount St Helens and contains more mass than the entire Sierra Nevada range in California. And yet, when viewed from a distance, with its gentle slopes and lack of an obvious summit, it barely looks like a mountain, certainly not a volcano.

Put that rock back!

As you feel deep black beach sand slipping through your fingers or feel the volcanic rock in your hands, you might begin to picture how a jar of that sand or one of those rocks would look in your collection back home. Before sticking those volcanic remains in your pack, however, think again. Not only is it against the law, but some people say that Pele, the Hawaiian goddess of the volcano, punishes those who remove her rocks.

Every year, the Hawaii Volcanoes National Park receives thousands of apologetic letters with accompanying rocks or sand from visitors who did not heed the legend of Pele and regretted it later. Remorseful visitors claim that Pele's curse has caused family deaths, sickness, divorce, financial difficulty, and more. Some claim that Pele has appeared to them on the island as a beautiful young lady or an ugly old woman with a white dog asking for favors to test the hospitality of the people. Not convinced? You'll have to decide for yourself, but if the law doesn't deter you, maybe your bad fortunes will.

Mauna Loa is classified as a shield volcano, built up by continual layers of lava flow, creating a rounded profile like a warrior's shield. One of the world's most active volcanoes, Mauna Loa has erupted 39 times since 1832, and much of the present summit surface is the result of a dramatic 1984 eruption. To this day the mountain continues to show signs of gas emissions and ground swelling but that doesn't stop people from being drawn to its flanks.

With an elevation gain of 7000ft and a round-trip distance of 39 miles, climbing Mauna Loa is not a light undertaking. And while the route is entirely nontechnical, it is not without risk. The surface terrain can be punishing, foot placements uneven, and there is the potential of breaking through a lava tube surface and dropping several inches while sustaining minor cuts and scrapes.

The ascent starts at the Mauna Loa Lookout at an elevation of 6662ft. It's the end of the road and a panoramic viewpoint for most visitors, but for you it's the trailhead where the adventure begins. From here hike briefly through shoulder-height vegetation before it opens to shadeless lava fields on the 7.5-mile ascent to the Pu'u 'Ula'ula (Red Hill) Cabin at 10,035ft. The cabin offers little more than eight bunks

Mauna Loa last erupted in 1984

PU'U 'ULA'ULA CABIN
ELEVATION 10,035 FT.

and a roof over your head, but it will feel sufficiently homey at the end of your first day, one likely spent in solitude. With no shade and no water to be found, plan on rising early to make your climb for the summit. Above 10,000ft, Mauna Loa is nearly lifeless – no vegetation or birds in sight, but no bothersome insects either. With nothing but surreal lava formations as far as the eye can see, you'll become somewhat of a connoisseur of the two types of lava that blanket the mountain. Rippling pahoehoe (pa-hoy-hoy) lava is smooth and has the appearance of coiled rope. The more physically challenging 'a'a lava (ah-ah), with its distinctive clinking sound, is more likely to catch your ankles as you walk by.

After walking the final twelve miles over lava rubble and lava beds you'll be relieved to reach the true summit at 13,679ft, on the west rim of the Moku'aweoweo caldera. Three miles long and a half-mile wide, with cliffs rising up to 600ft along much of the perimeter, the caldera is a fairly recent development which probably formed in the last 1500 years as the result of an eruption on the mountain's side. Peer into the desolate caldera and you'll see cinder cones, fumaroles, and fissures on the deceptively somnolent summit floor. It's an active volcano, remember, but you can be forgiven for feeling compelled to linger.

need to know

Since the great majority of those attempting the summit of Mauna Loa are coming unacclimatized from sea level, altitude sickness, resulting in headaches and vomiting, is a common problem. Take your time, stay hydrated, and be prepared to turn around if symptoms persist. Mauna Loa and the trail to the summit lie within Hawaii Volcanoes National Park (☎ 808/985-6000, ⓦ www. nps.gov/havo). Advance reservations are not required, but if you are staying overnight on Mauna Loa, you are required to register at the Kilauea Visitor Center and obtain a free backcountry permit.

guides and gear Mauna Loa is not offered as a guided climb, but the park visitor center is a great place to familiarize yourself with environmentally-friendly backcountry practices, and receive up-to-date information about the cabins, water, and weather. Gear should include a sleeping bag, sturdy hiking shoes, a wide-brimmed hat, raingear, plenty of water, and warm layers for cool summit temperatures.

when to go June through August offers the most comfortable weather and makes the best time for a summit bid. The volcano can be climbed in winter, but you may find the trail covered with snow.

getting there Fly into Kona or Hilo. The National Park is located 2hr 30min by car from Kona and 45 minutes from Hilo.

suggested reading Leslie Lang and David A. Byrne, *Mauna Kea: A Guide to Hawai'i's Sacred Mountain* (Watermark Publishing). The ins and outs of visiting and enjoying Mauna Loa's sister peak.

is this for me?

PHYSICAL ✦ ✦ ✦ ✦ ✦
Gentle, shadeless climb

PSYCH ✦ ✦ ✦ ✦ ✦
Mild weather and minimal risks

SKILL ✦ ✦ ✦ ✦ ✦
Maintaining adequate hydration

WOW! ✦ ✦ ✦ ✦ ✦
Hiking an active volcano

Canoeing in the Boundary Waters

>> Find complete wilderness

CANADA

USA

BOUNDARY
WATERS
CANOE AREA
WILDERNESS

Solitude is a rare commodity in today's world. Even in the United States' and Canada's expanse of national parks and wilderness areas, there are few opportunities to leave your car at the end of a road, turn your back on civilization, and spend days on end with just the sights and sounds of nature to stir your senses. The Boundary Waters of Minnesota and Ontario provides just that escape.

The Boundary Waters broadly refers to the network of lakes in and around Minnesota's Boundary Waters Canoe Area Wilderness (BWCAW) and Ontario's Quetico Provincial Park. It's a maze of waterways that flows to Hudson Bay, 550 miles to the north. Moose, deer, and reclusive bears make their homes here, beavers and otters frequent the channels, and bald eagles and osprey nest in the dense stands of white and red pine that blanket the land. It's a playground of 1500 miles of canoe routes with limitless opportunities for fishing, hiking, bird-watching, and simply getting lost in your thoughts. Two million acres with not one road, house, power line, or motorized craft.

You'll feel like you're among the first to arrive here, but this land has long seen its share of visitors. Over five hundred years ago Ojibwe hunters drew ancient pictographs on rock ledges and centuries later voyageurs plied the crystalline lakes, trapping and trading. While visiting the north woods in the late 1800s, John Muir told of "lakes gleaming like eyes, and silvery embroidery of rivers and creeks watering and brightening all the vast glad wilderness." In the time since, nothing has changed.

how to upright a swamped canoe

Finding yourself upside down in a canoe isn't the worst thing than can happen on a canoe trip if you are prepared with some basic rescue techniques. First, know that the rescue will be much easier if you are traveling with another boat and much safer if you're wearing a PFD (personal flotation device). If you ever get dumped in the water make sure to hold onto your paddle, keeping your feet pointed downstream from your body and never get downstream of your boat. The weight of a fully submerged canoe could be 500 to 1000lbs and the force of a canoe traveling downstream with that much weight behind it could potentially prove fatal if you were to get in its path on its way to a powerful collision with rocks in the river.

As quickly as possible, position yourself on one side of the dry canoe with your partner on the other side. Direct the end of the swamped canoe to the middle of the rescuing canoe, and angle the swamped canoe perpendicular to the rescuers. The rescuers then turn the swamped canoe over so the hull points up and pull the entire canoe over theirs to form a cross. Having now emptied the canoe of all the water the rescuers turn the boat right side up, put it back in the water and hold it firmly in place to allow those in the water to get back in the boat.

On the map, Ely appears to be at the end of the road. For people who love wilderness and beauty and solitude, on the contrary, it's at the center of the world.

Charles Kuralt

need to know

For self-guided trips, contact Boundary Waters Canoe Area Wilderness for permits and usage guidelines (☎877/550-6777, ⓦ www.bwac.org). Permits for the season can be reserved starting in November of the year prior to your planned departure. They go quickly, so early reservations are advisable. In Canada, permits are obtained from Quetico Provincial Park (☎888/668-7275).

guides and gear Local outfitters in Ely, Minnesota provide services and support for all types of trips; one of the most reputable is Canadian Waters (☎218/365-3202 or 1-800/255-2922, ⓦ www.canadianwaters.com).

when to go The canoe season in the Boundary Waters runs from May to September. Trips in May can be cold and made less enjoyable by pesky black flies. September cools quickly, but it's less crowded than midsummer and offers early fall colors. Prime-time is mid-June through the end of August.

getting there From Minneapolis-St Paul International Airport it's a four-hour drive to Ely, while it takes two hours from the smaller airport in Duluth. In Canada, Quetico Provincial Park is accessible by car at Dawson Trail Campground and Lac la Croix Ranger Station, located about two hours west of Thunder Bay, Ontario. Quetico Air Services offers seasonal floatplane flights to designated lakes and landing areas (☎218/993-2361 in the US, ☎807/485-2441 in Canada).

suggested reading Daniel Pauly, *Exploring the Boundary Waters: A Trip Planner and Guide to the BWCAW* (University of Minnesota Press). An excellent trip planner and guide to routes and natural history.

In such a vast region accessible only by water you can put in pretty much anywhere and find complete wilderness. Outfitters in the town of Ely, Minnesota, on the Boundary Waters' southern fringe, do brisk business helping people get on the water. Here you can sign up for a guided trip or, alternatively, work with an expert to design an independent excursion that matches your experience and interests. Permits, canoes, equipment, and meals are likewise on offer, though you'll need to come prepared with map-reading skills if you're heading out on your own.

Despite the high number of intrepid canoeists lured by the prospect of getting away on these waters, myriad route options mean that no two parties take the same trip. While you may have a general idea of where you want to go during a typical five- to seven-day expedition, you'll have the freedom to alter your plans from day to day and hour to hour. Choose an itinerary that inspires you, whether it focuses on waterfalls or wildlife, and plan your pace according to your canoeing skills and stamina: a family with young children may aim to cover five or six miles over four hours, while a more ambitious group might push for six hours on the water and cover ten to twelve miles.

Whatever your route, you'll inevitably encounter areas that require portaging, usually between landlocked lakes or around water hazards such as shallow, rocky rapids. Most Boundary Waters portages are fairly short, ranging from less than a 100ft to slightly over a mile. You'll need to be able to flip your canoe and balance it on your shoulders while carrying your remaining provisions in a backpack. Ultra-light Kevlar canoes weighing less than 45lbs make this feat considerably easier.

As you glide silently along, leaving behind only ripples, listen closely for the cry of the loon, a common call throughout the region. When the shadows begin to lengthen across the water, take refuge in one of many single-party campsites that include a fire grate and a wilderness box latrine. Kick back and relax, but if you must busy yourself before nightfall try climbing rock palisades and boulders, swimming, or berry picking. Around the crackling fire after a day's voyage, you'll hear the howl of the timber wolf and gain an inner confidence that comes from a self-reliant way of life in the wilderness.

is this for me?

PHYSICAL ◆ ◆ ◆
Paddling and portages

PSYCH ◆ ◆ ◆
Remote and on your own

SKILL ◆ ◆
Canoeing and camping

WOW! ◆ ◆ ◆
Deep in the woods

Skiing hut to hut in the Rockies

>> Pure backcountry bliss

USA
● DENVER

There is a way to ski Aspen and Vail in peak season without experiencing lift lines and crowds: traveling the backcountry from hut to hut. Carving pristine alpine bowls by day and arriving at a different cozy mountain hut each evening, you may soon forget why you ever bothered with a conventional resort vacation. While weekenders dodge each other on overrun slopes and pay dearly for a ski pass, you'll glide along remote wooded trails to a gorgeous overlook for a picnic in solitude. And you won't see a single SUV when you wake to a mountaintop sunrise and literally ski out your front door.

avalanche survival

The foreboding whump of an oncoming avalanche means that it's time to think – and act – quickly. While the best way to survive an avalanche is to avoid it, their unpredictable nature means that even the most prepared adventurer might encounter one of these icy torrents of destruction. The first thing to do when you hear the thundering rumble and find yourself in the avalanche's path is to yell to your group and get out of the way.

If you do get caught in the rushing snow, free yourself from your pack and ski poles and make swimming motions to stay near the surface. When the snow begins to settle, you'll have about three crucial seconds before the once-loose snow packs as hard as cement. During those three seconds you need to be extremely aggressive: create an air pocket in front of your face by making a shield with your forearms and punching the snow, take a deep breath to create chest space for future breathing, and if you are close enough to the surface, stick out an arm or a leg at the last second for rescuers to see. These measures will help rescuers find you and give you room to breathe until they do. The use of rescue equipment such as avalanche beacons, cords, and probes will enhance your chances of survival. Since proper training and preparation are the best ways to avoid getting caught in an avalanche, consider taking an avalanche safety course before skiing or shoeing a snowy mountain.

What you'll see from your front door is a bird's eye view of Colorado's Rocky Mountains, the largest collection of 14,000-foot peaks in the United States and home to some of the world's greatest backcountry ski slopes. The thirty or so huts that span the Rockies can serve as stepping stones for an extended ski tour or as a base for several days of in-and-out day-trips. Either way you'll be perfectly positioned to enjoy spectacular mountain scenery and still have the convenience and comfort of a place to call your own at the end of each day. Just don't expect room service and high thread count sheets – each hut is essentially a rustic wooden cabin equipped with padded bunks, wood stoves for heat, propane stoves for cooking, cooking and eating utensils and a large pot for melting snow. After your first day you wouldn't want it any other way.

Between three and nine miles of high bowls, gentle slopes, and wooded glades separate each hut, and you can expect a daily elevation change between 600 and 3000ft as you travel between them. The routes often follow existing trails and snow-covered forest service roads, though you may occasionally encounter sections that demand more ability, such as steep slopes and mountainous traverses, and from time to time you may need to break new trail. Most of your trip will be below the 11,400-foot treeline on routes that wind through silent, snow-covered forests of aspen, fir, and Engelmann spruce. When you ski out of the forests at higher elevations you'll be treated to dazzling one hundred-mile views of distant peaks.

need to know

The 10th Mountain Division Hut Association (☏ 970/925-5775, ⓦ www.huts.org) manages the system of backcountry huts. The huts experience highest demand in winter where peak season reservations are allocated on a lottery basis.

guides and gear Most skiers opt for a good metal edge backcountry ski with skins, but you also see Telemark, Alpine touring skis, and snowboards. If you are not already a skilled backcountry skier, you might consider traversing the terrain on snowshoes but you'll find travel to be slower. While most experienced backcountry skiers travel independently, novices should consider going with a guide. Paragon Guides (☏ 970/926-5299, 877/926-5299, ⓦ www. paragonguides.com) offers guided backcountry ski tours in winter and summer hut-to-hut hiking. Avalanche beacons, probe poles, and shovels are now standard equipment for backcountry skiers and can be rented or purchased prior to your departure.

when to go December through April is best for skiers, but huts are open July through September and mid-November through April.

getting there Fly to Denver and rent a car or take shuttle service to trailhead areas two to four hours away. Shuttle operators such as Dee Hive Transportation (☏ 888/266-2339) can take you to one trailhead and pick you up days later at another trailhead.

suggested reading Louis W., II Dawson and Warren H. Ohlrich, *Colorado Tenth Mountain Huts and Trails: The Official Guide to America's Largest Backcountry Ski Hut System* (Who Press). An extensive guide to Colorado's backcountry ski system.

Blue diamonds, and in wilderness areas, blazes notched into the trees mark the route. In either case, you could go a mile or more without any markings, so route-finding skills will be essential. Carry a compass and a detailed topographic map and know how to use them. A GPS can also be a helpful tool, but only if you have proven proficiency in its use, along with solid backcountry navigation experience. Your skills can be put to the test in a winter snowstorm where the trail can be obliterated, trail markings obscured, and some huts can be completely buried with snow. If your group is unfamiliar with the area or lacks the necessary skills, consider enlisting the services of a local guide.

While route-finding can be challenging, avalanches pose the greatest risk to backcountry skiers, and the Colorado backcountry is known for widespread and long-lasting snow-pack instability. Though the routes are positioned to avoid areas with the greatest avalanche risk, the risk can never be eliminated entirely. Skiers are often the trigger for a slide that can injure or kill them, so entering the backcountry with a current avalanche report, avalanche training and the proper equipment is essential. Learn to identify avalanche-prone terrain such as open slopes between 30 and 45 degrees, areas which show signs of previous avalanches, and cornices. Avoid these areas entirely or cross them quickly, one person at a time.

is this for me?

PHYSICAL ✦ ✦ ✦ ✦ ✦
Highly aerobic climbing with pack

PSYCH ✦ ✦ ✦ ✦ ✦
Severe weather, avalanche hazard

SKILL ✦ ✦ ✦ ✦ ✦
Route-finding, prior skiing experience

WOW! ✦ ✦ ✦ ✦ ✦
Stunning mountain scenery

Hiking the Pacific Crest Trail

16

>> **Alone in the wilderness**

MANNING PROVINCIAL PARK

CAMPO

A five-foot stone obelisk stands in the middle of the trail. An unfussy monument, it silently announces your arrival at the US-Canada border. There's no neon sign or cheering crowds, not even a bench to sit on waiting at the northern terminus of the 2650-mile Pacific Crest Trail (PCT). It's another seven miles before there's even a border guard to greet you, and further still to a hot meal and hotter shower to soothe five months' worth of weathered skin and wrinkled feet. You realized hundreds of miles ago why more people have climbed Mount Everest than have thru-hiked the Pacific Crest Trail, but with the end in sight you feel fantastic.

A trail of immense variety, the PCT dates back to 1930 when teams of hikers from the YMCA worked on connecting existing trails through the mountains of California, Oregon, and Washington. By 1968, with the passage of the National Trails System Act, the PCT along with the Appalachian Trail (AT) were the first two routes to be designated as national scenic trails. The two trails are routinely mentioned in the same breath, but they're vastly different. The PCT is nearly 500 miles longer than the AT and much less forgiving, with severe desert and mountain conditions. And while the AT is known as a social experience, the PCT is a true wilderness journey. PCT hikers camp alone most nights, travel distances up to 200 miles between road crossings, and deal with the fact that the number of hot showers along the trail can be counted on one hand.

Snaking up from the Mexican border to Canada, the PCT passes through six of North America's seven ecozones – missing out only the subtropical – and elevations ranging from just 180ft at the Columbia River to 13,180ft at Forester Pass in the Sierra Nevada; most hikers can't resist a short side spur to summit the tallest peak in the continental US, Mount Whitney (14,505ft). The journey is subject to the potentially dangerous whims of the region, whether it's water shortages in the desert, trail closures due to wildfires, or snowstorms in the North Cascades. Thru-hikers should start near the Mexican border in late April, before the Mojave Desert becomes unbearably hot but not so early as to hit mountain passes that can still be snowbound in May.

Southern California is the first of the trail's five distinct sections, where you'll witness the beauty of a desert in springtime and cross over the San Andreas Fault three times. The desert hums with life, from coyotes and cougars to rattlesnakes and hummingbirds. More than just lowland, you'll top out at over 9000ft in the San Jacinto Mountains before traversing the San Bernardino and San Gabriel ranges. Reliable sources of water can be

when mountain lions attack

Mountain lions are the only large predator that can be found throughout the PCT. The largest of North America's cats, males can reach 8ft in length and weigh up to 180lbs. Attacks are rare, but as more people encroach upon their habitat encounters have increased. Hikers are at greatest risk when alone or during the wee hours of the morning and night, when mountain lions are most active.

Should you cross paths with one, keep in mind that mountain lions usually aren't overly keen on attacking humans, so avoid cornering the animal and give it a chance to escape. In the unlikely event a mountain lion keeps stalking, scare it off by making yourself as big and loud as possible; try growling, baring your teeth, raising your arms, or fanning out your jacket. Never crouch, turn you back or run away as that can trigger the cat's chasing instincts. Should disaster strike and an attack occur, fight back ferociously. Anything you can find to throw at the mountain lion will help, and the best place to aim is the animal's eye. People have been known to fight a lion successfully with tree branches, their bare hands and in one dramatic attack, even a cheap plastic pen.

need to know

Hikers traveling more than 500 continuous miles on the PCT can obtain a Thru-Permit from the Pacific Crest Trail Association (PCTA; ☎916/349-2109, Ⓦ www.pcta.org). The permit allows camping along the trail, including within the national parks, along with entry into the Mount Whitney limited access zone. The non-profit PCTA also offers a toll-free number (☎1-888/PCTRAIL) for callers to report on trail conditions and receive recorded updates on the trail ahead.

guides and gear With no guides to lead the way, planning a thru-hike of the PCT is a monumental logistical task. At least a half-year of advance planning – including training and arranging supply drops at points along the trail – is to be expected. Lightweight backpacking is the new standard for most thru-hikers, who opt for running shoes over hiking boots and ultra-lightweight gear; some fanatics even skip the stove and fuel and eat raw food only.

when to go April to October, although the season may vary based on snowfall and the rate of spring snowmelt.

getting there The southern terminus of the PCT is located by the Mexican border on a low hill near the town of Campo, California and ends just over the Canadian border in British Columbia's Manning Provincial Park.

suggested reading Karen Berger and Daniel R. Smith, *The Pacific Crest Trail: A Hiker's Companion* (Countryman Press). A solid all-around guide for preparing for and hiking the PCT.Jeffrey P. Schaffer, *The Pacific Crest Trail: Southern California*; Jeffrey P. Schaffer, *The Pacific Crest Trail: Northern California*; Andy Selters, *The Pacific Crest Trail: Oregon and Washington* (Wilderness Press). Three volumes covering the complete trail; an essential series for thru-hikers, complete with maps, planning guide and trail details.

is this for me?

PHYSICAL ✦ ✦ ✦ ✦ ✦
Exceptional stamina over time and distance

PSYCH ✦ ✦ ✦ ✦ ✦
As much mental and emotional as physical

SKILL ✦ ✦ ✦ ✦ ✦
Planning and logistics, solid camping skills

WOW! ✦ ✦ ✦ ✦ ✦
A challenging, life changing experience

eight to twenty miles apart, so hikers must carry at least two liters of water and have a detailed route guide pinpointing upcoming sources.

The Sierra Nevada is the showstopper within central California. The PCT joins the John Muir Trail (see p.83) for 160 miles, ambling through the striking mountain scenery of Sequoia and Kings Canyon national parks and past the basalt columns of Devils Postpile before cutting through isolated stretches of Yosemite National Park. You'll be in the Sierra backcountry early, before the mass of hikers arrives, but you're far from alone. This is prime black bear country and bear canisters are required.

Northern California is logging country, and the trail progresses from the granite ridgelines of the Sierra Nevada to the southern Cascades, where volcanic peaks like Lassen and Shasta puncture the skyline. After crossing the Feather and Sacramento rivers, center stage for California's Gold Rush, the path enters the Trinity Alps Wilderness. Connecting the inland Cascade Range with the coastal ranges, the tall timbers and lingering snowfields here offer as good a chance of finding pure solitude for days on end as anywhere on the trail.

By now it's mid- to late-summer, when Oregon is a hiker's paradise with comfortable temperatures and decidedly wetter weather that makes for thick conifer forests laced with tiny treasures like berries and wild mushrooms. A spur trail in Crater Lake National Park leads along a caldera rim for stunning views of the deepest lake in the US, while the main trail skirts past other volcanic features including the recently active Mount McLoughlin and Mount Hood.

Washington continues the volcanic drama, treating trail-goers to views of Mount St. Helens, Mount Adams, and massive Mount Rainier. Crossing I-90 at Snoqualmie Pass, the trail cuts into the craggy peaks of the Alpine Lakes Wilderness, often picked as the scenic gem of the entire trail with seven hundred lakes, fearless mountain goats, and waving fields of wildflowers. A final treat, the steep glacial valleys, harsh terrain, and fickle weather of North Cascades National Park is the only zone on the trail that's home to grizzly bears. With the goal in sight, the days grow shorter. It's early autumn and the golden leaves and bright red huckleberry bushes signal the end of the trail as it crosses into Canada, the epic journey ending in British Columbia's Manning Park.

USA: ALASKA

KENAI FJORDS
NATIONAL PARK

17 Sea kayaking the Kenai Fjords

>> **Where the ice age still lingers**

You and your paddling partner barely break a sweat as your sea kayak pierces the small ripples of Alaska's Northwestern Lagoon. You've seen pictures of what awaits ahead, but no photo can capture its enormity. Skimming forward, you're struck by the luminescence of massive tidewater glaciers dangling at the edge of the earth. At the current distance, they seem like pale blue blocks of solid ice. But suddenly an unnerving crack snaps through the air. You stop rowing long enough to witness a massive column the size of a house split away and collapse, in slow motion, into the sea. You almost stop breathing as the thunderous roar rumbles into the distance and an invasion of swells rolls your way.

bergy bits and growlers

Glacial ice comes in so many sizes and formations that a specialized vocabulary has been created to describe the variety; you'd do well to become familiar with some of the most common.

bergy bit: A small chunk of ice generally rising 5–15ft out of the water; larger than a growler, but not big enough to actually be an iceberg.

floeberg: A massive piece of sea ice featuring large, upwelling pressure ridges.

growler: A chunk of ice usually smaller than a bergy bit and almost entirely submerged; dubbed a "growler" due to the sound it makes when air releases while the ice melts.

hummock: A large chunk of ice that has been pinched between two colliding ice floes and comes to rest above the water on top of the ice floe.

ice floe: A large, flat slab of ice floating freely on the surface of the water.

ice pack: Several large bodies of ice floating together and forming an extensive obstacle.

A calving tidewater glacier is a momentous event, a kind of mini-cataclysm that most people never get to see in person. To witness this natural wonder – and do so at water level in a sea kayak – you need to find a place where the ice age still lingers, where dozens of glaciers are constantly in motion, some moving several feet a day, then surging forward in dramatic bursts to expel huge bodies of ice into a glassy bay. Alaska's Kenai Fjords National Park is such a place.

The park's dominant feature is the Harding Icefield, which feeds most of the tidewater glaciers that flow into the fjords. The calving process, which involves enormous hunks of ice crashing to their new life in the ocean, happens quickly and often without warning, meaning it's more than a good idea to stay away from glaciers when paddling. At a safe distance, by the time you hear the sound, the collapse is in its final stages. Once spawned, these chunks of ices known as bergy bits or growlers, depending on their size – invite closer inspection. Don't be surprised to see these mammoth ice cubes floating by in an opposite direction to the wind; as most of an iceberg's mass is below the surface, its flow is directed more by currents.

To experience this unfolding drama, you'll need to head south from Anchorage across the Kenai Peninsula, one of the dangling jowls on the face of Alaska, to the town of Seward. Perched beside Resurrection Bay, this tiny spot is home to an active fishing port along with the park headquarters. It's the jumping off point for travel into the fjords, with most kayakers hopping on a water taxi or charter boat here to be dropped off at the more remote waters of Aialik Bay, Pederson Lagoon, or Northwestern Lagoon. You'll camp on backcountry campsites – more often than not equipped with bear lockers

What kind of sane man would pay that kind of money for an iceberg?

Opposition comment to US Secretary of State William H. Steward's agreement to buy Alaska for $7.2 million in 1867

need to know

In-depth information can be obtained from the Kenai Fjords National Park's visitor center in Seward (☎ 907/224-7500, ⓦ www.nps.gov/kefj). Advance reservations are essential for staying in Seward as the town's limited hotel space goes quickly during the peak summer season.

gear and guides With more than twenty years guiding in the fjords, Sunny Cove Sea Kayaking (☎ 907/224-4426 or 1-800/770-9119, ⓦ www.sunnycove. com) offers guided day-trips and multi-day sea kayaking and adventure vacations in Resurrection Bay and Kenai Fjords National Park. If traveling independently, you'll need prove you're experienced and be able to demonstrate a wet exit before local operators will rent you a kayak.

when to go Kenai Fjords National Park's peak visitor season is May to early September, with June and July offering the longest daylight hours. While southern Alaska has a relatively moderate maritime climate, cold rain and unstable weather conditions are still common in summer.

getting there The closest major airport is Anchorage International Airport; Seward is a 2–3hr drive to the south.

suggested reading David Wm. Miller, *Exploring Alaska's Kenai Fjords* (Wilderness Images Press). A comprehensive marine guide to the Kenai Peninsula outer coast. Ideal for planning sea kayaking trips.

to keep inquisitive visitors away – and either make day-trips from this base camp or pack up each day for more of a touring approach.

For paddlers unfamiliar with the area, traveling with a guide is strongly recommended. Most guided trips cover four to five days and can be adapted to suit a variety of skill and experience levels. Sea kayakers are particularly susceptible to rapidly changing winds and fast-mounting storm systems that frequent the fjords, even in summer. These can quickly take a novice kayaker out of their comfort zone. Even in protected waters, swells can rise up to 3ft, while tides can have a surprising impact on navigability. With few protected coves, icy waters, and some surf landings, this is not the most favorable place to learn sea kayaking. Fortunately, most tour operators favor double kayaks, which are more stable and also enhance the social element of your time on the water.

The stunning glacial scenery is just part of the package. Wildlife encounters, especially at sea, are virtually guaranteed. Sightings of soaring eagles and plump puffins always captivate. Orca whales – known as "killer whales", though actually quite friendly – have a curious fascination and an almost familial bond with sea kayaks, and pods have been known to spend hours with a small group of kayakers. Sea otters likewise seem to have a curious and playful bent with sea kayaks. But the highlight of any trip, if you're lucky, would be seeing a thirty-ton humpback whale hurl itself completely out of the water, in a dazzling acrobatic display known as breaching – a spectacle for which you can never be fully prepared.

is this for me?

PHYSICAL ✦ ✦ ✦ ✦ ✦
Paddling strength for winds, weather and tides

PSYCH ✦ ✦ ✦ ✦ ✦
Remote wilderness, wildlife encounters

SKILL ✦ ✦ ✦ ✦ ✦
Have wet exit and rescue techniques in place

WOW! ✦ ✦ ✦ ✦ ✦
Spectacular scenic wonders and wildlife

Canoeing the Bonaventure River

>> **A dreamlike float over liquid crystal**

GASPÉ
PENINSULA

CANADA

A little-known gem, Québec's Bonaventure River has all the elements of a perfect canoeing river – no portages, no crowds, and, best of all, no mosquitoes. A short season and remote source have kept it a little-known adventure; and it's estimated that less than a hundred people a year canoe its entire length. It typically takes six days to descend the full 114-kilometer journey through remote wilderness, and over that time paddlers cross oars with only a handful of other people.

The native Mi'kmaq got it right when they named the waterway "Ouagamet," meaning "clear water." The shockingly transparent water is the first thing newcomers notice about the Bonaventure River, a flow created by snow melts running off clean granite slopes. The river is reputed to be the clearest and cleanest in Canada, and one of the ten clearest in the world. Floating over pools ten meters deep, it's easy to see salmon swimming near the bottom. And even on rapids, paddlers experience an otherworldly sense of floating on glass.

From the seaside community of Bonaventure on Chaleur Bay, it takes the better part of a day to wind along rugged logging roads in a bus loaded with provisions and crowned with canoes. The put-in point is on Lac Bonaventure, high in the Chic Choc Mountains of Québec's Gaspé Peninsula, a region that is actually the northern tip of the Appalachian Mountains. As the river flows out of Lac Bonaventure, it's only ankle deep and about 6m wide. A fully-loaded canoe has just enough water to clear the rounded boulders lining the river's bottom.

Looming mountain vistas and forested gorges provide a beautiful setting for a river that, 60km from its headwaters, is still no more than 10m wide. Along the way, small feeder streams boost the Bonaventure's volume and speed. Rock outcroppings appear, and some runnable ledges cross the river, adding thrills to the nonstop Class I–II rapids. As the canoe rolls through these stretches you'll find yourself occasionally dropping a hand from the paddle to the gunwale to steady yourself, but the adrenaline isn't flowing freely quite yet.

About halfway down the river, the canyon walls constrict into a narrow gorge. Class III rapids begin to form as the river disappears around a long bend. If your helmet isn't already in place, now's a good time to strap it on. Through this two-kilometer gorge, the river's ledges and rapids become more challenging. Good balance and a strong paddle stroke must be maintained to stay upright and keep the canoe from being slapped around by the rush of water. As the river is joined by its only significant tributary, the West Bonaventure, it widens considerably, but remains relatively shallow. At some points, canoes zip along at 20km per hour, breakneck speed in a low-sitting craft.

But blazing through the trip at constant clip is the wrong way to travel on the Bonaventure. Chance encounters offer some of the most memorable moments, particularly in the magical mornings when the cool night air meets the early sun to create smoke-like mists over the river. Campsites nestled in

The river descends through deep canyons cloaked in fir and spruce

need to know

The Bonaventure can be descended by canoe independently or as part of a guided trip. The river is best for experienced canoeists with demonstrated whitewater canoeing proficiency. Both sternman and bowman should be capable with eddy turns, back ferrying, and in making quick correctional strokes to skirt rocks and other obstacles.

guides and gear Cime Aventure (☎ 1-800/790-2463, 🌐 www.cimeaventure.com) offer six-day guided expeditions, including meals and equipment. This local outfitter also does shorter sections of the Bonaventure in one- to three-day trips from its base camp and resort in the town of Bonaventure. If you prefer to outfit the trip yourself, they can provide shuttle service to the put-in at Lake Bonaventure.

when to go The Bonaventure's flow is heavily dependent on snowmelt and is run from mid-May through mid-July, with June being the prime season. During the peak runoff of early June, the river can even swell with occasional Class IV rapids.

getting there Fly into Bonaventure, located on the Gaspé Peninsula about 650km northeast of Québec City. Visitors can also arrive by VIA Rail to Bonaventure's train station.

is this for me?

PHYSICAL ✦ ✦ ✦
Prolonged paddling, some aerobic activity required

PSYCH ✦ ✦ ✦
Minimal risk, extended stay in an outdoor setting

SKILL ✦ ✦ ✦
Previous canoeing experience recommended

WOW! ✦ ✦ ✦ ✦
A week on an exceptionally beautiful wild river

stands of birch and spruce are often set up near still pools, and with coffee in hand you can watch Atlantic salmon splashing and jumping their way upstream. Mornings are the best times to see deer, black bear, and perhaps even a rare bobcat, and many a canoe has come around a bend only to find a bull moose standing in the river ahead.

Typical days involve six to seven hours in the canoe, paying constant attention to the rapids and flow of the river. While strenuous and demanding, the sweeping scenery and clear river itself are therapeutic. Unlike most other epic river trips, the Bonaventure feels intimate and friendly, never big and pushy. Tired paddlers can pull off to the side of the main channel to sit silently over a crystal pool, experiencing a dreamlike sense of hovering above the water.

By mid-afternoon, it's time to start looking out for a riverfront campsite, which you're most likely to find on flat bars that form on the inside of wide river bends. Join in the meal preparation, or take a short hike to look for moose or caribou. After a dinner of salmon grilled over an open fire, it's time for the evening tradition of storytelling around the embers. It won't take much pumping before your colorful Gaspésie guide starts to gush with stories of the river and backwoods.

poling down the river

The Bonaventure is the perfect place to observe and learn the time-honored tradition of poling – standing in the canoe and using a setting pole to propel and steer your way through the rapids. The ancient art and frontier tradition of poling predates paddling by centuries. By planting a 3.5-meter long pole firmly on the river's rocky bottom, the canoe feels like a ski, gaining maneuverability that allows a skilled guide to pick through the rapids without ramming a single rock. Experienced polers find the Bonaventure to be the best canoe poling river in the world, since you can literally run the entire length of the river standing up. This skill, which has been all but forgotten by most paddlers today, is still alive and well on the Bonaventure, preserved as part of a rich cultural legacy by Gaspésie guides.

Rock climbing
in Joshua Tree

>> **More about balance and physics than brute strength**

The rocky clusters that litter the otherwise sparse desert floor of Joshua Tree National Park practically beg to be climbed. They protrude from the scrubby vegetation at awkward angles, in evocative shapes and in all sorts of sizes, some as big as a mid-sized office building. More than five thousand established climbing routes exist along the many faces and crevasses, and you don't have to be Spider-Man to tackle a good portion of them. In fact, you don't even have to be capable of doing a pull-up . . . though it undoubtedly helps.

the Joshua tree

Have you ever seen a *humwichawa*? Odds are you have and you just don't know it, as that's the Cahuilla name for the Joshua tree, hallmark of the Mojave Desert. The Joshua tree is found only in California, Nevada, Arizona, and Utah, and even then just in well-defined ecosystems. Within Joshua Tree National Park, it's found only in the Mojave region and not in the park's warmer Sonora Desert or the higher Great Basin Desert. The slow-growing tree rises up no more than a few inches a year, eventually reaching a height of close to 40ft. Legend has it that they were named by Mormon pioneers, as the trees reminded them of the biblical prophet Joshua with outstretched arms leading to a promised land. Visually striking year-round, these small sentinels are at their most beautiful from February to late March, when they are laden with white blossoms.

Joshua trees can live to be 200 years old

Joshua Tree didn't start out as a rock-climbing hotbed. To the Native Americans, miners, and ranchers who scratched out a living in this harsh desert nearly 150 miles east of Los Angeles, the bizarre, almost alien, rock formations were a nuisance, making it harder to find lost animals and inhibiting wagon access. Indeed, when the area was designated a national monument in 1936, it was recognized more for its namesake yucca trees (actually giant lilies, not cactuses) than for its rocks. But with the emergence of climbing in the 1980s as a recreational sport, and with twenty million people living within easy driving distance, word spread quickly.

What draws devotees and aspiring climbers from all over is not just the quantity of routes, but also the quality of the rock. It's a largely exposed, beige-to-orange quartz monzonite, a type of coarse granite that provides a higher coefficient of friction than the Yosemite granite or desert sandstone popular among climbers in the western United States. In rather less technical terms, that means the climbing here is on a more secure surface, generally free of rockfall and loose, crumbly rock.

There are three main climbing styles on offer within the park. The least gear-intensive is bouldering, usually performed without a rope on large boulders or at the base of larger rock faces. Climbs tend to be limited to a height at which you can take a fall without sustaining injury. In traditional (or "trad") climbing, the roped climber places temporary protection (nuts or spring-loaded cams) into cracks or wedges in the rock, and limits the distance of a fall. The third style is sport climbing, which relies on permanent bolts set into the rock. Joshua Tree has hundreds of trad and sport routes that are

need to know

For experienced climbers, a trip to Joshua Tree National Park (☎ 760/367-5500, ⓦ www.nps.gov/jotr) doesn't demand a lot of advanced planning or logistical headaches; permits are not required for recreational climbing. The park's nine campgrounds are available on a first-come, first-served basis.

guides and gear Joshua Tree Rock Climbing School (☎ 760/366-4745, ⓦ www.joshuatreerockclimbing.com) provides individual and group instruction and guided climbing programs. They can supply all necessary climbing equipment, including shoes, harness, helmet, ropes, and hardware.

when to go The national park is open year round, although high temperatures – sometimes reaching 100°F – often make the summer unbearable; September through May is the most comfortable time-span for climbing. Temperatures at higher elevations in the park are cooler; these areas average about 3.5 inches more precipitation annually.

getting there Joshua Tree National Park is 140 miles east of Los Angeles and is convenient to Palm Springs International Airport, 45 minutes west by car.

suggested reading Randy Vogel, *Rock Climbing Joshua Tree* (Falcon). The most popular climbing guide to the park. He's also the author of *Rock Climbing Joshua Tree West: Quail Springs to Hidden Valley Campground* (Falcon), which is a comprehensive guide to 2300 climbs on the western side of Joshua Tree.

either single pitch or multi-pitch, as determined by the length and number of sections of rock face on which you are setting up a climbing system.

You can easily access most of the established routes from the various campgrounds and other public areas. Each route is rated for difficulty and given a name that is often a topical pun or tip-off to the challenge ahead. The Hidden Valley Campground in the heart of park, for example, boasts hundreds of climbs within a ten-minute walk. Some of the best climbs in this area include: "Double Cross," where intersecting lines on the rock face create a solid 5.7 single pitch of crack climbing; "Walk on the Wild Side," a moderate 5.8 face climb with three wildly meandering pitches; and the expert-only "Illusion Dweller," a classic single pitch 5.10b continuous hand crack, where the illusion lies in the crack's 70-degree slant. "Wonderland of Rocks", an area on the north side of the park, holds even more routes, with a good variety of bouldering, single and multi-pitch climbs. This rugged wash is filled with small pools, boulder caves, scrambles, and winding trails that are as tantalizing to hikers as they are to devout climbers. Even non-climbers will have fun trying a few moves on some of the lower-lying sculpted stones.

And if you've never rock climbed in your life, don't fear. For one thing, you'll have help (and probably some company in your status, too): local guides can quickly assess your skills and strengths, introducing you to suitable routes. Along with learning movements and techniques to leverage your capabilities and conserve energy, you'll discover that rock climbing is more about balance and physics than brute strength, more about surmounting mental challenges than physical challenges.

is this for me?

PHYSICAL ◆ ◆ ◆ ◇ ◇
Balance, upper body and hand strength

PSYCH ◆ ◆ ◆ ◇ ◇
Requires concentration. Falling protected by rope

SKILL ◆ ◆ ◆ ◇ ◇
Techniques can be developed on site

WOW! ◆ ◆ ◆ ◇ ◇
An ideal setting with limitless routes

Hiking the Appalachian Trail

>> In the company of others

KATAHDIN

SPRINGER MOUNTAIN

Standing on the summit of Katahdin, Maine at the end of a 2175-mile long, six-month thru-hike of the Appalachian Trail elicits all manner of celebratory responses: shouts, hugs, handstands, tears, and, if you've really come prepared, champagne toasts. It is the end of a monumental physical challenge and personal quest, the last step of a roller-coaster journey marked by intense highs and lows. Thru-hikers, known to each other by a trail name, speak glowingly of the trail's scenic beauty, while telling of deprivation, discomfort, and physical hardship. To each the trail is a transformative experience.

I hoped to think about future life direction while on the trail. That didn't really happen. I lived in the moment, absorbed the present.

Mama Bear

Starting at Springer Mountain, Georgia, in mid-March with a bulging backpack and a huge goal, you know that statistically your chances of finishing it are slim – only about one in four do. But soon you fall into step with others also intent on making it all the way to Maine's highest peak and you find yourself being carried along by the social bond formed with people from all walks of life. Sleeping in a three-sided shelter, sharing meals, and walking together on a sun-dappled or rain-soaked wooded trail, you gain an intimacy in a matter of days that you might not achieve with coworkers, neighbors – or even friends – in a lifetime. The pain, the vulnerability, the commitment, and the nature of the journey have a way of drawing people together.

As you wend northward, you'll experience days of deep-wooded serenity, strolling through Carolina hemlock, maple, and oak before opening to sunlit grassy balds. You'll traverse bucolic valleys, wildflowered meadows, rocky hillsides, airy ridgelines, and eventually subalpine forests of spruce and fir. That said, the AT is not a wilderness trail, and it can't really be deemed isolated or remote. Instead you'll find an ebb and flow of wild and pastoral, rural and small town, scenic and mundane.

the five best day-hikes

If you don't have the time to complete a thru-hike of the Appalachian Trail, you can still hike a portion of it and in so doing get a feel for what it's all about. The five day-hikes below will whet your appetite for dozens more found along the trail.

Clingmans Dome to Spence Field (Great Smoky Mountains National Park, Tennessee). Starting at Clingmans Dome (6643ft), the highest point on the AT, the next 22 miles heading north give you a superb sense of what the Appalachian ridgeline has to offer, with three mountains and numerous knobs, knolls and gaps,. It's a long day, so have your shuttle return ready when you arrive at Spence Field.

Crampton Gap to Harpers Ferry (Virginia, West Virginia). It's scenic, to be sure, but the real attraction is the trail's place in history. This ten-mile one-way section features Civil War monuments, follows an historic canal towpath, and crosses the Mason-Dixon Line and the Potomac River before arriving at Harpers Ferry, a National Historic Park.

Katahdin (Maine). No one wants to be a spoiler, but the final leg of the AT is a top-notch 10.4-mile (round trip) climb to the top of 5267ft Katahdin along the Hunt Trail. From the Katahdin Stream Campground you ascend through a spruce forest before breaking though treeline to a slope of immense, smoothed boulders leading to the tableland summit where you may share the final steps with elated thru-hikers.

Laurel Fork Gorge and Falls (Tennessee). Both peaceful and spectacular, Laurel Falls is one of many scenic highlights on the AT. For a day-hike you'll want to depart from main trail to explore the dark and exquisite gorge, which used to be part of the AT before it was rerouted, and a swimming hole if you're ready for a cool afternoon dip.

McAfee Knob (Virginia). It's a seven-mile round trip with a punishing 1200-ft ascent to the McAfee Knob from where you'll have commanding views into Catawba and Roanoke valleys – arguably the best in Virginia. The rock platform that juts out from the knob is a favorite photo-op on the AT.

need to know

With no guides or outfitters for the AT you'll want to turn to the Appalachian Trail Conservancy, a private nonprofit corporation responsible for management and protection of the Appalachian Trail and the surrounding lands in partnership with the National Park Service and a variety of other agencies. The best place to start for information is at their visitor center in Harpers Ferry, WV (Ⓦ www.appalachiantrail.org, ☎ 304/535-6331).

when to go Most of the trail can be hiked year round, but thru-hikers focus on March through October.

getting there At the southern end, the trail begins in northern Georgia at Springer Mountain, near Amicalola Falls State Park. The northern terminus is at the summit of Katahdin, the highest mountain in Maine, located in Baxter State Park.

suggested reading David Miller, *AWOL on the Appalachian Trail* (Wingspan Press). A first-hand account of leaving a job, hiking the trail, and what it takes to make it to the end. Cynthia Taylor-Miller, *Appalachian Trail Thru-Hikers' Companion* (Appalachian Trail Conservancy). Written for potential thru-hikers who want the *basic* information on towns, shelters, water, Laundromats, and post offices. David Lauterborn, *Appalachian Trail Thru-Hike Planner* (Appalachian Trail Conservancy) Chart your course, work out a budget, choose gear, plan meals, get in shape, and do it. Victoria Logue, Frank Logue, Leonard M. Adkins *The Best of the Appalachian Trail Day Hikes* (Menasha Ridge Press). Includes 45 days hikes that capture the trail's wonderful variety.

suggested viewing *Appalachian Impressions* (2005) Documentary on thru-hiking the AT that explores the experience without romanticizing it.

is this for me?

PHYSICAL ✦ ✦ ✦ ✦ ✦
Requires exceptional stamina

PSYCH ✦ ✦ ✦ ✦ ✦
Emotionally and physically taxing

SKILL ✦ ✦ ✦ ✦ ✦
Solid camping skills

WOW! ✦ ✦ ✦ ✦ ✦
Life-changing experience

ultralight hiking tips

In recent years, the concept of ultralight backpacking has become a growing obsession as a flood of new high-tech, lightweight products and fabrics have become available to hikers and backpackers who want to go farther and faster, without the exhaustion that accompanies a 40-pound pack. Here are some tips to help you lose some extra pounds.

- Choose items that are made out of lighter materials, like silnylon and titanium.
- Bring items that are adequate, but not excessive. For example, if you primarily hike in warmer areas, as is the case with the AT in summer, don't buy a sleeping bag rated for 15°F temperatures and below. Instead, wear a fleece in your sleeping bag on a record low night.
- Plan a menu around foods that don't require cooking and leave the stove and fuel behind.
- Creative hikers may want to look for ways to combine two items into one. For example, instead of bringing a pillow use a jacket or fleece, or maybe even leave the gloves behind and use a pair of socks as mittens. A wide tent stake can double as a trowel for digging a cat-hole, an essential Leave No Trace practice to be employed between privies.
- If you're really committed, there are always tags to be cut off and toothbrushes to be chopped in half.

The magnitude of it all never really set in – and still hasn't. Distance never seemed like much of a factor; we simply hiked, day after day, mile after mile. It was what we did.

Stinger

With five million steps and a vertical gain comparable to walking from sea level to the top of Everest and back sixteen times, even hikers who start out in reasonably good shape, find that by trail's end they have developed a level of conditioning they never thought possible. Beyond the physical challenge, there are enormous logistical and supply considerations. Most hikers make mail-drop food shipments to points along the way, and typically carry a three- to five-day supply of provisions in their backpack. Although it's advisable to carry maps and a compass, route-finding along the trail is the least of your worries, especially since the trail is marked with 80,000 blazes, an average of one every 144ft. If everything goes according to plan, an average thru-hiker will complete the length of the trail in just a week shy of six months – and more than likely in the company of others.

The AT is about being away from the "hurried life" that we all live – yet, it is not an isolated journey. What makes it so special is the people you meet.

Night Owl

CHERRY
CREEK

USA

21 Rafting Cherry Creek

>> Like riding a nine-mile rollercoaster

When whitewater aficionados get together and start bragging about the latest river they've run, someone's bound to cut to the chase by asking, "But how does it compare to Cherry Creek?" If the planet's top rafters got together to design a river as steep as possible with entertaining boulder placements and stunningly deep drops, it would look for all the world like the Cherry Creek section of California's Tuolumne (pronounced "too-ALL-uh-me") River. Without even the tiniest splash of hyperbole, those who regularly run the river refer to it as being "perfectly designed."

man overboard

You're racing down roaring, relentless rapids with water splashing and spraying all over your body when out of the blue it happens – you're body hurtles over the side of the raft into the raging water. Although flips on Cherry Creek are rare, their occurrence means a strenuous and chilly swim with no flatwater where you can easily aright your raft. Your safety hinges on preparation and the ability to act quickly. Once you've come to the surface and caught a breath, make eye contact with your oarsman or guide and listen for directions. Swimming in rapids can be both physically draining and dangerous. When you've connected with the raft and are holding on to a line or D-ring, the best defensive position is to float on your back with your feet up and pointed downstream. Move to the side of the boat, since the last place you want to be is between downstream rocks and the raft. Stay calm and hold tight while your guide aims for an eddy or calmer waters. Here, with some assistance from crew members, you'll be able to pull yourself back into the raft, shake off the water and be ready for the next rapid.

Known for its tumbling rock slaloms and heart-stopping drops, Cherry Creek is the most challenging commercially run whitewater in North America. Classified an "experts only" Class V+ run, the river is regarded as the benchmark for defining what a Class V river really is. Even experienced guides regularly shy away from running trips for fear of liability and the potential risks that can occur with clients, inexperienced or not.

"The Creek" spills out from the remote granite slopes of Yosemite National Park. In most rivers, rapids are formed by boulders deposited from above or from side streams. Cherry Creek is distinctive in that its rapids are formed primarily on bedrock granite sculpted by water, with the many boulders strewn about acting more as the frosting on the cake. This fundamental difference gives Cherry Creek a more "organic" feel and rhythm, and for rafters, it's like being a leaf in a millrace. With an astoundingly steep gradient dropping an average of 110ft per mile, Cherry Creek is ninety percent rapids – compare that to the famed Colorado River descent through the Grand Canyon, which is ninety percent flatwater. Still, numbers fail to tell the story. Only by experiencing the river's relentlessly dropping rapids and its maze of gigantic granite boulders can one discover the natural perfection of Cherry Creek.

Throughout the nine-mile, four-hour descent, you'll career through a pine-forested, V-shaped canyon where the river's width ranges from just 40 to 80ft. The first 1.5 miles kick in with solid Class III and IV rapids; these torrents would be showstoppers on most other rivers, but here they're just a warm-up act. At the confluence with the Tuolumne River, riders are given the chance to hike out if they have any last-minute doubts. In the first few miles below the confluence of the waterways,

rafts run through a gauntlet of Class V rapids in quick succession. First comes Jawbone followed by Mushroom, the longest and most intimidating of the river's rapids, where the final big drop is known as Toadstool. Guillotine rounds out this section of rapids, which together form a long slalom course with drops and turns requiring exceptional agility and skill to navigate.

These spectacular rapids all occur before the steepest section of the Tuolumne. Known as the Miracle Mile, a string of continuous Class IV and V rapids form as the river drops 210ft in a mile. There is simply no let-up in the action, and the waves, drops, and holes are unavoidable. Beyond here, the action mellows slightly, but the hair-raising thrills come back with a bang on Lewis' Leap, a highly technical rapid with an eight-foot drop halfway down. At Flat Rock Falls and Lumsden Falls plan on getting out and guiding or lining your raft from the safety of the shore, a practice followed by all commercial groups and sane private rafters. Runs conclude with several miles of Class IV rapids, including a thrilling ten-foot drop known as Horseshoe Falls, before taking out at Meral's Pool. Below here, the eighteen-mile section known as the Main Tuolumne River is one of California's most popular and family-friendly whitewater runs, with over a dozen Class IV and V rapids. If you're spending a few days in the area, consider doing this section first as preparation for Cherry Creek.

Gold was discovered in the Tuolumne River in 1849 and placer mined until 1856. You can still pan for gold in the Tuolumne today, but don't quit your day job.

Prepared or not, know that by surviving Cherry Creek, next time your whitewater friends are touting their favorite river, you're perfectly justified in casting a nonchalant glance and asking, "But how does it compare to Cherry Creek?"

need to know

Members of a Class V raft team will all be expected to demonstrate swift-water swimming skills by swimming across the river and back while wearing a wetsuit and lifejacket.

guides and gear Groveland's Sierra Mac (☎ 1-800/457-2580, ⓦ www.sierramac.com) runs one- to three-day guided trips on both Cherry Creek and the extended Tuolumne. Their trips on Cherry Creek include intensive pre-launch instruction including the use of all safety and protective equipment.

when to go For those who can handle the frigid water, Cherry Creek is run as early as March and as late as October, depending on snowmelt and releases from dams upstream. One of the most attractive features of the river is that because Cherry Creek is a dam release, it delivers exceptional rapids in mid-summer – the best time to come is June to August – something uncommon in North America.

getting there The staging point for most commercial trips is near the town of Groveland on Highway 120, located about three hours from Sacramento and an hour or two longer from San Francisco.

suggested reading Lars Holbek and Chuck Stanley, *The Best Whitewater in California: The Guide to 180 Runs* (Watershed Books). A classic mile-by-mile guide to the Tuolumne and other great whitewater rivers.

is this for me?

PHYSICAL ✦ ✦ ✦ ✦ ✦
Intense activity requires strength and conditioning

PSYCH ✦ ✦ ✦ ✦ ✦
Class V whitewater, lots of commitment

SKILL ✦ ✦ ✦ ✦ ✦
Strong swimming skills required

WOW! ✦ ✦ ✦ ✦ ✦
An exceptionally challenging whitewater experience

Climbing the Grand Teton

>> **A rite of passage**

GRAND TETON
NATIONAL PARK

USA

Who hasn't, at least once in their life, been seduced by a mountain? For many, the Teton Range is love at first sight. Its jagged spires stand stark against a sapphire sky, rising so sharply from the horizontal valley that foothills are expendable. These statuesque peaks at the heart of Wyoming's Grand Teton National Park have graced more calendars and postcards than any swimsuit model or pin-up girl, and attract four million shutter-snapping gawkers per year. But for some, simply eyeballing these young peaks isn't enough. Instead, they get roped in by the allure of climbing the tallest peak in the range, the Grand Teton (13,770ft).

The Grand Teton was first summited in 1898 by a party lead by William Owen and Franklin Spalding, and their route – still the most popular and easiest line to the summit – is known as the Owen-Spalding route. A few decades later, the Tetons ushered in a golden age of climbing in the 1930s when Glenn Exum, working as Paul Petzoldt's assistant guide, made a daring solo ascent of the ridge that now bears his name; he was only 18 at the time, and climbed the peak in football cleats without the use of ropes. In the years that followed, rapid advances in techniques and equipment opened dozens of new routes, and the era's top climbers made the mountain a proving ground for their ambitions. Into the 1960s, the Tetons

shared the climbing spotlight with California's Yosemite as the world's top mountaineers deliberately searched for difficult unclimbed routes and variations on existing routes. Thanks to the work of generations of climbers, there are now dozens of routes leading up "the Grand."

There's no question that the tower at the heart of the Teton Range is one intimidating peak. But one of its many wonders is that even fit novice climbers, provided they prove their mettle in training courses leading up to the ascent, can crest the peak by taking part in popular three- to four-day courses. In the course you'll learn to use basic equipment, develop rope skills, and become familiar with signals and commands. Learning all this from professional mountaineers on the rock faces of the Grand Teton is an especially memorable part of the experience. If you want a head start in your development as a Teton climber, here's a tip: never refer to the Teton Range as "The Grand Tetons." The proper term is "the Tetons" or the "Teton Range," as the Grand Teton is the dominant peak in the range.

Whether you're climbing the Grand as part of one of these guided trips or as an experienced independent climber, you'll more than likely begin your quest from the Lupine Meadows Trailhead along a trail that ascends quickly on slopes of aspen and fir shot through with sunbeams. It's easy to get swallowed up in the magnitude and beauty of Garnet Canyon, an eight-mile artery that leads to many of the Grand's best climbing routes, but odds are your mind will be fixed on the challenge towering ahead.

coming down the mountain

Rappelling, or abseiling as it is known outside the US and Canada, looks so graceful and daring as a climber glides down a cliffside on a rope. It's actually one of the easiest and safest of all down-climbing techniques, but not without inherent risks. Before you climb the Grand Teton and are faced with its lengthy free rappel, you'll want to have a few shorter and easier "raps" under your belt, and be familiar with climbing knots and the proper use of your harness and belay device. In one frequently used technique, you thread the rope to its midpoint through an anchor at the top of the climb and run the two sides of the rope through a belay device. With the anchor firmly in place and your harness and belay device properly attached, you walk backwards down the cliff. In this method you can descend up to half the length of the rope. Since the belay device applies friction and drag to the rope, you can control your descent by pulling on the ropes with your brake hand to increase the drag and even bring yourself to a complete stop in midair.

Climbers must always be aware of how long each rappel will be. For safety's sake, it's best to tie the two ends of the rope in a knot so you don't end up rappelling off of the end of the line. Extremely fast rappels, bouncing, or swinging can damage the rope. For repeated rappels, use belay devices that minimize heat build-up, sharp bends to the rope, and stressing of fibers which could damage the rope.

need to know

Within Grand Teton National Park (☎307/739-3300, ⓦ www.nps.gov/grte) a permit is not required for hiking or mountaineering, but you must obtain one for backcountry camping. The handiest stop for climbing information is the cluster of buildings at South Jenny Lake, including a visitor center (June–Sept; ☎307/739-3343), a ranger station dedicated to climbing (May–Sept; same number), and a general store.

guides and gear Guided climbing within Grand Teton National Park is provided by two companies: Jackson Hole Mountain Guides (☎307/733-4979 or 1-800/239-7642, ⓦ www.jhmg.com) climbs the Grand's Pownall-Gilkey route; Exum Mountain Guides (☎307/733-2297, ⓦ www.exumguides.com) has exclusive guide access to the Owen-Spalding route, along with an office within the park by Jenny Lake.

when to go The best climbing conditions are from June to mid-September; the rest of the year is challenging, with snow and ice climbing skills required.

getting there Grand Teton National Park is in northwestern Wyoming, due south of Yellowstone National Park. Regular flights are available to Jackson Hole Airport (JAC), located within the park boundaries. The closest town is buzzing Jackson, Wyoming, a fifteen-minute drive south.

suggested reading Leigh N. Ortenburger and Reynold G. Jackson, *A Climber's Guide to the Teton Range* (Mountaineers). You won't be carrying this hefty volume up the mountain, but it's an indispensable guide in planning and executing your climb. Richard Rossiter, *Teton Classics, 50 Selected Climbs in Grand Teton National Park* (Falcon). Excellent guide with maps to the best routes to the major summits.

is this for me?

PHYSICAL ✦ ✦ ✦ ✦
Requires solid physical conditioning and stamina

PSYCH ✦ ✦ ✦ ✦
Technical climbing with exposure

SKILL ✦ ✦ ✦
Climbing and rope skills are essential

WOW! ✦ ✦ ✦ ✦
A classic climb, a great accomplishment

As you arrive at top of the canyon, fixed ropes ease your ascent up the headwall to reach the 11,60-foot Lower Saddle, above which the summit looms to the north. Most summit-bound climbers spend at least one night camping on the rocky ridge of the lower saddle, enjoying the rarified air and memorable views to the east and west. Guided climbing trips will also often do their training here on the Grand's rocky upper flanks.

From your camp at the Lower Saddle on up, you need to have a few technical tricks in your bag. If climbing independently, solid route-finding, rope handling, and anchor placement skills are essential. Even the Class 5.6 Owen–Spalding route can demand exceptional skills in icy conditions, which are not uncommon even in mid-summer. The Pownall-Gilkey route, another popular guided route from the Lower Saddle, requires 4 pitches of Class 5 climbing and a demanding face with more than its share of exposure, followed by short belayed coils to the summit. Under normal conditions and steady climbing, you should make it from the saddle to the summit in about two hours.

The summit rises a precipitous 7000ft above the valley floor, and offers its most tantalizing views as you gaze along the tops of the other peaks in the range – Mount Moran, Middle Teton, South Teton, and Mount Owen – that are also popular climbing objectives. Jenny Lake looks like a glistening jewel below, while Bradley and Taggart Lakes sparkle for your attention to the south. There are commanding views of Jackson Hole further south and Idaho's Teton Valley to the west, but even if the summit is shrouded in clouds, as it often is, the realization that you're sharing that spot of craggy rock with generations of legendary climbers for whom the Grand was a rite of passage is reward enough. Welcome to the club.

The standard descent for most routes is the 100-foot descent of Sergeant's Chimney followed by the spectacular two-rope 120-foot Owen-Spalding free rappel to the Upper Saddle. There is a tendency for climbers to attain the summit, and then let their guard down on the descent, where climbing injuries and fatalities most frequently occur. On the way down, stay sharp and make sure your act is wired tight.

Exploring Isle Royale

>> **Between predator and prey**

CANADA

ISLE ROYALE
NATIONAL PARK

USA

What lies beyond the remote? Isle Royale, Michigan's hidden gem of a national park, is one answer. Reached via a three-hour ferry ride from the state's already far-flung Upper Peninsula, the island boasts a wild and distinct personality. Here you can swim out to an island located on a lake that's within an island within a lake. Howling wolves wake you up at dawn, while a large moose population keeps your camera always at the ready. Other surprises are more visceral, like the heady essence of spruce and the sweet taste of wild blueberries, or glorious Renoir-like sunsets followed by a night sky that lights up as bright as a Hollywood marquis.

new arrivals

Wolves and moose haven't always called Isle Royale home. In fact, both are relatively new arrivals. The first group of moose probably swam to the island from Canada around the year 1900, and for a half century they lived the high-life, feasting on the thick aquatic vegetation on an island lacking natural predators. All that changed when a pack of wolves wandered across an ice bridge from Canada sometime around 1950, instantly forming a unique relationship that exists to this day. The moose have no other predators, the wolves have almost no other prey, with the moose population providing ninety percent of the wolves' sustenance. This dynamic has made Isle Royale's wolves and moose the subject of the world's longest-running scientific study of predator-prey relationships and has produced valuable findings into the nature of predation and the viability of wilderness species in a harsh climate.

Although the potential mineral deposits and surrounding fish-rich waters have attracted notice for centuries, Isle Royale's most precious commodities are its untrammeled woodlands, rocky coastlines, and inland waterways. The largest island in Lake Superior – itself the largest freshwater lake in the world by surface area – Isle Royale is part of the US even though it's closer to Canada, and part of Michigan even though it's closer to Minnesota. Accessible only by boat or seaplane, simply getting here is an adventure requiring time and patience. And with no roads or cars on the island, and wheeled vehicles strictly forbidden – including bicycles and even canoe portage dollies – it's easy to see why Isle Royale is one of the least visited national parks in the United States.

Near the end of the boat ride across tempestuous Lake Superior, Isle Royale's defining features come into focus. Boreal forest rises from the shoreline while dozens of satellite islands and rocky outcroppings spangle the waters. Beyond the public docks at Rock Harbor on the island's southeast side, with its visitor center, small store, and lodge, or Windigo on the west, with its visitor center and store, the rest of the island is untrammeled wilderness.

After landing, your biggest dilemma will be how to best experience the pristine beauty: by foot, by paddle, or perhaps even both. On land you'll have 165 miles of marked hiking trails to explore, and ventures into to the woods typically include a moose sighting; a chance encounter with an animal five times your size is always an edgy thrill. The resident wolf packs are far more elusive, while the island's foxes are habituated to human contact and prowl

To step into Isle Royale is to leave behind one's own self and one's world and to begin a new exploration into the nature of life.
Napier Shelton

campgrounds looking for table scraps. To gain an appreciation for the island's size, try the Greenstone Ridge Trail, which runs lengthwise for forty miles down the spine of the island and offers views across Lake Superior into Canada. At lower elevations, you'll thread your way through peaceful forests of yellow birch and maple. If you'd rather a loop, one popular option is the thirty-mile Feldtmann Ridge Loop, starting at the Windigo ferry dock and making a traverse of the island's southwest sector, taking in an observation tower with commanding lake views, a camp on Siskiwit Bay, and some small, abandoned copper mines.

Also a playground for paddlers, the shoreline of Isle Royale is dotted with finger bays, barrier islands, and coves. Kayakers should be on the lookout for the occasional otters feeding on fish in both Lake Superior and the island's inland lakes. Around Isle Royale's southeast fins, the protected waters of Rock Harbor, Tobin Harbor, and Merritt Lane are ideally suited for peaceful paddles and laced with rocky beaches on which to land. For a more challenging adventure, consider the three-portage route connecting Chippewa Harbor, Lake Whittlesey, Wood Lake, Siskiwit Lake, and Intermediate Lake – a chain in which each lake becomes more remote than the last. Paddlers need to be aware of the possibility of rapidly changing weather conditions, and especially winds that can change without warning. The possibility of hypothermia is the top hazard on frigid Lake Superior, even during the warmest months of summer.

Nighttime is when the island's isolation comes into clearest focus, with the Northern Lights often lighting up the dark sky overhead and a hushed silence soothing tired bones. Both paddlers and hikers have access to comfortable accommodation at the island's campsites, which feature three-sided, wood-floored shelters lined with mosquito netting on the fourth side, tent campsites, and pit toilets. The shelters are available on a first come, first served basis, so you'd be smart to carry a tent. It may be a toss-up as to whether the mosquitoes or the black flies are the most abundant species on the island. Either way, you'll want to come equipped with repellant and maybe even plan your trip for later in the season when the bug population has tailed off.

need to know

Isle Royale National Park (℡ 906/482-0984, Ⓦ www.nps.gov/isro) has visitor centers at Rock Harbor and Windigo on Isle Royale, and in Houghton, Michigan; the basic park fee is $4 per person, per day. Backcountry use permits are issued onboard the National Park Service ferry while traveling to the island. For an understanding of the island's natural environment check in with the Isle Royale Natural History Association (℡ 906/482-7860 or 1-800/678-6925, Ⓦ ww.irnha.org) before leaving.

guides and gear You can bring your sea kayak or canoe on the ferry, though limited canoe and kayak rentals are available at Windigo and Rock Harbor. For guided adventures and outfitting services, the Keweenaw Adventure Company (℡ 906/289-4303, Ⓦ www.keweenawadventure. com), run out of Copper Harbor, offers four- to eight-day guided kayaking trips around Isle Royale.

when to go Peak season is late July through early September. Mosquitoes and black flies are at their worst in late June and early July and usually start to die off near the end of July. The park is closed November through April 15.

getting there Isle Royale is accessed by either the National Park Service ferry from Houghton on Michigan's Upper Peninsula, or by park-authorized private vessels leaving from both Copper Harbor, Michigan, and Grand Portage, Minnesota. Seaplane service is available to the island from Houghton County Memorial Airport (CMX). Fares, schedules, and reservation details are available on the park's website.

suggested reading Jim Dufresne, *Isle Royale National Park: Foot Trails & Water Routes* (Mountaineers Books). The complete guide to the island for both hikers and paddlers.

is this for me?

PHYSICAL ✦ ✦ ✦ ✦ ✦
Hiking and paddling in wind

PSYCH ✦ ✦ ✦ ✦ ✦
Remote but accessible wilderness

SKILL ✦ ✦ ✦ ✦ ✦
Know wet exit and rescue techniques

WOW! ✦ ✦ ✦ ✦ ✦
Spectacular scenery and sheer solitude

Windsurfing in the Columbia River Gorge

>> Catch a steady roller

COLUMBIA
RIVER GORGE

USA

Imagine zipping along a river at speeds that would allow for barefoot waterskiing, a glistening spray of water steadily splashing off your board, with the power of a 30-knot gust filling your sail. Welcome to the Columbia River Gorge, a rift dividing Oregon and Washington with such consistent winds that it's become one of the world's finest windsurfing destinations. It's so easy to get swept away by the winds on the Columbia River that you might miss the peripheral magnificence of the gorge itself, where basalt bluffs and wooded slopes rise dramatically above the mile-wide river, and where white-capped Mount Hood looms in the distance.

Eons before the arrival of boards and sails, thousands of volcanic eruptions flooded the region with layers of lava, ash, and mudflows. During the last ce age, some of the largest floods in the history surged to the sea and helped shape and scour the Columbia River Gorge, a spectacular eighty mile-long and up to 4000-foot-deep river canyon cutting through the Cascade Mountain Range. As the warm air to the east rises from the desert floor, it is replaced by cool marine air drawn in from the Pacific Coast. This air moves westward through the gorge like a giant wind tunnel, and the constriction produces an accelerator effect blowing from May through September.

Roll on, Columbia, roll on
Your power is turning our
darkness to dawn
So roll on, Columbia, roll on

Woody Guthrie

Winds of 20–30mph are considered ideal for windsurfing, and June through August you can expect to be treated to such conditions five or six days a week, with thirty-day stretches of great wind not uncommon. The wind blows steadily from the west as the mighty Columbia rolls on in the opposite direction, creating the characteristic rollers that plow their way through the river without breaking. On a normal summer day you can expect a 3–4-foot swell, and when the wind bumps to 35mph you'll find beautiful 6-foot rollers that create a launching pad for exhilairating jumps. For windsurfers, these rollers are a world apart from the choppy little whitecaps found on most freshwater lakes and are what makes the Columbia River Gorge superbly unique.

Beginners often make their first launch at the Hook, a protected waterfront lagoon in the funky town of Hood River, Oregon. It's named after the riverside jetty separating it from the main body of the river, and here you'll find shallow water and small chops on windy days. With a little experience on your side, you can move on to the Event Site, which can be crowded close to shore but offers an easy intermediate launch and good

opening the floodgates

About 15,000 years ago, the glaciers from the most recent ice age had reached their maximum size and began to melt. During this last glacial advance, a finger from the ice sheet moved down into the Purcell Trench in northeast Idaho, resulting in a 2500-foot-high ice dam across the Clark Fork River. The dam created what is known as Glacial Lake Missoula, and as time passed water behind the dam built up and overflowed into the east valleys, increasing the lake to the size of today's Lake Erie and Lake Ontario combined. The swelling water eventually exerted such extreme pressure that the dam became buoyant and water began to escape underneath it by carving sub-glacial tunnels. Once unplugged the water leaked so fast that it's estimated the lake emptied in less than a week, and waters gushed at a torrential 30–50mph across eastern Washington. The largest flood known in geological history had begun, and as it raced to the Pacific Ocean – more than 400 miles away – the landscape of eastern Washington was never to look the same. The flood stripped away the topsoil, carving barren black rock into plateaus, hills, and canyons. Though only one of more than one hundred major floods, the failure of the Missoula Ice Dam did much to create and shape the Columbia Gorge as we know it today.

It's so easy to get swept away by the winds on the Columbia River that you might miss the peripheral magnificence of the gorge itself

need to know

A windsurfing trip to the Columbia River Gorge is best centered at the city of Hood River, hub of the region's windsurfing scene. Mountain biking and mountain climbing are also popular local pursuits in the summer; the Columbia River Gorge Visitors Association is a good first source for planning assistance (Ⓦ www.crgva.org).

guides and gear Located in Hood River, Big Winds (☎ 541/386-6086 or 1-888/509-4210, Ⓦ www.bigwinds.com) offers windsurfing and kiteboarding instruction for all levels, including a camp for kids. They also have an excellent selection of high-performance rental equipment.

when to go Diehards start getting in the water in late March, but you'll find the best wind conditions from May to September, with the prime time being June, July, and August.

getting there Hood River is just off I-84, a scenic one-hour drive from Portland International Airport.

suggested viewing *The Windsurfing Movie* (2007). Conveys the beauty and excitement of windsurfing as it turns the camera on the best riders in windsurfing history.

is this for me?

PHYSICAL ✦ ✦ ✦ ✦
Strength, agility, balance, and coordination

PSYCH ✦ ✦
Challenging conditions in a safe setting

SKILL ✦ ✦ ✦ ✦ ✦
Requires patience, practice over time

WOW! ✦ ✦ ✦
Exhilarating experience in a beautiful site

westerlies. Four miles west of the Hood River Bridge on the Washington state side of the river is the Hatchery, known locally as "The Hatch." With excellent winds and deep water that forms large swells close to the shore, The Hatch is a top spot for experts as well as photographers looking to capture the action at close range. Numerous other launch sites dot both the Washington and Oregon shoreline for miles, offering more choices for all skill levels.

Although the sport of windsurfing is less than fifty years old, it has drawn devotees worldwide who see it as melding the best of surfing and sailing. Propelled by rapid technological advances in sailboard design, windsurfing allows for freestyle moves no surfer or sailor could dream of doing. The sport's learning curve is shaped by practice, patience, and good instruction. To get the most out of your initial outing, find a good instructor and take advantage of the shorter, wider boards that are easier to stand on, and smaller, lightweight sails that are likewise easier to balance – both recent developments that have helped get first-timers on the water more quickly. With a few days of instruction you'll be zipping across open waters, feeling the surges of adrenaline that come with each small swell of the river. With a modest amount of ability and a couple of seasons of windsurfing, you'll be transformed from one of the shore-bound spectators taking photos to one of the river-riding athletes getting photographed – but, more importantly, you'll be having a blast.

25 Hiking the John Muir Trail

>> Discover the backbone of the Sierra

The daily routine on California's epic John Muir Trail is a simple one. Starting with another in a long string of dramatic sunrises, you break camp with a quick breakfast and are back on track in the slanting light of dawn. After morning shadows peel away from the wooded valleys, you're treated to a crisp, bright blue morning and comforting mountain breezes while enjoying unobstructed views above the tree-line. Once you've switchbacked up a talus pass and skirted yet another isolated glacial lake, it's time to stop for a foot-soothing soak in a mountain stream and enjoy a snack propped up against a moss-padded granite boulder. After a long day on the trail and an energy-packed dinner, you'll sleep soundly on even the thinnest of foam pads.

being bear aware

Black bears rarely attack. But here's the thing. Sometimes they do. All bears are agile, cunning and immensely strong, and they are always hungry. If they want to kill you and eat you, they can, and pretty much whenever they want. That doesn't happen often, but – and here is the absolutely salient point – once would be enough.

Bill Bryson

The John Muir Trail has a reputation for attracting the most cunning black bears in the county. Counterbalancing food bags by hanging them high above the ground from a tree limb is a tried and true method for keeping food from bears in other parts of the country, but it's completely ineffective on most of the JMT. Similarly to how black bears in Yosemite have learned to break into cars for an illicit snack, those on the JMT climb trees to dislodge counterbalanced bags. What makes it worse is that these bears have a very broad definition of food: anything that smells like food or has had contact with food is food. Bears have been known to run off with liquor, toothpaste, deodorants, and scented sunscreens. The solution is a bear canister, a lightweight, high-impact plastic, aluminum or carbon-fiber barrel with a screw-on lid that even the smartest bear can't open.

Using bear canisters isn't only good for you, it's good for other campers and even the bears themselves. Bears that get to human food often abandon their natural resources and become a nuisance at campsites and sometimes have to be relocated. Should a bear somehow get your food, it's no longer your food. Don't even think about trying to retrieve it, as the bear will fight any attempts to take the food back. Never leave your food unprotected for even a short time during the day as both bears and marmots can rip into a pack quickly. While black bears are serious about your food, they don't pose a serious threat to you, and fatal attacks are rare. Still, if you see one in the wild, it pays to keep your distance.

Gliding through a great swath of Sierra Nevada wilderness, the John Muir Trail is officially 211 miles in length, but in practice it's a slightly longer 222 miles. On its meandering course, you'll discover the backbone of the Sierra backcountry in three majestic national parks – Yosemite, Kings Canyon, and Sequoia – while passing by dozens of 13,000 to 14,000-foot razorback peaks and hundreds of lakes. And if the stunning mountain wilderness wasn't enough of a draw, the Sierra Nevada is also blessed with typically mild and sunny summer weather.

While the weather makes the hiking more enjoyable, it doesn't make the trail any shorter or the slopes any flatter. The "JMT" has blistered more than its share of overly ambitious feet unaccustomed to carrying a heavy backpack and hiking a dozen miles per day. Considering the distances involved and remote setting, this isn't a hike to be done on impulse, and trail-goers need to have enough backpacking experience to realize the endurance required to complete a three-week trip.

Starting in the heart of buzzing Yosemite, the trail passes both Vernal Fall and Nevada Fall into Little Yosemite Valley. This is easily the most crowded portion of the trail, but also one of the most breathtakingly beautiful sections. Within an hour, the crowds thin and you're faced with the option of adding a four-mile round-trip spur to Half-Dome (see p.000) on the first day of a two-hundred-mile trip. From here, the trail continues on to Tuolumne Meadows, the starting point for some JMT hikers as permits are easier to obtain here; only consider doing so, however, if you've trodden the first leg on a previous trip and don't mind missing it.

From Tuolumne Meadows the JMT joins with the Pacific Crest Trail (see p.000) and turns to its general southward direction, gaining elevation and crossing the high tarns and creeks of the Ansel Adams Wilderness before arriving at Devils Postpile. While the fascinating formation of columnar basalt looks like the concrete pilings of a construction project gone wrong, it's actually the remnant of a Cenozoic lava flow.

The remaining 160 miles of trail only dips below 8000ft twice, averaging closer to 10,000ft as it weaves along the secluded eastern boundary of Sequoia and Kings Canyon National Parks. This is a realm where glacial cirques cradle shimmering lakes, with some of the most characteristically striking scenery on the trail. You'll also cross high streams that can be daunting, particularly when swollen by snowmelt in late spring. The last 100 miles of trail crosses five mountain passes in excess of 12,000ft, but the not-so-secret is that while these passes are high and rocky the hikes up them really aren't grueling quad-burners. The longest and toughest of the bunch is Mather Pass, which ascends 4000ft over ten miles – not terribly steep by most alpine standards. In any case, the views of scattered lakes below and peaks beyond make for thrilling uphill stretches.

The spine of rugged peaks on the sunrise side of Sequoia National Park culminates with a rise along the gently ascending backside of 14,505-foot Mount Whitney, the highest peak in the lower 48. Reaching the top earns sweeping views down into the Owens Valley and Death Valley, the lowest point in the Western Hemisphere, to the east. Whitney's summit marks the official end of the 211-mile John Muir Trail, but unless your backpack converts into a jetpack there's still another eleven miles of descent along the legendary 98 switchbacks and deep canyons of the Whitney Trail before you arrive at Whitney Portal. Here you'll be rewarded with the best burgers in the region at the Portal Store, along with a road that will take you back to civilization.

need to know

While the JMT is tackled in both directions, most thru-hikers choose a north-to-south route as it's easier to obtain the required entry permit at the northern terminus – Yosemite National Park – than at Whitney Portal to the south. All trailheads along the trail have a quota, but it's only an entry quota. Once you have a permit and are on the trail, you can stay as long as you like.

guides and gear Unless you're a trailrunner looking to break a record, plan your trip around the three primary re-supply stores along the trail: Tuolumne Meadows, Reds Meadow, and the Muir Trail Ranch. As food choices are limited, provisions can also be mailed to these re-supply points. Such logistical requirements, along with organizing transportation, are time-consuming, leading some to opt for a guided trip. Sierra Mountain Center is a good first stop for guided hikes (☏ 760/873-8526, Ⓦ www.sierramountaincenter.com).

when to go July to mid-September is ideal. You can usually plan a trip beginning in early July as the snow is melting from the higher elevation passes. The first snow generally hits in late October, but expect short, cold days by then.

getting there The airports in Reno, Las Vegas, Los Angeles, Sacramento, Fresno, and Bakersfield are within driving distance to the trail. High Sierra Transportation (☏ 760/827-1111, Ⓦ www.highsierratransportation.com) offers shuttle service between most major airports and trailheads. If driving, consider leaving your car at the large lot at Whitney Portal or in the town of Lee Vining and taking the YARTS bus (☏ 1-877/989-2787, Ⓦ www.yarts.com) to Yosemite Valley.

suggested reading Elizabeth Wenk and Kathy Morey, *John Muir Trail: The Essential Guide to Hiking America's Most Famous Trail* (Wilderness Press). A comprehensive guide to the trail complete with maps.

is this for me?

PHYSICAL ✦ ✦ ✦ ✦ ✦
Backpacking long distance requires stamina

PSYCH ✦ ✦ ✦ ✦ ✦
Takes planning and tenacity

SKILL ✦ ✦ ✦ ✦ ✦
Solid backcountry camping skills

WOW! ✦ ✦ ✦ ✦ ✦
The finest mountain scenery in the US

Dogsledding in the Yukon

>> Become a sled dog whisperer

WHITEHORSE

CANADA

If you think of dogsledding as a team sport, you're off to a good start. Your team's success, like any team's, is due in large part to its members' ability to effectively communicate with one another. The trouble is, you're the only one standing on two legs and you're in the middle of the arctic wilderness. Luckily your compatriots, tongues wagging as they gallop across the snow, are excellent listeners who provide constant cues. You, as the musher, just need to learn when to lead and when to follow.

St. Paul's Church

Using dogs to draw sleds can be traced back nearly one thousand years in both the Canadian and Siberian sub-arctic. Sled dogs performed well in Canada's eighteenth- and nineteenth century-fur trade, and even saw military service in the French and Indian War, where the command "*marche*" became "mush" and those giving the commands were mushers. But the most fabled dogsledding accounts come from the Klondike starting in 1896 and subsequent gold rushes along Yukon River which attracted tens of thousands of prospectors to the region and which made boomtowns of places like Whitehorse, Dawson, Fort Yukon and Fairbanks. While arctic rivers were navigable and provided reliable trade routes much of the year, once the long winter set in, sled dogs became the most reliable mean of transporting supplies, mail, and people.

Today, dogsledding has a competitive side found in some of the epic races like the Iditarod and the Yukon Quest, but it still provides the means to explore a remote land well beyond the reach of other forms of transportation. Here, you'll taste the legacy of the Yukon as you guide your team of sled dogs across a frozen landscape.

Before taking off across the tundra, take time to get to know your crew. Your teammates, thick-furred 23–30-kilogram Alaskan huskies, are the premier endurance athletes in the world of dogsled racing. Capable of running 160km a day for days on end, Alaskan huskies don't need to be forced to run – they love to run. The trick, rather, is getting them to stop. At the starting line of a dogsled race, it can take twenty people to restrain the forward thrust of a team yearning to take off.

being a sled dog whisperer

For their size, sled dogs are incredibly strong – pound for pound they're stronger than horses. But to harness that power they need training and conditioning. As a first lesson, trainers tie a light weight to an older pup, often a trailer tire, and then set the pup free to run. The pup pulls the weight for about 30m and the process may be repeated. Then the dog is placed on a small team of about four to six dogs with its mother or siblings and is taught to pull something larger. Mushers watch their dogs closely and if the dogs seem happy with pulling a certain distance the distance is lengthened until the dog is strong enough that it can pull a sled with a large team and still enjoy running. Mushers also train dogs to turn certain directions saying "gee!" for turning right, "hah!" for turning left, and "straight ahead" for running straight. "Hike!" is the most common command to start the dogs running, but words are rarely needed for this.

This is the Law of the Yukon, that only the Strong shall thrive; That surely the Weak shall perish, and only the Fit survive.

Robert W. Service

need to know

Whitehorse Visitor Reception Centre (☎867/667-3084, 800-661-0494, ⓦwww.travelyukon.com) provides general information regarding accommodation, tourist services and area attractions.

guides and gear Kennels and dog trainers near Whitehorse, like Muktuk Adventures (☎867/668-3647, 866/968-3647; ⓦwww.muktuk.com.), offer multi-day dog-sled training, tours and packages for beginners and experienced mushers, including accommodation and meals. Outfitters provides all necessary equipment including trained dogs, sled, guide, meals, accommodation, camping equipment, an outer layer of winter clothing and boots. Bring a warm thermal underlayer, sunscreen, and sunglasses.

when to go Mid-December to March, with weather conditions becoming generally more favorable into March.

getting there Fly into Whitehorse, Yukon Territory. Rental car and shuttle service is available to area kennels and dog training facilities.

suggested reading Brian Patrick O'Donoghue, *My Lead Dog Was a Lesbian: Mushing Across Alaska in the Iditarod – the World's Most Grueling Race* (Vintage). A novice competes in the Iditarod race with determination, luck, and a sense of humor.

is this for me?

PHYSICAL ✦ ✦
Requires strength, balance, endurance

PSYCH ✦ ✦ ✦
Requires patience and exposure to cold

SKILL ✦ ✦ ✦ ✦
Dog handling, sled rigging skills

WOW! ✦ ✦ ✦ ✦
A classic arctic experience

You'll also need a few days of preparation learning how to harness and "bootie" the dogs, handle a sled, motivate a dog team and read its dynamics. While the dogs will be doing the bulk of the work – and there's no way you can match the athletic prowess of an Alaskan husky at any rate – be sure to arrive physically fit. Mushing requires the same kind of balance, flexibility, and fluid turning skills required of a good skier. As well, you'll often need to run behind the sled or do a one-foot push kick to help on an uphill slope.

The sled, a two-meter chariot of fiberglass and ash, is held together with sinew for flexibility and improved torque on turns. It weighs 135kg when fully loaded for a touring expedition, not including the musher. Dogs are harnessed and clipped into what is typically a double-line six-dog team. Teams are generally a mix of both males and females, although females tend to be better leaders, smarter, with a better work ethic, and not as easily distracted.

When the dogs are roped up the barking begins in earnest, reaching a crescendo just as you give the command to go – not that one is needed. Hold on tight, because once released the sled surges forward with the thrust of a bullet train. On the trail, the team settles into a 16km per hour trot with galloping bursts of up to 32km per hour. To slow them down, step on a piece of snowmobile track attached to the back of the sled that produces drag. Once you're ready to handle a team with confidence, you'll find the Yukon provides unlimited opportunities for multi-day trips adaptable to all skill levels, including an extended tour that follows a portion of the epic 1600-kilometer Yukon Quest trail. One of its best sections is the fabled Dawson Trail of Gold Rush days where you'll travel along the Takhini River as you cross lakes and rolling hills on your way toward the Yukon River. The snow is dense and compact – ideal for dogsledding – and the trail is interspersed with stands of lodgepole pine, black spruce, poplar, and willows. Along slopes and basins you're likely to see wolverines, deer, elk, an occasional herd of caribou or bison, and elusive wolves. Temperatures well below −20°C make frostbite a real risk and the arctic winds quickly dehydrate both man and dog. There is always the potential of spilling the sled or losing the team. If you fall off the sled, the dogs won't return to pick you up; they'll only go faster without your added weight. But if all goes smoothly that won't be a concern, and you'll spend your days being mesmerized by the hiss of runners skimming the snow and the peaceful rhythm of 24 paws thumping on the white powder.

Climbing Colorado's Fourteeners

27

>> **A multiple-choice quest**

USA

● DENVER

Colorado's "purple mountain majesties" have long challenged and elevated the human spirit. And one collection of peaks, known affectionately as the "Fourteeners," have fired up the passions of both local and visting hikers more than any of the others. Straddling the heart of the Rocky Mountains, Colorado lays claim to more 14,000-foot peaks than any other state in the US, and the challenge found in climbing them has evolved into one of the region's prime outdoor pursuits.

the best of the bunch

All of the Fourteeners save for Longs Peak are located south of Colorado's main east-west highway, I-70. Each has a distinctive character, challenge, and appeal, and if you ask the members of any summit party which peak is the best, or the hardest, or the most beautiful, you're bound to get multiple answers. If just starting a quest to summit them all, these standouts make worthy starts.

Mount Elbert (14,433ft): Even though this is the highest of the bunch, Mount Elbert makes a great choice for a first-timer looking to bag a big one. Located in the Sawatch Range southwest of Leadville, it's a beautiful, nine-mile round-trip on a well-traveled and nicely groomed footpath to the peak, initially through woodland, then breaking out onto sunlit slopes. Take the more sustainable north route trail to hopefully let the more hammered south route recuperate.

Mount Sneffels (14,150ft): Sounding like a failed sneeze, this peak's name may be less than inspiring, but a ridgeline of exposed stone and angular spires near the summit make for a particularly photogenic and spectacular mountain. Located just five miles north of the buzzing resort town of Telluride, Mount Sneffels's already lofty 12,350-foot trailhead at Yankee Boy Basin makes the summit accessible by a short but steep 1.5-mile hike.

Mount Wilson (14,246ft): This reclusive mountain, located in the San Juan Range in the southwest corner of the state, is claimed by many peak baggers to be the toughest of the Fourteeners. It's just an eight-mile round trip to the top, but Mount Wilson dishes out some technical challenges with an exposed ridge right below the summit where some climbers choose to rope up.

Longs Peak (14,255ft): Located on the Continental Divide, Longs Peak is the highest summit – and sole Fourteener – in Rocky Mountain National Park. That helps makes it one of the most popular climbs in the state; on any given summer day you're likely to encounter hundreds of hikers on the fifteen-mile round-trip trail. It heads up to the dramatic ridgeline notch known as the Keyhole, then on to a series of ledge scrambles where a steep trough leads to the summit.

North Maroon Peak (14,014ft): A part of the famed Maroon Bells, North Maroon Peak is not only exceedingly picturesque, it's also a great climb. Though it appears higher than Maroon Peak when viewed from Maroon Lake, it's actually a lower spur and rises only 234ft above the connecting saddle. Among the number-crunchers its status as a Fourteener is disputed, but among hikers it's a sentimental favorite. Keep your wits about you when climbing here; the Maroons have earned their nickname of "The Deadly Maroons" due to their difficulty, with dangerous terrain and some route-finding required.

Great things are done when men and mountains meet.
William Blake

Certainly the 14,000-foot standard is arbitrary, but so is the 4000-meter club in the Alps or the 8000-meter quest in the Himalaya. Nonetheless it's a designation that hikers love to hang their hats on, and an estimated half-million people a year climb Colorado's Fourteeners. The sheer volume of human traffic on some of the peaks is an environmental concern, and trail organizations have spearheaded efforts to establish sustainable trails so that hikers can continue to enjoy the Fourteeners without loving them to death. Summit fever has led some zealous climbers to make a competitive sport out of climbing the Fourteeners, with goals like climbing all of them in winter or within a single month. That type of competition ultimetely puts too much stress on the delicate mountain resources; the encouragement now is to climb more responsibly, respecting the rights of private landholders and conserving the fragile ecosystems.

The exact number of 14,000-foot peaks in Colorado swings from 52 to 58, depending on who is defining the word "peak." The most widely accepted criterion is that an independent peak must rise at least 300ft above the saddle connecting it to its neighboring peak, and by this standard Colorado is home to a remarkable 53 Fourteeners. Its closest competitors, Alaska and California, have but 21 and 13 respectively.

For all their distinct charms, the Fourteeners share many similarities, from forests of Engelmann spruce, Douglas-fir, and ponderosa pine to stands of aspen that turn a radiant gold in the fall. Dotted throughout a band of six different sub-ranges, their trails ascend through fens and high mountain drainages that form the headwaters of some of America's great rivers, including the Missouri and the Colorado. And high treelines, near 12,000ft in the warmer southern part of the state, lead to rocky summits with commanding views. Another characteristic feature is lightning, which predictably accompanies afternoon thundershowers throughout summer, and is especially hazardous above the tree-line and on exposed ridges – it's best avoided by getting your summit in early in the day.

need to know

Coloradans are privileged to have the Fourteeners in their backyard and they enjoy sharing the joys of hiking them. To hook up with other hikers, consider joining the Colorado Mountain Club (☏303/279-3080, ⊛www.cmc.org) as they organize group climbs and other recreational activities. Similarly worthwhile is the Colorado Fourteeners Initiative (☏303/278-7650, ⊛www.14ers.org), an organization working to preserve the natural integrity of Colorado's 14,000-foot peaks.

guides and gear For most hikes, you'll only need the regular line-up of hiking gear, including sturdy boots, a waterproof jacket, and a good map. Telluride Mountain Guides (☏970/728-6481 or 1-888/586-8365, ⊛www.telluridemountainguides.com) offer custom adventures up many of Colorado's peaks and mountain areas.

when to go Many of the Fourteeners are climbed year round, but most of the hikers appear after the snow melts at higher elevations; June through mid-September is the ideal time.

getting there Trailheads are generally accessible from towns in central and southern Colorado, with the handiest airports being those in Denver, Colorado Springs, and Durango.

suggested reading Louis W. Dawson II, *Dawson's Guide to Colorado's Fourteeners, Vol. 1: The Northern Peaks* and *Dawson's Guide to Colorado's Fourteeners, Volume 2, the Southern Peaks* (Blue Clover Press). A year-round guide including snow climbs, technical routes, ski descents, and classic hikes. Gerry Roach, *Colorado's 14ers: From Hikes to Climbs* (Fulcrum). Informative, instructive, and accurate with up-to-date maps.

is this for me?

PHYSICAL ✦ ✦ ✦ ✦ ✦
Requires good overall aerobic conditioning

PSYCH ✦ ✦ ✦ ✦ ✦
Remote but accessible wilderness

SKILL ✦ ✦ ✦ ✦ ✦
Scrambling/climbing on selected peaks

WOW! ✦ ✦ ✦ ✦ ✦
A great challenge and memorable accomplishment

Sea kayaking in the San Juan Islands

>> Discover nestled coves and hidden inlets

THE SAN JUAN ISLANDS

USA

The San Juan Islands are proof positive that not all great island-hopping adventures take place in sun-soaked tropical waters. A close-knit archipelago of 743 islands in the not-exactly-balmy waters of the Pacific Northwest, the San Juans offer stunning vistas, brilliant sunsets, and fir-clad shores. Though ferries shuttle between a few of the forty inhabited islands off the coast of northwest Washington and southern British Columbia, only in a sea kayak can you discover nestled coves, hidden inlets, and see up-close the abundant marine life that make a journey on these waters so special.

The big surprise for most first-time sea kayakers coming to the San Juan Islands are the feisty currents that flush with the tides fed by the Strait of Juan de Fuca. Because the islands are really the tops of a mountain range within an inland sea, every time the tide changes – and it can be a change of 12–15ft – the water flows in an out between the islands with the force of river rapids. Exiting but treacherous, the currents bring food for the many marine mammals that thrive in the island waters. With a large number of both resident and transient orcas in the islands, whale-watching is a popular pursuit, and your best chances of seeing an orca in the Lower 48 will be on the west side of San Juan Island from June through September. Dall's porpoises, minke whales, harbor seals, otters, elephant seals, and sea lions are also commonly spotted; it's easy to see why Jacques Cousteau ranked the area one of the best dive spots in the world. Topside, you're likely to glimpse deer, sea and shore birds, as well as bald eagles, with over a hundred nesting on the mountainous and forested islands.

all in the family

Orcas (killer whales) can be found from the icy waters of Antarctica to all the way up to the North Pole, having a wider range of distribution than any other mammal on earth except for humans. Belonging to the same scientific family as dolphins, orcas have close family connections and travel in subpods, which are groups of two or three generations of a family headed by a female orca. During summer months, subpods often join with other subpods to hunt fish, creating super pods of over eighty orcas.

need to know

You can rent equipment in Friday Harbor, ; but for extended trips, be sure to make your plans well in advance. San Juan County Parks (℡ 360-378-1842, Ⓦ www.co.san-juan.wa.us/parks) manages campgrounds on all of the ferry-served islands. Reservations are not required, but are recommended during peak summer months. Washington State Parks (℡ 888-226-7688, Ⓦ www.parks.wa.gov) handles reservations for camping at Moran State Park on San Juan Island. Come prepared with some formal sea kayaking instruction, solid rescue skills, and some familiarity with tides and weather patterns.

guides and gear Unless you are familiar with the area, you would be well-served to use a local outfitter or guide who can use the currents to your benefit and paddle where the winds and tides take you. Discovery Sea Kayaks (℡ 360-378-2559, 866-461-2559, Ⓦ www.discoveryseakayak.com) offers customized and small-group sea kayaking adventures in the San Juan Islands. Most guided and outfitted trips use double kayaks that have rudders and provide a more stable platform, something you'll appreciate when you get into some charging currents or dicey weather.

when to go June through September is ideal, although paddle trips are possible year-round – if you can handle the cold weather.

getting there The San Juan Islands are served by Washington State Ferries departing from Anacortes, about 90 minutes north of Seattle. The ferries serve Lopez, Shaw, Orcas, and Friday Harbor.

suggested reading Terry Domico, *Natural Areas of San Juan Islands* (Turtleback Books) This comprehensive field guide to the natural history of the islands is a great companion for kayakers. Complete with access maps and photos.

is this for me?

PHYSICAL ✦ ✦ ✦
Paddling in strong currents

PSYCH ✦ ✦
Secluded but not remote

SKILL ✦ ✦ ✦
Have your wet exit ready

WOW! ✦ ✦ ✦ ✦
Spectacular scenery, challenging paddling

Your sea kayaking adventure in the San Juan Islands can take off in countless directions and is limited only how many days you've planned for your escape. You can circumnavigate larger islands or spend a week hopping from one to the next, exploring a different island or bay each day. One excellent multi-day loop starts on San Juan Island. After you arrive by ferry at the protected seaport village of Friday Harbor cross to the west side for your put-in. From here paddle north to Stuart Island, home to one of the few remaining on-room schoolhouses in America, and where without ferry service, things quiet down considerably. With favorable currents and long day of paddling you could stay the night on uninhabited Jones Island, a state park to the east no more than about one-half mile wide in any direction. Continue east to Orcas Island, the largest of the San Juans, whose small farms and villages give it a resolutely rural feel and make it a welcoming stopover. When the time is right to move on, ply the Harney Channel between Orcas Island and Shaw Island before looping back through Obstruction Pass where the channel bends and narrows to 250 yards.

Don't overlook some of the more out-of-the-way islands to the north that can easily be included as short extension to your loop. Two of these, Patos and Matia islands, include state parks and offer simple surprises like a native colony of prickly pear cactus, spring wildflowers and clam digging. Also north of Orcas Island is Sucia Island, a hand-shaped state marine park with a population of just four people. It was named *Isla Sucia*, meaning "dirty" or "foul" to warn sailors of the rocks and hidden reefs that made it a dangerous island to approach, though you'll find it anything but as you nose your sea kayak around rocky points and into narrow inlets tailor made for your boat. As you paddle throughout these islands you'll see sculpted sandstone crags in the north and harder rock formations in the south, and even an occasional cave to poke into.

By exploring several of the San Juans you'll come to appreciate the biodiversity of this archipelago as well as the cultural diversity, with each inhabited island having its own personality. When it comes time to stow your paddle and set up camp, you can have just as much fun beachcombing, hiking, or watching a sunset turn neighboring islands into a sea of silhouettes.

29 Hiking the Na Pali Coast

>> Seriously question your sanity

In an archipelago known for its beauty, the island of Kauai – the Garden Isle – has more than its share of eye-popping scenic wonders: Waimea Canyon, Hanalei Bay, and even some drop-dead gorgeous golf courses in Princeville. But the most stunningly beautiful landscape on the island is the remote northwest coast, where the only land access is by a muscle-burning foot trail etched along the cathedral cliffs and steep-walled valleys of the Na Pali Coast. No one ever told you paradise could be this rugged.

preserving the Hawaiian language

Aloha, ukulele, hula, muumuu, luau, lei – you probably don't know any more Hawaiian than this and unfortunately, neither do most Hawaiians. Hawaiian is a language spoken only in Hawaii, and even there, only by 0.1% of the population; today, only the isolated island of Ni'hau can boast a fluent Hawaiian-speaking population. Sadly, even Ni'hau, often termed "the Forgotten Island," is in danger of being taken over by English, as its struggling residents face exchanging their isolation for financial stability.

The language was first brought to the Hawaiian Islands around 1000 AD by Tahitian sailors, and in the hundreds of years of isolation before the arrival of Captain James Cook in 1778, the first non-Hawaiian visitor to the islands, the language had morphed from Tahitian into what we know as Hawaiian. Missionaries from New England created a Hawaii alphabet and written language, and translated the Bible into Hawaiian. In addition, they also managed to induce King Kamehameha III to form the first Hawaiian language constitutions in 1839 and 1840. This as well as Hawaiian language newspapers created by later missionaries brought Hawaiian to its peak of popularity around 1880.

Ironically, at this time, the processes were already at work for the downfall of the Hawaiian language. In 1885, public schools in Hawaii forbade the use of any language other than English for school instruction. Immigration to the islands caused the population of non-native Hawaiians speakers to increase and, through the introduction of deadly foreign diseases, caused the population of native speakers to decrease. Recent initiatives, including courses being taught in Hawaiian in elementary schools and the transferring of pages from nineteenth and twentieth century Hawaiian language newspapers to the Internet, are attempting to reverse the language's decline and been met with overwhelming approval throughout the state.

Formed roughly 3.5 to 5.5 million years ago, Kauai is the oldest of the major Hawaiian islands by about two million years. Perhaps the head start has given its rivers, deep canyons, and lush tropical covering more time to reach their full potentially visually. When humans arrived on the islands about 1600 years ago, many of them settled on this coast and in the verdant valleys that finger their way inland. Today, the route to the valleys of the Na Pali coast lies along the eleven-mile Kalalau Trail. Following in the steps of an ancient footpath, the trail is best experienced as a three-day backpacking trip, which allows time to soak under waterfalls, hike into canyons, and enjoy sun-kissed beaches.

Start your day early and head for the end of Highway 56 in Haena State Park, where the trail kicks off. You'll share the first two miles with day-hikers as you cross some steep sections along the coast from Ke'e Beach to Hanakapi'ai Beach. Here the trail turns inland and follows the stream up the Hanakapi'ai Valley for another two miles to Hanakapi'ai Falls; this is a spur trail, but one you don't want to miss. The stream crossings, muddy portions of narrow trail, and fallen trees and rocks are a precursor to the obstacles on the trail awaiting down the coast, making this a good spot to turn around and call it a day hike if you feel like you're in over your head.

Continuing down the coast from Hanakapi'ai the trail steepens and the crowds thin. The switchbacks climb 800ft as the trail plies the Hono O Na Pali Natural Area Reserve which protects rare plants and stream life and is a nesting site for the Hawaiian dark-rumped petrel. After some taxing switchbacks you'll arrive at the Hanakoa Valley and the Hanakoa Stream crossing. Here you're six miles down the coast, and if you did the Hanakapi'ai Falls spur, you have ten miles on your boots for the day, so plan on camping your first night near the stream, just below terraces where ancient Hawaiians planted taro. A poorly marked and dangerously eroded half-mile trail up the east fork of the stream will have you seriously questioning your sanity until you discover paradisiacal Hanakoa Falls with its black backdrop and rock-rimmed pool.

Leaving Hanakoa, you begin a five-mile, largely shadeless stretch of narrow trail to Kalalau Beach. Portions of this precarious segment are eroded with vertigo-inducing drop-offs down to ocean cliffs. With a full pack and the least bit of rainfall on the trail it would be easy to lose your footing – a fraction too far, and the drop of several hundred feet would finish you off, so use extreme caution. This harrowing section, and the trail itself, comes to an end at Kalalau Beach and a small waterfall after crossing the Kalalau Stream. Camping is permitted behind the beach and is a great choice for your second night.

A gentle two-mile trail leads up from the beach through Kalalau Valley to a pool in a stream. The valley sustained a small community of native Hawaiians until 1919 when they left their remote home for the conveniences of city life in places like Lihue. From the trail you'll see remains of their taro terraces and overgrown non-native species such as guava, mango and Java plum. You may also see wild goats, boars, and evasive tropical birds. Although people are no longer permitted to live in the valley, you will likely encounter hippies, some clothed and others nude, still living off the land until rangers come and evict them – although the eviction is usually a temporary deterrent for those so eager to return to Eden.

need to know

From mid-May to Labor Day (early September) no more than sixty people per day are allowed on the trail. That capacity shrinks to no more than thirty per day from Labor Day to mid-May, when the weather and surf conditions make the trail even more challenging. Permits to hike the Na Pali coast can be requested up to a year in advance, and no less than thirty days prior to your trip. Most permits are gone at least six months in advance. Permits can be obtained from the State Parks Office in Lihue ☏ 808/274-3444, ⓦ www.hawaii.gov/dlnr/dsp/NaPali.

guides and gear Although no commercial tour operators are permitted to guide on the Na Pali coast, Kauai Eco Tours (☏ 808/652-3390 or ☏ 1-877/538-4453, ⓦ www.kauaieco-tours.com) allows you to experience other scenic areas of Kauai in custom and small group tours with an emphasis on nature.

when to go The trail can be hiked year-round, however there are more permits available in the summer months. Winter surf can be dangerous and trail conditions more hazardous.

getting there The trail starts at Haena State Park in the overflow parking area for Ke'e State Beach at the end of Highway 56, about 45 minutes from Lihue Airport.

suggested reading Kathy Valier, On the Na Pali Coast: A Guide for Hikers and Boaters (University of Hawaii Press).

is this for me?

PHYSICAL ✦ ✦ ✦ ✦ ✦
Backpacking on a long trail

PSYCH ✦ ✦ ✦ ✦ ✦
Slippery sections and steep drop-offs

SKILL ✦ ✦ ✦ ✦ ✦
Be a surefooted hiker

WOW! ✦ ✦ ✦ ✦ ✦
Beautiful, remote setting

Climbing Mount Rainier

>> Topping out on an active volcano

30

MOUNT RAINIER

USA

On clear days around Washington's Puget Sound, when views stretch for nearly a hundred miles in every direction, Seattleites like to say, "The mountains are out." They're most often referring to the hulking mass of Mount Rainier (14,411ft), sixty miles away and a striking symbol on the city's southeastern skyline. Crowned in white, the mountain is the most extensively glaciated peak in the continental United States. Combined, the glaciers clinging to this still-active stratovolcano hold some 38 billion cubic feet of ice – enough to supply Seattle with water for two hundred years. It's also a preposterously snowy peak, at one time holding the world record for snowfall with nearly 94ft falling in a single year. Little surprise, then, that its name in the native Puyallup language, Tahoma, means "mother of waters."

These days, the mountain could also be described as the mother of North American mountaineering. Protected within Mount Rainier National Park, the mountain is laced with more than forty established routes converging on its summit cone. The routes offer near-limitless opportunities for both aspiring and experienced mountaineers, drawn to the distinctive physical and mental challenges inherent to an intensely glaciated peak like Rainier. Between the trailhead and the summit, climbers must conquer a grueling 9000ft of vertical gain in 24 hours to be successful. The combination of altitude, Pacific Northwest weather, and an active volcano encased in over 35 square miles of snow and ice make climbing Rainier a heroic experience.

As exalting as glacier climbing seems, there's a hitch: simply put, glaciers can kill you. There are thousands of ways for a trip up Rainier to turn fatal, from icefalls and avalanches to falling down steep glacial slopes or into a crevasse. Hypothermia, of course, is a constant threat as well. The single deadliest mountaineering accident in North America occurred here in 1981, when an icefall-triggered avalanche on Rainier's Ingraham Glacier killed 11 members of a 29-person climbing party in a matter of seconds. In recent years, there has been an average of two fatalities among the 10,000 climbers who annually seek Rainier's summit.

Somewhere in the neighborhood of sixty percent of climbers attempting the summit each year make it to the peak. The majority of them travel with a guide service via the Disappointment Cleaver route. This route begins at the park's Paradise Trailhead (5460ft) and quickly ascends through delightful alpine meadows spangled with fir and wildflowers to Panorama Point (6960ft), a rocky outcropping offering fine views of the surrounding ridges to the east. The Muir Snowfield then provides a snow-packed, though occasionally slushy, march to Camp Muir at 10,060ft. It's a non-technical walk up a moderately graded, snowy slope, but still a telling test of the endurance needed to reach the summit. If you're bone-tired by the time you get to Camp Muir, your chances of visiting the summit are already hanging by a thread.

arresting a fall

You're confidently ascending an icy slope, carefully focused on each step, when it happens. Your footing gives away, and instantly your body becomes a luge, bulleting down a slope with no run-out – just rocks, or even worse, a crevasse or cliff with a fatal fall waiting at the bottom. Survival hinges on your ability to safely stop the slide using the technique known as self-arrest. As your own life and the lives of fellow climbers rely on your ability to self-arrest, it's a fundamental skill that every climber must be proficient in. Rehearsed and honed in pre-climb instructional programs, it involves quick thinking and responsive action as you turn your body into the slope. With your side facing the slope, you're in position to forcefully plant the narrow pointed end of your ax – called the pick – firmly into the snow or ice. As you press your body weight against the ice ax shaft, you should be able to slow the slide. Snow will be flying and flecks of ice will sting your face, but by arching your back slightly and making every attempt to plant your crampons into the slope, you'll come to a secure stop.

need to know

It's essential to review climbing regulations and advisories posted by Mount Rainier National Park (☎360/569-2211, ⓦwww.nps.gov/mora) before attempting a climb. Available in advance or on arrival at the Paradise Ranger Station, permits are required for travel on glaciers or above 10,000ft. Unguided climbers need to approach Rainier with respect, armed with good judgment and technique gained from prior mountaineering experience.

guides and gear Rainier Mountaineering, Inc. (☎360/569-2227 or 1-888/892-5462, ⓦwww.rmiguides.com) has been guiding climbers up the mountain for nearly four decades. Additionally, International Mountain Guides (☎360/569-2609, ⓦwww.mountainguides.com) leads climbers on three of Rainier's top routes. Both also offer superb instructional programs.

when to go Rainier's climbing season runs from May to September, but as the summer wears on, safe climbing can become dicey as ice bridges thin, crevasses open up, and icefall increases. Late June through the end of July typically offer the best climbing conditions for a summit success.

getting there From Seattle it's a one-and-a-half hour drive to the Paradise Visitor Center in Mount Rainier National Park; shuttle services are available.

suggested reading Mike Gauthier, *Mount Rainier: A Climbing Guide* (Mountaineers). Preparation and route guide by Rainier's lead climbing ranger.

is this for me?

PHYSICAL ✦✦✦✦✦
Requires excellent aerobic conditioning and endurance

PSYCH ✦✦✦✦
Icefall, avalanche, crevasses, and steep slopes

SKILL ✦✦✦✦✦
Have solid mountaineering skills

WOW! ✦✦✦✦
Superb climbing on a classic glaciated peak

Nervous anticipation, howling winds, and the buzz of other climbers assure a brief and consistently interrupted rest at Camp Muir. Shortly after midnight, it's time to don a headlamp and get tied into a rope linking you up with two to four other climbers to begin threading your way through a maze of crevasses leading up the Ingraham Glacier. The pace up must be steady and intentional, always aware that the next step could take you or a partner diving into a hidden crevasse. Occasional rock outcroppings and some steep ledges of compacted snow and ice may require some hand placements, but for the most part it's one foot in front of the other, with the spike of your ice ax firmly planted on the uphill side of the slope with each step. In the predawn hours, you'll enjoy a reassuring ascent as your ice ax and crampons bite firmly into the glacial slopes. The early start minimizes the danger of weakening snow bridges and the intensified risk of ice and rockfall that occur later on as the sun bears down on the mountain.

At 13,000ft, the thinning oxygen, fatigue, and cold extract a noticeable toll. After long hours of climbing in the bluish glow of a headlamp, the arriving sun promises a broader spectrum of colors and views. Few things invigorate morale like the tantalizing hues of dawn bending its way over the eastern horizon. The climbing only gets tougher now, however, and you'll be required in several places to plant aluminum pickets in the ice as a running belay as protection from falling down slopes boasting inclines of 45 degrees. These tapering slopes lead to a crater rim that's nearly a half-mile in diameter. Fumaroles, steam vents, and ice caves dot the summit crater, a stark reminder of Rainier's persistent volcanic activity.

An easy crossing of the crater's indented bowl leads to the true summit at Columbia Crest. Clear views are never guaranteed in the Pacific Northwest, but lucky climbers are treated to an incredible summit panorama that takes in Seattle and the Puget Sound to the northwest, the volcanic sisters Adams, Hood and St. Helens to the south, and Mt Baker to the north. Rainier, however, is not a summit where you want to linger long. The rising sun glaring down on icy slopes only increases the risk of unfavorable conditions – melting ice bridges, slushy slopes, and icefall – meaning it's time to make your turnaround to begin a safe descent.

Paddling the Atchafalaya Basin

>> **Find yourself in dark, swampy corners**

USA

LAFAYETTE

Cypress trees dripping with Spanish moss over mist-shrouded backwater, and meandering bayous blend together in a haunting patchwork that is Louisiana's Atchafalaya Basin. As you paddle deeper into this eerie landscape an undeniable sensation starts to take hold of you: the feeling that help, should you need it, is a long way away. So far the GPS and detailed map that you brought along to keep you from getting completely lost have kept you on course, but neither can reveal just where the cottonmouth snakes and alligators lurk.

alligators in the Atchafalaya Basin

No matter how many times you've put-in to the Atchafalaya Basin, seeing an alligator is a spine tingling experience. Quietly paddling through smooth backwaters, you may see two golf ball-size bumps rising above the water level, only to disappear a split-second later as the alligator scrambles below the surface. Topside, gators are most frequently spotted sunning near the water's edge. It's especially exciting to come upon a large cow – the term used for a female alligator – surrounded by a dozen 18-inch hatchlings, all of whom scamper for the water as soon as you're spotted.

An adult alligator can snap its wide snout closed with thousands of pounds of pressure per square inch. When feeding, alligators typically sit and wait for prey rather than hunt it down. They strike with stunning speed and power; with a tail almost half the length of their body, gators can leap out of the water at incredible speeds and heights. While alligators in the Atchafalaya Basin have been known to attack swimmers, small children and dogs, they're not much of a risk to paddlers. The reptiles tend to be timid around humans and watercraft and normally take off when they see you. They have plenty more reasons to fear humans than we have to fear them; Louisiana hosts an alligator hunting season in September, and each year around 30,000 are taken.

The largest swamp in the United States, the Atchafalaya (ah-CHA-fa-LIE-ah) name comes from the native Choctaw *hacha falaia*, meaning "long river." A distributary of both the Mississippi and Red rivers, the Atchafalaya River acts as a safety valve that helps protect New Orleans from repeated flooding from the north. Thirty percent of North America's largest river system courses through here in any given year, bringing with it an enormous volume of silt, debris, and life-sustaining organisms.

While serious questions remain regarding the future of Louisiana's coastal lands, the upriver ecology of the Atchafalaya Basin is flourishing, both as a wetland environment and recreation area. Hundreds of miles of established paddle trails thread through the region, made accessible by dozens of public launch areas where one can park a car and be on the water in minutes. Day-trips mix paddling on still water with fishing and wildlife viewing, but with a wealth of primitive, boat-in campsites, spending days on end connecting trails is also an option.

A good place to dive into the swamp is at its northern end on Bayou Courtableau, located in the larger Indian Bayou district. After putting-in just west of Krotz Springs, water trails here can be explored as a chain of scenic loops. At the north end you'll start with stately forests of mature cypress, oaks festooned in wisteria, and stands of persimmon and maple. Paddling south, expect to see bald eagles and herons, both of which make a year-round home on the bayou. As half of North America's migratory species use the area, egrets, ospreys, ibises, pileated woodpeckers, and roseate spoonbills are other eye-catching winged species to watch for.

At points within Bayou Courtableau, you'll find yourself in dark swampy corners where the thick canopy blocks the sun's rays. Just as

need to know

While the paddling is for the most part easy enough, getting lost is a real risk. Those going deep into the Atchafalaya Basin without a guide need to be skilled in GPS navigation and have a map with waypoint coordinates plotted out. Water access is available from numerous spots, including Corp of Engineers managed areas, road crossings and public and private launch facilities.

guides and gear Paddlers use both canoes and kayaks, but those most familiar with the backwaters give a slight nod to the latter for the ability to more easily cut through dense swamp grasses; equipment rental is available at state parks and area outfitters. In Lafayette, Pack & Paddle (☎ 337/232 5854, ⓦ www.packpaddle. com) rent gear, guide private clients and sponsor group outings into the basin.

when to go Water levels vary by up to 9ft during the year. High water levels in April and May bring new sediments and more active wildlife to the wetlands, along with comfortable temperatures. September through December has lower water levels, revealing hidden terrain that makes it easier to find camping spots. There are plenty of pleasant days for paddling in the cooler months of January through March, but sweltering temperatures make June through August the least desirable time to visit.

getting there Lafayette, Louisiana, is a good starting point for extended exploration of the Atchafalaya Basin. Major carriers provide service to airports in Baton Rouge and New Orleans, one and two hours by car respectively.

suggested reading Mike Tidwell, *Bayou Farewell: The Rich Life and Tragic Death of Louisiana's Cajun Coast* (Vintage). A compelling tour of coastal erosion and the problems facing Louisiana's bayous.

you start wondering if perhaps there's no way out of this alligator's nest, the waterway opens to broad, sunlit marshlands and lakes. One of the largest, Henderson Lake, is lined with cypress that creep far into the water. Alligators are common here, while the flooded forests beyond the lake are home to beaver, river otters, and nutria, a large rodent originally imported for the fur industry that has become an invasive species. Large-mouth bass is the favorite catch of fishermen, while bream, crappie and white bass are also abundant. Henderson Lake has a number of take-out spots, but with adequate provisions and route-finding skills it's also possible to make it as far as the Gulf of Mexico in a few days.

Cajuns have lived in the basin for more than two centuries, developing a rich cultural tradition evident in their food and music. After a day on the water, slip into a small café and order up a plate of boiled crawfish or alligator stew. When your meal's done chances are the syncopated beat of zydeco music will call you to the dance floor.

is this for me?

PHYSICAL ✦ ✦
Relaxed paddling in still waters

PSYCH ✦ ✦
Exposure to alligators and snakes

SKILL ✦ ✦
Routefinding, navigation and basic paddling skills

WOW! ✦ ✦
Scenery and exploration in continent's largest swamp

Exploring the Escalante Canyons

32

ESCALANTE

USA

Within the labyrinthine expanse of Utah's Grand Staircase-Escalante National Monument are hundreds of colorful, unnamed sandstone canyons that have been visited by no more than a handful of people. If manicured trails, clear signage, and trailhead parking areas with flush toilets are of chief concern, you'll certainly be happier in nearby national parks like Zion or Bryce. But if you'd rather disappear altogether off the well-trod path, head to the Escalante Canyons.

Designated in 1996, Grand Staircase-Escalante National Monument spans nearly two million acres of southern Utah wilderness. The Grand Staircase, a giant plateau of sedimentary cliffs and terraces descending from southern Utah into the Grand Canyon, forms the west boundary, while the panoramic views and high juniper woodlands of the rugged Kaiparowits Plateau dominate the center of the protected terrain. And to the east are the fractal landscapes of the Escalante Canyons, a library of geologic formations where wind and water have etched countless washes, drainages, and slot canyons feeding into the calf-deep waters of the Escalante River.

When a Mormon militia scouted this area in 1866, they rightly noted "the utter impractibility of any trail crossing this basin." A few years later, John Wesley Powell led an expedition through the area, with his topographer and brother-in-law Almon H. Thompson writing that "No animal without wings could cross the deep sandstone gulches… that lay at our feet." The area remained one of the last sections in the country to be mapped by the US Geological Survey, and even then maps were drawn based on aerial photography. The only way to tell if a canyon is 10ft deep or a 100ft deep is by diving in.

Before venturing into the unknown, earn your desert legs on one of the more popular hikes around the sleepy town of Escalante. The trail to Calf Creek Falls is a well-traveled stroll up a sandy canyon floor, culminating with a 126-foot waterfall that scrubs down sandstone walls before landing in a shaded pool. The slot canyons of Peekaboo, Spooky, and Brimstone Gulches are full of twists, sandstone squeezes, and potholes that can be explored on foot in a few hours from the Dry Fork Trailhead on Hole-in-the-Rock Road. And Coyote Gulch is a favorite two-or three-day hike within a canyon graced with natural springs, ancient pictographs, and imposing natural bridges; for most of the route, a silty creek is the trail as it threads beneath towering redrock cliffs.

Once your feet are wet, it's time for a more out-of-the-way canyon. Heading into an uncharted slot canyon may be the last great undiscovered adventure in the United States. You might enter one to find a slickrock paradise lined with gaudy redrock formations, varnished canyon walls, or an oasis of willow and cottonwoods. You could drop into an emerald

Hole-in-the-Rock

Imagine an expedition of 80 freight wagons, 1000 head of cattle, 200 horses and a single piano heading through the steep crevices in Escalante. Such was the makeup of the San Juan Expedition, a group of 250 Mormon settlers that migrated across Utah in 1879–80. Intent on establishing a new settlement to the east, the expedition opted to take a shortcut through the present-day Grand Staircase-Escalante National Monument and Glen Canyon National Recreation Area, looking for a pass dubbed the "Hole-in-the-Rock."

The shortcut turned out to be anything but. The "Hole" needed to be widened for the wagons to squeeze through, while gaps and fissures in the rock had to be filled for them to pass over. They carved out a road and even improvised a bridge by drilling holes in the crevice wall, driving in oak stakes to secure the platform, then piling logs and dirt on top. Groups of men used ropes to lower the wagons down. Miraculously, all made it safely through; today's Hole-in-the-Rock Road follows the historic route.

The great plateau and its canyon wilderness is a treasure best enjoyed through the body and spirit … as a place for all who wish to rediscover the nearly lost pleasures of adventure.

Edward Abbey

need to know

Many of the popular recreation areas and well-known canyons within Grand Staircase-Escalante National Monument can be explored independently. Maps and trail guides are available at the Bureau of Land Management Visitor Center in Escalante (☎ 435/826-5499, Ⓦ www.ut.blm.gov/monument).

guides and gear Excursions of Escalante (Ⓦ 435/826-4714 or 1-800/839-7567, Ⓦ www.excursionsofescalante.com) run day hikes, multi-day backpacking trips, and canyoneering in less-frequented canyons. As with other local operators, they provide the equipment appropriate for each canyon, from ropes and harnesses to helmets and wetsuits.

when to go Mid-march through the end of October. The higher elevations of the Box-Death Hollow Wilderness are ideal in the hotter summer months, while the Escalante Canyons are more comfortable in the spring and fall.

getting there The administrative hub of Grand Staircase-Escalante National Monument is Escalante, Utah, 45 minutes east of Bryce Canyon National Park on Hwy-12. Additional visitor centers are located in the towns of Kanab, Cannonville, and Big Water. Scheduled air service is available into St George, Utah, and Page, Arizona.

suggested reading Steve Allen, *Canyoneering 3 – Loop Hikes in Utah's Escalante* (University of Utah Press). Dozens off hiking/backpacking trips in the Escalante Canyons with maps and photos.

is this for me?

PHYSICAL ◆ ◆ ◆ ◆ ◆
Hike 4-10 miles/day; canyoneering requires agility

PSYCH ◆ ◆ ◆ ◆ ◆
Rappelling, steep drops, surmounting obstacles

SKILL ◆ ◆ ◆ ◆ ◆
Skill with ropes and canyoneering gear

WOW! ◆ ◆ ◆ ◆ ◆
True exploration in distinctive and scenic setting

pothole and find the water is well over your head, or spend an hour trying to work your way around an obstructing chokestone the size of a bus. Most of the canyons in the backcountry are so infrequently explored that you'll want to find one of the few local guides who know the area intimately. These guides have discovered canyons unseen by botanists and archeologists, and may take you to explore Anasazi cliff dwellings abandoned centuries ago with ladders still in place, their granaries untouched. Such routes are jealously guarded, so don't be surprised if before heading out a guide asks you to sign a promise not to reveal these locations.

Many of the more dramatic canyons involve technical canyoneering skills, where you'll employ rappelling gear and learn techniques like *chimneying* (moving through a narrow canyon with your feet planted on one wall and your back on the other) or *smearing* (using the sole of your shoe to maintain friction). Few things feel more unnatural than leaning backwards over a cliff when rappelling for the first time, but you'll soon feel in complete control dangling high above a canyon floor. Along with scenic beauty, part of the appeal of slot canyons is that they're filled with puzzling obstacles; there's an empowering exhilaration that comes with figuring out a canyon conundrum and lowering your way down using only natural anchors.

Some of the more popular and accessible canyons are between Hole-in-the-Rock Road and the Escalante River. These include Zebra, Tunnel, and Bighorn canyons, each of which can be completed with a few basic climbing moves and without technical gear. Across the Escalante River to the east, working through Choprock Canyon requires some long cold-water swims and dicey downclimbs. And explorations of nearby Neon Canyon begin with an 85-foot rappel through one of three naturally carved holes in the dome of the Golden Cathedral, before landing in a broad pool. Then comes the crux – a long swim and two potholes. In many of the canyons, a wetsuit (even in summer) is needed to swim, drybag in tow, across large pools set in the shaded canyon depths.

Recent fatalities in these canyons prove the importance of going fully prepared and well equipped. The deceptive perils include flash floods, ice-cold water, and falling debris, so always check on conditions before heading out. Testing your limits in such majestic arenas is thrilling, but so is living another day to tell your friends about it.

Running the Grand Canyon in a dory

USA

GRAND CANYON

>> **Come to know the Colorado face to face**

The great appeal of experiencing the Grand Canyon from the Colorado River as it courses its way down through the geological wonder is the ability to take in the canyon's entire length – something even the most dedicated hiker could never do – and see it from the inside out. You come to know the river face to face, witnessing both the natural and human history of the canyon in a way no rim-gawker ever could. A trip through the Grand Canyon is more than just a series of whitewater rapids; it's an opportunity to bond with the side canyons, beaches, and waterfalls that lie at the heart of the mighty gulch, and connect with the explorers, miners, and ranchers who built their dreams here.

John Wesley Powell

John Wesley Powell (1834–1902) was the first man to successfully navigate and chart the Green and Colorado rivers: and he did it all with just one arm. Already an accomplished explorer of the Mississippi River Valley as a young man, Powell – a devout abolitionist – fought for the Union Army during the Civil War. He was shot in the wrist at the Battle of Shiloh in Tennessee, a wound so severe that doctors were forced to amputate his forearm as well. Even with his handicap, Powell continued fighting until the end of the war, after which he became a professor of geology at Illinois Wesleyan University.

Powell could have chosen the cushy life of a tenured lecturer, but his wanderlust was far too strong. He organized an expedition to the Rocky Mountains in 1867, and two year later set his sights on exploring the mighty Green and Colorado rivers. With a group of nine others, Powell launched the expedition in four wooden boats from Green River, Wyoming on May 24, 1869. The emotional turmoil, spoiled food, and lack of game over the tempestuous 100-mile journey led four members to desert – they were never heard from again – but after three months on the unknown river, Powell arrived at the mouth of the Virgin River and returned to those who had given him up for dead. He immediately made plans for a better outfitted second expedition, and by his return in 1872 he had contributed more to the body of scientific and ethnographic knowledge of the American Southwest than any man alive. Powell received his just rewards by becoming the Director of the US Geological Survey from 1881 to 1894, during which time he launched the effort to topographically map the entire US.

is this for me?

PHYSICAL ◆ ◆ ◇ ◇ ◇
Minimal aerobic activity; hiking side-trips

PSYCH ◆ ◆ ◆ ◇ ◇
Class IV–V rapids

SKILL ◆ ◆ ◆ ◆ ◇
All skills can be learned on site

WOW! ◆ ◆ ◆ ◆ ◇
The classic adventure in the American West

There are essentially three ways to run the Colorado River through the Grand Canyon. The largest, fastest choice is on a 40-foot motorized "baloney boat" that carries twelve to sixteen passengers down the river's length in just eight days. While undeniably efficient, these large crafts overwhelm and cushion the rapids with their size, dampening the overall excitement. An inflatable oar raft, carrying three to five passengers, is the most widely used craft on the Colorado, and over the years they have provided hundreds of thousands of river adventurers with the trip of a lifetime. But for those who yearn to connect with the river in the most intimate and traditional way, the hard-hulled dory is the quintessential whitewater vessel. It delivers the most responsive ride – particularly when thunderous whitewater sends the bow rocketing into the air before it reunites with the surface.

The dory evokes the pioneering 1869 voyage of John Wesley Powell, but with some modern refinements. Today's dory is a flat-bottomed, flare-sided craft, lighter and more maneuverable than Powell ever imagined. Brightly painted and made by hand, a dory can carry four passengers and about one thousand pounds of gear in its decked-over chambers. Seated in the center of the dory, facing forward with a ten-foot ash oar extending from his weathered hands, is one of the Colorado's legendary river guides.

Over one hundred rapids mark this stretch of the Colorado, some with celebrated names like Granite Falls, Crystal, and House Rock Rapids. As a dory passenger you'll share responsibility for keeping the craft level in these big waters by "high-siding," or shifting your weight toward an oncoming wave. You'll get a soaking smack of cold water when you do, but you'll help keep the boat from tipping and sending everyone overboard. A dory is more likely to flip than a raft, but it's also more easily set aright – as long as you avoid the urge to panic. Should your dory tip, keep calm and with the oarsman's assistance you'll be able to find and hold the flip line, a rope extending from the gunwales that allows you to stay with the swamped boat, and return it right side up. Even with a skilled oarsman at the helm, a dory is also prone to breaking on a rock – something that won't occur with inflatables. But despite these real risks, river trips in the Grand Canyon are relatively safe, and dory operators have an exceptional safety record.

Whitewater rapids feature prominently in the legendary tales of the Colorado River, but ninety percent of the waterway is actually flat-water that even a novice can handle in the oarsman's seat. Within these calm sections and silent eddies you'll discover that a river trip through the Canyon is just as much about kicking back and enjoying the sights and sounds around you. The silence is so sweeping that it's possible to hear the clicking hooves of bighorn sheep on the slopes above and the soothing calls of canyon wrens as they echo across the river. In the chasm's depths you'll see wildlife never glimpsed from the rim, including great blue herons and bald eagles, and giant California condor sightings are becoming more frequent in the Upper Canyon. And at night, you'll camp on cloistered beaches and have ample time to explore the wonders of the many side canyons, with their secluded waterfalls, grottoes, and gushing springs – the same ones which led John Wesley Powell to describe the setting as "a composite of thousands, tens of thousands, of gorges."

A complete run of the Grand Canyon in a dory is a sixteen- to nineteen-day journey, beginning at Lee's Ferry and ending on Lake Mead, 278 miles downriver. While a complete run of the canyon is very much like an epic novel – you don't want to start in the middle of the book – if need be outfitters can help you capture shorter sections such as the Middle Canyon, from Phantom Ranch to Whitmore Wash. If time is limited, start with the 87-mile Upper Canyon at Lee's Ferry and hike out at Phantom Ranch as part of a six- or seven-day trip. If time limits you to a shorter run, don't worry – you can always return again to experience the climactic Lava Falls, said to be the fastest navigable water in North America.

need to know

Permits for private or self-guided boat trips through the Grand Canyon are issued by the National Park Service; typical waiting time for these permits is several years. To obtain information about the permit process, go to Ⓦ www.npas.gov/gcra; the site also lists support companies who provide equipment rental, shuttle services and guides.

guides and gear Commercially guided trips by paddle rafts, motorized rafts, and dories are offered through officially licensed outfitters. O.A.R.S. (☎ 1-800/346-6277, Ⓦ www.oars.com), the first company to bring back dory trips, runs fully outfitted trips varying in length from four to nineteen days via both paddle raft and dory.

when to go Though private river runs can be made year-round, commercial trips are typically offered from April to October, when comfortable temperatures and longer days allow for more enjoyable trips and exploring of side canyons.

getting there Most commercial trips begin by flying into either Flagstaff Pulliam Airport, a three-hour drive from Lee's Ferry, or Page, about 45-minutes away; both are in Arizona. Shuttle transportation is often provided to and from the river. If you plan on joining a river trip at Phantom Ranch, the journey will start with a seven- to ten-mile hike to the bottom of the Grand Canyon from the South Rim.

suggested reading David Sievert Lavender, *River Runners of the Grand Canyon* (Grand Canyon Association). Meet the men and women who have dared to brave the most challenging whitewater in North America. Edward Abbey and John Blaustein, *The Hidden Canyon: A River Journey* (Chronicle Books). An account of a dory trip down the Colorado with legendary boatman Martin Litton. Michael P. Ghiglieri, *Canyon* (University of Arizona Press). Narrative by river guide that captures the excitement and lore of the Colorado. John Wesley Powell, *The Exploration of the Colorado River and Its Canyons* (Penguin Classics). The classic account by the man who first explored the Colorado.

Hiking Half Dome

34

>> Yosemite's lightning rod

A proud sentinel at the head of Yosemite Valley, Half Dome (8836ft) has snuck its way not only onto most postcards of the national park, but also California's official State Quarter and the logo of the Sierra Club. Even in a spot with more granite domes than anywhere else on the earth, the tower cuts a commanding and instantly recognizable profile, its sheer frontside soaring a mind-bending 4700ft above the valley floor. The smooth face is where rock-climbing legends are made, but hikers can experience the thrill of topping out on Half Dome by ascending the steep granite backside.

The familiar form seen today looked quite different millions of years ago, before the dome was undercut near the base by the same glacial system that carved out Yosemite Valley. As glaciers struck fractures extending up the northwest face of the larger dome, around a quarter of the granite mass was carried away, resulting in the sheer vertical northwest face seen today. Like a shattered vase, rubble from the lost section remains scattered throughout the valley below.

Daring and enticing hikers in equal measure, the eighteen-mile round-trip slog from the valley floor to the top of Half Dome is Yosemite's most irresistible hike. It's also a popular one, with around five hundred people a day committing to the trip in summer. To avoid the crowds, plan a hike in early September, when you can expect the same generally perfect weather and far fewer trail neighbors. Half Dome can also be included as part of a longer backpacking trip by staying the night at Little Yosemite Valley Campground (6100ft), about half-way up the trail from the valley floor, or as a four-mile spur hike from the John Muir Trail (see p.000).

The main trail begins on the west side of the Merced River near the Happy Isles Nature Center. After a mile, the trail crosses the Merced River on a footbridge and leads to a junction with two distinctive routes to the same place. The John Muir Trail to the right is shaded and nearly a mile longer, its gentle gradient being a better choice for backpackers. The two miles of asphalt at the start might offend some purists, but it helps reduce erosion on one of the park's most widely used trails. The other option is the Mist Trail, a shorter route with granite steps in the steeper sections. Take the John Muir Trail in the morning and save the Mist Trail for the return, when you can take a dip in the refreshing pools above Vernal Fall as a late-afternoon break.

The two trails eventually reunite above Vernal Fall for the onward trek up the canyon. The trail ahead is a scenic show-off, especially as it bridges the boisterous Merced River and follows the waterway along its granite trough. This flat and thinly wooded section of trail features expansive views up the river and the slopes on both sides. The section also marks the halfway point, making it a good point to take a snack to recover energy for what's ahead. Turning away from the river and to the north, the forest cover thickens as the trail makes a peaceful wooded ascent. Until the last mile, the path is largely shaded, with the scents of red fir, ponderosa pine, and incense cedar heavy in the air.

taming Half Dome

Of all Yosemite's landmarks, none have borne more names than Half Dome. Failed titles include Rock of Ages, Goddess of Liberty, Mt Abraham Lincoln, Cleft Rock, Spirit of the Valley, Sentinel Dome, and, funny enough, both North Dome and South Dome. Whatever its name, people have long wanted to tame the tower by climbing to its top.

Even before the initial geological survey proclaimed the dome "perfectly inaccessible," an unsuccessful attempt was made in 1859. Failed assaults continued until local trail builder and guide George G. Anderson – called "an indomitable Scotchman" by another indomitable Scotchman, John Muir – hiked to the base of the upper dome, near where the cables begin today. By drilling his way up, inserting bolts and ropes every five to six feet, Anderson was able to reach the summit on October 12, 1875. Four days later he led a group of six tourists to the base of the dome. One of the two who made it to the top was Sally Dutcher, the first woman to climb Half Dome – an impressive feat accomplished while wearing a long dress. Anderson's fixed ropes were eventually destroyed by avalanches and the Sierra Club installed steel cables near Anderson's original route in 1919. Since then, the cables, stanchions, and crossplanks have been replaced several times.

It is a crest of granite ... perfectly inaccessible, being probably the only one of the prominent points about the Yosemite which never has been, and never will be, trodden by human foot.

Josiah Whitney, California Geological Survey Report, 1865.

need to know

Half Dome is most frequently topped as a day hike from Yosemite Valley, for which backcountry permits are not required. Since the trailhead parking area is often full, day-hikers often use the lot at Curry Village and walk an additional mile, or else use the conveniently sited Upper Pines campground. While the handy Yosemite Valley Shuttle stops at the trailhead, you'll want to be on the trail before the shuttle begins operating at 7am as the hike takes between ten and twelve hours to complete; overnight accommodations in the valley are recommended. Contact Yosemite National Park (℡ 209/372-0200, Ⓦ www.nps. gov/yose) for options and additional information.

guides and gear Yosemite Mountaineering School (℡ 209/372-8344, Ⓦ www.yosemitepark. com) offers guided hikes to the top of Half Dome during the summer season.

when to go The cables are in place from mid-May to mid-October, and Yosemite's mild weather makes the summer season particularly enjoyable for hiking. There have been lightning strikes every month of the year, and numerous lightning fatalities on Half Dome; never begin an ascent if you see lightning anywhere in the Yosemite area.

getting there Yosemite Valley is located a two-and-a-half hour drive from Fresno and four hours from Sacramento or San Francisco.

suggested reading Michael P. Ghiglieri & Charles R. Farabee, *Off the Wall: Death in Yosemite* (Puma Press) A fascinating and morbid chronicle of deaths within the park. Suzanne Swedo, *Hiking Yosemite National Park* (Falcon). Choose from 59 Yosemite hikes, planning a trip best suited to your time, energy, and experience.

is this for me?

PHYSICAL ✦ ✦ ✦ ✦ ✦
Require aerobic conditioning and stamina

PSYCH ✦ ✦ ✦ ✦ ✦
Climbing a steep protected slope

SKILL ✦ ✦ ✦ ✦ ✦
Ascending cables placed in a 45° slope

WOW! ✦ ✦ ✦ ✦ ✦
A breathtaking hike to an iconic granite dome

Get as close to the edge as common sense permits

Nearing trail's end, a conifer forest gives way to exposed granite and the route up the eastern slope of Half Dome comes into full view. A trail of granite blocks leads to the base, where the hike's biggest adventure begins. Like a spine made of metal, 450ft of cable handrail runs up the peak's back. Sturdy and secure, these cables are strung through steel stanchions set into the rock every eight feet. The only thing left to do is take a deep breath and start climbing. Sure footing on the steep, nearly 45-degree incline is aided by wooden crossplanks placed on the granite at each of the stanchions.

While the cables make an otherwise insurmountable slope accessible to the average hiker, the route is not foolproof – there have been nine fatal falls from the Half Dome cables since 1971. Wear comfortable rubber-sole shoes or boots with good traction, and bring a pair of leather-palmed gloves to protect your hands and improve your grip. The cable route is off-limits in wet or stormy weather, and rangers typically take them out in mid-October and don't put them up again until late May.

After a few minutes of huffing, you'll top out on a surprisingly large, thirteen-acre field of smooth granite that forms a nearly perfect natural

observation deck. You can get as close to the edge as common sense permits, soaking in spectacular views of the towering granite monuments surrounding Yosemite Valley. And if you're not one to back away from dizzying heights, take a wander over to the "Diving Board." This overhanging rock ledge hovering nearly a mile over the valley floor attracts thrill seekers out for the ultimate view, but sends far more walking comfortably in the opposite direction, sweaty palms firmly gripping the cables for the downward descent.

35 Climbing Devils Tower

WHERE Wyoming, USA

WHEN May & July to September

PHYSICAL	✦ ✦ ✦ ✦ ✧
PSYCH	✦ ✦ ✦ ✦ ✧
SKILL	✦ ✦ ✦ ✦ ✧
WOW!	✦ ✦ ✦ ✧ ✧

On the vertical rock faces of Devils Tower National Monument, geology and geometry come together to create something far more appealing than those school subjects. Reaching some 1200ft into the sky, the tower consists of naturally formed, stacked hexagonal columns; what you see on the surface are hundreds of clean vertical lines where the columns join one another. Each crack represents a potential climb: just imagine the ideal rock gym without a ceiling and you'll get the picture.

The small, hard nature of the rock's crystal structure makes the tower great for full body friction moves such as jamming, lay backing, and stemming. Let your moves take you up the unpredictable routes as high as your strength and stamina allow, and don't be surprised if you're exhausted when you top out – the tower's longest crack stretches to a length of 400ft. But you don't have to climb until you drop. With difficulty ratings ranging from 5.7 to 5.13, you can either go all out or just relax and enjoy a more leisurely climb. Whatever the type of ascent, register first with the ranger station, and be sure to bring water, keep hydrated and wear a helmet, to protect from falling rock. During June there is a voluntary climbing closure, supported by the park service, to show understanding and respect for Native American people who regard the tower as sacred.

36 Hiking the Continental Divide Trail

WHERE Western US

WHEN April through October

Fewer than ten people a year, on average, tackle the length of the rough Continental Divide Trail. Little wonder – it takes a full six months to complete. Its 3100 miles slice vertically from Canada right down through the Rockies, eventually winding up at the Mexican border; along the way the trail takes in parts of grand landscapes like Glacier National Park, Idaho's Bitterroot Range, Yellowstone National Park, San Juan Mountain National Park in Colorado, and the Zuni Mountains of New Mexico. The path is a work in progress, with as much as a third of it not well-defined and still subject to the whims of the western wilderness and private land holdings. As a result, you're left to navigate the true route – a source of constant debate by hikers – on your own.

The dedicated paths and small roads that do make up the trail snake through woodsy Alpine terrain in the north, the sharp scent of lodgepole pine a hiker's frequent companion. The scenery is starker, though no less beautiful, as you move south, in and out of swirling red dust and past dry desert shrubbery.

If you don't have half a year to make your way from the bottom of the country to the top or vice-versa, you can get a taste of the trail's ruggedness on one of any shortened hikes, like the thirty-mile section that starts in El Malpais National Monument and Conservation Area, not too far west of Albuquerque, New Mexico. There you can cross bridges of lava built by Ancestral Puebloans and walk through the Chain of Craters, a piñon and juniper moonscape surrounded by lava tables and crumbled volcanoes.

37 Tracking polar bears in the tundra

WHERE Manitoba, Canada

WHEN October and November

You are surrounded by a serene frozen wilderness. From the comfort of your warm tundra buggy, you watch the world's largest land predators emerging from an endless white blanket of snow and ice. Seemingly oblivious to the elements, they casually survey their icy domain, sniffing the winds for the scent of their next meal. You're off the coast of the Hudson Bay near Churchill, "polar bear capital of the world," and you're witness to one of the most magnificent migrations on earth.

In fall these creatures head to the coast in preparation for the freezing of the bay, so they can end their summer of tundra starvation to begin feasting on seals again. The best way to catch a glimpse is on a group tour; knowledgeable guides lead the way, driving so-called tundra buggies across the barren landscape of Wapusk National Park and reciting how the bears are coping with the effects of climate change as well as other tidbits about the local culture and landscapes. Keep your camera poised for a shot of a half-ton *ursus maritimus*, though don't forget about the other animals that thrive in this harsh environment, among them Arctic foxes and snowy owls. At the end of the day return to your lodge situated right on the tundra and illuminated by the countless stars in the wide-open night sky.

38 Hiking in Glacier National Park

WHERE Montana, US

WHEN May to September

Hikers are spoiled for choice in Glacier National Park. Hundreds of miles of trails lace the area, over high grassy meadows populated by bighorn sheep, around deep blue lakes, on hills covered in wildflowers, even past old disused mine shafts from the heady prospecting days of the 1800s. It all makes your visit extremely customizable, with a wide variety of trail lengths and difficulty levels available.

The most popular backcountry hikes lead over the divide of the Rocky Mountains. The physically fit can set aside ten days to cover the full length of the park: a chain of interconnected trails nearly 100-miles long leads over the back of mountain ridges to the Canadian border at adjoining Waterton Lakes National Park. Easier options exist on bite-sized portions and day-hikes, such as Two Medicine Trail, an incredibly scenic 9.4-mile walk over the Continental Divide. It leads past the sapphire-blue Medicine Lakes and by Running Eagle Falls, also known as "Trick Falls," where, depending on the season, the upper falls' abundant flow may hide the lower falls or, conversely, the lower falls may almost exclusively constitute the water flow. A little further north, the 5.4-mile Cut Bank trail ascends to the place where the park's streams divide, one heading down to the Gulf of Mexico and the other to Hudson Bay. Another option is a 7.6 mile-trail to Red Eagle by way of the Triple Divide Pass. You can revel at the magnificence of the deep Red Eagle Lake and stand in awe in front of Rainbow Falls, a 47-foot waterfall plunging over a sheer ledge of sandstone.

39 Canyoneering in Paria River and Buckskin Gulch

WHERE Utah, US

WHEN March through October

PHYSICAL	✦ ✦ ✦ ✧ ✧
PSYCH	✦ ✦ ✦
SKILL	✦ ✦ ✦
WOW!	✦ ✦ ✦ ✧

Dipping just below the surface of one of the most barren and monotonous territories in the southwest United States is the longest slot canyon in the world, a technicolor terrain with textures, hues, and shadows that alter with the position of the sun and the movement of water. Part of the charm of Buckskin Gulch is its cool daytime shade in the middle of the desert – more shadows than sunlight. In some places, the canyon walls reach 500 feet (152m) above the streambed. The sun does not hit the floor of the canyon very often and when it does it can't stay for long. Be prepared for cooler temperatures than you might expect.

Not more than three yards wide for most of the sixteen miles (26km), this slot canyon presents little elevation change, but distinct hiking challenges. You'll encounter unpredictable trail surfaces, such as unstable dry sand, wet solid sand, wet sticky clay, thick mud, waist-deep pools, and car-size boulders. Flash floods, which occur about eight times a year, send torrents of water through the slot, scouring rough edges, tossing hefty sandstone boulders, snapping cottonwood trees, transporting sand and gravel, and facilitating rockfall; as fascinating as that might sound, you definitely do not want to be around to watch, since there are limited escape routes once you're in the canyon. Consult the weather forecast as well as the local ranger station before entering the canyon.

Best done as a three- or four-day trip, the 26-mile (42km) loop trail winds its way along the narrow canyon floor before opening up into a brilliant amphitheater as it meets with the Paria River. Overhangs, beaches, and flat rocks provide camping spots near the river; you'll need a permit for an overnight stay.

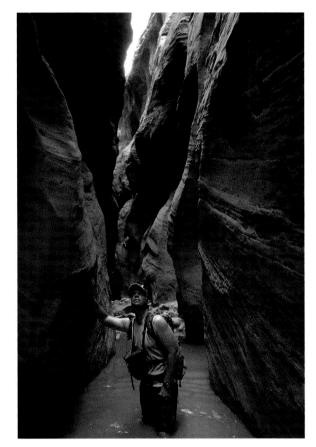

40 Rafting the Klinaklini River

WHERE British Columbia, Canada

WHEN July and August

PHYSICAL	✦ ✦ ✧ ✧
PSYCH	✦ ✦ ✧
SKILL	✦ ✦ ✧
WOW!	✦ ✦ ✦

The Klinaklini River is so remote and difficult to navigate that most of the natives in the region have never even attempted it – in fact, they were never even aware of the river's upper reaches until helicopters first accessed the area. This is no casual float trip; be fully prepared for some Class V rapids as you whirl through steep glacial canyons with unexpected twists and turns. The reward, besides the adrenaline rush from the heart-stopping chutes and wild runs, is some of British Columbia's most exquisite scenery and wildlife.

The weeklong wilderness journey begins by helicopter, which delivers you to your put-in. Rimming the water are unspoiled forests and fields of delicate wildflowers; bighorn sheep, wolverines, moose, weasels, wolves, and grizzlies populate the river's edge. Dramatic blue icefields and epic mountain ranges cast their shadows into the water. It's chilly water (and air, for that matter), too, requiring that you wear a drysuit.

This kind of river calls for your constant attention, and portages demand strength and tenacity; it's echoed in the names of the runs. Your first day on the water will have you plunging through the Class V "Little Drop of Horrors," the next confronting "Nobody Moves," where guides will have to gauge water levels to determine whether you can run it. The toughest single passage, the spectacular Klinaklini Canyon, can be neither run nor easily portaged, so a helicopter comes to carry you to runnable downriver rapids. The adventure ends at Knight Inlet, as the wild Klinaklini flattens and gently empties into a deep 60-mile long fjord on the Queen Charlotte Strait at the north end of Vancouver Island.

41 Ice-climbing in Québec

WHERE Parc de la Chute-Montmorency, Canada

WHEN January and February; longer if conditions allow

You are clinging precariously to a sheer face of ice. In each hand you hold an ice axe; you wear crampons on your feet. Again and again, you hurl one of the axes at the ice, trying to gouge a crevice secure enough to hold your body weight as you edge another painful inch up the ice. But you can't find a hold. "You must start from back here," your guide, who belays you now, had explained when you were safely on the ground. He held the ice axe high above his shoulder as if he were going to throw it and said, "And then you just flick your wrist at the end." He then demonstrated, scampering up the ice face like a squirrel. "Well," you'd thought, "this is going to be easy." You were wrong.

Your whole body is trembling as bit by bit you edge up the frozen chute of water. Just meters away, the 83-meter Montmorency Fall still tumbles, even in winter. You're in Parc de la Chute-Montmorency, which attracts hikers and sightseers in summer and is popular in winter for snowshoeing as well as ice-climbing. To the sides of the cascading water extraordinary formations of ice descend like the melted wax of ecclesiastical candles. But for now, you're not interested in the natural wonders around you. Slowly, you're making progress up the ice. When, finally, you reach the top, endorphins flood your veins and you could shout to the world of your achievement

42 Diving with manta rays in Kona

WHERE Big Island of Hawaii, US

WHEN Year-round

It sounds like a giant fish story: sitting on the ocean floor at night, shining a flashlight and having a group of thirteen-foot manta rays swim by close enough to touch. Along the coasts of Kona, on Hawaii's Big Island, it's a reality.

To see this matchless underwater spectacle, you'll need to be a certified diver. Outfitters take boats along the shoreline to bay areas of concentrated coral. From there, it's an 18- to 32-foot descent to a gravelly, rocky area between patches of coral; you and your fellow divers form a circle on the bottom of the ocean floor. When the bright underwater lights are shone above, plankton quickly gather, and manta rays follow, in search of their evening meal.

You can expect to see four to six manta rays on a dive, although up to as many as 28 mantas have been seen within a period of just a couple hours; the success rate of seeing rays on any given dive is in the 80 to 90 percent range.

43 Mountain biking on the Kokopelli Trail

WHERE Colorado & Utah, US

WHEN April to October; best in spring and fall

Legendary in mountain biking circles, this remote desert trail is no pedal in the park. Sandy single tracks, slickrock and rough four-wheel drive roads take turns providing the drama. The 142-mile length connects Loma, Colorado, and Moab, Utah, and leads you through beautiful canyons, arid plateaus, wooded mountain slopes, and sheer wall cliffs – all lightly touched with a coat of red dust.

It generally takes about five to six days to complete, as you'll bike anywhere from 15 to 40 physically challenging miles a day, depending of course on the terrain. Teetering along the ledges of ragged mountains, you'll weave through numerous canyons along the Colorado River and steeply climb the La Sal Mountains to elevations of over 9000 feet. You'll dodge rocks, bumps, and scurrying lizards on rugged terrain roads and likely come across mule deer, desert bighorn sheep, and bald

pattern of waves as they roll to shore in sets. Deep blues and even darker greens mix with the white spray in a pulsating rhythm; soon, you won't be able to hold out much longer. Even a surfboard won't suffice.

So bodysurfing it is. The peerless breakwater offers overhead and even double overhead opportunities. The waves are noticeably cold, with water temperature never getting much above 60°F; no wonder the first full body wetsuit was developed here. The depth of the water and strong currents require fins for bodysurfers to catch a wave; other lesser breaks nearby are better for the inexperienced bodysurfer. Whatever wave you intend to catch, make sure to consult the surf report first. Local surf shops can help you find the best spot for your skill level and ensure you have the necessary gear and information.

45 Paddling Tatshenshini-Alsek Park

WHERE Alaska, US
WHEN June to August

Floating in an inflatable raft or kayak around mammoth icebergs can be downright humbling. Part of it is realizing that ninety percent of the mass of these jagged iceblocks is hidden below the surface; they seem mountain-sized as it is.

The Alsek and Tatshenshini rivers help make up the glacial wilderness of Tatshenshini-Alsek Park, nestled in the northern reaches of the Alaskan panhandle. The pace of navigating these waters alternates between leisurely, almost languid, and frenetic and frenzied; at times icy water will slap your face and put your paddling to a severe test. The latter mostly happens on the turbulent rapids of the Alsek, which flow against the backdrop of the Fairweather range. Rafters are supported by helicopters to portage past Turnback Canyon as survival would be severely questionable if you advanced into those unforgiving hydraulics and frigid waters; expert kayaker Walt Blackadar, after taking on the canyon in 1971, deemed it just plain "unpaddlable." The Tatshenshini is less wild and remote but no less compelling, with wildflowers blooming along the riverbanks and meadows all summer, moose wading in marshes, and gnomelike kingfishers hunting the waters with precision. You hit some whitewater here, but not with the frequency and drama found along the Alsek.

This trip requires expert logistical support, and a number of companies provide services on the river. Remember to bring good raingear as Mount Fairweather, belying its name, receives significant annual precipitation, much of it in the summer.

eagles. You'll even cruise through the deserted, rusting ghost town of Cisco, Utah, where the only movement you might be aware of is the figure you cut through the whistling wind.

Campsites dot the way, even some right on the Colorado River, perfect for taking a breather and cooling off (though bring a copious amount of water, as well as clothing that provides thermal insulation and dries quickly). As each day promises to be physically exhausting, be content to wrap up warm each evening and lie back to watch the fire-sky sunset.

44 Bodysurfing Steamer Lane

WHERE California, US
WHEN Year-round

Well before they were immortalized in the Beach Boys' hit, "Surfin' USA," the beaches of Santa Cruz held rank as a surfing hotspot. Those who wanted to ride the crest of powerful beach-pounding waves gathered – and still gather – at Steamer Lane, where the geology and ocean currents work together to create the ultimate natural thrill ride. This is where California surfing started.

Stand on the shore and be hypnotized by the predictable

46 Hiking the West Coast Trail

WHERE British Columbia, Canada

WHEN May to September

PHYSICAL	✦ ✦ ✦ ✦ ✧
PSYCH	✦ ✦ ✦ ✧ ✧
SKILL	✦ ✦ ✦ ✧ ✧
WOW!	✦ ✦ ✦ ✦ ✧

It all began with a shipwreck. When the SS *Valencia* ran aground on Vancouver Island's west coast in 1906 and all 126 passengers perished, the government built a trail between Port Renfrew and Bamfield, originally named the Shipwrecked Mariner's Trail, to provide coastal access in the event of future wrecks. Hiking the 77km West Coast Trail may make you feel you're part of a heroic rescue party as you ford streams, ride in cable cars, cross suspension bridges and footlogs, and climb backcountry ladders. It's an object lesson in ingenuity for getting from point A to point B.

Challenges abound – muddy beaches and surge channels, incoming tides, and steep slippery slopes – but so do rewards.

There's the wide-open Pacific sunset for example, or the lovely Douglas fir and red cedar forests. You might listen to a humpback or gray whale from a sandy beach one day and spot a bear or cougar on another.

Plan on five to seven days to complete the route and come prepared for rain even in July and August. Once on the trail, there's no opportunity for resupply or an easy exit, so you'll need to stock up on provisions beforehand. The trail can be easily accessed from Victoria on the southern end of Vancouver Island, and its popularity requires that you have a permit – as there's a quota system, it is best to plan far in advance so that you can get reservations. Walk-on permits are available but extremely limited.

47 Magpie river rafting

WHERE Québec, Canada

WHEN June to August

PHYSICAL	✦ ✦ ✦
PSYCH	✦ ✦ ✦
SKILL	✦ ✦ ✦
WOW!	✦ ✦ ✦ ✦

It takes some daring to tackle Québec's Magpie River. This rushing chute of water cuts through a largely untouched wilderness larger than the whole of Scandanavia and offers rapids from Class III to V, with a put-in so remote that it can only be reached by float plane.

Beginning at Lac Magpie, an 80km-long lake, it often takes six or seven days to travel the full 190km down the river, but every bend and ripple is worth it. The river flows through granite-enclosed canyons smothered with deep, green pines and littered with bright colored moss and lichen. Moose and bear can be spotted along the shoreline and in wooded areas, and the camping is excellent, especially under the magnificent colors of the aurora borealis, best seen in summer. Another natural phenomenon are the waterfalls along the way, the most impressive of which is Magpie Falls, where the entire river drops 100 feet down in a cascade of rushing water wider than it is tall by 25 feet. Of course, rafters must portage around a huge gorge that swallows the river to reach the entrancing falls. The trip's powerhouse rapid is the Class V run that starts directly below Thirty Foot Falls and runs into a lovely little lake; the takeout occurs near the confluence of the Magpie and the St Lawrence River.

The weather can be shifty, so bring warm, waterproof clothing. You can arrange for the float-plane put-in and run the river idependently, or book with an outfitter for a guided trip. Inflatable kayaks work well for smaller rapids, while large whitewater rafts are preferable for the larger rapids, of which there are plenty.

48 Hiking the Hoh Rainforest

WHERE: Washington, US

WHEN: April to October

PHYSICAL	✦ ✦ ✦ ◇ ◇
PSYCH	✦ ✦ ✦ ◇ ◇
SKILL	✦ ✦ ◇ ◇ ◇
WOW!	✦ ✦ ✦ ◇ ◇

Nearer the Arctic Circle than the Tropic of Cancer, Olympic National Park's Hoh Rainforest is one of the few temperate rainforests in the world. Rather than a tropical rainforest, it's a cool, wet, coniferous paradise, full of immense trees and shrouded in perennial fog. What makes this ecosystem so special is, quite simply, rain – lots of rain – about 12 to 14 feet (3.6 to 4.2m) per year. This not only nourishes the old growth forest and its wildlife but frequently causes the Hoh River to erode its banks, change its course, and regenerate the forest as it deposits alluvium, topples old growth, and fosters new growth.

The exoticism of the environment is the main excitement here. Two short interpretive trails near the national park visitor center, the Hall of Mosses Trail and the Spruce Nature Trail, give you a good overview of what lies further in the misty wooded depths. The Hoh River Trail is a 36-mile (58km) round-trip slog into a dense canopy of spruce, hemlock, and cedar. Along the way you might espy deer, mountain goats, or a member of the world's largest herd of Roosevelt elk. Rarer species thriving in this habitat include the northern spotted owl, Pacific tree frogs, and a bewildering variety of mushrooms. The path moves into snowbound territory as it ascends to Glacier Meadows, and serious hikers can consider tacking on the climb up Blue Glacier; bring crampons and an ice axe. Raingear is a must in all seasons.

the first mountain bike

In 1953 American John Finley Scott cobbled together various bike parts into something that we would recognize today as a mountain bike. But riding off-road didn't gain serious traction until the mid-1970s on the rocky trails around Mount Tamalpais, just north of San Francisco. The first mountain bike to have a significant impact on the cycling world was Joe Breeze's 1977 "Breezer," which came with lightweight tubing, fat tires and quality hubs and rims.

"Without wilderness, the world is a cage."

David Brower

FIVE UNUSUAL SURF SPOTS

▶ **Cortes Bank**, California. Around a hundred miles off the coast, these waves (up to 60ft high) are for professional tow-in surfers only.

▶ **Jackson Hole**, Wyoming. The Class III whitewater rapids on the Snake River aren't just for rubber rafts any more.

▶ **St Lawrence River**, Canada. Montreal has some the world's best river surfing on two-meter standing waves.

▶ **Sheboygan**, Wisconsin. Lake surfers come for summertime's "Dairyland Surf Classic."

▶ **Yakutat**, Alaska. You'll need a thick wetsuit to ride these North Pacific breaks.

"All other things being equal, choose a john with a view."

Colin Fletcher

lightning capital of North America

Mountaineers and backcountry hikers face real risks in lightning storms, with several deaths each year from lightning strikes. But if you think that mountainous regions are the most lightning prone, think again. The lightning rod for the US is Florida, which is also the flattest state in the US, with no land elevation over 345 feet. Florida averages about 10 lightning fatalities per year. Alaska and Hawaii, both of which have some sizeable mountains, have the lowest number of lightning deaths.

AN INUIT CULINARY ADVENTURE

After a long day paddling your kayak on cold Arctic water you've probably burned several thousand calories. What better way to replenish your stores of fat than a bowl of Eskimo ice cream, a concoction known as Akutuq? Combine reindeer fat with a little seal oil, whip in some ice, and then add fresh seasonal berries – blackberries, salmonberries, or blueberries . . . just keep in mind that it's something of an acquired taste.

"Life is like a dogsled team...If you're not the lead dog, the scenery never changes."

Lewis Grizzard

you can hide, but you can't run

In the mountainous regions of North America, bears, wolves, and cougars still crown the food chain, and if you want to avoid that chain, stay out of the way. Running is a poor way to protect yourself from large carnivores. Not only does it trigger the predator's "chase and hunt" instincts, but there is simply no way you can outrun one of these animals. The human speed record, held by the world's fastest sprinters, is around 27 mph. Both cougars and wolves can run at 40mph for several miles and a grizzly bear can sustain speeds above 30mph. North America's fastest land animal, clocked at a speed of 61mph, is the pronghorn antelope, a timid herbivore that will usually be running away from you.

FROM SKIS TO SNOWBOARDS

The invention of the snowboard is usually credited to American Sherman Poppen, who in 1965 gave his daughter a water ski to allow her to "surf" down the snow covereddunes near their Michigan home. It was such a hit with the kids that he went to his workshop and crafted a wider board with a rope handle. This became known as a "Snurfer", which over the next two decades was further developed by half a dozen manufacturers. Jack Burton of Vermont, who in the late 1970s was the first to create a snowboard with bindings, helped fuel the craze with his design and in the 1980s the sport underwent a massive boom. Though shunned at first by many traditionalists, it has now gained enough acceptance to be an Olympic sport, and most ski resorts have some sort of halfpipe or terrain park.

"Wild rivers are earth's renegades, defying gravity, dancing to their own tunes, resisting the authority of humans, always chipping away, and eventually always winning."

Richard Bangs

world's longest cave

With more than 365 miles explored and more still remaining to be discovered, Mammoth Cave in Kentucky is the world's longest cave system. Other caves around the world have larger chambers, bigger passages or lie deeper, but Mammoth's length exceeds the length of the world's next three longest caves combined: Optimisticeskaja in Ukraine, Jewel Cave in South Dakota, USA, and Holloch in Switzerland.

HIKING THE TRIPLE CROWN

For most people, hiking just one of America's long distance trails is an epic lifetime achievement. But in 1999, "Flyin'" Brian Robinson became the first person to hike the length of the Appalachian Trail, Continental Divide Trail, and Pacific Crest Trail in a calendar year. Averaging 30 miles a day, he covered a total of 7400 miles through 22 states, conquering a combined total of over a million vertical feet of ascent. In the process he consumed about 6000 calories a day and wore out seven pairs of running shoes.

"Everyone must believe in something. I believe I'll go canoeing."

Henry David Thoreau

five adrenaline-charged rafting runs

Beyond the whitewater adventures detailed in this section, there are plenty more spots to get a soaking and a thrill.

▶ **Gauley River**, West Virginia. Try the 16-mile, Class IV–V upper stretch from Summersville Dam to Peters Creek.

▶ **Frasier River,** British Columbia. The wild upper span from Moose Lake to Robson confluence is eleven miles of big-volume Class III–IV+ runs.

▶ **Upper Animas River**, Colorado. From Silverton to the Powerhouse you get cold water, Class V+ rapids to keep you awake.

▶ **Stikine River**, British Columbia. A dangerous river with Class V–VI through the "Grand Canyon" section. Good whitewater throughout its 400-mile length.

▶ **South Fork**, American River. This dam-release year-round ride delivers consistent Class III–V thrills.

STEEP SLOPES

Mount McKinley in Alaska is North America's tallest mountain, at 20,320ft; Canada's Mount Logan, in the Yukon, comes in second at 19,551ftt.

Yosemite system exposed

The Yosemite Decimal System, the standardize method for rating the difficulty of hikes and climbs, was actually developed outside of Yosemite. The initial 1–5 scale was developed throughout the Sierra Nevada, but the more specifically designed and commonly used method of rating rock climbing routes (5.0 through 5.9 and above) was a Southern California concoction, originating at Tahquitz Rock in Idyllwild. There, in the 1950s, members of the Los Angeles chapter of the Sierra Club rated the easiest climb as a 5.0 and the most difficult climb humanly possible as a 5.9. Since then, the system has been expanded and subdivided with several climbs rated up to 5.15.

speak Mi'kmaq like a native

The Mi'kmaq are a First Nation or Native American people indigenous to New England and Canada's Atlantic Provinces, including the Gaspé Peninsula. Several of their words have found their way into English, including "toboggan," which means "sled," and the word "kayak" which is used in several Arctic languages. "Caribou" is a word meaning "snow-shoveler," because the animal paws through the snow for its food. One Mi'kmaq word that never quite bridged the divide is "abigjilu," their word for "skunk" which literally means "an animal that steps backward and farts."

POISONOUS SNAKES THAT DON'T RATTLE

Not every slithering creature is poisonous and not every poisonous snake has the courtesy to warn you with a rattling alert. And for that matter, not all poisonous rattlesnakes have rattles. But here are few silent but deadly North American snakes to watch for in the wild:
Copperhead. Native to Southeast US, Texas and Oklahoma on rock outcrops and hillsides.
Cottonmouth. This aggressive snake is often longer than 6ft and is found near water ways and swamps in the Southeast US
Coral Snake. The Western, Eastern, and Texas species are found through much of the southern US. Their distinctive bands have led to the reminder "red and yellow kill a fellow."

old and new

Yellowstone National Park, in northwest Wyoming (and crossing over into Idaho and Montana), is the oldest national park in the world, designated as such in 1872; Alberta's Banff National Park followed in 1885 and was Canada's first such park. More recently, Ukkusiksalik National Park, in Nunvaut, Canada, was granted its status in 2003, and Colorado's Sand Dunes became a national park in 2004.

LATIN AMERICA AND THE CARIBBEAN

49 Kayaking in the Sea of Cortez

>> **Share water with whales**

SEA OF CORTEZ

MEXICO

With hundreds of unexplored coves, uninhabited islands, and miles of mangrove-lined estuaries that play host to sea lions, turtles and nesting birds, it's easy to see why Baja California has become a favorite destination for a growing number of sea kayakers. Of course, a famously mild climate, relaxed pace of life and an overabundance of sunny days only adds to the peninsula's allure. From sunrise to sundown the shimmering waters of the Sea of Cortez beckon, calling kayakers to explore coves bathed in light, languid lagoons, hidden caves and natural sandstone arches. With such a beguiling invitation, who could say no?

ceviche

If you thought it was only the Japanese who ate their fish raw, then you ought to spend some tine on the Sea of Cortez, where ceviche is a local delicacy. While the dish originated in Peru, it is popular throughout Latin America, particularly on the Pacific coast where fresh fish is readily available.

There are as many variations as there are cooks, but they all start with cutting fresh fish into bit-sized chunks, and pouring lime juice over the fish to cover. When the fish turns opaque, drain the lime juice, and add a diced tomato, chopped green pepper, finely diced onion, cilantro and a dash of Tabasco or a touch of chilli pepper for a little fire. Ceviche can be served as a salad or as a main dish, but either way it is best enjoyed while you're relaxing on the beach at sunset after a day of paddling.

One classic route is a circumnavigation of Isla Espíritu Santo, an uninhabited island with a washboard topography, sandstone cliffs and fingerlike coves in the Sea of Cortez five miles off the peninsula north of La Paz. You and your kayak are taken to the island by motorboat, whose crew will set up camps along your planned clockwise route, leaving you to travel light, explore caves, *arroyos* and beaches, and still have a comfortable camp and delicious cooked meal awaiting you each night. You may see a few other kayaks out on the water as well during the day, but for the most part it's just you, the local marine life and whispering zephyrs.

Paddling north along the west coast of Isla Espíritu Santo in largely protected waters, you'll come to Isla Partida. At low tide the two islands are connected by an isthmus, but at high tide you can paddle through the channel that separates them. Along the way you'll make occasional acquaintances with sea lions cruising the coastal waters, but the greatest congregation is found on the north side of Isla Partida at Los Islotes, a world-renowned rookery with a large natural arch at its center. Here, secluded from natural predators you can swim with sea lion pups, and if you approach them slowly, they can become especially playful, even mimicking your underwater movements before performing a ballet of their own.

After rounding the top of Isla Espíritu Santo, continue south on the island's east side where the open waters are potentially more challenging, and the coast, with high cliffs separated by long stretches of sandy beaches, becomes more uniform. Some of these striking cliff formations

The Gulf of California is the natural aquarium of the world.
Jacques Cousteau

take on a personality of their own, like *la maschera*, where cavities in the rock form a ghoulish face with deep-set eyes and a growling mouth. Though the topside scenery never fails to impress, keep your snorkeling gear near the hatch cover for a quick escape to an underwater world teeming with life. Just the shell of your kayak separates you from thriving coral reefs and over six hundred species of colorful fish. The Sea of Cortez is also a haven for dolphins, orcas, humpback whales, blue whales, grey whales, sperm whales and pilot whales. With so many whales migrating to and from these waters throughout the October through May season you'll stand a good chance of spotting one – a magical and potentially intimate experience from the seat of your kayak.

A circumnavigation of Isla Espíritu Santo takes five to seven days,

giving you ample opportunities to stretch your legs on shore and take part in some of the island's land pursuits, such as beachcombing, birding and climbing peaks. Or you may be content to simply lie on white-sand beaches and feast on freshly made ceviche. No matter – when the sun sets you'll surely be pondering ways to extend your stay.

need to know

The calm waters of the Sea of Cortez make for easy surf launches and smooth paddling. While sea kayaks are quite stable – especially when loaded with 45 or more kilograms of gear – you'll still want to be comfortable with a dunk test and wet exit before venturing too far from shore.

guides and gear Sea kayak tours, including single-day trips or expeditions lasting three to seven days, can be outfitted from many towns along the Sea of Cortez. Both Loreto and La Paz offer outfitting, guided expeditions and accommodation, with La Paz providing the easier access to the Isla Espíritu Santo and more rental options for the independent kayaker. Baja Outdoor Activities (T 52/612-125-5636, W www.kayactivities.com, or www. kayakinbaja.com) offers a variety of custom and group adventures from La Paz into the Sea of Cortez and nearby islands.

when to go October to May is the best season, before the summer heat sets in; avoid the August and September hurricane season. November is exquisite since the water is still warm, with comfortable daytime temperatures and cooler evenings.

getting there Fly into La Paz, located on Baja's southeastern coast about two hours north of Los Cabos.

suggested reading Adromeda Romano-Lax, *Adventure Kayaking in Baja* (Wilderness Press). A collection of popular short routes (three to five days) with maps and trip summaries.

is this for me?

PHYSICAL ✦ ✦ ◈ ◈ ◈
Paddling in mild currents

PSYCH ✦ ✦ ✦ ◈ ◈
Remote, warm waters

SKILL ✦ ✦ ✦ ✦ ◈
Know how to make a wet exit

WOW! ✦ ✦ ✦ ✦ ◈
Spectacular coastline and marine life

Trekking the Paine Circuit

50

CHILE

>> On the trail of the three towers

PARQUE
NACIONAL
TORRES DEL
PAINE

Your flight into the small gateway of Punta Arenas or Río Gallegos gives you a hint of the unpopulated terrain that lies ahead, but little of its majesty. You have arrived at the southern tip of South America in wind-carved Patagonia, an austere province of *gauchos*, grass tussocks, ice fields, barren plains and spectacular mountainscapes. For over five hundred years adventurers have been drawn from mild climes and the comforts of home to explore the breadth and length of this fabled region, though nowhere has the lure proved stronger than in Chile's Parque Nacional Torres del Paine. It is a dramatic landscape of gleaming lakes, deep fjords, pristine glaciers and pink-granite spires that can only be truly appreciated in one manner: on the Paine Circuit.

Begin the ten-day 100-kilometer trek at the Laguna Amarga entrance and make the circuit in a counter-clockwise direction, strategically saving the best for last, as most do. You'll spend the first day in a steady ascent with the mountain views to your left and the Río Paine close at hand on the right. The next three days on the backside of the circuit offer up quintessential Patagonian vistas: jeweled blue lakes dotted with icebergs, grassy meadows, a swollen gorge, waterfalls and a maze of fallen trees. Along this section you'll have a good chance to see Patagonia's wildlife, which is every bit as distinctive as the scenery. Guanacos, a camelid similar to the domesticated llama, can be found grazing on tundra slopes and meadows, and rheas, an omnivorous, flightless bird similar to an ostrich, are also commonly sighted. With a bit of luck you may even spot a majestic Andean condor, the biggest bird found on the continent. Patagonian pumas are the largest predator, feeding on guanacos and smaller mammals, however these big cats are elusive and rare.

need to know

The two principal routes in Torres del Paine are the "W" and the full circuit. If you're traveling independently, plan on purchasing all supplies before entering the park, ideally at Puerto Natales, then register and secure your permits at the park. Accommodation options range from wilderness camping, to basic *refugios* with food and hot showers, to luxury lodges.

guides and gear US-based Mountain Travel Sobek (☎510/594-6000 or 1-888/687-6235, ⓦ www. mtsobek.com) offers guided and supported treks on the Paine Circuit.

when to go Mid-November to the end of February is the best season for a visit, and even then rough weather is possible.

getting there Parque Nacional Torres del Paine can be accessed by bus service from Punta Arenas, Chile where bus service takes you to Puerto Natales 250km to the north, then on to the park entrance, another 145km to the northeast.

suggested reading Carlos Brebbia, *Patagonia: A Forgotten Land : From Magellan to Perón* (WIT Press). Five centuries of Patagonian history and culture, richly illustrated with maps and photographs. Urruty and Zagier, *Torres del Paine Trekking Map*. Excellent detail and topographic features, including reasonable hiking times.

is this for me?

PHYSICAL ✦ ✦ ✦ ✦ ✦
Active hiking and some scrambling

PSYCH ✦ ✦ ✦ ✦ ✦
Slippery trails and rough weather

SKILL ✦ ✦ ✦ ✦ ✦
Trekking, backpacking experience handy

WOW! ✦ ✦ ✦ ✦ ✦
A scenic environment like no other

Patagonia's camelids

While trekking in Torres del Paine, you may come across a number of indigenous species – perhaps one even as tall as you. Herds of the spunky and tan-furred guanaco, a close relative of the camel, are numerous in the park. Though they spend much of their time grazing on plains, they can sometimes be seen foraging on mountainsides where they can move about with surprising agility. With their pointy grey ears, large snout, elongated neck, and soulful eyes, guanaco might seem cuddly, but they're known to have an aggressive side, particularly during mating season. A picture of one, with the Torres as a backdrop, is as close as you should get.

From John Garner Pass (1241m), the scenery only gets better as the trail, often marked by colorful wildflowers and orchids, turns south and crosses streams, boulder fields and scree slopes, accompanied by breathtaking views of the electric blue Glacier Grey. The massive face of Glacier Grey spans the head of Lago Grey and resembles an army marching into the water, with the occasional cracks and rumbles of icebergs falling into the lake resonating across the landscape. The route now rejoins the "W" trail, with two side trips that should be considered mandatory. The first crosses a large suspension bridge and ascends Frances Valley to an arresting view of the Cuernos del Paine (the Horns of Paine), the eerie and iconic sculpted granite spires for which the trek is most famous. The second side hike, and on this itinerary the final day of the circuit, is the vista most worth waiting for – the impossibly jagged Torres del Paine (Towers of Paine). Crossing a suspension bridge over the Río Ascensio and climbing steeply up the Ascensio Valley you arrive at a small glacial lake and a lookout point where you'll have the perfect view of the Torres del Paine, not only a classic Patagonian vista, but one of the most mesmerizing mountain scenes in the world. The descent from the Torres returns you to the *Hosteria Las Torres* and the park entrance.

The trail can present some challenges with boggy sections, stream crossings and some slick mud in places. But the most significant hindrance on the Paine Circuit is the weather – always windy, and often cool and wet even in January and February, the warmest months of the austral summer. At some points along the circuit you'll face winds which consistently average a stiff 64km per hour. In a Patagonia wind, rain is horizontal and walking downhill can be an uphill battle, though one well worth it in Torres del Paine.

Diving in Belize

AMBERGRIS CAYE

BELIZE

51

>> **Go for a swim with nurse sharks and manta rays**

You might naturally expect that diving in waters with sharks, barracudas, manta rays, moray eels and a limestone sinkhole over 100m deep is out of the realm of possibility to all but the most expert diver, but not so in Belize. With startlingly clear water and shallow depths at many of the very best dive sites, Belize is a great place to learn the basics of diving in a safe and comfortable setting. Whether or not you're a beginner, plan on at least a week; with world-class options like the Great Blue Hole and the barrier reef, there's almost too much on offer to consider anything less.

lightning on the water

"*When thunder roars, go indoors*" – that simple advice has saved thousands of lives during lightning storms. Even on the water, being inside the enclosed cabin of a boat is safer than being in a small boat with no cabin, but it is not risk free. But what are the risks to scuba divers when lightning strikes? First of all, the fact that you're scuba diving makes you safer than anyone around you who may be swimming or boating in an open craft. This is because lightning follows what physics calls the skin effect – that the electricity in lightning travels on the surface, or skin, of an object it strikes. So, instead of deeply penetrating beneath the water, a lightning strike will travel along the surface. Lightning may penetrate about 3m beneath the water's surface at the point of impact, but not much more than that. So if your boat doesn't have a safe cabin to be in during a lightning storm, then you are safer diving deep into the water for the duration of the storm or as long as possible. If lightning strikes when you're scuba diving, you should be spared from any harm if you're 6m or more underwater. Being knowledgeable and attentive when scuba diving around lightning can literally save your skin.

Belizeans think the Great Blue Hole, the most popular dive site in Belize, should be one of the Seven Wonders of the World – and maybe they're right. From the air it appears as a nearly perfect circle of royal-blue water surrounded by Lighthouse Reef and the shallow aquamarine waters of the coral atoll. The Great Blue Hole came to the attention of divers worldwide when Jacques Cousteau first explored its depths in his one-man submarine and televised its towering stalactites suspended from overhanging walls – like giant tree trunks plunging into the abyss – and eventually probed to its maximum depth of 126m. It's now an essential part of any dive holiday in Belize and easily reached a day-trip from the mainland.

Descending slowly to around 43m into this circular limestone sinkhole, you'll be dazzled as the intricacy of the formations become more dramatic the deeper you go. The limestone twists back and forth and forms overhangs, allowing you to swim around columns and into underwater caves and passageways. Enjoy navigating the maze-like surroundings and check your trail from time to time – a reef shark just might be keeping you company.

After a day at the Great Blue Hole, most of your remaining dive time in Belize will be spent on the barrier reef, which is essentially a 300-kilometer long continuous dive site, and the second largest barrier reef in the world. Between the mainland and the reef are sandy, shallow waters with several hundred cayes (pronounced "keys") which are palm-clad coral sand or mangrove-covered islands. The heart of the barrier reef dive scene is the

The Great Blue Hole should be one of the Seven Wonders of the World...

need to know

The perfect diving vacation in Belize could be achieved with 2 or 3 local two-tank days on the reef at Ambergris Caye, combined with a full-day excursion to the Great Blue Hole, and a half-day dive at Hol Chan. Water temperatures range from 26–29°C throughout the year, making it an appealing year-round choice. Visibility is a lengthy 25–40m which you will appreciate, especially if you're a photographer.

guides and gear Belize Academy of Diving (☎ 501/226-2873, Ⓦ www.belize-academy-of-diving.com), located in San Pedro on Ambergris Caye, offers local dives and diver education plus trips to the Great Blue Hole and Hol Chan. Belize's only hyperbaric chamber is a Double-Lock Recompression Chamber located in San Pedro on Ambergris Caye.

when to go Belize is a year-round diving destination. November to March generally provides the best visibility, and the cooler water invites a greater variety of wildlife. March to May offer the bonus of whale sharks which come through in migrations.

getting there International flights arrive at Philip Goldson International Airport in Belize City. Scheduled and charter boats or planes continue on to Ambergris Caye.

suggested reading Ned Middleton, Diving Belize (Aqua Quest). Detailed reviews of specific sites with maps, illustrations, and color photos. Also covers accommodation and dive services.

town of San Pedro on Ambergris Caye. Within just five minutes by launch from San Pedro are dramatic drop-offs and warm waters with manta rays, whale sharks and porpoises. If it's photogenic diving you're after, bring your camera for the many colorful tropical varieties like butterfly fish, angelfish and parrot fish near the cayes, as well as turtles and lobsters.

Along the reef, 6km south of San Pedro by road and just off the southern tip of Ambergris Caye, Hol Chan Marine Reserve has become a premier dive site thanks to its successful protection of habitats previously on the decline. Since 1987 the protected waters of Hol Chan have witnessed a remarkable resurgence of marine species rarely seen elsewhere, including barracuda, moray eels, groupers and red snappers. Nurse sharks, abundant in the Caribbean, swim here in just 2 to 3m of water; if the circumstances are right, recreational divers and snorkelers stand a chance of seeing these four-meter long sharks up close.

For divers attracted to atolls, a unique type of island marked by an organic reef, Belize has an unusual appeal. Most atolls are located in the Pacific, where they form on the top of a submerged volcano, and only five occur in the Caribbean – of which three are located in Belizean waters. At the southeastern edge of Hol Chan is the aptly named Shark Ray Alley. As your boat approaches this dive site, dark shadows shift to and fro just beneath the water's surface – telltale signs of graceful nurse sharks, manta rays and possibly even barracuda.

To avoid decompression sickness count on taking a no-dive day at the end of your stay. But there needn't be any downtime, since Belize has plenty of adventure options for active travelers from exploring Mayan ruins to zip-line canopy tours.

is this for me?

PHYSICAL ✦ ✦ ✦ ✦ ✦
Good balance and coordination

PSYCH ✦ ✦ ✦ ✦ ✦
Normal risks associated with diving

SKILL ✦ ✦ ✦ ✦ ✦
Certification required, obtainable on site

WOW! ✦ ✦ ✦ ✦ ✦
Exceptional and varied diving

Rafting the Futaleufú

52

CHILE

>> Test your mettle on Big Water

CHAITÉN

Patagonia has a longstanding reputation for life on a grand scale. When Magellan first encountered the native inhabitants in 1520, he was supposedly so awed by their towering stature and oversized appendages that he named them *patagones*, or "big feet". Subsequent reports from Sir Francis Drake seem to confirm the notion that the southern tip of South America, now claimed by both Argentina and Chile, was a mythical "land of giants". This larger-than-life mystique is palpable on Patagonia's greatest whitewater adventure river, the Futaleufú (foo-tah-lay-oo-FOO), which derives its name from the indigenous Mapuche word for "big water".

damming the Bio Bio

Running from the snow-capped Andes to the Gulf of Arauco in the Pacific, the rugged canyons and cascading waterfalls of the Bio Bio River were once a whitewater paradise. Volcanic formations, natural hot springs and the local Pehuenche Indians made it an unforgettable adventure for any visitor. In 1992, however, ENDESA, Chile's largest power company, broke ground on the Pangue hydroelectric plant, the first in a series of Bio Bio River dams built to sustain the country's growing power needs. The gates of the dam were shut in 1996, drowning the Canyon of a Hundred Waterfalls and the Royal Flush rapids and cutting off access to the final leg of the exhilarating raft route. In 2002 the Ralco Dam was completed, transforming most of what remained of the route, along with local flora and fauna, into a placid reservoir.

To make matters worse, the Pehuenche, who for centuries had lived on and defended the land south of the river, were forced to relocate. Although some bitterly fought the dam's construction, in the end they were no match for the government-backed plan. The fate of the Pehuenche and the Bio Bio is being repeated all over the world: while economic development is an important and inevitable aspect of progress, we too often pay a price in the tales of adventure that will be forgotten – or never lived at all.

need to know

The Futaleufú's remote location means it is best rafted as part of a five- to seven-day trip. Stay at an area lodge and enjoy a bevy of other activities, such as hiking, mountain biking, sea kayaking and horseback riding. Rafters should be capable swimmers and strong, responsive paddlers – expect to demonstrate your swimming skills and dexterity in a pre-trip training session and test.

guides and gear California-based O.A.R.S. (☎ 209/736-4677 or 1-800/346-6277, ⓦ www.oars.com) offers trips with transfers, accommodation, meals, rafting and a variety of other adventure sports. Since flipping is possible (albeit rare), wetsuits are advisable, particularly in the early season and on cool, wet midsummer days.

when to go Short summers are the norm in southern Chile; December to April is the length of the season.

getting there Fly into Puerto Montt, Chile. Continue to Chaitén by ferry (10hr) or chartered flight, then reach Futaleufú by private shuttle or bus (3hr) along a mountain road.

suggested reading Tyler Curtis, *Futaleufú Whitewater* (Heliconia Press). A world-champion kayaker takes visiting paddlers on a tour of the river.

is this for me?

PHYSICAL ◆ ◆ ◆ ◆ ◆
Extended physical activity

PSYCH ◆ ◆ ◆ ◆ ◆
Challenging whitewater and wilderness

SKILL ◆ ◆ ◆ ◆ ◆
Prior experience recommended

WOW! ◆ ◆ ◆ ◆ ◆
Lots of thrills, untrammeled setting

The Futaleufú is a large-volume river with 80km of raftable whitewater. Originating in the glacier-fed lakes of Los Alerces National Park in Argentina and fed by the wet, western slopes of the Andes, it has carved a canyon through which it charges with unrelenting speed and power. With a flow of 370 cubic meters per second, it's been compared to a big Tuolumne, with plenty of turns and boulder action rarely found in rivers of its size. It demands the highest level of judgement and skill from its guides, who are required to act with lightning speed and expert agility.

The river's legendary grandeur has been preserved thanks largely to its remoteness. Its unpolluted water has a blue, glacial tinge and such glistening clarity that few rafters can resist scooping a mouthful. There is no direct road access here from Chile's more populated northern half, so you'll need to take a ferry or small plane to the seaside town of Chaitén and then a three-hour trip on a single-lane dirt road to the village of Futaleufú. This journey through a landscape of volcanoes, hanging glaciers and turquoise lakes is an essential and rewarding part of the adventure.

Typically run in four or five days, the Futaleufú is conceptualized in sections ordered by difficulty rather than by the river's natural flow. By staying at a base camp lodge, you can raft those sections best suited to your skills and interests and in the order of your choice. Most trips start with either the "Heart of the Futaleufú" or the "Bridge to Bridge" section, the latter boasting fourteen Class III–IV rapids along 14km of water. The second day typically features two Class V showstopper rapids, "Mas o Menos" and "Casa de Piedra", the second named after a hefty, house-sized boulder. "Infierno Canyon" may be the most exhilarating stretch of commercially rafted whitewater in the world, with huge, furious rapids and multiple Class V drops. Once you commit to the canyon's four walloping rapids, there is no possible portage and no way to politely back out. Spectacular "Zeta" is considered Class VI for rafts and is always lined; under the right conditions, though, you may see expert kayakers running it. By far the longest and most challenging rapid is the "Terminator", a complex boulder garden with powerful hydraulics and deceptive drops. This section is normally saved for last, since it's generally regarded as one of the most technically demanding rapids anywhere.

In spite of its world-class reputation, the Futaleufú is relatively undiscovered by the masses; since Patagonia is the edge of the earth for most travelers, fewer than a thousand raft the river each year. Nevertheless, the river has not escaped the notice of Chile's leading energy producer, which has long eyed the pristine waters and explosive rapids for potential dam sites. Thankfully, the proposal to build a series of hydroelectric dams appears to be on hold for the moment, but a similar project has already stilled the waters of the Río Bio Bio to the north, with the first of six planned dams already in operation (see box, p.135). What is unquestionably the best multi-day whitewater stretch in South America, and arguably one of the top three in the world, deserves to flow wild and free forever – and any dedicated rafter deserves to experience it.

Exploring the Amazon Basin

>> **Like nothing you've seen**

How big does something have to be before you really can't hope to comprehend its vastness? Take the Amazon, for example. It constitutes one-fifth of the world's total river flow. No less impressive than the river itself, the Amazon Basin is home to one-third of the entire world's species, including at least 2.5 million insect species and one-fifth of all the world's bird species. One square kilometer of Amazon rainforest may contain over 75,000 types of tree and 150,000 species of higher plants. All of this enormity and biological density means that any river journey to the heart of the Amazon Basin is guaranteed to expose you to life forms and natural wonders you've never seen before and can find nowhere else.

ECUADOR ● COCA

BRAZIL

PERU

the Huaorani

The Huaorani are the indigenous people of the Amazon Basin living within Ecuador and parts of Peru. Today their population numbers less than two thousand as their traditional homelands have been threatened by hunting and logging. Prior to 1950 they were semi-nomadic hunters and gatherers, had almost no contact with the outside world, and spoke a language related to no other. They were known for their fierceness and inter-clan murders especially by men who would kill other males to obtain an additional wife. The Huaorani hunted monkeys and peccaries with Stone Age tools and blowpipes with curare-laced poison darts. Today they live in small permanent settlements of about fifty people, and although some Huaorani still hunt with a large spear, most engage in small-scale farming of maize, sweet potatoes, fruit and cassava. While some Huaorani clans have contact with outsiders and many of their children attend school and learn to speak Spanish, there are still two clans that have refused any outside contact.

Since the Amazon drains most of South America east of the Andes, you could focus your adventure in Brazil, Ecuador, Peru, Bolivia, Columbia or Venezuela. That said, as much of the Amazon is navigable, exploring its most remote headwaters is best accomplished on a paddling expedition along its tributaries in Ecuador, Peru or Bolivia. One exceptional opportunity for witnessing the rich biodiversity of the Amazon Basin and entering the world of indigenous people of the Amazon Basin can be found on the Río Shiripuno in eastern Ecuador, where in a sea kayak or canoe you will soon find yourself deep in the Amazon jungle.

Coca, served by scheduled air service from Quito, isn't much of a destination in its own right, but it's a great jumping-off point for this guided journey often accompanied by one of the local Huaorani Indians. A two-hour trip south on a jungle track brings you to the banks of the Shiripuno, where the dense vegetation spills right into the river. Once you find an access point – not always easy in the thick undergrowth – you'll find the slow-moving water perfect for leisurely paddling a canoe or sea kayak and soaking in the sounds.

By late afternoon, with several enjoyable river hours behind you, a clearing near the shore makes for an ideal improvised campsite. There is no one waiting for you at the campsite, nor any signs of civilization nearby, but out of the clearing some Huaorani might make a silent appearance; you are a guest in their backyard, after all.

In the morning, you're met in camp by a tribal elder whose pierced dangling earlobes have a hole about 6cm around. Despite his fierce appearance and the two-meter spear carried over his shoulder, he's really quite pleasant and even chatty in his broken Spanish. After following him through the jungle along a damp path for about thirty minutes, you arrive at a small settlement of traditional thatched huts surrounded by small vegetable plots. He instructs you in the use of a spear and blowpipe, although it's unlikely you'll ever hit anything – and even if you did, a meal of monkey or tapir is an acquired taste.

For the next two or three days you'll continue downriver, staying in jungle lodges or camps supported by a cook staff and guides. You'll be in good hands with your Huaorani guide who will introduce you to his jungle world with its enchanting birdlife and abundant land animals. Within the forest canopy you're surrounded by a variety of monkeys such as the red howler monkey, spider monkey and the woolly monkey, while a rustle in the underbrush could be a white-lipped peccary. Your guide will also introduce you to carnivorous plants which in the nitrogen-depleted soils of the rainforest obtain some of their nutrients by devouring insects. Living in the rainforest, the Huaorani have also learned to use the abundant variety of flora to their advantage with both medicinal plants, which they use to treat common ailments, and poisonous plants, from which they prepare curare to use on their hunting darts.

On hikes through the jungle you'll find giant anthills and encounter jaguar tracks. By night the jungle and the riverbanks come alive with nocturnal species like owls, bats, caimans, frogs and insects. After four days in the Amazon, a motorized canoe takes you back to a waiting shuttle for the return trip to Coca. Perhaps you'll appreciate the comforts of civilization all the more, but you may also find that your most relaxing night's sleep was found deep in the jungle, when its sounds eased you into a peaceful slumber.

need to know

You can explore the headwaters of the Amazon and the jungle of the Amazon Basin by sea kayak, canoe from lodges or on camping expeditions from Ecuador, Peru, Bolivia or Brazil.

guides and gear US-based Adventure Life Journeys (☎406/541-2677, 1-800/344-6118, ⓦ www.adventure-life.com) offers several different custom and small-group expeditions into the headwaters of the Amazon on a year-round basis including programmes that offer involvement with the Huaorani.

when to go With its equatorial climate, the Amazon headwaters are accessible year-round. June, July, and August are the wettest months, but still offer great wildlife viewing and enjoyable travel.

getting there Fly to Quito and take an onward flight to the frontier town of Coca. A hired vehicle will take you to a river put-in about two hours away.

suggested reading Peter Matthiessen, *At Play in the Fields of the Lord* (Vintage) A classic novel of the conflict between the forces of development and indigenous peoples. L. Ziegler-Otero, *Resistance in an Amazonian Community: Huaorani Organizing Against the Global Economy* (Berghahn Books). Traces the Huaorani struggle for survival against oil companies, capitalism and politics.

suggested viewing *End of the Spear* (2006). A docudrama recounting the 1956 killing of five American Christian missionaries who attempted to evangelize the Huaorani.

is this for me?

PHYSICAL ✦ ✦ ✦
Easy paddling, walking on jungle trails

PSYCH ✦ ✦ ✦
Jungle wildlife; fascinating cultural encounters

SKILL ✦ ✦
Paddling skills learned on site

WOW! ✦ ✦ ✦ ✦
An eye-opening immersion into Amazonia

Trekking the Inca Highlands

54

>> A route to the lost city

PERU

CUSCO

The Inca Empire, once the largest nation on earth, stretched more than 400km from Colombia to Chile. Its masterwork was a system of over 20,000km of roads, running the length and breadth of the Andes and connecting the highlands with the coast. These ancient highways reached altitudes of nearly 5000m and provided access to over 2.5 million square kilometers of territory. Though the jungle has long since reclaimed many of these stone-paved trails, others are still used today by direct descendants of the Inca.

A trek through the Cordillera Vilcabamba, eventually joining with the classic Inca Trail and its renowned culmination at Machu Picchu, is like none other on Earth. Along the way you'll make a half-circle around towering Mount Salcantay and traverse the Inca Highlands before arriving at the otherworldly "lost city of the Inca". The trek captures stunning Andean peaks, high mountain passes, deep valleys and cloud forest trails overgrown with ferns and orchids – not to mention an archeological treasure trove that reveals insights into a mysterious civilization.

The staging point for this adventure is the Inca capital of Cusco, the oldest continuously inhabited city in the Americas, still rich with Andean custom and surrounded by countless Inca ruins. At 3350m, Cusco is also a great place to acclimatize for the higher elevations awaiting you. When you're ready, a drive to the village of Mollepata strategically positions you on the southwestern slopes of the Cordillera Vilcabamba. Ascending a route still used by local farmers, you'll pass small plots of corn and potatoes as you move from terraced slopes to uncultivated higher hills.

Soon the trail nears the base of snow-covered Mount Salcantay (6270m), the highest peak in the cordillera, whose spectacular profile you can admire from a secluded campsite. The next day you'll pass the same mountain's base as you ascend to 4880-meter Abra de Incachiriaska, "the pass where the Inca turns cold". As you come face-to-face with the steep slopes and rugged glaciers of the sacred mountain, you'll hear the distant thunder of rockslides and avalanches. Descending the southern slopes of the range and following the trail through grassy meadows and small settlements, keep an eye out for Andean condors riding the wind.

The camp of Huayllabamba signals your arrival at the classic Inca Trail. Having already traversed the Cordillera Vilcabamba, you'll be better acclimatized than the steady flow of trekkers plodding along the path. Mountain passes offer sweeping views of deep valleys, and the trail's stone paving becomes more evident as you progress. Periodic ruins of Inca waystations and fortresses continually whet your appetite for the more impressive sites ahead. Climb a precipitous stone stairway to marvel at the

Hiram Bingham

If there were ever a real-life Indiana Jones, Hiram Bingham would claim the fedora. A college professor, lieutenant governor, aviator, US senator and discoverer of Machu Picchu, Bingham wore many hats during his life. His interest in adventure began early: raised in Hawaii as the son of Protestant missionaries, he read about great explorers and dreamed of going to Africa, but instead earned degrees at Yale and Harvard and married into the Tiffany jewellery fortune. Appointed by Woodrow Wilson to lecture in South American history at Princeton, Bingham soon tired of teaching and headed to Peru to search for the last Inca capital – a journey that led to his most famous discovery.

The first time Bingham laid eyes on Machu Picchu, he wasn't convinced he had discovered anything special. In fact, he stayed at the ruins for just a few hours and thought of them only occasionally during his other explorations in the country. A year after his initial visit, however, Bingham returned to the site, where his crew had meanwhile been excavating the great city. After taking hundreds of photographs of the expansive ruins, Bingham headed home and worked with the National Geographic Society to publish an issue of their magazine devoted entirely to his findings. He continued exploring areas around Machu Picchu, uncovering more historical artefacts, but soon returned to his family and teaching and eventually entered politics. Still, his explorer's instinct never faded, and until his death he upheld his theory that Machu Picchu was the "lost city" where the last Incas lived after the fall of Cusco to Pizarro in 1533.

The Intihuatana stone (meaning "hitching post of the sun") at Machu Picchu is a precise indicator of both equinoxes

need to know

Access to Machu Picchu is restricted, and only five hundred hikers are allowed on the Inca Trail per day, so make your travel plans months in advance. Visitors must be accompanied by a local guide. The complete trek from Mollepata to Machu Picchu typically takes seven to nine days.

guides and gear Peaks and Places Travel (☎ 1-970/626-5251, ⓦ www.peaksandplaces.com) guides and outfits small-group treks in the Inca Highlands, including Machu Picchu.

when to go April to October is the ideal season to trek the Inca Trail.

getting there Fly to Cusco and take local transportation to the trailhead.

suggested reading Hugh Thomson, *The White Rock* (Weidenfeld & Nicolson). An explorer's search for Inca archeological sites throughout the Peruvian Andes, with background on earlier travelers. Ruth M. Wright and Alfredo Valencia Zegarra, *The Machu Picchu Guidebook; A Self-Guided Tour* (Johnson Books). An excellent guidebook to one of the world's greatest destinations.

is this for me?

PHYSICAL ◆ ◆ ◆ ◆ ◇
Extended trekking at high elevation

PSYCH ◆ ◆ ◆ ◇ ◇
Fatigue and possible sleep disruption

SKILL ◆ ◆ ◇ ◇ ◇
Camping and some route-finding

WOW! ◆ ◆ ◆ ◆ ◇
Exceptional highlands and ruins

impeccably terraced Wiñay Wayna, a beautifully restored Inca site overlooking the Urubamba Valley.

As the trail dips along the hillside, you walk through a dense, moist jungle on your way to Intipunku, the Sun Gate. Passing stone walls shrouded in thick vegetation, don't be surprised if you feel you're the very first explorer to stumble upon the magnificent sight below you. The gate's ridge-crest position gives you a commanding view of Machu Picchu and allows you to approach the ruins as the Incas once did.

With its breathtaking mountaintop setting, Machu Picchu can be described only with superlatives, as it has been since its discovery in 1911 by explorer Hiram Bingham. Led here by a 10-year-old boy, Bingham found Machu Picchu smothered in jungle, but even before its extensive excavation and restoration he proclaimed its scenic perfection: "In the variety of its charms and the power of its spell, I know of no place in the world which can compare with it. Not only has it great snow peaks looming above the clouds more than two miles overhead, gigantic precipices of many-colored granite rising sheer for thousands of feet above the foaming, glistening, roaring rapids; it has also, in striking contrast, orchids and tree ferns, the delectable beauty of luxurious vegetation, and the mysterious witchery of the jungle."

An archeological showpiece, Machu Picchu is an unequaled complex of temples, terraces, storehouses, residences and staircases. Perfectly interlocked stones, placed without mortar, attest to the technical and aesthetic craftsmanship of the Inca masons. Don't miss the dramatic stone stairway leading to the temple and mountaintop terraces of Huayna Picchu, which towers atop its own spire above the main site.

Below Machu Picchu lies the town of Aguas Calientes, where you can relax your aching muscles in thermal springs, find comfortable accommodation and return by train through the Urubamba Valley to the Inca fortress of Ollantaytambo. Most importantly, get to know the locals; conversing with direct descendants of the Inca is a fitting way to conclude this strenuous trek through an unforgettable landscape of natural and manmade wonders.

ALBERT TOWN

JAMAICA

55 Exploring Cockpit Country

>> Sinkholes, caves, and underground rivers

Every year over a million vacationers come to Jamaica to unwind on white-sand beaches beside warm Caribbean waters. Most stay in large, enclosed resorts, their primary defence from the elements being SPF 30 sunscreen. Helmets and climbing ropes, on the other hand, are the protection of choice for the few who venture into Cockpit Country. Uncharted by roads, this nearly impenetrable wilderness is crisscrossed by hundreds of kilometers of footpaths – and here the adventure begins. Hiking through the mountainous jungle, abseiling down waterfall-laced cliffs and following rivers into caves will mean you'll miss some tanning time, but you'll come away with sights and experiences never imagined on the beach.

the Maroons

During eighteenth-century British rule, runaway slaves, or Maroons, used the caves and rugged terrain of Cockpit Country to evade the pursuing redcoats. By using secret trails, precipitous ravines and the dense forest, they disappeared at will. The Maroons eventually settled in the area, establishing some of Jamaica's first free villages.

karst topography

Stranger even than the eroded limestone landforms known as karsts is the fact that their name comes from the Slovenian "Kras", meaning "a dry, waterless place". Quite the opposite, most karst landscapes are lush areas overlying extensive subterranean aquifers. More than a quarter of the earth's population relies on these aquifers, which have their own built-in purification system: before water reaches the underground chambers, it seeps through porous rocks that filter out particles and bacteria.

Water plays an important role in forming the karst landscape. Once the subterranean chambers are entirely filled, water levels rise above ground to create pools. Eventually this water drains back down, further eroding the earth's surface on its way. This process occurs over and over, gradually making sinkholes, alternating bowl-like depressions and conical hills and occasionally, where erosion and water-level fluctuation is more dramatic, the huge plateaux that you'll see throughout Cockpit Country.

Cockpit Country covers over 500 square kilometers of wilderness atop a rural plateau in Jamaica's western interior. Its namesake "cockpits" are the more than five thousand conical hillocks and depressions formed over the past hundred million years, creating a karst topography with the appearance of an inverted egg carton. Ongoing erosion of the soluble limestone continually changes the landscape of cliffs, sinkholes and over three hundred caves. Wet forests in this region serve as the primary watershed for three of Jamaica's largest rivers, while smaller rivers meander through the cockpits and disappear abruptly into underground caverns.

Cockpit Country's rugged beauty is easily reached on foot from the communities of Bunkers Hill and Albert Town, both acting as bases for guided day-hikes of roughly four hours, though longer hikes can be arranged. A favourite destination within reach of Bunkers Hill is Dromily Cave via the Dromily Roaring River. As you leave the village on rural dirt back roads, you'll pass expansive trees from which the world's largest tree fruit, the ten-kilogram, watermelon-sized jackfruit, dangles dangerously overhead. Descending into the cockpits you come to the Dromily Roaring River, whose peaceful flow belies its name. The riverbank trail weaves through a thick undergrowth filled with some of the five hundred fern varieties found within Cockpit Country. In all, there are more than a hundred plant species found nowhere else in the world – some are endemic to a single hillock. Dozens of bird, butterfly, reptile and amphibian species make their homes here, too; keep an eye out for endangered yellow and black-billed parrots, the Jamaican boa and the giant swallowtail butterfly. Ascending from the river the trail to the Dromily Cave entrance involves a short climb up a 45-degree slope; the cave is easily explored and is marked by sparkling white stalactites.

From Albert Town there's an excellent hike to the limestone cathedral of the Quashie River Sink Cave, accessed by way of ladder-lined cliffs and rope handrails. Scrambling over boulders and cutting through undergrowth, you'll reach the cave's mouth, and enter the spacious and backlit Cathedral Room. As you descend into the depths of the cave you'll come upon of an underground river that leads to a waterfall. After exploring this amazing natural wonder, cool yourself outside the cave at the base of a six-meter waterfall near the entrance.

need to know

Cockpit Country can be explored in a single day or as a multi-day side-trip from Jamaica's popular beach resorts. Despite its wealth of attractions, be advised that Cockpit Country has its share of hazards. Its overgrown trails and indistinguishable hills can be disorienting, and thin layers of limestone may suddenly give way to sinkholes; falling into one can spell serious injury or death. In this wild and confusing terrain, the company of an experienced guide is essential.

guides and gear Cockpit Country Adventure Tours (☎ 876/610-0818, ⓦ www.stea.net) offers a variety of hiking, caving and climbing tours in the area, and can also assist with local accommodation for longer visits. They also provide helmets, lights and other safety equipment.

when to go Cockpit Country can be visited and enjoyed year-round. With its higher elevations, temperatures are comfortable even in mid-summer. Jamaica's rainy season is from May through June and Sept through Oct.

getting there Fly into Montego Bay's Sangster International Airport and take local transportation (2–3hr) from the coast to Albert Town or Bunkers Hill. Tour operators can also arrange transport from the beach resorts.

suggested reading Kathleen Monteith & Glen Richards, *Jamaica in Slavery and Freedom: History, Heritage and Culture* (University of West Indies). Essays on everyday life and the development of national identity in Jamaica.

Also close to Albert Town is the maze-like Printed Circuit Cave, which can be reached by hiking through the community of Rock Spring along the Mouth River. This complex and still-uncharted cave contains fascinating limestone formations and dozens of chambers throughout its 2.5-kilometer descent. Finish off your visit with a swim in the nearby pools of the Mouth River cascades.

Deforestation threatens the region as land is cleared for cultivation, firewood and charcoal production. Since 1996 the Southern Trelawny Environmental Agency (STEA) has spearheaded efforts to protect Cockpit Country forests by providing villages in the area with viable alternatives to destructive practices. STEA, with its staff of local guides, is now responsible for marketing and managing hiking, caving and heritage tours of the region. Still, mass tourism has not yet arrived in Cockpit Country; only a few hundred people enter the forest sanctuary each year. Groups remain small – often just two or three individuals – giving visitors unfettered access to a one-of-a-kind landscape.

is this for me?

PHYSICAL ✦ ✦
Some steep descents and scrambling

PSYCH ✦ ✦
Sheer drop-offs, caves, and jungle wildlife

SKILL ✦ ✦
Abseiling and some roped climbing

WOW! ✦ ✦ ✦
Exotic setting and captivating scenery

Kiteboarding at Preá

58

>> Wind, water, palms, and dunes

Bob Dylan made it clear: "You don't need a weatherman to know which way the wind blows." For kiteboarders looking for consistently idyllic side onshore winds day after day, heading to the beaches of Preá on Brazil's northeast coast is the closest you'll ever come to a guarantee of consistently perfect conditions. If you need to make the decision any easier, consider that at 2.5 degrees below the equator, the water temperature throughout the year swings wildly between 27° and 28°C, and that the entire coastal area is a national park. It all combines for great wind, water, and sweeping shore views to enjoy as you ride.

While kiteboarding, also known as kitesurfing, has quickly propelled its way into the mainstream of watersports in the past decade, owing much of its success to innovations in kite design (see box), many new destinations have emerged as kiteboarding hotspots, with beaches like Preá in the state of Ceará receiving some much-deserved attention. With hundreds of kilometers of white sand beaches, previously uncelebrated fishing villages are becoming mini-Meccas for kiteboarders.

Initial instruction, ideally from a professional at a well-established kiteboarding school, is essential, and will give you the foundation from which you can build your expertise. No kiteboarding education is complete without a few faceplants and some frustrating failed launches.

As you're building your skills, pray for days on end with steady side onshore winds in the 15–20 knot range, at which time you'll be able to ride for as long as your patience and endurance will allow. In a destination like Preá that's an easy prayer to answer, as the winds during the July through January season are as predictable as the sunrise. After a satisfying Brazilian breakfast, hit the beach to rig up and ready yourself for a launch with the winds that come in around 10am. After a morning session and lunch break you'll be ready for the superb afternoon winds that will make for an epic day with great conditions and sustained rides.

The turning point in every kiteboarder's learning curve comes as you start riding upwind – meaning you can leave the beach and come back to the same spot. Eventually, with enough practice you can thread a needle with your kite and board. You'll see a small buoy out on the water, and you'll be able to go to it and return. By the end of the week you'll come to understand the pressures of the board and the art of managing your kite. You'll find that the essence of kiteboarding is 85 percent flying the kite and 15 percent riding the board.

There's an incredible, almost electric, surge of energy transmitted from the kite through the lines and into every muscle of your body as you hold the bar and feel the humbling power and force of the wind. If kiteboarding is an extreme sport, then at least it allows you to choose where you want to be on that scale. On the extreme – and expert – side, you can ride the 40-knot winds and take the ten-meter jumps. But even as a one-week wonder, you'll feel an exciting connection with the wind and ocean, accompanied by a liberating sense of openness and freedom – not always common in extreme sports.

need to know

The northeastern coast of Brazil from Recife to Fortaleza and on to Jericoacoara features hundreds of kilometers of pristine beaches, and with the favorable tradewinds, a growing number of kiteboarding and windsurfing resorts. Although no windsport or boardsport background is required before beginning kiteboarding instruction, you should be a good swimmer.

guides and gear For a novice kiteboarder, a great holiday hinges on both the destination and the instruction available on site. Ozone Travel (☎ 305/213-0288, Ⓦ www.ozonetravel.com) specializes in custom kiteboarding holidays for beginners and independent riders, and can include a variety of destinations in Brazil with accommodations, transportation, kiteboarding instruction and other services.

when to go Wind averaging 25 knots starts in July and blows steadily through January. Winds are strongest from mid-September to the end of November.

getting there From Fortaleza private transportation in a 4x4 vehicle for passengers and kiteboarding equipment is available and takes about 4hr for the trip to Preá and Jericoacoara.

is this for me?

PHYSICAL ✦ ✦ ✦ ✦ ✦
Requires balance, coordination, endurance

PSYCH ✦ ✦ ✦ ✦ ✦
High winds can overpower novice riders

SKILL ✦ ✦ ✦ ✦ ✦
Learning curve to overcome

WOW! ✦ ✦ ✦ ✦ ✦
Exhilarating watersport in dream destination

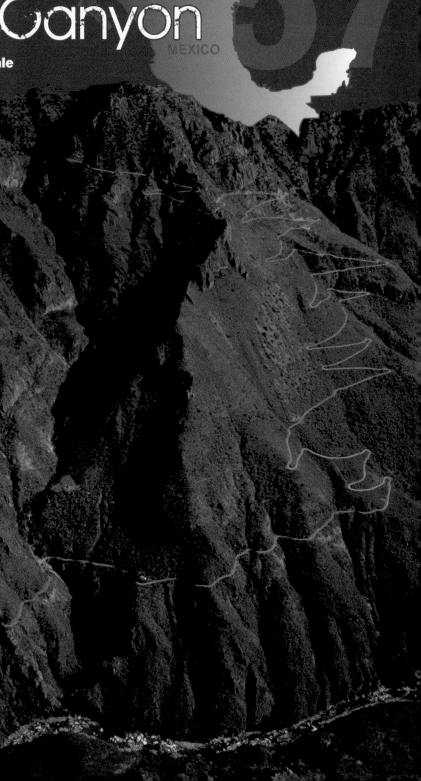

Exploring Copper Canyon

>> Nature on a gargantuan scale

● EL FUERTE

MEXICO

57

If you were asked to name the largest canyon in North America – one that's miles across, thousands of meters deep and the centerpiece of a renowned national park – you'd probably say the Grand Canyon. But while it's certainly grand, it's not the largest on the continent. That title belongs to Copper Canyon, a convoluted series of over two hundred smaller canyons comprising four major systems, portions of which are deeper than their neighbour to the north. While less well known than the Grand Canyon, enormous Copper Canyon will quickly entice you into its depths.

Running through northern Mexico's Sierra Madre mountain range, Copper Canyon, or Barrancas del Cobre, is 72,000 square kilometers of rugged ravines, piñon plateaux and yawning river gorges. You'll find adventure on many different levels, from scenic viewpoints at the rim, to extended backpacking below, to first descents of uncharted canyons. All excursions in Copper Canyon have one thing in common: if you want to get from point A to point B, you're going to have to work at it.

The first step is simply getting there. Most visitors still arrive on the famous Chihuahua al Pacífico railroad, affectionately known as "el Chepe", which crosses breathtaking chasms and skirts the canyon rim as it gains over 2440m of elevation in fewer than 290km. One of the world's most scenic railways, it covers 36 bridges and 87 tunnels on its route from Los Mochis to Chihuahua. The train makes stops in the towns of Divisadero and Creel, giving you access to the canyon's backcountry.

Arriving at the rim, you'll find engaging day-hikes to nearby caves and a box-canyon waterfall. The more challenging and rewarding destinations, however, are below the rim, where the high pine and juniper forest gives way to vast, oak-covered highlands and finally subtropical thorn forest near the canyon floor. One popular route, both for backpacking and mule-packing, connects the villages of Batopilas and Urique through remote wilderness. During the fifty-kilometer trek, you'll stay in primitive campsites below indigenous villages that cling to the canyon walls and are accessible only by mule or on foot. Leaving Batopilas Canyon, you ascend nearly 1830m to camp on high mesas before dropping into Urique Canyon and the deepest point in Copper Canyon. Since backpacking here means hiking for three to six days along unmarked trails where water sources aren't always apparent, a guide with intimate knowledge of the area is strongly suggested.

Though it would take a lifetime to complete all the backpacking routes in Copper Canyon, you may be drawn to more technical canyoneering challenges, a great way to explore uncharted rivers and side-canyons – if you don't mind getting wet. A typical canyoneering trip requires abseiling down cliffs and waterfalls and fording and floating along some sections of river. Experienced guides and canyoneers start such adventures by strapping a buoyant, watertight drybag to a traditional external pack frame so that, when they encounter deep water or a pool, they can remove the pack and float behind it like a frog. Be prepared for some shallow wading, too – depending on the season, some sections can be a torrent one day and a trickle the next. As the rivers scour the canyon floor, they leave pools, boulders and other obstacles you'll need to work your way under, over or through. More rugged sections may require three full days to cover just 25km. It's hard work, but this is beautiful, virgin wilderness, largely unknown to technical canyoneering aficionados.

foot runners of Copper Canyon

For the Tarahumara, a people known for their ability to run for hours on end, running is both sport and a way of life. Their innate prowess may be attributable to where they live – one of the coldest parts of Mexico, with a mix of high altitudes and a warm canyon floor – and their custom of farming, herding and hunting at various elevations throughout the year. Running from village to village to trade goods and communicate news likely boosted their endurance. They also practised persistence hunting, often chasing a deer or boar for over a hundred kilometers until the exhausted animal allowed its pursuer to approach close enough to kill it with a spear.

Beyond its practical applications, running also plays competitive and ceremonial roles in Tarahumara culture. One pastime involves kicking a wooden ball along the ground as participants run in either solo or relay races that can last for hours or even days. In traditional footraces (without the ball to slow them down) they regularly run a 120-kilometer course through the night, with many competitors finishing in ten hours after maintaining a constant near-sprint.

need to know

Most begin an exploration of Copper Canyon from either Divisadero or Creel on the canyon's north rim. Both offer a variety of accommodation, tourist services and transport into the canyon.

guides and gear The man known as Copper Canyon Guide (☎ 406/587-3585, ⓦ www.coppercanyonguide.com), called Santiago by the Tarahumara, offers custom backpacking or animal-supported adventures.

when to go Lower elevations are best from October through April. The rainy season is June through September.

getting there Fly into Los Mochis on the Pacific coast, where you can board the train or head east to the frontier town of El Fuerte for a convenient and scenic starting point on the rail line.

suggested reading *The Copper Canyon Companion* (California Native). An in-depth look at the people and history of Copper Canyon. Jeff Biggers, *In the Sierra Madre* (University of Illinois Press). A memoir based on the author's yearlong journey among the Tarahumara. M. John Fayhee, *Mexico's Copper Canyon Country: A Hiking and Backpacking Guide to Tarahumara-land* (Cordillera Press). A personal narrative with route descriptions of day-hikes and multi-day backpacking trips. Bernard L. Fontana, *Tarahumara: Where Night is the Day of the Moon* (University of Arizona Press). An insightful and beautifully photographed treatment of the Tarahumara.

suggested viewing *The Unholy Tarahumara* (1998). A documentary by Kathryn Ferguson about the Tarahumara, produced in the area around Norogachi.

is this for me?

PHYSICAL ✦ ✦ ✦ ✦ ✦
Aerobic workout with some steep ascents

PSYCH ✦ ✦ ✦ ✦ ✦
Wilderness camping in challenging terrain

SKILL ✦ ✦ ✦ ✦ ✦
Hiking and backpacking experience advised

WOW! ✦ ✦ ✦ ✦ ✦
Scenic and cultural appeal

While Copper Canyon is nature on a gargantuan scale, don't forget to appreciate its smaller treasures. Hundreds of bird species live here, among them some endangered varieties like the military macaw, the eared trogon and the thick-billed parrot. Although many mammals, such as the black bear, have been hunted out, Mexican wolves, pumas, deer, coatimundi and coyotes still roam these parts, and river otters frolic in some remote areas.

Copper Canyon is also the ancient home of the Tarahumara Indians, who call themselves Rarámuri, or foot runners (see box, p.149). For centuries they have subsisted on corn, beans, squash and livestock, which they herd in the high country during the summer rainy season. In the winter they descend deep into the canyon to grow oranges, avocados, papaya and bananas. Although most speak Spanish and have adopted modern culture, there are still isolated groups that retain their traditional lifestyle. In these places, far from roads or contemporary conveniences, the Tarahumara live in caves, wear traditional dress and preserve such customs as peyote healings and ceremonial masked dances. Meeting the people who have made this wild land their home is but one of the many rewards of Copper Canyon's hidden depths.

Bask in the canyon's hidden depths

COSTA RICA

● SAN JOSÉ

Wildlife viewing in Costa Rica

>> Surprises around every corner

Wild rivers, fiery volcanoes, iridescent ocean reefs and dense rainforests all combine to make Costa Rica one of the world's prime adventure travel destinations. But before the rafting, surfing, sportfishing, cozy hotels and canopy tours that have become a staple of the country's economy, there were arkloads of animals – in fact, there still are. In an area smaller than West Virginia, Costa Rica has more biodiversity than all of North America or Europe. The result is a panoply of mangroves, lowland rainforest, misty cloud forests and subalpine mountain slopes teeming with birds, mammals, frogs and butterflies.

Arenal Volcano

When a 1968 earthquake awoke the Arenal Volcano from a 400-year sleep, the eruption devastated the town of Arenal and the surrounding area, and it caused three new active craters to form. This volcano, 145km northwest of San José, is the youngest and only active volcano in Costa Rica. Rising 1657m over Lake Arenal, Arenal Volcano is almost always surrounded by thick cloud cover at its peak; if you happen to spot the volcano free of cloud cover consider that a good omen for spotting wildlife. Its frequent, moderate eruptions are quite a sight (especially at night), attracting numerous travelers each year who come to view the glow of the incandescent rocks, enormous ash columns, fiery explosions and spilling red lava – from a safe distance.

Aside from standing as an awesome spawn of nature, Arenal Volcano harbours many tourist attractions including tours of the nearby hot springs that are heated by the volcano, river rafting and kayaking on the nearby lakes and rivers, sky tram tours and much more. Among these attractions are many opportunities to observe the areas surrounding the volcano, which are teeming with wildlife. A tour along the hanging bridges within the forest to the west of Arenal allows a broad exposure to rich vegetation and wildlife. Early bird-watching tours take you through the lush rainforests that are full of rich biodiversity.

Progressive environmental decisions have led to the protection of a quarter of the country as national parks or reserves, making its natural wonders – including its wildlife – readily accessible. To have the best opportunities to see animals you often can't see anywhere else while seeing a wide variety of habitats, plan a trip that takes in three of the crown jewels of Costa Rica's vast protected areas: Corcovado, Monteverde and Tortuguero.

Corcovado National Park, on the Pacific's Osa Peninsula, has the most untamed and physically challenging park terrain the country, but it rewards with some of the finest unspoiled scenery and best wildlife viewing. Over 480cm of annual rainfall nurtures the last significant virgin rainforest in Central America. The absence of roads means that to reach the Sirena research facility in the heart of the park you must hike 13 to 26 kilometers from the ranger stations on the periphery. On the trek in you're certain to

see the local wildlife since the park hosts six hundred species of mammals, birds, amphibians and reptiles. Look skyward and listen for noises in the forest canopy; up there you might see scarlet macaws and howler, spider, white-faced and squirrel monkeys. Five species of tree sloth are found in Corcovado, and while you'll never hear them, if you look closely – and quietly – chances are good you'll see one clinging to a tree. Roaming on the ground in the thick undercover are white-lipped peccaries – wild pigs that look frightening, but are basically harmless unless put in a threatening position. Even though you're most likely to see the more common animals, there are several endangered species in the park that over a few days hiking you might spot: the Baird's tapir, poison dart frog and puma are just a few.

A trip from Corcovado on the Pacific coast to Tortuguero National Park on the Caribbean side of Costa Rica takes you from lowland rainforest to a mosaic of lagoons, canals and marshy islands. Tortuguero is a vital turtle nesting site and one of the last remaining and most important breeding grounds for the endangered green sea turtle as well as hawksbill and leatherback

species. During the nesting season from March to May and July to October expect to be both captivated and entertained by the procession of turtles clumsily making their way from the sea to their sand nest. Except for the marked trail along the beach to observe turtles, the best way to see other wildlife in Tortuguero is from a boat, either on a guided tour or in a canoe or kayak through the canals and lagoons. While plying a placid lagoon in search of a rare West Indian manatee, don't miss the aerial sideshow featuring the raucous banter of great green macaws and the swooping of bulldog bats feeding on fish.

After several days in the humid coastal parks, a retreat to the higher elevations of a cloud forest will be refreshing. Straddling the slopes and chasms of the Tilarán mountain range, whose rivers drains to both the Pacific and the Atlantic, Monteverde Cloud Forest Reserve shelters hundreds of mammal, bird and plant species in its green cathedral. Because of its high altitude (1400m) clouds here tend to hang in trees – hence, a cloud forest. The signature species is the resplendent quetzal whose magnificent tail plumage can reach over half a meter in length. Although it's found in Monteverde year-round, your best chance of seeing this rare and striking bird is during the March and April nesting season. But the quetzal is just one of 425 bird species found in Monteverde, sharing the cloud forest canopy with 800 species of epiphytes (plants that grow on other plants), colorful bromeliads and orchids absorbing their moisture from the mist. From the reserve entrance you have instant access to a well-designed and maintained 10km network of trails that are ideal for day-hikes; huts are available if you want to spend the night in the forest. While spotting colorful birds, or odd-looking larger mammals like a collared anteater or a coatimundi, don't miss the continual sideshow of

insects, reptiles and amphibians. In Monteverde and throughout Costa Rica you will find some of the most fascinating discoveries in small packages as you watch leaf-cutter ants carrying debris ten times their weight, a furry tarantula scampering into its burrow, or a snake struggling to swallow a frog. Whether you're up with the birds or out at night in search of a three-toed sloth or opossum, surprises are plentiful.

need to know

The best advice for birding and wildlife viewing in Costa Rica is to connect with an experienced local guide, whose eyes and ears are sharply turned to the lights and sounds of the forest. Though you stand a great chance of spotting wildlife during the day, since sixty percent of Costa Rica's rainforest wildlife is nocturnal, night walks with nothing but you, a trail, a guide and a lantern, are a real treat.

guides and gear A leading operator and a national pioneer in eco-tourism, Costa Rica Expeditions (☎506/2257-0766, Ⓦwww.costaricaexpeditions.com) offers both group and custom itineraries to wildlife viewing hotspots throughout the country, including Corcovado, Monteverde, Arenal, Tortuguero and others.

when to go December to April is the dry season, which locals refer to as "summer". It's an ideal time to go, although if you're willing to put up with some warm tropical rain, you can have a great visit anytime.

getting there Fly into San José. Car rentals and ground operators provide access to parks and reserves.

suggested reading Les Belestsky, *Costa Rica: Travelers' Wildlife Guides* (Interlink). Fully illustrated field guide aimed at those who find glimpses of wildlife in natural settings the best parts of any trip.

is this for me?

PHYSICAL ✦ ✦
Extended walking on generally easy terrain

PSYCH ✦ ✦
Potential exposure to wild animals

SKILL ✦
Be alert, with open eyes and ears

WOW! ✦ ✦ ✦
Unusual and varied wildlife in a beautiful setting

Trekking in the Cordillera Huayhuash

>> A circuit in the clouds

HUARAZ

PERU

Along Peru's Andean backbone lies the Cordillera Huayhuash (WHY-wash), a range of icy peaks that, until recently, remained largely unknown to international trekkers. This compact cluster of stunningly vertical, 6000-meter-high mountains, exquisitely mirrored in freshly-fed glacial lakes, practically begs to be circumnavigated. The jagged mountains along the challenging circuit rise 1500m from the valley floor, and the echoing roar of avalanches and tumbling ice is the perfect soundtrack for the trek. While it's not as heavily trodden as the Inca Trail to the south or the Cordillera Blanca to the north, the Cordillera Huayhuash is deservedly considered one of the most beautiful mountain treks in the world.

There are several ways to access the circuit, but most people start from the town of Huaraz, about 80km north of the cordillera. At an elevation of over 3000km, Huaraz is a pleasant place to acclimatize and arrange logistics. You can hire private transport to Llamac, a village on the western fringe of the range and a good launching point for the excursion.

As you loop the range on a guided trek of ten to fourteen days, you'll cover a distance of about 180km, depending on your exact route and side-trips. Along the way you'll cross seven mountain passes, six of which exceed 4600m, and drop into camps where the elevation hovers around a lofty 4200m. Most treks are supported by *burros* and a cook staff, allowing you to carry a light pack, eat well and enjoy the adventure.

On a clockwise circuit you'll get breathtaking views of Jirishanca (6094m), whose name means "hummingbird beak of ice" and which some call the "Matterhorn of Peru" because of its distinctive sculpted summit. Circling the western slopes of the Huayhuash, you'll have splendid vistas of Yerupajá (6617m), Peru's second-highest peak. The route skirts four other towering mountains all over 6000m, including Siula Grande, the site of Joe Simpson's harrowing survival account, *Touching the Void* (see box opposite).

When you reach the crest of the pass at Portachuelo de Huayhuash (4785m), stop for a moment to breathe in the rarefied air and appreciate that you are right atop the South American continental divide. All the rain that falls in front of you flows to the Pacific Ocean, 120km to the west, though what collects in Laguna Viconga in the valley below becomes Lima's water supply. Any raindrops falling behind you drain into the Río Huayhuash, where they begin a 5600-kilometer journey through the Amazon Basin to the Atlantic Ocean.

Despite the tropical latitude, nighttime temperatures at this elevation frequently drop below freezing, and even in good weather trekking here puts some unique physical demands on the body. Proper acclimatization won't entirely inhibit the effects of high altitude as you slowly ascend a pass. Interrupted sleep cycles are common, with most people experiencing a periodic breathing pattern during sleep known

Touching the Void

In 1985, two climbers in their early twenties attempted the 1370-meter west face of the Andean peak Siula Grande. Despite the fact that no one had yet completed the route, Joe Simpson and Simon Yates decided on a lighter and faster expedition than the classic mountaineering siege, which required many men, tons of equipment and several days. Their story, the subject of the book and film *Touching the Void*, is the kind of legendary tale shared on cold nights in the glow of mountaineers' headlamps.

Their stripped-down approach brought them to the summit, but, due to their limited provisions, required them to descend quickly. During the descent, Simpson took a devastating slide that pushed his tibia through his kneecap, and the partners agreed on an improvised, one-man rescue operation. Yates made a small belay seat in the snow, then lowered Simpson down the mountain. When Simpson reached the end of the rope, he tugged on it to signal that Yates should descend. Over and over the two climbers performed this routine until, after lowering Simpson down a particular section, Yates didn't feel a tug on the rope. Simpson had been lowered over a cliff, and, hanging in midair, was unable to reach the rock face or otherwise rescue himself. After bearing Simpson's full weight for over an hour and calling to him with no reply, Yates – his snow seat gradually giving way – cut the rope, deciding to give at least one of them a chance rather than allowing both to be pulled off the mountain. After this harrowing decision, Yates believed his partner to be dead and gingerly descended the mountain alone, eventually reaching camp.

What Yates didn't know was that Simpson, after plummeting through the ceiling of an ice-covered crevasse, was still alive. Slipping in and out of consciousness, he made his way through a side-opening and onto the face of a glacier, where he began an excruciating three-day crawl back to the campsite. Yates, resigned to his climbing partner's death, was about to break camp when Simpson appeared on his hands and knees. Both men eventually made full recoveries and, despite some mountaineers' claims that Yates should never have cut the rope, Simpson has always maintained that Yates did the right thing.

need to know

Hiring an experienced guide is the best way to enjoy a scenic and challenging route without risking getting lost. Guided treks are accompanied by a team of cooks and mule-drivers. You can hire pack animals for an unguided excursion, but the driver and mules will stick to the easiest route.

guides and gear US-based Peaks and Places (☎ 970/626-5251, Ⓦ www.peaksandplaces.com) has offered custom treks with certified mountain guides in the Cordillera Huayhuash for more than twenty years. La Cima Logistics in Huaraz (☎ 043/721203, Ⓦ www.cafeandino.com) provides logistical services (transport, porters, guides, cooks and mule-drivers) for both guided and independent treks.

when to go During the May to September dry season you're likely to have clear weather and mild daytime temperatures. August is windier and may bring the occasional afternoon thundershower.

getting there Fly into Lima's Jorge Chavez International Airport, then take a motorcoach to Huaraz for acclimatization and staging.

suggested reading *Cordillera Huayhuash Topographic Map* (Peaks and Places). A detailed map of the Huayhuash, with key trekking routes.

is this for me?

PHYSICAL ◆ ◆ ◇ ◇ ◇ ◇
Long-distance trekking and high elevations

PSYCH ◆ ◆ ◆ ◇ ◇ ◇
Potential sleep disruption and extreme weather

SKILL ◆ ◆ ◆ ◆ ◇
Route-finding and outdoor skills required

WOW! ◆ ◆ ◆ ◆ ◇
Exceptional scenery in the high Andes

as Cheyne-Stokes respirations. This can be unnerving at first, as you listen to your tentmate shift from shallow breathing to deep sighs, stop entirely for a few seconds and then return to shallow breathing. Often the restless sleeper will suddenly wake with a feeling of suffocation, making a full night of sleep nearly impossible. To minimize this and other effects of high altitude, you should be an experienced camper in good physical condition and familiar with elevations above 3000m.

Unsurprisingly, relatively few living things thrive in this alpine terrain. At lower elevations you'll pass the occasional farming settlement or remote pasture where villagers still speak their native Quechua language. A smaller but more abundant inhabitant of the cordillera is the vizcacha, a chinchilla-family rodent that resembles a rabbit with its long ears and tan coat. It browses above the tree-line for tundra plants and low shrubs. Birds don't seem to mind the harsh climate quite as much; scan the deep blue skies and you may catch sight of a soaring Andean condor.

The Cordillera Huayhuash is a pristine and fragile mountain ecosystem. While most commercial groups have acted responsibly toward the environment, recent years have seen an increasing problem with rubbish and human waste. Trekkers should stay on established trails and pack out all rubbish. Human waste must be buried: groups should dig a proper toilet hole for communal use, and refill the hole and restore the sod when they leave. Although the Cordillera Huayhuash is a reserved zone, it is not a national park. The absence of official protective regulations means that the cordillera's future depends on the wilderness ethic of those who explore it.

COSTA RICA

● SAN JOSÉ

60 Rafting the Pacuare

>> **A heart-pounding ride**

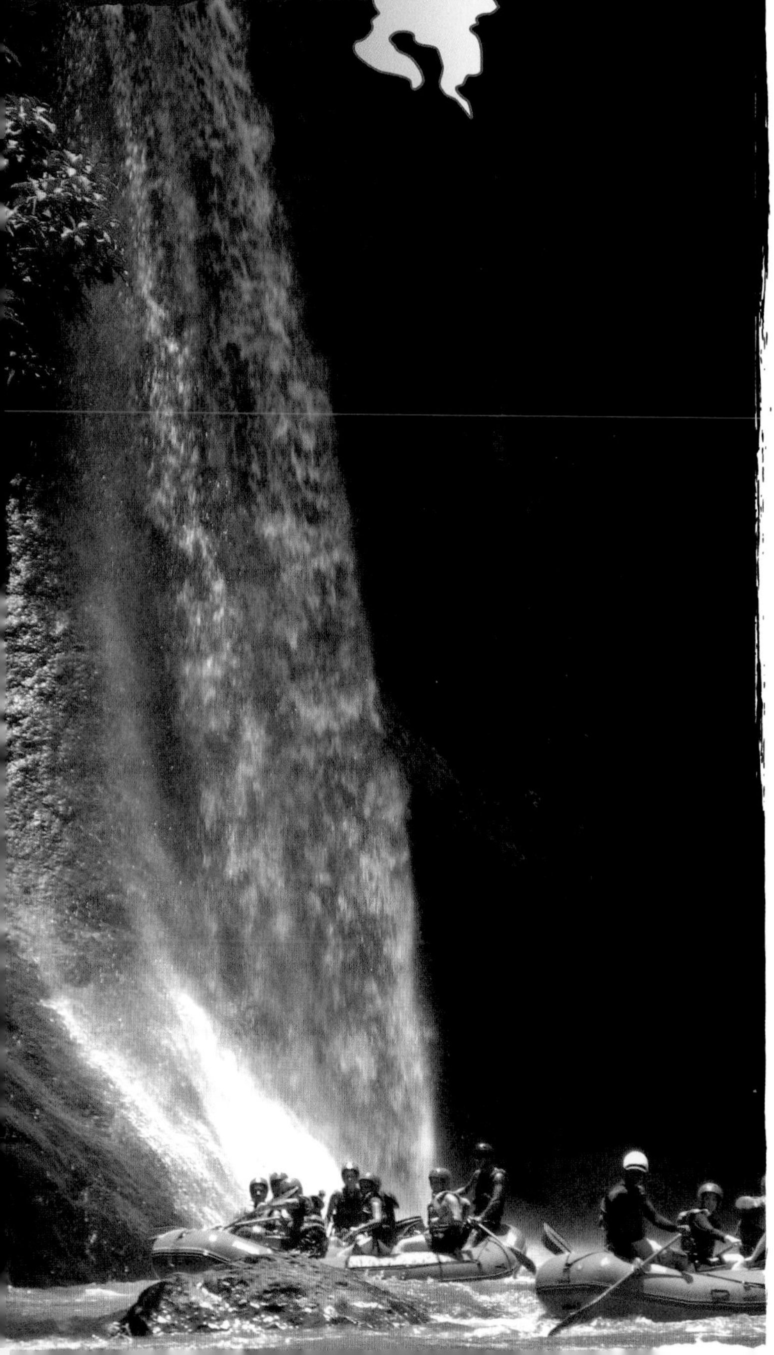

The Río Pacuare (pah-KWAH-ray) is everything you imagine a tropical river to be. Surrounded by towering cliffs coated with luxuriant vegetation and dotted with stunning thirty meter waterfalls, the river races through a virgin rainforest home to monkeys, ocelots, blue morpho butterflies, toucans and a bewildering variety of plants. In the dry season (usually mid-December to May) the river is intimate, friendly and fun-loving. But the Pacuare is nothing if not temperamental, and this idyllic gateway to the country's stunning biodiversity has a more wild side, too. When seasonal rains deluge the high tributaries of the Talamanca range, water levels swell, placid dark-blue pools disappear, rapids run together, big waves and holes form and flips are frequent. In short, the river wields a power that demands the utmost respect – and one that makes for a heart-pounding ride.

preserving the Pacuare

The Pacuare's steep gradients and abundant water have long been a tempting resource for the Electricity Institute (ICE), Costa Rica's national utility, who in 1996 formulated a plan for a complex set of dams, diversions and reservoirs along the river. The centerpiece of the plan was a towering 180-meter hydroelectric dam at the Dos Montañas gorge, which would have flooded the river all the way to the traditional whitewater put-in location and destroyed much of the rainforest's flora and fauna, indigenous villages, and the river's widespread ecotourist appeal.

Efforts to protect the Pacuare were quickly mounted by environmental advocates and whitewater enthusiasts who pushed for it to be included in Costa Rica's exemplary national park system. These efforts also received the support of several international conservation organizations anxious to preserve this magical river. A much smaller dam located above the put-in at Tres Equis was roundly defeated by a local referendum and in 2005 Costa Rica's National Environmental Organization (Setena) rejected the construction of the Dos Montañas dam. The ICE has since made no further attempts to dam the Pacuare, perhaps recognizing that the short-lived boom that such a project would represent doesn't equal the hold this wild river has on the local population.

You can test your mettle on a one-day trip with a put-in at a wide arc of the river near Tres Equis where easy vehicle access and shallow waters make for an inviting start. From there the river quickly drops through Class II–III runs, the canyon narrows and verdant slopes close in around you. Boulder gardens punctuate this initial section, but the approach is straightforward enough, with no complex turns or nasty hydraulics. That said, don't let the almost predictable course lull you into a false sense of security – it still requires careful maneuvering to avoid being pinned. From there the Pacuare constricts into a vertical-walled canyon, the river's gradient increases and the Class IV rapids begin. The toughest rapids in this section are the aptly named Upper and Lower Huacas – Burial Sites – which consist of two 135-meter stretches of solid Class IV ledges and boulders separated by a pool into which a 30-meter waterfall plunges into the river from the canyon rim. Of the two sections, Lower Huacas is the least forgiving and the most likely to send your adrenal glands into overdrive.

After the Huacas you get a much-deserved breather before taking on the Cimarrón rapids, a steep maze of boulders through which the river scatters into several channels. Kayakers can negotiate these rapids with ease, but as a rafter you'll find it's more challenging to make a quick change of course in a less agile craft – though your oarsman's steady hand and good teamwork should keep you from wrapping your raft on one of the many boulders.

As the Pacuare nears the Caribbean Sea, you are carried into the Dos Montañas rapids, below which is a steep-walled, dark chasm of the same name – its tranquil waters are a perfect place to take a dip. When the canyon walls open up, the river eases back into its more relaxed self and signs of civilization start to appear. Soon you'll reach the pull-out at Siquirres, a broad beach on the river's north bank. After a full day on the Pacuare, you'll have enough endorphins bouncing in your brain to keep you laughing and and swapping river stories all the way back to San José.

need to know

At normal water levels the trip is not extremely strenuous, but rafters should be physically fit. No previous whitewater experience is necessary. While most adventurers experience the Pacuare on a day-trip, there are longer commercial trips available, some of which start with the Class V Upper Pacuare.

guides and gear Guided one- and two-day rafting trips on the Pacuare, including transportation from San José and lunch are offered by Rios Tropicales (℡506/233-6455 or toll-free from US ℡866/722-8273, Ⓦ www.riostropicales.com). Outfitters provide all the river gear, and you only need to bring shorts, sandals or shoes that can get wet, plenty of sunscreen and a change of clothes.

when to go The Pacuare can be successfully and safely run year-round, however the dry months of January through April are especially popular. The river swells to its highest water usually in October, sometimes making it unrunnable. Keep in mind that unseasonable rains can make the put-in inaccessible at any time of the year.

getting there Most day-trips leave from San José and take you to the put-in about three hours southeast of the capital.

suggested reading Michael W. Mayfield & Rafael Gallo, *The Rivers of Costa Rica: A Canoeing, Kayaking and Rafting Guide* (Menasha Ridge Press). A scientist and a paddler team up to guide you to Costa Rica's best whitewater. Primarily for kayakers, but great for serious rafters.

is this for me?

PHYSICAL ✦ ✦ ✦ ✦ ✦
Minimal aerobic activity, easy paddling

PSYCH ✦ ✦ ✦ ✦ ✦
Class III whitewater

SKILL ✦ ✦ ✦ ✦ ✦
No prior experience required

WOW! ✦ ✦ ✦ ✦ ✦
A fun, exceptionally beautiful whitewater river

Wildlife viewing in the Galápagos

61

>> Giant turtles, tropical penguins, and blood-drinking finches

What on earth makes these animals so fearless? Sea lions blow bubbles in your face as if to mock your underwater ineptitude. Blue-footed boobies blithely stand and nest on trails, forcing you to walk around them. Birds don't scatter in your presence and turtles don't swim away. The cormorants are flightless and couldn't escape even if they wanted to, while slow-moving marine iguanas saunter across sandy beaches, secure in the knowledge that they're not going to be your next meal. This is what it's like to grow up in an environment lacking natural predators, to never have been hunted by humans.

Lying in the Pacific Ocean and straddling the equator about 1000km west of the South American continent, the Galápagos are a province of Ecuador consisting of thirteen main islands and six smaller islands. Famously the site where Charles Darwin's theory of evolution took shape, the Galápagos Islands are a living laboratory of evolutionary oddities and biological wonders. Where else can you see penguins in the tropics, blood-drinking finches, iguanas that swim, giant 225-kilograms tortoises, frigate birds with inflated air sacs that look as if they've swallowed a red beach ball, and Sally Lightfoot crabs that spit saltwater from an outlet near their eye?

The Galápagos National Park, which takes in about ninety percent of the islands' land area and most of the surrounding ocean waters, has strict controls in place to protect this amazingly unique habitat and all visitors must be accompanied by a certified naturalist guide. The islands are served by a variety of vessels of varying sizes and types offering tours ranging from three to fifteen days. The longer trips will generally give you more variety by allowing you to experience the outer islands. For the best experience, look for operators with a strong educational and conservation-minded approach. The sixteen smaller passenger yachts give you flexibility in shore access and a more personalized approach.

Once on the tour, your best bet is to get on the islands early in the day for the best light to take photos and to find the celebrated local animals at their peak of activity. You'll also find that the trails are less crowded in the early morning hours. A ten-passenger *panga* or Zodiac, an inflatable craft lowered from the transom of the yacht, will bring you from your vessel to land. Trails are short and most days involve no more than 5km of walking. Mid-morning or afternoon snorkeling forays will give you opportunities to swim with sea lions – always a highlight – and encounter other marine species like Galápagos penguins, golden rays, damsel fish, parrot fish and goldrim surgeonfish. Always close at hand will be a knowledgeable naturalist to tell you all you'd like to know about everything that you see.

Charles Darwin

The largely barren volcanic islands hosted their most famous visitor in 1835 when Charles Darwin, a 25-year-old English naturalist, arrived on the *HMS. Beagle* and spent five weeks in the islands. His painstaking observations suggested that species change over time to suit their environment and led him to develop his theory of evolution based on natural selection. Darwin never returned to the islands, and didn't publish his first book, *On the Origin of the Species*, until 24 years after his visit to the islands.

need to know

Tours are best arranged in advance of your trip, though operators can be chosen once in Ecuador. There is a park entrance fee of US$100 that must be paid in cash upon your arrival at the airport.

guides and gear Galapagos Travel (☎831/689-912, or 1-800/969-9014, ⓦ www. galapagostravel.com) specializes in natural history, educationally-oriented eleven- and fifteen-day trips to the Galápagos Islands on sixteen-passenger yachts, with year-round departures.

when to go Agreeable weather throughout the year means there is never a bad time to visit the Galápagos, though the islands typically see the most visitors from mid-June to August and from December until mid-January.

getting there There are two airports that receive flights from mainland Ecuador; the most frequently used is Baltra.

suggested reading Jonathan Weiner, *The Beak of the Finch: A Story of Evolution in Our Time* (Vintage). A Pulitzer Prize-winning book that demystifies evolution by showing that evolution is happening now and in a very short time frame. Barry Boyce, *A Traveler's Guide to the Galapagos Islands* (Hunter). The essential guide for trip planning and making the most of your time on the islands. Michael H. Jackson, *Galapagos: A Natural History* (Michigan State University Press). The bible of Galápagos field guides is also a valuable pre-trip resource.

suggested viewing *Galapagos: The Islands that Changed the World* (2007). A 150-minute documentary that beautifully showcases the islands with stunning cinematography shot from air, sea and land.

is this for me?

PHYSICAL ✦ ✦
Walks on generally easy trails

PSYCH ✦ ✦
Comfortable vessels and amenities

SKILL ✦ ✦
Come prepared, use observation skills

WOW! ✦ ✦ ✦ ✦ ✦
Ideal for photographers and naturalists

As you travel from island to island you, like Darwin, will be able to see how each species has adapted, or evolved, to suit its environment. Though the beak adaptations of finches particularly fascinated Darwin, chances are you'll find a giant tortoise – endemic to nine of the islands with minor subspecies variations from island to island – more compelling subject matter. You'll also discover the unique nature of each island, some of which are largely flat and others that have volcanic features, creating a wider range of altitudes, weather patterns and foliage. The outer horseshoe-shaped island of Genovesa is home to red-footed boobies, while blue-footed boobies are found throughout the archipelago. Fernandina is the best place to find well-populated colonies of large marine iguanas as well as flightless cormorants and Galápagos penguins, both of which are also found on Isabela. The outer island of Española is one of the few places in the world where you can find breeding colonies of waved albatross, the only tropical albatross.

For all their fearlessness and accessibility, the wildlife of the Galápagos do not live free of threats. The greatest environmental threats to the Galápagos Islands come from non-native species such as rats, pigs, goats and cats. These introduced species tend to reproduce quickly and often overtake the habitat or eat the eggs of native species. Although the islands have over five hundred native and endemic species, there are now over seven hundred introduced species. Skyrocketing tourism and a human population explosion, are also taking their toll on native species habitats, prompting the National Park to implement sweeping changes to promote sustainable development for the islands' growing resident population, regulate tourism, manage fishing in area waters, and shut down or restrict some sites that have suffered from overuse so that habitat restoration can take place. These restrictions, along with ongoing conservation and research efforts, will enable future generations to enjoy the natural wonders of the Galápagos Islands and witness evolution in progress.

62 Climbing in the Cordillera Blanca

>> Beat the tropical heat

HUARAZ

PERU

Imagine mountains of staggering dimensions, girded with vertical ice faces and covered year-round with snow; glaciers with yawning crevasses and avalanches that roar down steep valleys. This is likely not your vision of the tropics. But this is Peru's Cordillera Blanca: the world's highest tropical mountain range, offering expert climbers accessible, high-altitude adventure found nowhere else on earth. If you love mountaineering, glacier travel and breathtaking peaks, but hate waiting for days in a tent for a chance at summit success, then the Cordillera Blanca is just what you've been looking for.

acute mountain sickness

It's not always easy to tell the difference between acute mountain sickness (AMS) and dehydration. Both can be accompanied by headache, sleep disturbance, fatigue, shortness of breath, dizziness, loss of appetite and vomiting. Whereas dehydration occurs when your body can't absorb enough water, AMS is a symptom of gaining altitude too rapidly. If you've been getting plenty of fluids and your urine is clear and copious, there's a good chance you are experiencing AMS. Either way, the best course of action is to stop ascending, rest and drink more fluids. Treating AMS is simple, but your body may need several days to acclimatize to lower oxygen levels. Pain medications like aspirin or ibuprofen and high-carbohydrate foods can also be beneficial; sleeping pills, alcohol and smoking should be avoided.

AMS on its own is not life-threatening, although in rare cases it can develop into more serious illnesses caused by swelling in the lungs and brain. If symptoms appear to worsen, immediately descend 600m or more if possible, keep the victim warm and hydrated and get medical assistance. Doctors can prescribe medication to prevent AMS before you leave for a mountaineering adventure, especially useful to those who have experienced AMS in the past and are therefore more likely to experience it again.

Just nine degrees south of the equator in the Peruvian Andes, the Cordillera Blanca – Spanish for "white range" and usually shortened to just "the Blanca" – stretches roughly northeast to southwest. It includes over three hundred major summits, 25 of which exceed 6000m. The range's focal point is massive Huascarán (6768m), the highest peak in Peru and the highest tropical peak in the world; most of the Blanca is neatly encompassed within Huascarán National Park. All of the range's peaks are incomparably rugged and interspersed with deep, plunging valleys, or *quebradas*.

What makes the Blanca so appealing to mountaineers, other than its height and magnificence, is its accessibility. Its peaks don't require weeks or even days of expedition-style approach, nor shuttling equipment to establish successively higher camps. Routes on many of the more challenging summits typically start from a base or moraine camp below 4900m, then proceed to a glacier camp before ascending to the summit. On some climbs you can enjoy breakfast in the city of Huaraz and be at the toe of a glacier by the afternoon. Such ease of access enables you to fit more climbing into a shorter trip, often tackling some easier acclimatization climbs before a more challenging 6000-meter summit.

Such a selection of great peaks to choose from means you'll have no trouble finding a climb or group of climbs suited to your skill level and preferences. With towering granite walls and aquamarine lakes, the Quebrada Llanganuco is the most impressive valley in the range and a great place to start, providing access to the popular and beautiful Pisco Oeste climb. From the first day's base camp at just over 4600m, it's a short hike up to a moraine

camp right below the glacier, where you can stay the night and make preparations for the summit bid. Once you're on the glacier, the route leads toward a high saddle with the four Huandoy peaks on the left – each over 6000m – and the ridge to Pisco on the right. The only obstacle between you and the summit is a wall of ice, usually scaled without too much difficulty. The highlight of Pisco's apex (5752m) is its in-your-face views of Pirámide and the two Chacraraju summits, just a few kilometers away.

Called "the most beautiful mountain in the world", although it's most gorgeous when viewed from the northwest, Alpamayo lies at the northern end of the Blanca. It is one of the range's most sought-after peaks, usually climbed along its famous "Ferrari Route". Although the exact route changes from year to year, you can expect a dramatic summit day as you scale its fluted face with an ice axe in each hand. Other challenging and noteworthy climbs start in the Ishinca Valley, which, because of its proximity to Huaraz, sees its fair share of climbers. Huascarán, normally accessed from the village of Musho, is an especially great ascent, although the standard route has become quite dangerous due to icefall.

The Blanca's beauty and accessibility sometimes mask the dangers inherent in any mountain environment. Avalanches, rockfalls, crevasses and altitude sickness all take their annual toll in the form of serious injuries and fatalities. But such isolated incidents will be forever overshadowed by a single catastrophic day in 1970, when an earthquake dislodged an enormous section from the west face of Huascarán's north peak. The heat and force of the falling rocks triggered a chain of avalanches and mudslides that rumbled down the Quebrada Llanganuco for more than 18km at over 160km per hour, instantly burying seventeen thousand villagers in a sea of rock and ice. Throughout the region, nearly eighty thousand died in the worst natural disaster in South American history. While the terrifying memories still haunt the area's older residents, today youthful, avid *andinistas* are taking to the peaks in record numbers and introducing this brilliant range to eager climbers from around the world.

need to know

The city of Huaraz provides accommodation and easy access to climbs. Check current conditions before departing on any climb; an experienced guide is highly advised. Hiring well-trained and hardworking local porters, *arrieros* (mule-drivers) and cook staff is relatively inexpensive, supports sustainable tourism and promises a more enjoyable climb.

guides and gear Peaks & Places Travel (℡ 970/626-5251, ⓦ www. peaksandplaces.com) specializes in custom climbing and trekking adventures with certified mountain guides and over twenty years of experience. La Cima Logistics in Huaraz (℡ 043/721203, ⓦ www.cafeandino.com) provides logistical services (transport, porters, guides, cooks and mule-drivers) for both guided and independent treks.

when to go The May to September climbing season offers the best weather and chances of success on the summit.

getting there Fly in to Lima and take a comfortable, scheduled motorcoach (8hr) to Huaraz, at the head of the Huaylas Valley.

suggested reading Brad Johnson, *Classic Climbs of the Cordillera Blanca, Peru* (Western Reflections). Exceptional maps, photography, route descriptions and additional tips and resources.

is this for me?

PHYSICAL ✦ ✦ ✦ ✦
Excellent conditioning and endurance required

PSYCH ✦ ✦ ✦
Mountain hazards and potential sleep disruption

SKILL ✦ ✦ ✦
Glacier travel and crevasse rescue knowledge

WOW! ✦ ✦ ✦ ✦
Stunning peaks; exciting, accessible climbing

Windsurfing in Bonaire

>> Catch the good air

63

As you drive along Bonaire's quiet backroads, you'll notice that all car licence plates bear the inscription "Divers Paradise". It would be just as fitting if they read "Kayakers Paradise", "Mountain Bikers Paradise", "Hiker's Paradise" – or simply "Paradise". As if these descriptions weren't enough, Bonaire has also become a world-class windsurfing destination – and why not? Beautiful days here are a dime a dozen, there is no rainy season and temperatures consistently range from 22°C to 31°C. For windsurfers, the warm and constantly blowing trade winds that give the island its name (it means "good air") are the biggest appeal.

Bonaire is a dogleg-shaped island about 8km wide and 32km long, lying just 80km north of Venezuela. Claimed for Spain by Amerigo Vespucci in 1499, it was captured by the Dutch in 1633 and today is an independent protectorate of the Netherlands. While Dutch remains the official language, Papiamentu, a form of Creole also spoken in Aruba and Curaçao, is more widely used, and English and Spanish are commonly spoken as well. On the water, though, the wind is the lingua franca, and your windsurfing skill will speak for itself.

Bonaire's windsurfing epicenter is Lac Bay, on the southeastern side of the island. This eight-square-kilometer protected marine park is a perfectly pristine place for the sport. Graced with fine white sand, Lac Bay is a rarity on the rather beach-deficient island, which is better known for its diving and abundant coral. While the surf off the island's eastern coast is usually rough, Lac Bay is a kiddie pool sheltered by a natural barrier reef. Since nearly half the bay is waist deep and sandy bottomed, your launch couldn't be easier – just wade a few steps out into the warm water, step on your board and catch the wind.

If you're a novice, start on the beach side of the bay. It's smooth sailing, and even if you fall, recovery is a cinch. With a little more practice under your harness, shoot for the light swells across the bay – still nicely protected, but with a little more movement in the water and the wind. Big-leaguers looking for competitive conditions, on the other hand, should head for the outskirts of the bay, where the waves are mast-high and the winds exhilarating.

The trades blow on shore and almost always out of east-northeast. For nine months of the year – December through August – the winds come in at 17–21 knots, known as a "fresh breeze" or a 5 on the Beaufort wind force scale. Although Bonaire lies outside the hurricane belt, the winds can be interrupted from September through November by hurricane season disturbances or Caribbean depressions. Even then, though, winds are typically at 12–18 knots, the weather is pleasant and you can get in plenty of good time on the water.

No matter the conditions, Bonaire is a safe place to windsurf, and probably the best in the world to learn the sport. With no breaking waves, Lac Bay is perfect for beginners, and even though it's internationally known among windsurfers, it's relatively quiet. Regardless of your skill level, get yourself to Bonaire's windward side and, with some practice, you'll soon be skimming the turquoise waters of the Caribbean.

need to know

Facilities, rental equipment and instruction available on the island cater to all ages. Since the water is shallow and warm and getting atop your board is easy, you can spend entire days honing your skills. In addition to being the ideal learning environment, Bonaire is also a great place for an intermediate windsurfer to work toward a more advanced level.

guides and gear Bonaire Windsurf Place, located at the Sorobon resort area on Lac Bay (☎599/717-2288, Ⓦ www.bonairewindsurfplace.com), offers expert instruction, rental packages and accommodation.

when to go You can enjoy Bonaire windsurfing year-round, but count on December to August for the best wind conditions.

getting there Bonaire is served by Flamingo International Airport. Lac Bay is on the island's southeast side, about fifteen minutes from the airport and accessible by taxi, shuttle or rental car.

is this for me?

PHYSICAL ✦ ✦ ✦ ✦ ✦
Strength, agility and balance

PSYCH ✦ ✦ ✦ ✦ ✦
Idyllic conditions in a safe environment

SKILL ✦ ✦ ✦ ✦ ✦
Extended practice required

WOW! ✦ ✦ ✦ ✦ ✦
Exhilarating experience in a beautiful setting

64 Trekking to Angel Falls

WHERE Canaima National Park, Venezuela

WHEN April to October

PHYSICAL	✦ ✦ ✦	
PSYCH	✦ ✦ ✦	
SKILL	✦ ✦ ✦ ✦	
WOW!	✦ ✦ ✦	

Imagine a dizzying drop of nearly one thousand meters – well over half a mile – in fourteen seconds. That's how long it takes for the water that rushes from the top of Angel Falls to hit the river below, much of the spray evaporating before it hits the ground. The tallest falls in the world seem to cascade straight out of the heavens, even if they are situated on the Auyántepui, or "Devil's Mountain."

Be ready to canoe and hike your way to the base of the falls. The surrounding jungle area is so dense, over-grown and rugged that it takes several days to hike through to a point where you can put in. It's another couple of days paddling up the river, sleeping in hammock camps along the way. Once you've canoed as far as you can go, it's about a one-hour trek to the actual base. During the wet months, April through October, the waters are easier to navigate, but there are more visitors and the top of the falls is usually shrouded in fog. The rest of the year it's more or less the opposite: fewer people, but lower water levels that are more difficult to manage and a less spectacular cascade.

To reach the sharp-edged cliff where the falls begin their tumble, you'll need to conquer three bluffs stacked like enormous steps one above the other, setting up camp for the night on each. A final push through a giant cleft passing by some of the most exotic plants you'll ever see and you're at the flat mountaintop where the ribbons of water originate.

65 Caving in Camuy

WHERE Río Camuy Cave Park, Puerto Rico
WHEN Year-round

Deep in the tropical rainforest of Puerto Rico, the Río Camuy has carved an exquisite 268-acre subterranean network of limestone caverns. Hidden beneath vine- and fern-covered hills are calcified spectacles of a magnitude found few places in the world. Lush green openings into the monstrous caverns allow filtered sunlight into the dark depths. These rays of light reflect off trickling water and flowstone cave walls to create a type of underground aurora borealis. Amazingly, the Camuy cave system, the third largest in the world, remained largely unexplored until 1958.

Cueva Clara, one of the most spectacular caves within the park, yawns an astonishing 52 meters, making it wide enough for a seventeen-story building to fit inside. Massive chunks of stalactites broken off from the ceiling litter the cave floor. A startling 122m deep sinkhole, the Sumidero Empalme, lies at the south end, opening the cave up to the sky. From a platform nearby, you can view the immense Tres Pueblos sinkhole which drops 110m, allowing you to see the underground river that continues to change the topography of the cavern.

Cueva Angeles (Angel's Cave), near the town of Lares, may be even more heart-stopping. You begin by repelling 61m into a dark sinkhole where you swim in chilly water through an underground narrow passage and then slither down a mudslide to the edge of the Río Camuy. From there it's body-rafting through cave passages to another sinkhole where you can exit.

Reservations must be made in advance. Shoes that have good tread are needed for slick surfaces, and clothing that will dry quickly and keep you warm is a must.

66 Seeing the jungle in Manu Biosphere Reserve

WHERE Western Amazon, Peru
WHEN Year-round

From a cool, dark understory and tropical evergreen cloudforest to high-altitude tundra-like puna, Manu National Park, the largest rainforest reserve in Peru, pushes the limits of eco-diversity available in one adventure. While trekking overgrown trails by day and camping on damp forest floor by night, you share the forest with thousands of mostly unseen, but not necessarily unheard, creatures. The reserve is home to scampering howler monkeys, giant otters, iridescent squawking parrots, dancing cock-of-the-rocks (Peru's national bird), skulking jaguars, harpy eagles, lumbering tapir, and leathery black caimans. Glistening moist ferns and tumbling vines frame the cascade of colorful orchids that thrive in this humid natural greenhouse. In all, some 1000-plus species of birds, 200 species of mammals, and 15,000 species of flowering plants populate the place.

On the western reaches of the Amazon, Manu is accessible either by air or gravel road, but both routes require a short river trip. To see as much of the forest as possible, you'll almost certainly need to be on a guided tour, most likely organized in Cusco, which is about a 161km southwest from the reserve entrance. Multi-day jungle treks plumb the depths of the accessible part of the reserve, though just outside, the privately owned Manu Wildlife Center offers a kind of "best-of" what lies deeper in the jungle and serves as a base for visiting tapir and macaw salt-licks and a couple of 37-meter-tall wildlife observation platforms.

67 Climbing the Masaya and Maderas volcanoes

WHERE Masaya and Ometepe, Nicaragua
WHEN Year-round

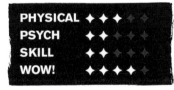

Back in the days of fire and brimstone, Nicaragua presented the Spanish with a vision of damnation itself: Volcán Masaya. So perturbed were they by the volcano's miasmic, black-slurry depths they got a priest in to exorcize it. Come the twenty-first century, the threat is physical rather than spiritual; as one of the most consistently active and unpredictable volcanoes in the world, climbing its deceptively undulating slopes is still – forgive the pun – one hell of an adventure. Not that the ascent itself is particularly strenuous, although robberies aren't uncommon, so safety can be a concern, and the lack of tree cover can make for a broiling (two- to three- hour) climb. The reward is a staggering, sulphurous, smoking gun of a crater, where you'll dare yourself to crane your head as far as it'll go without choking on the fumes. Curiously, a species of small green parrot – chocoyo del cráter – spends its entire life up here, but don't hang around birdwatching for too long; you might just need to make an exceedingly quick exit.

A different proposition entirely is Volcán Maderas, sequestered in cloudforest on the far side of Isla Ometepe. Here, bird calls unceasingly mock those foolhardy enough to attempt the climb in trainers. Boots at the ready then, and armed with a personable guide from nearby Finca Magdalena, you can wrestle with outsized tree roots in a dripping twilight before (some three hours further up) descending a rock wall – down a rope – and emerging into what can only be described as an unlikely Eden, a cloistered crater lagoon on top of a world seemingly yet to exist.

68 Trekking to Panama's Caribbean Coast

WHERE Boquete, Panama

WHEN Late December to April

As the downpour finishes and dusk encroaches, a deafening chorus of tree frogs starts up. You collapse under the corrugated iron shelter (the night's accommodation), grateful for the firewood that someone has left that will ensure a hot meal and the means to warm, if not actually dry out, your soggy socks. You're so exhausted, yet exhilarated from the first eight-hour day of your four-day trek – up the cool mountain slopes from Boquete village and through mist-clad cloudforest topping the continental divide of the Cordillera Talamanca – that you scarcely notice the leaks as the heavens open again. You burrow in your sleeping bag, hoping that the makeshift drainage channel can keep the rising water at bay. Night two promises a more comfortable sleep in a rustic farm owned by guide Feliciano's uncle while night three is spent on the floor of a hut in a traditional Ngöbe Buglé village.

After the first day the going gets progressively easier – though the amount of rain, and therefore mud, may have some bearing on the matter – as the 50-kilometer route wends its way (predominantly) downhill. Occasional breaks in the tree-line afford fabulous views towards the coast, your final destination. The hiking is hard but rewarding, through lush tropical rainforests interspersed with flashes of colorful orchids and heliconia. Keep an eye out too for parrots, toucans, and hummingbirds – more likely sightings than the elusive pumas and ocelots that also inhabit the more remote areas. Your energy may wane during the countless river crossings on the final day, but the prospect of easing your aching limbs into the warm waters of the Caribbean will keep you going.

69 Riding with gauchos in the pampas

WHERE: Buenos Aires Province, Argentina

WHEN: Year-round

The gaucho is Argentina's equivalent of the American cowboy – a splendid, freedom-loving figure in beret and *bombachas* (baggy riding pants), who roams the country's vast pampas heartland on horseback, looking after the cattle raised on the centuries-old *estancias* (ranches). Take some time out from the capital to stay on one of the many *estancias* scattered around Buenos Aires province and you can spend a day riding out with them, perhaps helping out with tasks such as rounding up, lassoing, or branding. This is not for beginners, though – if you want to keep up you'll need to be able to hold your own in the saddle and, if necessary, adjust to the Western style of riding.

There is something hypnotic in galloping over the pampas, the utterly flat grassland stretching as far as the eye can see in every direction, met by a cornflower blue sky. The horizon is broken only by the occasional distant ranch building, surrounded by a clump of windbreaker trees. The sole sound is the whipping of the wind, the thud of your mount's hooves, and the occasional call from your companions to rein in and take a break to share a few rounds of *maté* – a bitter tea, sipped via a metal straw from a gourd, which has invigorated pampa residents since pre-Columbian times. Return by nightfall to the homestead, a little sore but much exhilarated, to warm your feet by the fire and swap stories over a glass of red wine or two.

70 Hiking in the Serra do Mar

WHERE Paraná state, Brazil

WHEN Year-round, though nicest in spring and autumn

Lining 1609km of the Brazilian coastline, from Rio de Janeiro to Santa Caterina in the southeast, lies the Serra do Mar, a dramatic range of mountains separating the ocean from a high inland plateau. This is far from the Amazon and yet these mountains' slopes are enveloped by an

equally diverse rainforest, the *Mata Atlantica* contains over three hundred bird species, primates such as howler, spider, and capuchin monkeys, as well as rarely-seen mammals like ocelots, jaguars, and black-faced lion tamarins.

The region is rich in clearly laid hiking trails, many of them challenging mountain ascents with ropes or rock handles already placed for your convenience on the steeper stretches. One of the best treks is 1547m Mount Olimpo, a formidable peak in the Pico do Marumbi park in the state of Paraná. The adventure begins on an exciting train journey which descends from the plateau through canyons, tunnels, and cloudforest, with rocky peaks exposed above and sweeping forested valleys below. Moments after starting your hike you are engulfed in deep jungle, the greens and browns of the canopy accompanied by bright orchids and the noises of crickets and bird songs. The paths are broken occasionally by gushing streams and tumbling waterfalls strewn with boulders. Climbing is strenuous, and you can only speculate what might await you at the summit. But as you progress the vegetation becomes thinner, the terrain rockier, and the air even fresher. At Olimpo's peak you're eventually rewarded by a spectacular view to two horizons, the deep blue Atlantic on one side and the vast plateau on the other. On your descent, a bathé in one of the cool river pools provides the ideal antidote for tired muscles.

71 Widlife viewing on Península Valdés

WHERE Chubut Province, Argentina
WHEN September to November

It's difficult to pin down precisely the slapping sound that emanates when six tons of blubbery wet flesh collides, but while I was still working out if it's more of a "schlop" than a "schlurp", the two huge bull elephant seals thundered together again, sending gallons of seawater flying in their titanic battle.

This is October on the Península Valdés, a scrubby blob of land clinging to the side of Argentina's Atlantic coast that, other than being the only continental breeding ground for southern elephant seals, also happens to be one of the most significant marine reserves on earth. The strip of sand on which the seals try prove their prowess is also crammed with some of the area's twenty-thousand-strong sea lion population, while along the coast a colony of Magellanic penguins have pocked the rugged hillside with their burrows.

Huge numbers of southern right whales – half the world's population – gather in the sheltered waters of the Golfo Nuevo each summer to raise their calves. And there are killer whales, too, though their mood is far more belligerent: it is here, on the shingle spits of Punta Norte, the peninsula's northern tip, that they famously beach their gigantic bodies in an attempt to snap up a baby sea lion or young elephant seal.

It must rank as one of nature's most incredible sights, but back at the beach, the elephant seals aren't interested. The fatties are still fighting, and behind them both, two more gigantic males square up, clashing with such force that the sand shakes.

72 Birdwatching on the Pipeline Road

WHERE Parque Nacional Soberanía, Panama
WHEN September to November

The logbook at Parque Nacional Soberanía's headquarters reads like a "Who's Who?" of exotic bird species. There are mealy Amazons, shining honeycreepers, and red-capped manakins. Ocellated antbirds make a regular appearance, alongside gray-headed chachalacas and thick-billed motmots. Each entry is more gushing than the last – someone had almost torn through the page describing their chance encounter with a rufous-vented ground cuckoo. But if there's one place on earth that's guaranteed to send twitchers into a frenzy, it's the seventeen-kilometer-long trail at the heart of Soberanía: a dirt track they call The Pipeline Road.

The "road," a thin stretch of track constructed by the US during World War II to maintain a fuel pipeline, holds the world record for the highest number of bird species identified in a 24-hour period – in 1996, the Audobon Society counted an incredible 360 different specimens amongst the foliage. A network of side tracks, creeks, and rivers can be followed into the surrounding forest, but the road itself is as good a place as any to start running up your own tally, especially in the soft light of dawn or the cool hours around dusk, when activity is at its greatest. Army-ant swarms attract birds by the hundreds, while the trail is a popular location for leks – an incredible avian dance-off where males gather at the same spot each season for the purposes of elaborate (and very competitive) courtship displays. Just don't be surprised if you find yourself rushing back to HQ, pen at the ready.

73 Biking down the World's Most Dangerous Road

WHERE La Paz, Bolivia

WHEN April to October

PHYSICAL	✦ ✦ ✦ ✦ ✦
PSYCH	✦ ✦ ✦ ✦ ✦
SKILL	✦ ✦ ✦ ✦ ✦
WOW!	✦ ✦ ✦ ✦ ✦

When you're ready to take mountain biking to the literal edge, there's no better place than the aptly named World's Most Dangerous Road, the Apolobamba. This hair-raising route leads from high in the Cordillera Real outside La Paz down to the heavy moist Amazonian jungle at the base of the mountains – a drop of almost 3600m. Even for the adventure seeker, it's a heart-thumbing ride that borders on the terrifying as you roll along a road that takes you to the very brink of some of Bolivia's highest mountains.

In the morning you'll start out in the clouds and travel down a road that begins as asphalt, but soon becomes rugged dirt and mud. The descent takes you through the mists of small waterfalls and near ledges with sheer drops of 600m – and all the while you'll be sharing the road with four-wheeled traffic. Fortunately, vehicles can only travel downhill in the morning; after 5pm traffic direction switches to uphill. Since the road is 90 percent downhill, it will take only four to five hours to complete the ride. It will be an intense and immeasurably thrilling ride through some of the most beautiful country Bolivia has to offer.

Several tour companies in La Paz lead guided tours down the road, and each ensure that the quality of their bikes is high – and that the brakes are strong. When riding this daring trail, keep in mind the rules of the road: yell if you are passing someone, check your brakes regularly, and always keep your eyes on the road. April to October are the driest months and have the most stable weather, so they are the best times to ride.

74 Sea kayaking to the San Rafael Glacier

WHERE Patagonia, Chile

WHEN Best undertaken October to March

PHYSICAL	✦ ✦ ✦ ✦	✦
PSYCH	✦ ✦ ✦ ✦	✦
SKILL	✦ ✦ ✦ ✦	✦
WOW!	✦ ✦ ✦ ✦	✦

The Andes' central reaches, with their great mountains and soaring condors, are the range's most naturally dramatic parts. Down south, as the peaks retreat into increasingly cold fjords and the weather moves in, great birds are less visible and people are rarer, too. This weatherbeaten landscape is almost unremittingly tough: paths are few and roads fewer, and as you move away from the cities you pass less inhabited settlements and deserted fisherman's huts. Crossing the great fjords on a kayak is a frightening business. Tip over into the water and you'll need to be hauled up, teeth chattering, as the waves crash around you, and paddle onto the nearest patch of land, to be revived with hot tea, a fire, and the warmth of those around you. Leeches sit malignantly in the rainforest and sandflies lurk on the beaches, waiting to turn your skin into a large sweaty itch.

Yet the rewards of this landscape are truly inspiring. The channels you kayak down are so icy it can feel like moving through a Slush Puppy; you can spot seals and seabirds and hear the eerie cry of the sea lion while moving into the great laguna that surrounds the San Rafael glacier, which stretches down the mountain and into the sea, icebergs calving off in apparent slow motion. It's far easier to get a cruise – traveling independently, you'll have to negotiate with the park authorities to spend the night, carry your own supplies and emergency kit, and probably get a boat to drop you part of the way from Puerto Chacabuco. But far better to have earned your time in front of this great retreating wall, resting your hands in the cold water and feeling your kayak shift beneath you as the glacier crunches its way into the sea.

Judgment comes from experience and experience comes from bad judgment.

Simon Bolivar

naming rights

Anybody can get a stadium or university building named after them for a few mil, but how about a whole continent? Currently, only two continents are named after an individual – North America and South America – and the individual is not Amerigo Vespucci as has been widely taught, but Richard Amerike, a British merchant born in 1445 who funded the voyages of Giovanni Caboto, or John Cabot. Cabot arrived in Newfoundland in 1497, two years before Vespucci, and mapped much of the American continent's North Atlantic coast as far south as Maine. While no records exist on the amount of Amerike's investment, it would likely have been well under £300,000 in today's value based on similar voyages of the period.

Many will call me an adventurer – and that I am, only one of a different sort: one of those who risks his skin to prove his platitudes.

Che Guevara

OJOS ODDITIES

Aconcagua in Argentina is the highest peak in the western hemisphere and a formidable mountaineering challenge, but Chile's Ojos del Salado, at 6891m just 71m shorter than Aconcagua, is virtually ignored by mountaineers because it's a largely non-technical hike. Thanks to its location in the dry Atacama region it receives little snow except in winter. But Ojos del Salado has some distinctions that no other mountain in the world can match: it's a massive and still-active stratovolcano, and is the world's tallest volcano. The crater lake on its eastern slope, at an elevation of 6390m, is the highest lake of any kind in the world. In 2007 a Chilean team set a new high altitude record for a vehicle as they drove across bounder fields, sandy slopes and glacial ice to an elevation of 6688m. According to the driver, crossing the main glacier required "very technical driving."

Human-sized rodents

Crossing a grassy meadow or passing by a riverbank in South America, don't be surprised if you see a brown, stout-bodied, flat-nosed rodent that can tip the scales at over 70kg. The capybara is the largest living rodent, is the only animal that can crack a Brazil nut without tools. It is found near water in the temperate and tropical regions east of the Andes. While these lumbering, aquatic herbivores are harmless to humans, one has to wonder if the capybara's extinct ancestor would have been quite as gentle. It was a 3m long and weighed in at 700kg.

"Don't let it end like this. Tell them I have said something."

Pancho Villa's final words

BOLEADORES

Watching one of Argentina's gauchos at work is an impressive sight. In addition to being skilled horsemen, they are proficient with a lasso and with the *boleadores* which they keep slung over they belt, always at the ready. *Boleadores* are fist-sized balls of metal or stone bagged in leather, two of which are attached to woven strands of leather about a metre long and tied to a third strand with a smaller ball at the end. Holding the small ball in hand, with a few swift overhead swings the gaucho hurls the *boleadores* at a running wild horse, guanaco or ostrich, aiming at the legs. As the flying *bolos* strike the leg of the running animal, they wrap around and bind the legs, often breaking one or at least causing the animal to stumble to the ground. But the whole technique is easier said than done, and only after years of practice on the pampas can a gaucho master the *boleadores*.

My undertaking is not difficult, essentially. I should only have to be immortal to carry it out.

Jorge Luis Borges

ANDES LONG AND SHORT OF IT

The Andes are the longest *exposed* mountain range in the world, stretching over 7000km. But the longest mountain range on earth is the Mid-Atlantic Range, which runs below the Atlantic Ocean north to south and only rises above sea level in places like the Azores. Within the Andes, Aconcagua, at 6962m is the highest peak and also the highest peak in the Western Hemisphere, but falls far short of higher peaks in the Himalaya. However because of the equatorial bulge, the summit of Mount Chimborazo in the Ecuadorian Andes has the distinction of being the point on the earth's surface most distant from its center.

The world's southernmost city

Argentina and Chile have had occasional diplomatic squabbles over the years, including who can claim the title of the world's southernmost city – Ushuaia, Argentina or Puerto Williams, Chile. Ushuaia has long claimed the title, boasting that it is a fully functioning city with a hospital and an institution of higher learning. Puerto Williams has only 2400 inhabitants, and none of the urban amenities of Ushuaia, and is primarily a Chilean naval station. Recently, however, in an act of diplomatic harmony, Argentina and Chile agreed to bestow the "Southernmost City" title to Puerto Williams. It should be noted that there are other continuously inhabited settlements further south of either Puerto Williams or Ushuaia, such as Orcadas, South Orkney Islands, and Esperanza, each of which has fewer than 100 residents.

It's a willing horse they saddle the most.

Jamaican proverb

Crossing a piranha-infested river

It's a clichéd adventure movie scene – someone is crossing a tropical river, falls from the boat and is instantly devoured by piranhas. Possible? Yes. Likely? No. But piranhas, a tropical freshwater fish found only in still or slow-moving South American lakes and rivers, can be a threat. First, know that piranhas almost never attack a large mammal or human except in the dry season when water levels are low and food is scarce. Second, avoid areas where piranhas may have been habitually feeding, such as near docks where fish have been gutted. Third, they are attracted to blood, so avoid potentially infested waters if you have an open cut or wound. Finally, if you do have to cross a piranha-infested body of water, it's best done at night, since piranhas are most active in the morning. Move quickly, but make as little disturbance as possible to the water. If you have any doubts always ask experienced locals about the water's safety.

GREAT HIKES IN THE CARIBBEAN

You might associate the Caribbean with white-sand beaches rather than rewarding tramps, but there's more to the region than postcard manufacturers might have you believe.

▶ **Cayman Brac, The Cayman Islands**
Located around ninety miles northeast of Grand Cayman, quiet, isolated Cayman Brac is crossed by numerous trails, exploring the island's iconic limestone bluff, hundreds of caves and a reserve where you can spot rare parrots.

▶ **Morne Trois Pitons, Dominica**
Perhaps the Caribbean's finest wilderness, this dramatic national park stretches over much of southern Dominica, encompassing volcanic features, thick rainforest and sparse woodland. Boiling Lake, the Valley of Desolation and Trafalgar Falls live up to their evocative names.

▶ **Saba, Netherlands Antilles** Tiny, unspoilt Saba offers some splendid short walks, including the march up Mount Scenery, which heads past elephant ear ferns and mahogany trees and up to a viewpoint offering great views on sunny days, with the chance to spot hummingbirds, butterflies and iguanas.

Sierra del Escambray, Cuba Just northwest of Trinidad, itself a World Heritage Site, these pine-covered mountains climb to 1140m. Several trails – generally half-day walks or less – take in fine sights including waterfalls and natural pools for swimming. Tours can fill you in on the area's contexts and provide lunch.

▶ **St Lucia Forest Reserve, St Lucia**
The beach crowds soon drop off as you head into the beautiful, teeming forests of St Lucia's interior. Easy walks contrast with more substantial loops – for which a guide is useful and transport often essential.

Skiing the roof of the world

Bolivia's only ski resort, Chacaltaya, is also the world's highest, set at 5421m. Unusually, most skiing takes place in the southern hemisphere summer and autumn, when temperatures are tolerably high. But Chacaltaya is dying. More than 80 percent of the glacier, reached by a tortuous dirt road, has melted in the last twenty years, leaving a bare, rocky expanse and a sliver of snow and ice that repels all but the most determined skiers and snowboarders. The only lift – powered by a car engine – stopped working in 2007. Bolivia's skiing tradition (the country last sent a team to the Winter Olympics in 1992) looks destined to wither, one of global warming's early casualties.

LA QUEBRADA

Cliff diving's roots are allegedly found in Hawaii, where King Kahekili encouraged his warriors to leap into the sea from a great height to prove their loyalty. The activity's more famous modern manifestation takes place in Acapulco, Mexico, where so-called *clavadistas* fling themselves off La Quebrada ("The Break"). Inevitably, the landing – into a shallow, rocky channel – is the difficult part, as divers must time their jump to coincide with incoming waves that provide the necessary depth. The details of the jump are cloaked in tourist-baiting mystery: some claim the highest platform is 45m above the sea, while more conservative estimates put it at less than 30m.

EUROPE

75 Climbing the Matterhorn **76** Walking England from coast to coast **77** Via ferrata climbing in the Dolomites **78** Sea kayaking in Iceland **79** Trekking the GR20 **80** Mountain biking in Cappadocia **81** Climbing Ben Nevis **82** Hiking the Haute Route **83** Cross-country ski touring in Norway **84** Climbing Mont Blanc **85** Hiking Hadrian's Wall **86** Hiking Kungsleden **87** Hiking the North Devon Coast **88** Diving the Zenobia **89** Cross-country ski touring in Lapland **90** Walking in the Cévennes **91** Cycling in the Southern Piedmont **92** Hiking in the Pindos Mountains **93** Mountain biking King's Trail **94** Walking the Kerry Way **95** Hiking in the Carpathians **96** Walking the West Highland Way **97** Sea kayaking in the Ionian **98** Horseback riding in Andalucia **99** Hiking the Snowdon Horseshoe **100** Walking the Camino de Santiago **101** Walking across the Llŷn **102** Ice diving in the White Sea **103** Coasteering in Anglesey **104** Caving in the Banat **105** Bagging a Munro **106** Kayaking the Ardèche gorges

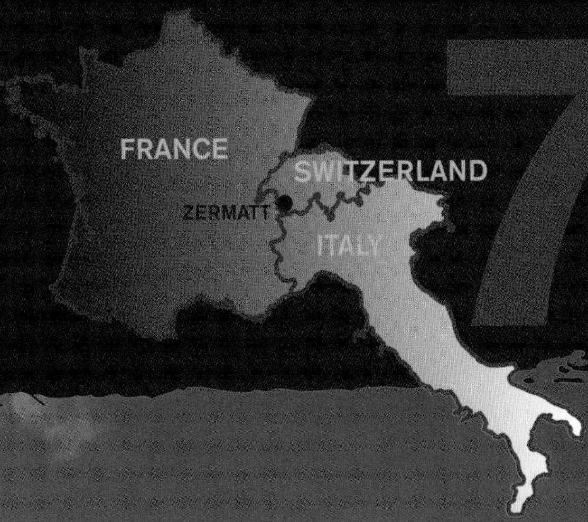

FRANCE

SWITZERLAND

ZERMATT

ITALY

75 Climbing the Matterhorn

>> **Scramble amongst the Alps**

Its unmistakable, angular profile makes the Matterhorn the most recognizable mountain in the world. It was also the last major peak of the Alps to be climbed, not so much because of its altitude – at 4478m it's a full 330m lower than Mont Blanc – but because its steep angles terrified early mountaineers, who lacked the technical apparatus available to climbers today. It's still a challenging climb and an exhilarating one at that, but with fixed ropes on key pitches and with a throng of other climbers for company, you can rest assured that your first ascent will be far different from that of British explorer Edward Whymper.

Whymper's ascent

Seven men reached the summit of the forbidding Matterhorn on July 14, 1865, but only three returned to the bottom to give an account. Whymper's ascent, as it has come to be known, is one journey that Edward Whymper described in *Scrambles Amongst the Alps*. But six other men were a part of the expedition that constituted the first successful climb of the sharp peak: arguably the grand finale to the age of alpinism.

The other six men were French mountain guide Michel Croz, surefooted British mountaineer Charles Hudson and his inexperienced companion Douglas Hadow, 19-year old Lord Francis Douglas, and a father and son guiding duo from Zermatt, both named Peter Taugwalder. The seven companions were tied together as they descended the slope one by one, but the rope that was meant as a safety net became a deadly anchor when Hadow slipped and knocked Croz, who was leading the way, off the mountain. As both men fell, the dead weight of the rope caught Hudson and Douglas unprepared, and pulled them off the end. With four men falling, there were just three left to brace the weight, but as they did so the old rope snapped. Whymper's last sight of the men alive was as they struggled to get a hold on the mountain before plummeting, one by one from precipice to precipice, until they reached the Matterhorn glacier 1200m below.

Whymper's account states that he and the remaining two members of the party – the Taugwalders – remained motionless for nearly half an hour. Once they had safely descended, a search party found the bodies of Croz, Hadow and Hudson entrenched in the glacier at the bottom of the mountain. Lord Francis Douglas' body was never found.

Every night, do you understand, I see my comrades of the Matterhorn slipping on their backs, their arms outstretched, one after the other, in perfect order at equal distances – Croz the guide, first, then Hadow, then Hudson, and lastly Douglas. Yes, I shall always see them.

Edward Whymper

After seventeen failed attempts over the course of eight years, Whymper made an ascent via the Hörnli route and found it easier than its sharp angles had led him to believe. His party finally reached the summit on July 14, 1865, but their triumph was short-lived: tragically, just minutes after leaving the summit, a slip and a broken rope sent four of Whymper's teammates hurtling 1000m to their death.

Since Whymper's fateful climb, the Matterhorn has been scaled in all seasons and along all of its faces and ridge routes. The addition of fixed ropes and an abundance of guides enable thousands to climb the popular Hörnli route each summer. About sixty percent of climbers are without a professional guide – typically two-man teams who have honed their skills on similar rock faces and alpine routes. The climb is rated AD (fairly hard), and its technical demands should not be underestimated, and nor should the strenuous sustained climbing at high altitude required to attain the summit. Simply put, this is not a theme park attraction: don't climb the Matterhorn without a clear sense of what you're getting yourself into. Loose rock and large numbers of inexperienced climbers on a crowded route result in several deaths each year – more than on Everest or McKinley.

A climb of the Matterhorn generally begins in Zermatt, an idyllic, car-free and extremely touristy Swiss village. While Zermatt is a good place to rent gear, connect with a guide and meet other climbers, at 1615m it's not a great place to acclimatize. For that, there are several easily accessible training climbs in the area. Local guides require Matterhorn aspirants to undergo a safety test which can require climbing one or two nearby peaks, such as Breithorn, Riffelhorn or Pollux – all day hikes from Zermatt.

A mid-morning departure from Zermatt takes you by tram to Schwarzee (2590m). From there it's a two-hour trek to the Hörnli Hut (3260m) at the base of the mountain, where you can check in, grab some lunch at the restaurant and scout the route for an hour or so. This advance preparation will give you daylight familiarity with an area that will be dark the following morning. Have your gear laid out and be ready for bed by 9pm.

Allowing four to six hours for the ascent and the same for the descent, expect to rise at 3.30am – time to dress and grab a quick breakfast before starting your climb by 4.15am. Be aware that there is an unspoken pecking order on the ascent: the Swiss guides leave first, followed by the Germans, Italians and other Europeans, in that order. Unguided climbers take a back seat and have to fend for themselves, or forego breakfast to get an early start. Route-finding on the lower flanks can be tricky, where staying to the left of the ridge is the best approach. You'll be climbing by headlamp and in the weakest light of dawn, and many inexperienced climbers have lost valuable time by drifting off-track in these lower rubbly regions. You're likely to be comfortable climbing unroped up to the Solvay emergency hut at 4000m, at which point you'll probably have daylight, putting your route-finding challenges behind you. From here the rock faces of the lower and upper Moseley slabs and the steep shoulder of the Matterhorn provide the greatest risks. While the crux of the ascent is 5.4 climbing with fixed ropes and anchors, the real challenge is the endurance required to complete 1200m of mostly Class 4 and 5 climbing in a matter of seven hours. Stamina is the key, and looking up to see the summit getting closer with each step is a huge motivator.

Climbing hand over hand right up to the top, you'll find yourself suddenly on the Matterhorn summit, a rocky ridge about 3m wide and 30m long. The summit defines the Swiss-Italian border, so be sure to step into Italy – about a meter lower than the 4478-meter Swiss summit. The descent is made safer, though not much faster, by ten to fifteen extended rappels. After a long day on the Matterhorn, staying an additional night at the Hörnli Hut may not be as comfy as your hotel back in Zermatt, but it's certainly convenient.

When you return to Zermatt the next morning, stop by the Matterhorn Museum where you'll find Whymper's frayed rope on display, along with his admonition:

"Climb if you will, but remember that courage and strength are nought without prudence. Look well to each step; and from the beginning think what may be the end."

need to know

You'll need to be in top physical condition for a long and demanding summit day. If climbing unguided and during the peak season, reservations at the Hörnli Hut (☎027/967 22 64) are also essential.

guides and gear A number of companies offer guided climbs of the Matterhorn, on both the Hörnli and the Italian route. Guide to client ratios are always 1:1. In Zermatt, guides can be hired at the Zermatt Alpin Center (☎027/966 24 60, Ⓦwww.alpincenter-zermatt.ch).

when to go Mid-July to mid-September brings the best weather, great climbing conditions and the heaviest crowds.

getting there Fly to Zurich or Geneva, from where there are trains and shuttles to Zermatt. The Hörnli Hut can be reached from Zermatt on foot or by tram to Shwarzee, then on foot to the base.

suggested reading Edward Whymper, *Scrambles Amongst the Alps in the Years 1860–69* (Dover). The classic account of the first ascent of the Matterhorn, with masterful engravings by the author.

suggested viewing Walt Disney personally supervised the filming of *Third Man on the Mountain* (1959), a fictionalized story about the first ascent of an alpine peak, while on location in Zermatt. He was so inspired by the Matterhorn's profile that he built a mini-Matterhorn, which incorporated a bobsled ride, as the centerpiece attraction in Disneyland.

is this for me?

PHYSICAL ✦ ✦ ✦ ✦
Grueling sustained climbing

PSYCH ✦ ✦ ✦ ✦
High altitude, risk of falling

SKILL ✦ ✦ ✦ ✦
Climbing experience required

WOW! ✦ ✦ ✦ ✦
Feat of physical, mental stamina

Walking England from Coast to Coast

75

ST BEES   ROBIN HOOD'S BAY

UK

>> The stuff of poetry

Adventure treks may lead you across swollen rivers or up icy mountains; very rarely do they inspire you to write Romantic poetry. But the sweeping, pastoral valleys of England's Lake District and the wild moorland of the Yorkshire Dales aroused the creative spirit in Wordsworth, Coleridge, Keats, Tennyson and, more recently, Beatrix Potter and James Herriot. Even if England's famous Coast to Coast Walk, which traverses these stirring landscapes, fails to make a poet out of you, it is undeniably romantic.

Before you set out on the walk, make sure you understand some essential English geographic terms. The names of the many lakes that dot the Lake District usually include the word *water* or *mere*, as in Ullswater or Windermere. A *tarn* is a small pond in a glacial bowl or hollow, known as a *corrie*, and *beck* denotes a creek or steam. If a creek or stream moves fast or forms a waterfall, it's called a *force*.

A rugged rock cliff is a *crag*, and a *moor* is a boggy, grassy area in a *moorland*. A *fell* is a hill or mountain; a fell with a peaked summit is a *pike*. Names such as Stonethwaite and Rosthwaite incorporate the Norse word for "forest clearing". Along the route lie hundreds of *stiles*, or steps over a fence – be on guard, as some will deposit you in a field belonging to a potentially aggressive bull. A long detour around pastures is sometimes worth the extra effort.

For all its literary and historic appeal, the Coast to Coast Walk is fairly young as a popular excursion; its pioneer was Alfred Wainwright, who first visited the Lake District in 1930. "I was utterly enslaved by all I saw", he said. "Here were no huge factories, but mountains; no stagnant canals, but sparkling crystal-clear rivers; no cinder paths, but beckoning tracks that clamber through bracken and heather to the silent fastnesses of the hills. That week changed my life."

Starting in 1953, Wainwright published a series of seven pictorial guides to the area, followed in 1968 by a similar walking guide to the Pennine Way. He didn't devise his Coast to Coast Walk until 1972, when he declared that its scenic beauty "puts the Pennine Way to shame". The route links the Irish Sea on England's west with the North Sea to the east, winding through the hills, moors and valleys of the North Country. It crosses the Pennine Range, known as "England's backbone", and traverses three of the country's most magnificent national parks: the Lake District, Yorkshire Dales and the North York Moors.

Dip your boot in the Irish Sea or pocket a pebble from the rocky beach before you start the 300-kilometer journey at St Bees Head. Walking the route from west to east is a sensible choice since that's how the guidebooks describe it; there's also some advantage in having the prevailing winds at your back and enjoying the affable company of more walkers. On the other hand, hiking in the opposite direction saves the best scenery – the Lake District – for last. Many locals walk it sequentially over several weekends, while the great majority do it as a through hike in ten to fourteen days, staying at cozy pubs and bed and breakfasts along the way.

Despite its established reputation, the Coast to Coast Walk carries no official designation and no markings. There are several variations of the route, all of which use existing paths and occasional sections of paved road

need to know

No permits are required to enjoy England's Coast to Coast Walk. In the peak summer season, when accommodation is in high demand, you should plan your daily route and lodgings carefully.

guides and gear You can opt for a guided, self-guided or independent walk; if you forego a guide, be sure to bring a map, route guide and compass. Given the long distances and unpredictable weather, however, having an operator arrange logistics, shuttle your luggage and reserve accommodation is often worth the extra cost. Footpath Holidays (℡ 01985/840 049, ⓦ www.footpath-holidays.com) and the Sherpa Van Project (℡ 01609/883 731, ⓦ www.sherpavan.com) provide luggage transfers and pre-booked accommodation. Both companies offer guided and self-guided tours.

when to go May through September, with July and August offering the best weather and September seeing the smallest crowds. Even in midsummer, English weather never guarantees sunshine, so bring raingear. Patches of fog and morning mist are common, bestowing a supernatural aura on valleys and lakes.

getting there From Manchester, take a shuttle or local transportation to St Bees Head (1hr 30min).

suggested reading Henry Stedman, *Coast to Coast: British Walking Guides* (Trailblazer Publications). Detailed, hand-drawn maps show which routes to take and which to avoid.
Alfred Wainwright, *Coast to Coast Walk: A Pictorial Guide* (Frances Lincoln). Wainwright's classic is still the standard guide.

suggested viewing *Miss Potter* (2006) is a warm historical drama/romance surrounding the life and works of Beatrix Potter, whose efforts have preserved much of the Lake District.

is this for me?

PHYSICAL ✦ ✦ ✦
Moderate to strenuous terrain

PSYCH ✦ ✦
Extended travel with minor challenges

SKILL ✦ ✦
Nothing beyond normal walking experience

WOW! ✦ ✦ ✦ ✦
Beautiful cross-country walking

where walkers may share narrow stretches with vehicles. Lower versions take fairly unchallenging valley routes, while higher ones involve steep climbs to splendid views from the tops of fells. No scrambling is required, but switchbacks are virtually nonexistent and trails often head straight up mountain slopes. Other minor hazards may include boggy paths in the moorlands and erosion in the dales, both possibly requiring detours.

The first 5km of the route follow the red cliffs of St Bees Head before turning inland. After about 22km of fairly easy terrain on the first day, you'll arrive at the edge of Lake District National Park. With elevations over 900m, this is England's only true mountain region. It's a captivating expanse of craggy peaks and rising fells that cradle lush, glacier-sculpted valleys. Green dales hold tiny, idyllic settlements and are crisscrossed by stone walls and footpaths. The village of Patterdale, one of the park's many highlights, gives exquisite views of Ullswater, a beautiful lake set in a broad, green valley bowl.

Leaving Lake District National Park, you cross the Pennines, England's watershed, and tramp along gentler hillsides. Soon you'll reach the walk's approximate halfway point, marked by Nine Standards Rigg, a mysterious cluster of ancient hilltop cairns lining an escarpment. While their origins are uncertain, one theory claims that they were Roman decoys built to resemble troops or fortifications from a distance. You'll then wind your way through the Yorkshire Dales as you behold a landscape of weathered limestone pavements and serpentine rivers. The final few days of the walk take you through wild and pastoral North York Moors National Park, with its deep valleys and grassy moorland. It's at its best in August and September, when miles of heather become a carpet of delicate lavender blossoms.

The walk ends just as it began, with 5km of welcome coastal views along dramatic cliffs as you approach the village of Robin Hood's Bay. Here you descend a steep cobblestone path and cast your pebble into the North Sea. It's a fitting end to a truly classic walk filled with inspiring landscapes and constantly unfolding beauty.

CORTINA
D'AMPEZO

ITALY

Via ferrata climbing in the Dolomites

>> Steel yourself for "the iron way"

An exhilarating sense of triumph overtakes you as you climb the crest of a jagged, snow-laced limestone peak. From your roost far above the valley floor, Cortina's campanile and the *albergo* where you had breakfast this morning are barely visible, and the most spectacular routes in the Dolomite Alps are within your grasp. You've joined the ranks of the world's elite alpine climbers – or so you'd like to think. Actually, most of the credit must go to the ingenious system of cables, ladders, rungs and bridges known as via ferrata, or "iron way." This network of fixed-protection routes puts forbidding alpine peaks within the reach of even novice climbers – and allows you to marvel at the stark, dramatic beauty of the Dolomites up close.

the iron way to an upper hand

Until World War I the town of Cortina d'Ampezzo was know by its German name of Petsch-Hayden, as the Dolomites were part of the Austro-Hungarian Empire. When Italy allied with Britain, Russia and France, Austria shifted its forces along a defensive line that ran through the rugged Dolomites. The opposing Italian and Austrian forces battled not only against each other, but against the hostile terrain, struggling to gain control of mountain peaks, where firing positions and lookouts could be established. Just getting to those peaks was extremely hazardous. Never mind gunfire – avalanches, falls and freezing temperatures claimed tens of thousands of lives in the Dolomites. To speed troop movements and to provide safe routes, permanent cables were attached to rock faces, and ladders were installed so that soldiers could more easily ascend steep faces with heavy packs laden with ammunition, weapons and supplies. Some similar cables and ladders had already been placed by climbing guides in the 1880s, but it was during the war that the comprehensive via ferrata system that can be used today was established.

On several routes it's still possible to see dugouts, trenches and other relics of the conflict. You can wander among the fortifications, tunnels, and armaments as part of an open air museum with interpretive displays on Cinque Torri, and Mount Lagazuoi, where some of the heaviest fighting occurred. As Italian and Austrian troops fought for control of Lagazuoi they built tunnels through the mountain and set off dynamite to destroy each others' fortifications. Along the via ferrata you can follow these tunnels – now restored – for a speedy descent.

The Dolomites range in northeastern Italy has a solid reputation as a superb climbing destination, but it's not just prized for its sheer faces and rewarding routes. The region holds the overwhelming majority – about 180 – of the world's via ferrata climbing paths, first created by alpine guides as early as the 1800s to give ambitious climbers access to more challenging routes. During World War I, existing routes were developed to aid troop movements and secure mountaintop lookouts.

The Brenta region on the western edge of the Dolomites harbors some excellent climbs near the town of Madonna di Campiglio, but the densest concentration of routes is centered around the town of Cortina d'Ampezzo in the eastern Dolomites, where a lush, rolling valley is flanked by soaring faces of grey limestone topped with jagged ridges and spires. The steep rock faces, narrow ledges and gaping chasms which elsewhere would be the exclusive territory of experienced rock jocks, can here be tackled without a rope, specialist footwear or pricey hardware, thanks to in-built, protective iron bars drilled and cemented into the rock, and threaded with a heavy-gauge steel wire. With just a helmet, a harness, and a Y-shaped lanyard, you clip your carabiners into the fixed cable, position your foot on one of the iron rungs and start climbing. It's an amazing way to boost your climbing confidence, conquer some stunning vertical terrain and quickly ascend to airy alpine paths. Beginners will find a secure and surefooted excitement in this aerial playground, and the craggy peaks that ring Cortina offer commanding views and satisfying personal rewards.

Mountains are the means, the man is the end. The goal is not to reach the tops of mountains, but to improve the man.
Walter Bonatti

While via ferrata routes don't require polished technique, exceptional strength, balance, or even rock climbing experience, what they do demand is decent aerobic conditioning for a sustained ascent of several hundred vertical meters. Paths vary in distance, duration, vertical ascent and difficulty. Some can be polished off in an hour or so, while others are full-day affairs. Typical routes will include sections of hiking and scrambling where protection is not required, coupled with rocky ledges, cliffs and traverses where serious exposure to a deadly fall is protected with fixed cables, stemples and ladders. A chairlift from Cortina accesses some higher routes, while others can be climbed directly from the village, with the lift available for the return trip. Intrepid climbers can link routes to form a multi-day excursion with overnight accommodation in a remote alpine *rifugio*.

A well-trodden route, and one of the more challenging, is Punta Anna in the Tofane Group, which is rated a 5 – the maximum on the scale of via ferrata difficulty – requiring serious climbing skills. It can be done as two separate sections – both with strenuous sustained climbing – or as a longer combined route with 800m of vertical ascent. Gloves – particularly the fingerless cycling type – are helpful and a helmet is essential protection from falling rock, often inadvertently dislodged by climbing partners. Starting at a chairlift in Pietofana just west of Cortina, the path arcs its way up a spiny ridge. A stretch of mountain walking and scrambling on scree leads to the second leg of the route.

Here the jaggedness of the rock provides plenty of handholds and the squared edges offer a firm purchase for your feet. The white-knuckle traverse over the crest of the ridge to the soaring pinnacle of Punta Anna is spine-tingling. The views from this spire over the valley below trick you into feeling that you're on the top of the world – though the summit is still several hours skyward. Following the mountain's crest, you approach the final leg: a spectacular exposed climb up the face of an immense tower, followed by several ladder sections. By the time you hit the summit of Tofana di Mezzo you've earned your cable-car ride back to Cortina, where a sound sleep will ready you to take on a new route tomorrow.

need to know

For one-day climbs, base yourself in Cortina, where a wide range of accommodation is available, or create a longer excursion by exploring connecting routes and staying at scenic mountain huts (*rifugi*). Information about accommodation and services is available from the Cortina d'Ampezzo Tourism Board (Ⓦ www.dolomiti.org). Shops in Cortina cater to independent climbers with maps and equipment rental.

guides and gear Gruppo Guide Alpine (☎ 0436/868-505, Ⓦ www.guidecortina.com) offer guided day-trips around Cortina d'Ampezzo, while Ferrate Tours (☎ 570/675-7835 or 1-866/744-0775, Ⓦ www.ferratetours.com) specialize in personally guided via ferrata adventures, with transport and accommodation included. Climbers can bring their own helmet, harness, gloves and lanyard, or use equipment available from the guide.

when to go The season runs from late June to mid-September, with August bringing fair weather and busy routes.

getting there Fly into Venice and take shuttle transportation to Cortina d'Ampezzo in the Dolomites, about two hours to the north.

suggested reading John Smith and Graham Fletcher, *Via Ferratas of the Italian Dolomites: North, Central and East* (Cicerone). A guide to the popular routes in the Cortina area with schematic climbing maps.

suggested viewing Although the story is set in the Rocky Mountains, the Sylvester Stallone movie *Cliffhanger* (1993) was actually filmed in the Dolomites. The Bond action-thriller *For Your Eyes Only* (1981) and *The Pink Panther* (1963) were also filmed in Cortina d'Ampezzo.

is this for me?

PHYSICAL ✦ ✦ ✦ ✦
A good aerobic challenge

PSYCH ✦ ✦ ✦ ✦
Exposure to serious falls

SKILL ✦ ✦ ✦ ✦ ✦
Requires technique and gear proficiency

WOW! ✦ ✦ ✦ ✦
Exceptional scenery on great routes

Sea kayaking in Iceland 78

ICELAND

REYKJAVIK

Icelandic sagas, the complex and heroic historical tales of Iceland in the tenth century continue to shape and define Iceland, its people, and culture. They describe the struggles and conflicts of those who journeyed by sea to Iceland, Greenland, and beyond. The best-known saga tells of Erik the Red, a Norwegian exiled to Iceland, who was later temporarily banished and settled Greenland, before returning to Iceland. For Erik and his band, survival depended on expert seamanship in the most basic of vessels and an ability to find life's essentials in Arctic waters. Though you won't have to resort to eating a beached whale like they did, nothing can come closer to capturing the spirit of Erik the Red than sea kayaking on Iceland's isolated coast.

Ragged and rugged, Iceland's western shoreline is a mix of 400-meter high sea cliffs, low rocky bluffs, white sand beaches and black sand beaches. On this unforgiving test of seamanship and navigation in open waters and sheltered fjords there's no such thing as help waiting in the wings; you could easily paddle for days without seeing another person.

Though only minutes shy of the Arctic Circle, the coast, ports, and fjords along the west coast of the island remain ice-free year round because of the steady stream of warm Gulf Stream waters. The coastal landscape can even be hospitable, as it reveals patches of lush greenery; but once inland, the land quickly turns to barren uninhabitable highlands. So not surprisingly Iceland's population and culture has developed around the sea. Summers on the coastal waters are characteristically cool and damp, but frequently sparkle with clear and pleasant days. Still, the record high temperature for Reykjavik has never exceeded 25°C, so spraydecks and paddling splash jackets are essential.

The town of Stykkishólmur, located about two hours north of Reykjavik by road, is an ideal jumping-off point for a sea kayaking adventure in the Breiðafjordur Bay with its hundreds of islands. Low-slung Flatey Island has been a year-round outpost since the Middle Ages and the site of a monastery established in 1172. Throughout some of the forty smaller islands surrounding Flatey various auks, skuas, gulls and terns feast in coastal waters and comfortably nest on shore and cliffs, safe from Iceland's solitary land mammal, the arctic fox. The cute puffins you see from the nose of your kayak on nearby rocky islets are also a popular and traditional item on the menu and dinner table. You have plenty of options and flexibility with a sea kayak in Icelandic waters. Short land walks will lead you to ruins of Norse settlements and long-deserted fishing communities. Charming fishing villages, the cultural backbone of the country, line the coast.

fire and ice

Iceland is a paradox, often better known for its heat than its ice. Formed by eons of volcanic activity, this tiny island nation is covered by less ice than you might expect considering its frigid location at the edge of the Arctic Circle. Volcanic ridges, hot springs, and geysers bisect the island and reveal its superheated geologic history.

Lacking the drama of glowing hot lava, evidence of volcanic activity can be easily seen in the abundant displays of spurting steam through various cracks in the surface. Iceland's most famous geyser, Great Geysir in Haukadalur, regularly shoots a sixty-meter tall column of boiling hot water into the air – with displays lasting as long as an hour. No surprise that the word geyser is Icelandic, meaning "to gush."

Iceland's subterranean volcanic activity generates warm rivers that in places create a verdant landscape of moss and ferns. Of course, residents have discovered that Iceland's inner heat is also surprisingly useful. The heat was originally used by Icelandic natives for washing clothes, cooking, and baking bread. Today, geothermal heat is used to warm homes and is converted into electricity, providing an endless source of renewable and inexpensive energy.

Active nearby volcanoes continue to create new real estate. In November 1963, an underwater eruption south of Iceland pushed enough lava to the surface to produce a new island mass, which was named Surtsey after the Norse god of fire, Surtur.

need to know

Sea kayaking in populated areas and the protected waters near Reykjavik is an easy and enjoyable recreational activity. But a journey to remote and wild coastal areas is serious business. You'll need to be a strong paddler, have solid navigation skills and be familiar with the regions changing weather patterns. Lacking proficiency in any one of these areas, stick with a trusted and experienced guide.

guides and gear Sea Kayak Iceland (☎ 354 690-3877, Ⓦ www. seakayakiceland.com) operates on the west coast from Flatey, Stykkishólmur and Reykjavik and offers tours and instruction all over Iceland. They have a fleet of both one- and two-man sea kayaks.

when to go The best time for sea kayaking is mid-June to mid-August when days are long and temperatures are most favorable.

getting there Fly into Reykjavik's Keflavik Airport where kayaking destinations on the west coast are easily accessible by car or shuttle.

suggested reading David Roberts and Jon Krakauer (photographer) *Iceland: Land of the Sagas* (Villard). Two first-rate adventurers examine Iceland through its literary heritage of sagas.

suggested viewing In searching for dramatic outdoor scenery, filmmakers have gone to Iceland to shoot portions of films such as *Flags of our Fathers* (2006), *Die Another Day* (2002), and *Lara Croft: Tomb Raider* (2001).

is this for me?

PHYSICAL ✦ ✦ ✦ ✦ ✦
Upper torso strength for paddling

PSYCH ✦ ✦ ✦ ✦ ✦
Open cold water

SKILL ✦ ✦ ✦ ✦ ✦
Have wet exit and solid rescue skills

WOW! ✦ ✦ ✦ ✦ ✦
Great scenery, waterfowl, marine life

In the water your wildlife encounters will be dramatic and on a large scale. Seeing a humpback whale, with a nose to tail span of 15m and tipping the scales at nearly 35,000kg, from the seat of your slender five-meter sea kayak is an awe-inspiring and heart-stopping occasion. They come to Iceland in the summer to feed on krill and small fish before returning to warmer waters in autumn to breed, completing an annual migration cycle of over 25,000km. You're likely to see surfacing minke whales, and though they're just half the size of a humpback, they can still command your attention on the water. Orcas, bottlenose whales, sperm whales, and pilot whales also frequent Icelandic waters and summer sightings are not uncommon. Nearer to shore, you'll spot sea lions both in the water and sunning on the shore.

After a long day of ocean paddling, spending time on terra firma is appealing. It may be tempting to gobble down a meal and snuggle into your warm down bag, but don't forget to look heavenward. With summertime bringing twenty hours of sunlight and a fairly constant cloud cover, a star-speckled night is a rarity. Even rarer, but definitely worth the effort, is a glimpse of the ethereal aurora borealis pulsing overhead. Before bounding back into your kayak the next morning, you may want to explore some of the remarkable landscape that makes up the coastal rim of Iceland. Geysers, fumaroles and hot springs bring a nice change of scenery and temperature, and some of Iceland's geothermal features can be found right on the coast with several thermal pools that can be accessed by kayak.

Along this wild coastline the weather can change unexpectedly and it demands that you be alert and constantly aware of your surroundings. To disregard a changing weather system on the open water could be treacherous, and even in protected waters you'll want to know that your can make it to shore safely and quickly if things turn nasty. Once on shore, you'll camp near the beach or on an escarpment where the wind never dies, the waves never cease lapping, and the sun never sets.

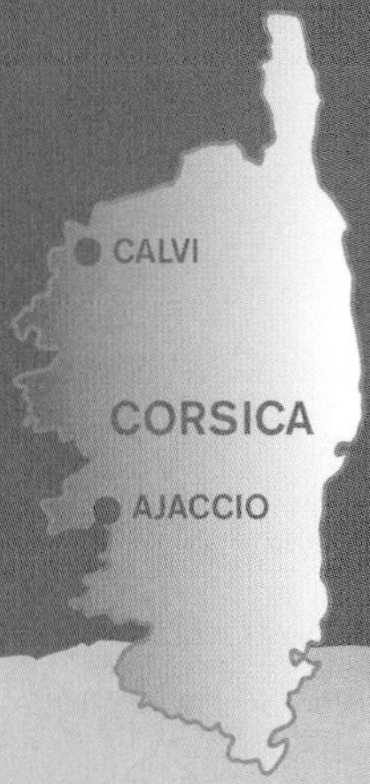

79 Trekking the GR20

>> Know a traditional mountain way of life

CALVI

CORSICA

AJACCIO

Of all the Grand Randonnée, or "great walks" – Europe's network of long-distance walking paths – Corsica's GR20 is widely considered the most challenging and visually arresting. This will come as no surprise to those who know Corsica, Homer's "mountain in the sea". Steep, rugged terrain and striking scenery are this Mediterranean island's defining features, and the trail that diagonally bisects its mountainous core delivers inspiring views along an unspoiled, often demanding route. Since no Corsican peak is more than twenty-five miles from the coast, many of those vistas sweep down valleys and across ridges to the Mediterranean Sea.

With the famously mild climate and elegant sun-soaked beaches of the French Riviera just a hundred miles away, it's easy to underestimate the severity of the route and the unforgiving nature of the distinctly alpine environment

With the famously mild climate and elegant sun-soaked beaches of the French Riviera just a hundred miles away, it's easy to underestimate the severity of the route and the unforgiving nature of the distinctly alpine environment. Only a third of those who start the GR20 each season complete all sixteen *étapes*, or stages, and many hikers have started a June day in shorts and a light shirt only to ascend 450m and be pelted with hailstones while traversing a snowfield. The trail reflects the island's jagged topography as it follows high ridges, descends into deep chasms, and curls its way around granite outcroppings. Although the trail requires no technical climbing skills, it is uneven, precipitous, and stony, and demands surefooted balance and respect.

Much of Corsica is covered by a dense growth of aromatic lavender, myrtle, rosemary, and heather called *maquis* – which Corsica-born Napoleon said he could smell while exiled on Elba – and it is through the sweet pungency of this sun-kissed brush that much of the trek winds. Though the Mediterranean is never far from view, you'll spend much of your days traversing the island's upper reaches where you'll come to know a traditional mountain way of life. Over their 4000-year history, Corsicans have migrated to the mountains to avoid coastal invasions, to graze sheep, or simply to enjoy summer in cool grassy meadows. You'll see rustic shepherds who make their own cheese and converse in the native Corsican tongue, then cordially change into French when you approach. You'll also cross paths with the island's original inhabitants, reddish-brown mouflon sheep with curled and spiraling horns that perch on rocky crags, while pigs and wild boar roam freely on the lower elevations.

If you're intent on hiking the length of the GR20, start at the hamlet of Bavella under a cluster of pink-granite pinnacles. Though the route can be walked either northward or southward, by starting in the south you'll have the trek's most ruggedly scenic sections awaiting you at the end – just rewards for the toll they'll exact on your lungs and legs. On a fifteen-day trek you'll pass through forests of pine and chestnut, across green spongy meadows, and along spring-fed streams and waterfalls. Ridgelines are crowned with wind-mangled juniper and bedded with fragrant laurel. As you move north, the magnitude of the mountains intensifies, slopes steepen, and you come face-to-face with Monte Cinto, at 2706m the highest peak in Corsica. The challenge and scenic drama culminates at the Cirque de Solitude, a wildly craggy bowl of granite with stark, sheer faces, and shingled slopes. It can be quite intimidating as you stand gingerly on the lip and wonder how you'll ever make in through alive. Fixed cables provide protection on some of the steeper inclines, but you'll still need a careful, sure-footed approach to make it up and back down again.

If the GR20 is Western Europe's toughest hiking route, it's also one of the more crowded, drawing an estimated 17,000 hikers each season. With no wilderness camping permitted, the refuges, which can accommodate forty to fifty trekkers, regularly fill to capacity. Rather than race through exquisite mountainscapes in the hopes of beating the crowd to the next refuge, consider a self-guided option that provides pre-arranged lodging. You'll stay in conveniently located camps, refuges, and shepherds' cabins, enjoy prepared meals in the evenings, and appreciate the social aspects of the adventure. Whether through the island's gastronomy or its people, you'll see firsthand the shared respect for *"l'humeur de la nature,"* or nature's will – a respect that will surely have found its way into your heart well before your trek is over.

need to know

The route is surprisingly well defined, with red-and-white painted waymarks every six meters – but stray from the waymarks and you can very quickly find yourself in trouble. Water sources are marked on the map with blue teardrops, and it's not necessary to burden yourself with more than a couple liters of water at any time. While your average daily elevation will hover around 1500m, you can expect to climb and descend 1000 vertical meters on any given day, so you should be in good physical shape and able to walk comfortably and confidently uphill with a pack weighing 10 to 15kg.

guides and gear Tour Aventure offers a wide range of self-guided and small-group guided options including pre-arranged accommodation, meals, airport transfers and luggage transfer services (℡ +04.95.50.72.75, Ⓦ www.tour-aventure.com/gb). This supported hiking approach, similar to hiking from hut to hut in the Alps, allows you to travel light without a sleeping bag, tent, stove or food. You'll want sturdy trail shoes or hiking boots, trekking poles and a small daypack to carry snacks, a camera, raingear and a layer of warmth, in case some unexpected cool or wet weather blows in.

when to go You can start hiking in early June as the snowfields are melting and expect to find a trail and accommodation through September. July and August offer the warmest weather, but draw the largest crowds.

getting there From Ajaccio's Campo Dell'Oro airport on the island's western side, take a two-hour shuttle to the Bavella trailhead in the south. When you've reached the northern terminus consider returning to the mainland from the convenient Calvi Airport.

suggested reading Paddy Dillon, *GR20 – Corsica: The High-level Route* (Cicerone Press). A handy trekking guide with maps, photos and detailed route descriptions.

is this for me?

PHYSICAL ✦ ✦ ✦ ✦ ✦
Long distances over steep terrain

PSYCH ✦ ✦ ✦ ✦ ✦
Requires commitment and emotional stamina

SKILL ✦ ✦ ✦ ✦ ✦
Some routefinding and mountain navigation

WOW! ✦ ✦ ✦ ✦ ✦
Stunning scenery and landscapes

Mountain biking in Cappadocia

>> Rock cones and fairy chimneys

For most mountain bikers, the exhilaration of hurtling along a primitive trail or single track, the air filled with the aroma of moist earth and fir needles, is usually enough to get the adrenaline pumping. But in Cappadocia the usual thrills are amplified by a dazzling natural landscape: instead of a forest of aspen or spruce you'll be riding through stands of rock cones, spires and pillars known as "fairy chimneys." And there are plenty of man-made wonders too: monasteries with frescoed walls, Byzantine art, and fascinating cave houses. One glimpse at this fantasy landscape and you'll know you're in for a treat.

In ancient times, Cappadocia (cap-ah-DOKE-ya), a mountainous region in central Turkey, covered a much larger expanse of the Anatolian Plateau, but today it is generally considered an area within the Nevşehir province, centering on the valleys of Göreme and Ürgüp. It's a land of exceptional natural beauty, dotted with fantastic pinnacles, caves and minaret-like rock formations. Thanks to its distinctive landscape, the region has become a mountain biking hotspot, playing host to the European Mountain Biking Championships and attracting enthusiasts to its annual international mountain biking festival. It's also a favorite destination for mountain bikers worldwide, who thrill at the thought of racing along trails that have been compacted over four thousand years. Although you're in a mountainous region with elevations ranging from 1000m to 1700m, the trails aren't brutal or jarring, so a full suspension bike really isn't necessary. The air is invigorating and clear days are easy to come by, providing the perfect setting for magical rides: here you'll roll alongside streams, down tight canyons, and over low-lying mountain passes. You'll dart and skirt round surrealistic rock forms – some soaring to 45m in height – and on a typical day lay down over eighty percent of your tracks on off-road trails.

But Cappadocia's appeal goes beyond its extraordinary scenery and geology. The region has been a cultural, trade and military crossroads since the Bronze Age, when Hittites ruled the roost and established it as a trading point along the Silk Road. Successive waves of invaders, from the Persians to Alexander the Great, the Romans and later, Arab warlords, forced the region's inhabitants to seek refuge in caves and underground. The region's true fascination lies in its human history: how its inhabitants have used the stone to create monumental, rock-hewn churches, cave houses, monasteries

Cappadocian cave houses

Cappadocian legend says that every once in a while a fairy falls in love with a man. She emerges from her tall, rock-hewn "fairy chimney" and takes the man she loves back to her home, and he is never seen again. While the naturally formed fairy chimneys – conical structures with a rock cap – are steeped in legend, other tales surround Cappadocia's man-made structures. In the high conical rocks are networks of caves dug out by hand from the soft porous rock called tuff stone: a melting pot of ancient civilizations, cultures and religions developed by people who shared a distinctive way of life – as cave dwellers. Hermits came to this desolate area and dug simple cave houses with built-in benches and tables carved right out of the rock. Monks created elaborate monasteries within the tall spires, with intricate arches, columns, pillars and labyrinthine stairways that led to a single door opening to the outside world – but most cave houses were simple, functional and unadorned. Their diminutive size leads you to believe that these dwellings harbour gnomes, hobbits or other impish troglodytes – until you discover that their (fully-grown) inhabitants are among the most warm and hospitable people you could encounter.

need to know

With so much to see and do, both on and off the trail, Cappadocia is well-suited to mountain bikers of all levels of skill and endurance, including couples and families. On a multi-day trip you can stay in a different village each night, enjoying comfortable inns and cave hotels, and delectable Turkish cuisine. The tourist office in Nevşehir (☎ 0384/213 3659) is a good source of information on local hotels.

guides and gear Custom and group mountain biking trips of varying length and difficulty are offered by Argeus Tourism and Travel, (☎ 0384/341 4688, ⓦ www. cappadociaexclusive.com), located in Ürgüp. Prices include meals, accommodation, guiding, the services of a support vehicle and luggage transport. Rental of front suspension bicycles is available, but if you're a serious mountain biker on a longer trip you may prefer to bring your own bike.

when to go With comfortable riding temperatures, May, June, September and October are ideal months for a visit. July and August bring searing temperatures, while from November to April you're likely to be faced with rain and even snow. The international mountain biking festival takes place in late June or July.

getting there Daily flights from Istanbul serve Kayseri. Ürgüp, in the heart of Cappadocia, lies 70km southwest of Kayseri.

suggested reading Patrick Leigh Fermor, *A Time to Keep Silence* (New York Review Books Classics). One of the great travel writers explores monastic life in Cappadocia.

is this for me?

PHYSICAL ✦ ✦ ✦ ✦ ✦
Good aerobic riding in hills

PSYCH ✦ ✦ ✦ ✦ ✦
Some drop-offs

SKILL ✦ ✦ ✦ ✦ ✦
Basic mountain biking skills

WOW! ✦ ✦ ✦ ✦ ✦
Visually captivating setting

carved out of tufa and entire underground cities. Incredibly, the whole valley is honeycombed with underground dwellings. Mountain biking in Cappadocia never gets too strenuous or exhausting because you seldom go more than a few minutes without spotting something so intriguing that you need to dismount and explore. Your shutter finger will get as much exercise as your legs.

Spend a day exploring the Ihlara Valley in the neighboring Askaray province, the first of several Cappadocian sites where fourth-century Christians sought refuge from persecution under Emperor Diocletian's edict. Following the river through the 14-kilometer long valley, you'll see over a hundred ancient churches carved out of the volcanic stone dotting the gorge. In the valley, and throughout Cappadocia, you'll ride in the shade of apricot, walnut and Russian olive trees. You'll see very few hikers, and your bike will give you access to some of the remoter sites not swamped by large groups of visitors. Although the area has a long history of human habitation, the trails are surprisingly primitive; expect some steep uphill sections near the end of the valley.

The Red Valley and the adjoining Rose Valley to the east of Ilhara form the heart of Cappadocia, yet they're surprisingly removed from the tourist traffic. A single track winds through beautiful villages cut in cream-colored stone, and past vineyards, churches and pigeon houses; pigeons have historically been a source of food and fertilizer in Cappadocia and are provided for with thousands of man-made lofts hewn into the soft tufa. In the nearby Göreme Valley you can pedal your way through the Göreme National Park, an ethereal land of fairy chimneys and a UNESCO World Heritage site, then park your bike to wander through the open-air museum with ten Byzantine churches adorned with colorful tenth-century frescoes. After a full day of riding, walking and exploring four thousand years of Cappadocian history, you can check in to a luxurious cave hotel, feast on authentic tandoori dishes slow-cooked in a clay pot – and still have time for an evening ride.

FORT
WILLIAM

SCOTLAND

UK

81 Climbing Ben Nevis

>> A spirited, dangerous peak

In Gaelic mythology, the winter witch, Cailleach, holds the spring nymph captive over the cave where rises the tallest peak in the British Isles. On most days Ben Nevis (1344m) wears a crown of clouds that hints at its regal stature and does little to hide its rugged grandeur. Once in a while, on days of rare clarity, the sky will open and the mountain gives its guests a view of distant Highland peaks and valleys. Aside from that rare clear day, as you ascend the rocky summit of the Ben, you may feel like the winter witch holds her dominion well beyond the spring thaw.

taking the Ben's temperature

Though few people know it – even those who climb Ben Nevis – at the summit of Britain's highest mountain lie the ruins of a meteorological observatory. Established by the Scottish Meteorological Society (SMS) in 1883, the observatory was staffed for twenty years by weather observers who lived in the summit station year round to obtain weather data. Ben Nevis was considered an ideal spot for an observatory because the mountain is located near the west coast of Scotland, directly in the path of storms inbound from the Atlantic.

This location is also the site of extreme weather conditions. A sturdy building was required for observations because of the harsh weather atop the summit, and trying to obtain information proved difficult. Because temperatures were often well below freezing, instruments would ice over, making manual observations of weather necessary, and only two stoves provided heat – an open one in the kitchen and a closed one in the office. Supplies were brought up by pack ponies that trudged along a rough-made bridle path, and men faced high speed, icy winds to reach the top. After the first heavy winter with many feet of snow, a tower was erected to allow access to the building for the following winter in case the building became completely covered by snow. All of these challenges made determining weather information difficult and the data collected did not seem particularly noteworthy at the time. In later years, however, the weather data that was obtained proved invaluable and is still today the most detailed source of weather information for British mountains.

The Highlands' down-to-earth culture and mythical tales makes Ben Nevis one of the top draws for UK adventurers. John Keats climbed the mountain in 1818 and compared the ascent to "mounting ten St Pauls without the convenience of a staircase." No doubt many have indignantly said to themselves, "if a Romantic poet with tuberculosis can climb it, then so can I!" And so they come – 100,000 climbers in any given year – a seemingly never-ending stream of summer traffic. Some are shod in sturdy hiking boots, while others wear flip-flops. Still, don't let the Ben's popularity and the questionable footwear of some of its hikers fool you – this is a respectable climb, that's been known to go haywire very quickly. Although the mountain may seem tame when compared to the heights of those on any continent, it's a spirited peak with its own set of dangers. With the Gulf Stream and the Atlantic Ocean bringing a constant supply of mild and cool air, storms and even blizzards are common occurrences. Gale-force winds blow an average of 261 days per year, and the summit receives 4350mm of annual rainfall, over twice as much as falls at the base. And even if the weather is mild at the base, treat the Ben as if it could get angry at any moment – it often does.

The most popular route to the top is the Pony Track built in 1883 to supply the meteorological observatory. The trailhead is just 20m above sea level in Achintee on the east side of Glen Nevis about 2km from the town of Fort William. A steep initial ascent has several stream crossings made easy by footbridges and takes you to 570m and a saddle between Ben Nevis and a lower hill to the west called Meall an t-Suidhe (pronounced "MEL-an-tee" and meaning "lump of the seat"). Beyond the saddle, a scree track with a single switchback up the rocky west flank captures the remaining 700m of vertical gain.

While about three-quarters of those who summit take the Pony Track, there are also other routes to choose from. Next in popularity is the more challenging hike that starts at Torlundy just 5km to the northeast of Fort William, following a path along the Allt a' Mhuilinn before ascending the Carn Mòr Dearg. Although it involves some scrambling and a bit of exposure, you have the advantage of viewing the cliffs on the north face which you'll miss along the Pony

Set a stout heart to a steep hillside
Scottish proverb

Six hours is a decent amount of time to allot for this activity in the summer. If you are doing the mountain summit hike you will do just fine with a map and compass. If you are planning to do some climbing, you should contact a guide company and talk to some local experts.

guides and gear Alan Kimber West Coast Mountain Guides (☎ 1397 700-451, Ⓦ www. westcoast-mountainguides.co.uk) is located in Fort William and provides individual and group instruction and guided climbing programs. They can supply all necessary climbing equipment, including boots, crampons, ice axes, ropes, helmets and hardware, and even offer bunkhouse accommodation onsite.

when to go The mountain can be hiked year round, with June to September providing the most comfortable hike. Even in the summer there is no guarantee that you will get sunshine and a clear sky, and it can be very windy at times. Winter requires more gear and planning.

getting there Trains and buses provide transport for the trip from Glasgow to Fort William in the west Scottish Highlands.

suggested reading *Ben Nevis: Scottish Mountaineering Club Climbers' Guide* (Scottish Mountaineering Trust). One of the most authoritative climbing guides to Ben Nevis. Alan Kimber, *Winter Climbs: Ben Nevis and Glen Coe* (Cicerone). A great guide to Ben Nevis and surrounding areas.

Track. On the kidney bean-shaped summit of Ben Nevis no commanding views are promised, since its clear only one day in ten. Still, it's a sociable place where you can enjoy a packed lunch with hundreds of other summer hikers. Leaving the summit on any route other than the Pony Track can be decidedly tricky. The north face of the mountain is riven with sheer cliffs and buttresses; you must have a map and compass and be competent in their use.

Summer hikes are comparatively straightforward affairs, but the logistics of a winter outing give a summit bid in that season a more serious tone. Knowing how to use a compass and map will aid in a safe trip no matter the time of year, but in winter a compass is crucial. The Ben's famously brutal winter weather, and the challenging nature of an alpine climb requiring crampons tends to ward off all but the hardy, but that means you'll also have a more intimate experience Outside of the summer months visibility turns very poor in fog and cloud. In these situations the mountain typically claims two or three lives per year, often as climbers get lost and wander off a cliff or walk too far out on a cornice.

If rock climbing is your game, you'll discover a variety of difficulty levels on the 700m cliff faces on the north side of Ben Nevis. All grades are catered for, and no one will go away without having something that pushes their levels to some degree. World-class ice and mixed climbs abound. With beautiful buttresses, arêtes, and cracks dotting the north face, the mountain stands as a worthy proving ground for even bigger technical alpine climbs.

is this for me?

PHYSICAL ◆ ◆ ◆
Good endurance for steep ascent

PSYCH ◆ ◆ ◆
Weather can obscure route

SKILL ◆ ◆ ◆
Route-finding skills essential in off-season

WOW! ◆ ◆ ◆
On a rare clear day the views are amazing

Hiking the Haute Route

82

FRANCE
SWITZERLAND
ZERMATT
CHAMONIX
ITALY

>> **From Mont Blanc to the Matterhorn**

In the classic story
Heidi – still as integral
to Switzerland's national
identity as fondue and
gadgety knives – the plucky
alpine heroine invites her
sickly cousin Clara to leave
Frankfurt and come to the
Alps to witness their beauty
and enjoy their clean,
mountain air. As Clara rises
from her wheelchair in the
curative embrace of an alpine
meadow, Heidi's friend
Peter pushes the chair off
the mountain, never to be
needed again. The scene is
a perfect expression of the
Alps' effect on the body, mind
and soul.

Even though the Alps have been settled, farmed and otherwise tamed for over ten thousand years, only within the last two hundred have they become a playground for adventurous Europeans. Considering the popularity of mountain sports like hiking, mountaineering and skiing, it's no surprise that most of the range has been thoroughly explored. Still, plenty of restorative power remains, as numerous villages in deep, glacial valleys, larch woods, wildflower-dotted meadows and high mountain passes will prove to you.

With thousands of miles of trails crisscrossing the Alps as they arc through France, Switzerland, Italy, Austria, Germany and Slovenia, you could easily spend a lifetime hiking here. But the Haute Route, linking Chamonix, France to Zermatt, Switzerland, delivers more scenic splendour in one achievable trek than any other alpine walk. It takes you through some of the highest hikeable terrain in Europe, passes beneath ten of the Alps' twelve highest peaks and connects the tallest, Mont Blanc (4808m), with the Matterhorn (4478m). Weaving through pine forests sprinkled with wild mushrooms and berries, you'll frequently emerge onto grassy slopes where herders graze their cows, goats and sheep throughout the summer.

The Haute Route, or "high route", was pioneered on an 1861 expedition to establish a trail from Chamonix to Zermatt over a series of glacier passes in the Pennine Alps, the sub-range that forms much of the border between Switzerland and Italy. Today the route is both a popular spring ski-mountaineering tour and a 180-kilometer summer trek known as the "Walker's Haute Route". The trek requires no technical mountaineering skills, avoids the high glacier crossings and is well suited to healthy hikers who can walk for twelve to fourteen days while gaining nearly 14,000m in total elevation.

The journey links remote alpine hamlets with wild corries and high meadow, crossing eleven passes along the way. A network of huts offers hikers simple accommodation, hearty meals and even the occasional hot shower. You'll hike for days without having to carry a tent, sleeping bag, stove or food. But while eschewing the very thought of a cable lift or a cosy chalet hotel is certainly an option for the purist, it is not obligatory. You'll have plenty of flexibility along the way and you'll likely exercise options such as these on your first rain day.

Although the Haute Route is bidirectional, most hikers start in Chamonix since that's how the guidebooks are written; this also puts the morning sun at hikers' backs as they ascend the steepest mountain slopes and passes. From the base of France's Mont Blanc you'll make a quick ascent past the *aguilles*, the dramatic needles that glisten in front of the mountain's white dome, to a refuge at Col de Balme, the pass at the unmarked border between France and Switzerland. The remainder of the Haute Route lies in Switzerland, and though Mont Blanc will be behind you, a string of equally illustrious peaks awaits.

Considering the concentration of ski lifts, runs and utility roads in the area, the Haute Route does an admirable job of avoiding them, especially along the forest path between the deep valley village of Le Châble and the lofty Cabane de Mont Fort mountain hut, which smoothly skirts the immense Verbier resort. The path brings you to a rugged, mountainous stretch where the three-peaked Grand Combin massif crowns the southern skyline and where your chances of seeing ibex and chamois are excellent. Both species are happiest on remote alpine slopes, where the chamois, a goat-like bovid, can ascend 1000m in fifteen minutes – something you'd be hard-pressed to do in three hours.

glacial retreat

Gazing into the deep blue hue, zigzagging crevasses and beautiful run-off streams of a glacier, it's hard to imagine that it's something your grandchildren might never see. Alpine glaciers are quickly shrinking, or retreating, due to increases in global warming at high altitudes. Retreating glaciers have created or changed existing lakes and rivers, altered landscapes and affected plant and animal life in drastic ways. Shrinking glacial mass, for instance, means run-off to some rivers has dropped 65 to 80 percent, greatly reducing their fish populations. Just as ice cubes melt faster and faster as their ratio of surface area to volume increases, glaciers shrink increasingly faster as they retreat. Scientists predict that most of today's 160,000 glaciers will be considerably smaller, if not gone altogether, within the next hundred years.

need to know

The Haute Route can be hiked in its entirety from Chamonix to Zermatt or divided into shorter sections. Trains and postbuses serve all valleys along the route, so taking a rest day or skipping a stage is always possible. Hikers typically walk five to sseven hours per day.

guides and gear Several operators offer guided treks. The Adventure 100 (☎ 1-801/226-9026 or 1-800/532-9488, ⓦ www.theadventure100.com) offers small-group and custom treks on the Haute Route, the Matterhorn Circuit and other classic alpine walks, with all meals, accommodation, and luggage transfers included. This leaves you with just a small daypack for water, snacks and raingear.

when to go Mountain passes are often covered with snow well into June. The best conditions are from mid-July to early September, with August generally offering favourable weather but heavy crowds.

getting there Start in Chamonix, France, served by train and private shuttle (2hr) from Geneva, Switzerland.

suggested reading Kev Reynolds, *Chamonix−Zermatt: The Walker's Haute Route* (Cicerone). A step-by-step guide with maps, elevation profiles and detailed daily itineraries.

is this for me?

PHYSICAL ◆ ◆ ◆ ◆ ◆
Steep ascents, strenuous mountain trails

PSYCH ◆ ◆ ◆ ◆ ◆
Occasionally dicey alpine weather

SKILL ◆ ◆ ◆ ◆ ◆
No technical climbing required

WOW! ◆ ◆ ◆ ◆ ◆
Superb mountain scenery

As you pass beneath the snout of a once-giant glacier that filled the rocky bowl known as the Grand Desert, observe the exposed moraine – barren and rubbly evidence of glacial retreat. The next day, take a relaxing morning stroll along the western shore of Lac des Dix, the snaking reservoir behind the Grande Dixence Dam, before an hour of boulder-hopping to rocky Riedmatten Pass, the toughest on the route. Descending the Forcletta Pass into the quiet valley of the Turtmanntal, you'll begin to hear new greetings from people you encounter, from "bonjour" to "guten tag" or the Switzerdeutsch "grüezi". Gruben, the first German-speaking waypoint, is a seasonal hamlet where, gazing across a meadow at a distant object, you'll be unsure whether you're seeing a horse or an exceptionally large European red deer.

A steep ascent to the Augstbordpass, used as a trade route since medieval times, leads to a sweeping view of the last valley, the Mattertal, but the ultimate prize of the Haute Route is still a day away. Finally, as you climb slowly out of the valley to Zermatt, you'll be blessed with the mesmerizing sight of the legendary Matterhorn – the perfect ending to a magnificent alpine trek.

Cross-country ski touring in Norway

>> Self-reliance on the Hardangervidda Plateau

NORWAY

In Norway, skiing is more than a sport, more than a means of transport – it's a way of life. With a network of nearly 350 mountain huts linking 18,000km of trails across some of the world's most impressive ski terrain, Norway offers great cross-country adventures for aspiring and experienced skiers alike. It's not just the excellent ski conditions that draw enthusiasts year after year: even in the depths of winter, with the land transformed into a harsh wilderness, you'll find security and camaraderie in the most extensive system of trails and huts in the world. As you warm your toes by the log fire in a mountain hut at the end of the day, you'll understand why cross-country skiing is such an integral and enjoyable part of Norwegian life.

The word "ski" comes from the Norwegian meaning "stick of wood."

Norwegian gold: Bjorn Daehlie

Fans arrived in droves, waiting for hours in subzero temperatures, just to catch a glimpse of passing skiers in the cross-country relay of Lillehammer '94. With Norway as the host country, parades of fluttering blue crosses, outlined in white on a red background, were everywhere to be seen. The birthplace of skiing, where a quarter of the population are avid cross-country skiers, has long dominated cross-country competition – a tribute to their national pride and toughness. Norway has won more Winter Olympic gold medals – and more medals in total – than any other country.

It's no surprise, then, that Norway has also produced arguably one of the greatest Winter Olympians of all time. Bjorn Daehlie, who reigned supreme in the 1994 Olympics, won twelve medals, of which eight were gold: more than any other Winter Olympics athlete. During the 1990s, the press compared his fame in Norway to that of Michael Jordan in the United States. He even had his own trademark – more often than not, he finished the race by falling down in exhaustion. In Daehlie's last Olympic race, at the 1998 Olympics in Nagano, he skied for over two hours before crossing the finish line in first place. He then collapsed into the snow, and more than five minutes passed before he was able to get to his feet again. Daehlie understood that in a sport as grueling as this, winning means holding nothing back.

Intrepid skiers can travel the entire length of the country on skis – but ask any Norwegian to pick one unmissable cross-country ski tour and they'd name the Hardangervidda. Located on Northern Europe's biggest expanse of mountain plateau, the region encompasses Norway's largest national park. Most of the plateau is above 1000m, placing it clearly above the tree-line, and snow is all but guaranteed from December to mid-May. Midwinter travelers can still expect bitterly cold temperatures and fearsome winds to sweep across the treeless landscape; in January, short days, fresh snow and daytime highs that never make it above -15°C can slow your pace to less than 2km per hour. But spring ushers in longer days, warmer weather, and more stable snow conditions that transform the Hardangervidda into a scenic wonderland, attracting enthusiasts from throughout Norway and much of Europe.

The classic crossing of the Hardangervidda normally begins with a train journey from Oslo to Finse on the northern side of the plateau, and traversing the plateau to Haukliseter at the south end. Much of the central plateau is a matrix of lakes and streams, providing plenty of level terrain. The south and west offer more in the way of rolling hills and mountain ridges, but overall, the slopes are gentle and routes follow the safest and simplest lines. A typical day involves about six hours on the trail and

There is no bad weather, only bad clothing.
Norwegian saying

covers about 20km, making a complete crossing of the Hardangervidda achievable in five days. Because of its elevation, Hardangervidda has become the southernmost habitat and breeding ground for many Arctic and sub-Arctic species. As you plow through pristine expanses of snow, you're likely to encounter the local wildlife: the plateau is home to the largest herd of wild reindeer in Europe, as well as colonies of lemmings, Arctic foxes and snowy owls.

Arctic explorer Roald Amundsen twice attempted a winter crossing of the Hardangervidda and was twice defeated by weather, forcing him to turn back (later polar expeditions proved more successful). Crossing the Hardangervidda is not an adventure for beginners. You need solid winter backcountry travel experience, a proven level of aerobic conditioning, self-reliance and the stamina to keep going under demanding weather conditions. Also essential are a pair of light touring skis, a modest-sized pack, and adequate winterwear; a basic level of technical skills will serve you well as you strengthen and refine your ski technique along the way. Under favorable spring conditions and with prior navigation experience, route-finding is not too daunting, and wands mark the route to the next hut. If this is your first time in the area, you should opt for a guided ski tour which will eliminate any route-finding concerns.

Bedding down in one of the surprisingly efficient and comfortable huts, run by the Norwegian Touring Association (DNT), is one of the pleasures of a visit to the Hardangervidda. In winter, unmanned huts have beds, blankets, pillows, wood stoves and canned food, while melted snow provides the water supply – all you need is a sleep sheet or bag liner. The honor system is one of the most appealing aspects of hut life: when you depart, you tally up the number of nights and the items you've used from the communal pantry, sign a credit card slip and leave it in the payment box. During spring most of the huts are manned. Some are small, with only four to six beds, while others accommodate up to forty and offer comforts such as hot showers, drying rooms and delicious meals. A night's rest will have you revived and ready to take on another day of physical challenge and scenic rewards in this inspiring winterscape.

need to know

Mountain huts in Norway are operated by the Norwegian Touring Association (Den Norske Turistforening, or DNT; ☎ 40 00 18 68, ⓦ www.turistforeningen.no) and its 55 local affiliates. Membership allows access to staffed and unstaffed mountain huts and offers reduced accommodation rates.

guides and gear UK-based Haymark Holidays (☎ 870/950 9800 in UK, 1-800/843-4272 in US, ⓦ www.waymark holidays.com) offers guided ski tours on the Hardangervidda including transportation from Oslo to Finse, hut accommodation and meals. Necessary equipment includes waxable metal-edged touring skis, climbing skins, a sheet sleeping bag and a daypack. The cold weather combined with the wind speed on the plateau can result in a severe windchill factor: take extra precautions for dehydration and frostbite.

when to go March and April offer longer days, warmer temperatures and the best conditions for a hut-to-hut tour. To avoid the crowds, steer clear of Easter week, when Norwegians flock to the plateau for reliably perfect skiing conditions and enthusiastic crowds at the huts.

getting there Fly into Oslo, from where trains provide access to both the northern and southern sides of the Hardangervidda Plateau.

suggested reading Constance Roos, *Walking in Norway* (Cicerone). Once the snow melts, these mountains and plateaus are great for walking, too.

is this for me?

PHYSICAL ✦ ✦ ✦ ✦ ✦
Demands aerobic conditioning and endurance

PSYCH ✦ ✦ ✦ ✦ ✦
Remote area with adverse weather

SKILL ✦ ✦ ✦ ✦ ✦
Backcountry ski experience recommended

WOW! ✦ ✦ ✦ ✦ ✦
Beauty, solitude and challenge

Climbing Mont Blanc

84

>> La Dame Blanche

FRANCE

SWITZERLAND

MONT BLANC

ITALY

Dragons in the Alps? Chronicles from the eighteenth century are replete with tales of monsters lurking in caves and surprising hikers, soldiers and wandering merchants. Even a nineteenth-century German physicist confirmed the reports after exploring the Mont Blanc Massif. Such accounts fanned travelers' long-smouldering fears and convinced them of the mountains' supernatural powers. Residents of Chamonix, at the base of Mont Blanc, invited the Bishop of Geneva to exorcise the advancing Mer de Glace glacier, which threatened farms and villages in the valley. Not until the "golden age of exploration" in the mid-nineteenth century did an onslaught of climbers, in many cases wealthy Brits on their "Grand Tour", spend enough time in the Alps to debunk the dragon stories.

Dragons or no, it took a hefty cash prize to convince early adventurers to attempt Mont Blanc's summit. In 1786 Pacard and Balmat made the first successful climb, generally considered the earliest instance of alpine mountaineering. But subsequent expeditions were few and far between, and it wasn't until the popularization of guided climbing and the establishment of mountain huts in the twentieth century that Mont Blanc's 4808-meter summit, the highest in Western Europe, became accessible to a wide range of climbers. Today the ill-defined massif is one of the continent's most frequently climbed mountains, with some thirty thousand people pursuing the summit every year.

On his honeymoon in 1886, future US President Theodore Roosevelt climbed Mont Blanc. Four years later, Achille Ratti, the future Pope Pius XI, also made the ascent.

A climb to the top can follow any of the dozen or so established ascents, although the most reliable and popular is the Goûter Route, commonly known as the "standard route". From the town of Les Houches, just south of Chamonix, take the Bellevue lift and transfer to the Tramway du Mont Blanc, which whisks you to the Nid d'Aigle (Eagle's Nest) at 2372m. From here, a couple hours on a worn mountain path brings you to Tête Rousse (3167m). Overnighting at its large refuge permits an early-morning crossing of the scarred slopes of the Grand Couloir before midday temperatures increase the likelihood of rockfall; the *couloir* is sometimes called the "bowling alley" due to the effect of tumbling boulders on hapless climbers. You'll also beat the crowds to the Goûter, assuring yourself a bed and a carb-laden dinner – both essential if you want to be alert for the recommended 2am departure for the summit.

With headlamp aglow, crampons locked in and ropes firmly secured, you'll climb the Dôme du Goûter up an exposed slope whose whiplash winds can prevent passage on an otherwise clear night. Fortunately the route is well established and the minor crevasses are an insignificant hazard. At 4362m

the birth of mountaineering

It's difficult to imagine climbing icy peaks with only a long pole for support, but this is just what early alpinists like Dr Michel Gabriel Pacard and Jacque Balmat used, when mountaineering was as much a scientific pursuit as an adventurous one. On August 8, 1786 Pacard and Balmat made the historic first ascent of Mont Blanc after repeated failures by other climbers. Their success was due in part to Balmat's near-fatal attempt in June of the same year, during which he discovered the optimal route.

Equipped with only long, pointed staves and axes, the two men braved the mountain's frigid upper slopes, crossing snowfields and treacherous crevasses. Upon reaching the summit, Pacard used a barometer to perform a number of scientific tests. The mission successfully completed, Balmat headed to Geneva to collect a cash prize from Horace-Bénédict de Saussure, who had promised a reward for the first viable route to Mont Blanc's summit. One year after Pacard and Balmat's feat, Saussure led another successful expedition up the mountain.

The concept of scaling a mountain for a reason other than science and financial gain – that is, for pleasure – evolved from these early expeditions. Mountaineers' tools likewise advanced from everyday wood axes and steel-tipped poles to modified ice axes and crampons, and continued to evolve through the following centuries as climbing transformed into a recreational sport.

Mont Blanc is the highest mountain in the world with a tunnel through it: the Mont Blanc Tunnel runs for 11.6km between Chamonix, France and Courmayeur, Italy

need to know

While the summit is not technically challenging for experienced climbers, it still requires mountaineering skills and should not be regarded as a trek or walk. Arrive with experience on other glaciated peaks and be prepared for over 2400m of sustained vertical ascent. In summer, crowds require that you have advance reservations at the refuges, or you'll likely end up sleeping on the floor. The Office d'Haute Montagne in Chamonix (Ⓦ www.ohm-chamonix.com) is an excellent source of mountain assistance and information.

guides and gear Certified guides in Chamonix have a longstanding reputation for excellence. Mont Blanc Guides (☏ 682/497-510, Ⓦ www.montblancguides.com) offer instruction and six-day guided climbs, providing a guide for every two clients, equipment and accommodation.

when to go July and August are the best months, but even in midsummer the weather can change suddenly. Extreme heat, sometimes the cause of rockfall, can be as likely to close the route as inclement weather.

getting there Most climbs of Mont Blanc begin in the Chamonix Valley, about 100km southwest of Geneva, Switzerland and easily reached by train or private shuttle (2hr).

suggested reading Chamonix, Mont Blanc Massif (IGN). Its detailed topographic map (scale 1:25,000) for both sides of the mountain lets you preview route options, hut locations and elevations. Fergus Fleming, Killing Dragons: The Conquest of the Alps (Atlantic Monthly Press). An engaging and entertaining chronicle of Alpine exploration and mountaineering. Gaston Rébuffat, The Mont Blanc Massif: The 100 Finest Routes (The Mountaineers). The history, lore and beauty of the mountain in large format, as told by a legendary local guide.

you'll pass Refuge Vallot, marking the start of the Bosses Ridge; don't expect a rest, though, as the dozen beds are for emergency use only. Here the ridge narrows to a boot-width trough, along which the throngs of ascending and descending mountaineers collide – the rare inconsiderate climber is your primary risk. Ascending steadily, you'll reach the summit just after the morning sun has cast a magenta glow over the icy slopes.

From the mountain's broad dome, take your time enjoying the coveted, panoramic views of the magnificent peaks spreading below you. Then, once you've feasted your eyes, start your careful descent back to Chamonix.

is this for me?

PHYSICAL ✦ ✦ ✦
Endurance for climbing at altitude

PSYCH ✦ ✦ ✦
Steep slopes, exposure to falls

SKILL ✦ ✦ ✦
Solid mountaineering skills required

WOW! ✦ ✦ ✦
Classic climb, commanding views

85

NEWCASTLE

UK

Hiking Hadrian's Wall

> Ancient wonders and scenic thrills

The Roman army dominated Europe for five hundred years, leaving behind thousands of monuments to its strength and ability. But the greatest of these is Hadrian's Wall, which took ten thousand men eight years to build. Originally 117km long, up to 4.6m high and 2.5 to 3m wide, it stretched across England from coast to coast as the ultimate Roman power statement, intended to intimidate the barbarian tribes to the north during the second century AD. The barbarians are long gone, but as you gaze out from one of the hilltop mileposts at the stirring scenery on all sides, it's easy to understand why the emperor was so dedicated to protecting his picturesque domain.

the Roman presence in Britain

In 410 AD, after nearly four hundred years as a valuable outpost in a far-flung corner of the vast Roman Empire, Britain received word that the occupation was over. Roman troops had withdrawn and Saxon invaders were threatening, but the Romans' only response to a plea for help was a missive telling the British to "look to their own defences". The unstoppable empire – an empire that had redefined British language, culture, geography and architecture – was crumbling.

Long after the fall of the empire, however, a remarkable legacy remains. Sights such as Hadrian's Wall and the Roman Baths are just the most well known: Roman villas, amphitheatres, roads and walls are still easily accessible. The imposed Roman order was often brutal, but the conquerors also bestowed many good things upon the island's scattered Celtic tribes, including reading and writing, standard units of measurement, hot-water bathing, sewage systems and even some animals and plants, such as chickens and the sweet-chestnut tree.

The Hadrian's Wall Path is a newly designated and well-marked 135-kilometer trail which follows the wall and much of its remains as it marches across England, taking in its stride riverside farmland, pastures, rocky uplands and salt marshes. The creation of a national trail not only guarantees the preservation of this cultural icon and UNESCO World Heritage Site, but promotes public awareness of the wall and its cultural legacy. The wall hasn't always been prized as a symbol of national heritage: after the fall of the Roman Empire it was cannibalized as a convenient source of ready-cut stone to build hundreds of local houses, castles, churches, and even other walls. The greatest destruction of the wall occurred in the medieval period, reaching a peak during the Norman invasion in 1066, which launched a period of sustained stone-robbing. Portions of the wall built in terrain too rocky for farming were less susceptible to robbery, and as a result, these sections, forts and room layouts have stayed more intact.

Much of the path can be done as a long-distance walk of five to eight days depending on whether you're a purist – stopping for in-depth study at every fort and granary – or simply interested in the overall experience and the countryside scenery. Along the Hadrian's Wall Path you're never too far from the motorway, and public transport is convenient – useful for dodging urban areas and focusing on the most scenically striking sections. Campsites are limited and camping rough is prohibited, but there's plenty of accommodation, ranging from hotels and traditional inns to B&Bs and farmhouses. The entire walk, or the best sections as described here, can be approached as guided, self-guided or independent treks.

Hadrianus murumque per octoginta milia passum primus duxit, qui barbaros Romanosque dividert. (Hadrian was the first to build a wall, eighty miles long, to separate the Romans from the barbarians.)

Scriptores Historiae, Vita Hadriani 11,2

The ideal starting point for an adventure that takes in both the most intact sections of the wall and the most appealing scenery, while avoiding the more congested urban areas, is Heddon-on-the-Wall, about 16km west of Newcastle. From here to Shield-on-the-Wall at Milecastle 33 – a 19-kilometer stretch – the trail follows the wall, which is also closely paralleled by the road to the south. Breaking ranks with the road, the best-preserved portions of the wall lie between Sewingshield Crags and Walton, a stretch of about 30km, where the landscape combines heather-covered moorland with open grassland and meadows. The beauty of the surroundings calls for frequent stops, as craggy outcrops and rumpled hills afford sweeping views

need to know

A walk along Hadrian's Wall can be enjoyed as a series of day hikes or as a continuous through-hike. Hadrian's Wall Heritage Ltd (℡ 01434322-002, Ⓦ www.hadrians-wall.org) coordinates site management and visitor information services for the wall corridor, and can help you plan a trek.

guides and gear Guided and self-guided treks along Hadrian's Wall and other walking destinations in England and Scotland are provided by Footpath Holidays (℡ 01985/840-049; Ⓦ www.footpath-holidays.com), while the Sherpa Van Project (℡ 01609/883-731, Ⓦ www.sherpavan.com) specializes in door-to-door baggage transfer and accommodation booking along the wall.

when to go The trail is accessible and open year-round, with May through September offering the best weather for extended hikes. Public transport serves various points along the wall from late March through early November.

getting there From Newcastle travel by bus – the appropriately named AD122 – to Heddon-on-the-Wall or other access points along the trail.

suggested reading Henry Stedman, *Hadrian's Wall Path: Wallsend to Bowness-on-Solway* (Trailblazer Publications). A pocket guide with excellent mapping and detailed itineraries. David J Breeze & Brian Dobson, *Hadrian's Wall* (Penguin). The life and times of Hadrian's Wall and its builders.

across the countryside. Between these points along the wall you'll discover well-preserved forts at Chesters, Housteads and Birdoswald; slightly off the route, but well worth exploring, are Corbridge, a garrison and supply base, and Vindolanda, with its extensive remains of a fort and civilian settlement, with ancient textiles, pottery and tools. Rare clay tablets inscribed with mundane information such as party invitations, recipes and clothing orders, give a rare glimpse into the daily lives of second-century Romans.

The central section of the wall and trail is particularly spectacular because it follows a geological fault known as Whin Sill as it crosses the grazing uplands of Northumberland. The wall tracks the jutting face of the sill which frequently rises and erupts onto the surface in outcrops to form a dramatic ledge. The Romans used this natural feature to their strategic advantage by building the wall along the crest of the volcanic escarpment.

As you walk along the trail within arm's reach of ancient, moss-covered stones, it's easy to imagine that Hadrian's Wall has always been there: it's so much a part of the landscape that it almost feels like a natural, organically evolved feature. When you remember that every stone was carried here and placed by hand, you're reminded of the boundless efficiency of the ancient Roman army and their mighty reach throughout the world.

is this for me?

PHYSICAL ✦ ✦ ✦ ✦ ✦
Full days of walking

PSYCH ✦ ✦ ✦ ✦ ✦
Mostly comfortable setting

SKILL ✦ ✦ ✦ ✦ ✦
Well-marked trail

WOW! ✦ ✦ ✦ ✦ ✦
Compelling historical connection

Hiking Kungsleden

86

ABISKO

SWEDEN

>> Nature in the raw

If you want a hike in the lone wilderness with absolute freedom of choice – how long you take, what trails you hike, even where you camp – head to Abisko, Sweden and embark on the aptly named Kunglesden, or King's Trail. On this epic journey you'll pass through expansive glacier-carved valleys where wild herds of reindeer roam; walk through beautiful birch forests; meander alongside rushing rivers and streams and deep lakes and ponds; and pass hundreds of sparkling mountain tarns. This is nature in the raw.

Lapland languages

While Lappland is the largest and northernmost of Sweden's 25 provinces, the broader Lapland is a cultural region of northern Europe that's spread out over Norway, Finland, Sweden, and Eastern Russia. The region is inhabited by the Sami people whose traditional language Sami (or Saami) is actually a family of a dozen languages, all of which are presently extinct or endangered through continually declining usage. Linguist have noted the precision of Sami languages in describing landforms. For example, more than one hundred words to describe the shape of hills, forty words to describe bogs and swamps, and sixty to describe valleys. In many cases Sami will describe in one word what in Finnish or Swedish takes several words.

Extending through four national parks and a natural reserve, the Kungsleden stretches 438km from Abisko to Hemavan in Swedish Lapland, requiring at least one month to hike in its entirety. Although either town can serve as a starting point, most people begin in Abisko and journey south. The Kungsleden straddles the Arctic Circle, so facing south keeps the sun on a hiker's face – a real bonus in this neck of the woods. The trail is usually tackled in four week-long sections, each segment unveiling different landscapes: grassy, rocky and sometimes even marshy, from mountain peaks and river valleys to sweeping plains of tundra. The first portion, a little more than one hundred kilometers from Abisko to Nikkaluoka, is the most popular and arguably the most attractive, taking in the highest mountain peak in Sweden, the Kebnekaise (2114m). Closer to the end of the trail, the 166-kilometer stretch between the village of Kvikkjokk and the larger town of Ammarnäs requires four lake crossings and is more rugged and isolated, which might be particularly to your liking if you've come seeking solitude in Lapland's stunning scenery.

In this vast region, one thing there's a lot of is water: sturdy suspension bridges permit passage over rivers, and you can take boats across lakes to shorten trail distance or to continue further on a trail. Refreshingly, you can take advantage of the water's purity, drinking right from freshwater streams and refilling your water bottle as necessary. You can also camp wherever you want without restrictions; just leave the area as you found it. If camping in a tent doesn't appeal, stay in one of the cabins or fell stations maintained by the Tourist Association; you'll find 21 of them about a day's hike apart all along the trail.

need to know

The Swedish Tourist Association (STF), created the Kungsleden in the late nineteenth century to enable visitors to discover Lapland's wild beauty. Today the STF (Ⓦ www.svenskaturistforeningen. se) manages a network of fell stations (huts), with restaurants, showers, and other amenities at various points if you need a more comfortable place to relax before continuing your hike.

guides and gear The trail is well marked and no guides are necessary. Bring rubber boots or waterproof shows, as well as clothing to deal with any kind of weather. A hiking map, acquired from one of the cabins along the trail, is useful too.

when to go The best time of the year to hike the trail is between late June, when the last of the snow has melted, and mid-September, when the deep autumn colors of the leaves and mosses are quite spectacular.

getting there From the capital of Stockholm, fly to Kiruna then take the train to Abisko; alternatively, you can take the train all the way from Stockholm, a nineteen-hour trip. The trailhead is walkable from the train station. Buses serve various towns and villages along the way at the end of your route.

suggested reading Derek Ratcliffe, *Lapland: A Natural History* (Yale University Press). Examines the flora and fauna across Lapland's major habitats. Lantmäteriet Kartförlaget, *Norra Norrland*. The definitive map to Swedish Lapland (scale 1:400,000).

is this for me?

PHYSICAL ✦ ✦ ✦ ✦ ✦
Requires stamina for distance

PSYCH ✦ ✦ ✦ ✦ ✦
Well-crafted trail, dicey weather

SKILL ✦ ✦ ✦ ✦ ✦
Walking, easy route-finding

WOW! ✦ ✦ ✦ ✦ ✦
Wild Lapland landscape

87 Hiking the North Devon Coast

WHERE Braunton to Lynmouth, England

WHEN Year-round

PHYSICAL	◆ ◆ ◆ ◆ ◆
PSYCH	◆ ◆ ◆ ◆ ◆
SKILL	◆ ◆ ◆ ◆ ◆
WOW!	◆ ◆ ◆ ◆ ◆

With some of the finest scenery the country has to offer, the North Devon coastline brings together the best elements of the English countryside – high, rocky cliffs; barren moorland; deep, wooded valleys that cut through to the sea; and some fantastic dunes and beaches. The South West Coast path hugs the coastline here as it does throughout this region of the country, and is one of the world's great walks – not for its strenuousness, but rather for the riveting variety of its scenery, and the sheer drama of the coastline here. If you only hike one stretch of the South West Coast Path, it's worth knowing that the North Devon stretch is among the most spectacular.

In the west it's the beaches that predominate, and there are some of the UK's finest surfing beaches at Saunton Sands and Croyde. Just south of here, the weird dunescape of Braunton Burrows is quite unlike anywhere else in the country. Beyond Croyde, the sandy expanses and magnificent dunes continue at Woolacombe, before you climb up to the rockier stretches around and beyond the seen-better-days seaside town of Ilfracombe. From here the cliff paths roughens towards Watermouth Bay and the cliffs of Exmoor, which plummet into the sea. Hike out of the small seaside town of Combe Martin to the Great Hangman and Little Hangman hills, which tower above the bay, and continue on for a break at *Hunter's Inn*, a few miles inland down a dark, wooded valley or "combe". The coast reaches its most stunning heights at red-tinted Countisbury Hill, the highest sea cliffs in England, just beyond the almost alpine, old-fashioned twin resorts of Lynton and Lynmouth, which are joined to each other by funicular. You can walk this entire stretch, from Braunton to Lynmouth – probably about forty miles in total – in a couple of long days with an overnight stop, and although you need to be reasonably fit, it's not overly demanding. On the other hand, why not take longer, assume a more leisurely pace, and continue right along the Exmoor coast into Somerset?

88 Diving the Zenobia

WHERE Larnaca, Cyprus

WHEN June to August & December to March

Lying on its portside in the Mediterranean seabed is a shipwreck that divers from all over dream about exploring. The 10,000-ton, 178-meter long Zenobia ferry was built in 1979, registered to carry 140 passengers, and meant to operate in the Eastern Mediterranean and the Middle East. In May of 1980, the ferry departed on its maiden voyage from Sweden to Syria. A month in, it sank near the Larnaca fishing harbor in Cyprus. It took two days for its two decks, two stern doors, two seven-cylinder engines, 104 articulated lorries, and miscellaneous cargo to descend to the dark sea bottom. Today, merely a 15-minute boat ride from Larnaca port, you can discover the massive wreck for yourself.

The dive reaches a maximum depth of 42m and maintains an average depth of 25m; a low current and excellent visibility of about 20 meters makes for easy navigation. Parts of the ship seem to have been abandoned only days ago: much of the cargo – industrial machinery, air conditioners, timber, Tonka toys, eggs, and paint – can still be seen within the ferry's interior or close by. Check out the ferry's winch gear, canteen, bridge, oil slicks, and lorries that are still tethered to the decks by slowly rusting chairs. You can even take time to sit in the life boats and watch barracudas, groupers, amberjacks, and many other fish enjoying their new digs.

89 Cross-country ski touring in Lapland

WHERE Finland

WHEN November to May

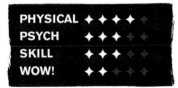

You're gliding along and suddenly a herd of reindeer steps right into your path. If you're not used to skiing in the Arctic Circle, such an occurrence might just stop you in your tracks. On the shimmering slopes of Finland's Lapland, it's the norm. So is the quality of the cross-country experience: because of the dry climate, the cold isn't as piercing as you might expect from the low temperatures, allowing you to ski longer and harder. And with Lapland's

northerly latitude, a mere blue dusk illuminates the sky during the day in the winter months. Luckily, the spotless snow reflects even the slightest illumination, so you can ski quite easily in the dark. In the spring, both the day and night are much lighter, and the snow a bit harder, making for a completely different skiing experience. The farther north you go, the lighter the sky and the longer you can ski.

Plenty of ambitious skiers take extended ski tours of the area, hitting trails in excess of fifteen kilometers and staying in cabins along the way. At day's end, the still nights are excitement enough, with a full moon that rivals the brightness of the noonday sun.

90 Walking in the Cévennes

WHERE South-central France

WHEN March to October

For a glimpse at man's struggle to integrate with nature, take a walk through France's last undiscovered region – if any could said to make such a claim – the Cévennes. Part of the Massif Central, it was remote and largely inaccessible country until well into the twentieth century. A seven-day self-guided walking tour takes you through a wild, undeveloped terrain of steep slopes, narrow valleys, and countless hills. Its extensive natural and human history has been well-preserved, so traveling around is a bit like seeing all the points on a timeline at once: from cave dwellings and stone circles, to Roman roads and twelfth-century castles and fortifications, the past blends seamlessly with the present.

Most walking trails are moderately challenging, but you can choose options with varying degrees of difficulty; GRs 6,

7, and 60 cross all or part of the range, while the GR67 is a 130km Tour des Cévennes. W . The landscape is scattered with a wide variety of trees including green oak, pine, chestnut, and the strawberry tree. You might also come across vultures, short-toed eagles, European bison, Przewalskis horses, wild boars, red foxes, deer, Praying Mantises, small lizards, and crickets.Nestled among the hills, too, are nineteenth-century homesteads, made exclusively out of the natural materials on offer, a reminder of man's ability to adapt to living in a wild and rugged environment.

91 Cycling in the Southern Piedmont

WHERE Piedmont and Liguria, Italy
WHEN Spring and autumn

It is always exciting to experience something before others have. Bicycling through the Southern Piedmont takes you away from some of the better-known and more heavily traveled cycling routes in Italy to a region with little traffic and lots of lovely terrain, from flats and gentle roads to rolling hills and steep climbs. There's clean, floral-scented air to breathe and medieval villages and majestic castles to admire. There's the great food and wine of the region, which you'll sample when stopping off in any number of quaint towns, one known for its exquisite Barbaresco reds, another for Robiola, a creamy goat's milk cheese. Traveling either guided or independently, the charming town and surrounding vineyards of Barolo make it an enjoyable starting point as you wind your way over the course of a week or so to the coast. Theoretically, it's downhill to the coast, but you'll have your share of rolling hills and a few steep climbs. Consider yourself brilliant if you plan your route through the fertile Langhe Hills where you can indulge your visual senses in flowing hills swathed in vineyards and orchards, then tease your taste buds by night with local truffles, hazelnuts, wine, and cheese. Take your time and proceed at your own slow pace before continuing on to the sparkling waters of Paradise Bay in Camogli on the Ligurian coast; this area is, after all, where the Slow Food movement caught hold.

92 Hiking in the Pindos Mountains

WHERE Epirus, Greece
WHEN May, June, September & October

The Path of the Pindos is a multi-day, moderately strenuous trek that winds in and around snow-capped mountains, dense forest, colorful meadows, gushing rivers, and trickling streams. It starts off with a spectacular, steep descent into the Vikos Gorge, tapped by the Guinness World Records as the world's deepest canyon (in proportion to its width) with 1100m-high walls only 900m apart. Not long after, the path brings you up out of the gorge and into a protected village view filled with ancient trees, old houses, and churches. If you want a little break, you can take a leisurely swim in the nearby Kolymvitirio River. The path continues on through fields, dense birch woods, alpine meadows, and small mountain passes, along which you're likely to encounter wild horses and cows, sheep, tortoises, bears, and the well-known Pindos sheep dogs – which direct most of their attention to passing hikers. Toward the end of the hike, you will cross plateaus and ravines leading up to Mount Smolikas, which at 2637m is the second highest mountain in Greece, just below Mount Olympus. You'll traverse its snowfields before finally beginning your descent to the path's end.

93 Mountain biking King's Trail

WHERE Gran Paradiso National Park, Italy
WHEN June to September

Snaking through the northwestern Alps, the so-called King's Trail or King's Road is the highlight of Gran Paradiso Park. It's an old path that was constructed by miners under King Vittorio Emanuele II of Italy in the seventeenth century, so that the king could easily reach his hunting huts (the area around the trail was his private game reserve) by carriage. You can tackle it in a number of ways – on foot, by horseback, or even with skis (in the winter months). Mountain biking, however, is probably the preferred method. The trail is considered easy in terms of technical difficulty, with the challenge in its steep climbs and rigorous switchbacks: it covers some 1200m and is around 55km long. As the area is now a sanctuary for wildlife, you'll enjoy rare alpine flora and encounter such animal species as deer, ibex, marmots, and eagles. Refuges along the trail are available for food and shelter.

94 Walking the Kerry Way

WHERE Killarney, Ireland
WHEN Year-round

The longest signposted walking trail in Ireland at over two hundred kilometers, the Kerry Way loops around the Iveragh Peninsula in the southwest and takes around eleven days to complete. It consists mostly of old abandoned and overgrown drovers' and traders' tracks, now closed off from the public and not particularly rough-going, but the walk still requires substantial physical endurance. The starting point is Killarney, a town whose pretty setting – amid shimmering lakes and heath-covered valleys – is its best asset. Just south of town the Killarney National Park begins, a lush vegetative woodland with lakeside gardens full of rhododendrons and azaleas in the early summer. The trail leads you straight through the mist of the twelve-meter high Torc waterfall, canopied by leafy trees, and alongside Bronze Age forts in the surrounding countryside. You'll soon find yourself in the contrasting rugged wilderness outside of Killarney – the red sandstone

mountains to the east burdened by ominous storm clouds and illuminated by multiple rainbows lingering overhead from the last rain. Between the dark peaks are ancient glens carved out by glaciers thousands of years ago. As you move along the circuit, through deep peat boglands and moors to dramatic coastal scenery, you'll get to observe the scattered wildlife of hares, foxes, red deer, skylarks, meadow pipits, bilberries, cowberries, and greater butterwort.

95 Hiking in the Carpathians

WHERE Romania and Ukraine
WHEN May to October

Extending in a 1500-kilometer arc from Slovakia and Poland to Ukraine and Romania, the Carpathian Mountains offer an Eastern European alternative to hiking in the Alps. It's a land of fir-tree forests, majestic peaks and panoramas, with endemic flowers and other vegetation throughout. If you're interested in an option with a more cultural bent, Romania is probably the best bet, where you can trek through Transylvania and fit in a visit to Bran Castle – a residence of Vlad the Impaler, whose history provided the inspiration for Bram Stoker's novel *Dracula*. Mountain paths through deep forests are well established and you're likely to see species that were long ago hunted to extinction in the Alps to the west, including bears and wolves.

Ukraine's Carpathians are perhaps the least developed region of the unspoiled mountain range, so hiking there may often mean bushwhacking or hiking through areas with little trail maintenance. Winter ski resorts like Slavsko serve as good jumping off points to mountain hiking, and the historic cities of Lviv and Uzhhorod provide access to trail networks in the area. While this makes for a great opportunity to get away from civilization it also makes it more difficult to go trekking without a guide or prior knowledge of the area. But if you can't find an organized tour you'll often find a willing local guide. With the exception of a few nature reserves that are restricted for camping, you can normally camp in tents or existing camp shelters.

Towns along the way offer accommodation in simple hostels and comfortable inns, so that you can relax for the night before stepping back on the 152-kilometer trek, which runs from Milngavie north up to Fort William. There are also many companies that lead walking tours or can transport your luggage from town to town so that you are not weighed down. Still, if you wish to camp, some areas are marked as designated camp spots. You can also camp in the wild so long as you make sure to take care of the area you stay in and leave nothing behind. Be sure to bring good shoes and come prepared for Scotland's famously changeable weather.

97 Kayaking in the Ionian

WHERE Ionian Sea, Greece
WHEN May to October

Cast out onto the calmest sea in Greece with nothing but the warm, sapphire Mediterranean waters lapping at your kayak and a guide wistfully telling stories about the surrounding sea and land . . . all in all, not a bad way to start the day. Bordered by Italy's boot and the west coast of Greece, the Ionian Sea is home to some islands with great natural appeal, like Corfu, and plenty of them, unlike Corfu, still undeveloped. To get on the water, you have the option of a one-day or multi-day tour: the calm waters allow for some nice crossings of bays and channels, pleasant coastal paddling, and exploration of intriguing sea caves. Marine life, such as loggerhead turtles which can reach up to one meter in length, monk seals, dolphins, and even sperm whales can be spotted on your journey. On land, lizards and many small reptiles bask in the sun, while skyward watch for kingfishers, terns, or even eagles.

As you slowly paddle through the sea, you'll be cupped by sandy coves buried amongst rigid cliffs – part of Greece's scenic 15,000km of coastline, almost half the shoreline of the entire Mediterranean. Nestled into that coastline are quaint villages rich in history and culture. When you're not out to sea or mingling with some of the islanders, you may be sleeping under the stars on the sandy beach of one of the uninhabited islands nearby. Awakening to the sights and smells of pine or fir forests, olive and cypress groves, prickly pear cacti, and wild herbs such as thyme and oregano may well tempt you to stay land-based for a spell, but the sea will no doubt call to you again in no time.

96 Walking the West Highland Way

WHERE Scotland
WHEN May to August

It takes around a week to walk the West Highland Way, its moorlands, forested tracks, evocative pools, and scattered mountains your principle companions. The route takes in some of the largest freshwater lochs in Scotland including the biggest of all, Loch Lomond, which has a number of artificially made islands, called crannogs, within its parameters. These were created by settlers in the area as safe havens from enemy attack. The rest of the scenery measures up as well: grassy, rolling hills, wooded forests with fir, pine, birch, and willow trees, and the highest mountain in Scotland, Ben Nevis (1344m). You even pass by a cave that was supposedly the hide-out of Scotland's outlaw Rob Roy – also the same cave guessed to be the one where Robert the Bruce hid for a while during the turmoil in Scotland.

98 Horseback riding in Andalucia

WHERE Andalucia, Spain

WHEN March to November

PHYSICAL	✦ ✦
PSYCH	✦ ✦
SKILL	✦ ✦ ✦
WOW!	✦ ✦

In southern Spain, the autonomous communities of Andalucia border the Atlantic on the west and the Mediterranean Sea on the east. It's a vast, often mountainous landscape with a centuries-old tradition of horsemanship firmly linked to the culture. In short, it's one of the best places to ride a horse in all of Europe.

You'll spend your days galloping along golden sandy beaches, cantering through the desert landscape or pine forests, and viewing breathtaking panoramas of flower-filled valleys and stunning sierras. As much a part of the adventure as the land around you is your steed, a fabled Andalucian horse – long the choice of European royalty and of filmmakers. One of the oldest known breeds, Andalucian horses are famous for their intelligence, strength, and elegant demeanor. At home they might be used in a bullring or for herding cattle, but in the world's equestrian arenas they shine in classic dressage.

Different outfitters cater to riders of all experience levels, and most offer training. You can enjoy a few hours on a horse, or, if your legs and back can handle it, stay for seven to ten days. Most guided experiences include room and board, and nights away from the riding facility are usually spent in hotels. Outfitters may also offer Spanish, English, or Western saddles.

99 Hiking the Snowdon Horseshoe

WHERE Snowdonia, Wales

WHEN April to October, unless you like snow and ice

PHYSICAL ✦ ✦ ✦ ✦ ✦
PSYCH ✦ ✦ ✦ ✦ ✦
SKILL ✦ ✦ ✦ ✦ ✦
WOW! ✦ ✦ ✦ ✦ ✦

Standing by the busy access road, Crib Goch looks less like a viable route and more like a broken-backed beast, stretching its spine to the sky and burying its head in Snowdon's great bulk. Standing atop "the red ridge" is even less reassuring. It feels impossibly exposed, wind whistling over the protruding rocks that make up the path, the ground dropping almost straight down away from you, the comforting flat of the valley a long way away.

Crib Goch is the most worrying part of the Snowdon Horseshoe, a circuit that eschews the busy, straightforward paths (not to mention the incongruous railway line) that climb up Wales's most famous peak for some serious scrambling. It's rarely that technically difficult and holding on tight, your heart pumping, you may see an experienced group waltz by, apparently unconcerned by the certain death lurking a few meters away. But it's a wonderfully rewarding route, taking in a cruel and beautiful landscape, featuring exhausting scree, delightful ridge walks and lovely views – when the clouds break.

If you're feeling hardcore, you could tackle the Welsh 3000s, a series of fifteen peaks that takes in three mountain ranges, including most of the Horseshoe, in a long day of pain – and requires proper preparation. But start off with the Horseshoe, a challenging enough route on its own terms: you won't have just walked Wales's highest mountain; you'll have done it in style.

100 Walking the Camino de Santiago

WHERE Spain
WHEN Early fall or late spring

It's not an adrenaline-filled adventure somewhere out in the wild and it's most definitely not off the beaten path. In fact, the path has been well-worn for a thousand years. Still, making the pilgrimage along the Camino de Santiago is the kind of experience you'll look back on with a sense of accomplishment, wonder, and shared purpose – especially if you manage its entire 800-kilometer length. The most popular route these days, the Camino Francés, begins in the Pyrenees and ends in Santiago de Compostela, where the remains of St James are said to be buried (though if you like, you could even start further back in France, as many of the pilgrims did in medieval times).

On any of the varied routes, you'll march down warm, dusty trails that weave through old Spanish villages and past some of the country's loveliest rural scenery, with the sun's rays beating down on your weary limbs. It is meant to be physically demanding, to prove the devotion of those who choose to make the journey. You might do it in less than two weeks or you might let your spiritual side take over and spend months on the trail; there's no shortage of agreeable hostels – or fellow pilgrims – to help you out along the way.

101 Walking across the Llŷn

WHERE Northwest Wales
WHEN Year-round

Grab a backpack, a good pair of walking boots, and a map, then set loose on a walk across the emerald-green Welsh countryside. If you're in for the long haul, the entire walk is 84 miles long, going from Caernarfon to Porthmadog. Much shorter walks are available, each one varying in landscape and difficulty. Walks range from moderate to challenging, as you change elevation between sandy beaches, higher-grounded heath land, and steep cliff edges that overlook the streamlined joining of lush vegetation, shoreline rocks, and the aquamarine sea.

Aside from its enchanting scenery, the Llŷn maintains its fair share of history. Pilgrims used one of the walking paths to reach Bardsey Isle, a nearby island that legend deems a halfway point between this world and the next. Pass by old hill forts and crumbled ruins that date back to the Stone, Bronze, and Iron Ages, by ancient archeological sites and historic churches such as St Beuno's Church, which was founded around 630 AD. You may as well take the opportunity to visit St Mary's Holy Well (only safe to visit at low tide), which was said to have been blessed by the Virgin Mary herself and was the last chance pilgrims had to get a blessing before crossing to Bardsey Isle. The peninsula is also quite abundant in beautiful fauna, most notably birds. Birds such as choughs, Manx shearwaters, ospreys, pigeons, curlews, grebes, and puffins are commonly seen around the area. It's worth taking it slow, so you can enjoy plenty of inns, cafés, restaurants, and pubs along the way.

102 Ice diving in the White Sea

WHERE Kindo Cape, Russia
WHEN February to April

The only European sea fully covered with ice in the winter – and one of the few places in the world where the ocean actually freezes – Russia's White Sea is a diver's adventure paradise. Brave the cold and come explore in late winter after the snows have melted, when the melon-headed Beluga whale swims giddily below the surface despite average water temperatures of -3°C.

Head out across the lake surface by snowmobile and don your wetsuit in a heated, mobile wooden shelter that rests atop the ice. After sawing through the 1.5m-thick ice, hop through the surface with your underwater flashlight, connected to the world above via a single safety rope.

That's when the adventure really begins. Follow your guide down 30m past ice hummocks, rifts, cavities, and caves, minnowing past tall underwater arches and vertical rocks overgrown with sea anemones, sponges, and hydroids. Underwater rocks abruptly disappear into the pitch black depths of the ocean, while kelp sways gently atop laminaria gardens and mussel plantations. The sea's soft coral is home to a unique marine life: wolf-fish, basket fish, and pinogor, as well as more exotic species such as lancet fish, eelpout, gunnels, and the rare scorpian fish. In some parts you'll even come upon parts of shipwrecked fishing and patrol boats, while up above – visibility can reach a crystal clear 50m – the masses of surface ice appear as glowing green castles bobbing atop the air bubbles. After surfacing, let yourself be guided by the glimmering northern lights above as you retire to your cottage for some Russian hospitality and comradeship.

103 Coasteering in Anglesey

WHERE Anglesey, Wales

WHEN Best in summer, May to September

The wet and wild coast of the island of Anglesey, tethered to the Welsh mainland by two bridges and long associated with the druids, is most comfortably viewed from a pub interior. If that sounds a little staid, coasteering offers a more direct way of getting stuck in. The sport, in which wetsuited, lifejacketed, and helmeted participants clamber from one squall-whipped rock to another, traverse mini-ridges, and leap into frothing inlets, was invented in the UK in the 1970s and first taught by adventure companies in the 1990s – one outfit even tried to trademark the term. Yet once you're hanging off the edge of Britain, coarse granite in one hand and moist, pungent seaweed in the other, nothing feels particularly modern or novel about the activity, which essentially encourages you to treat obstacles as your playground – a kind of free running for people who don't mind getting their trainers wet.

It's exhilarating stuff: the water hits you with a shock, but once you're actually in it the adrenaline kicks in and the fun starts. There are technical moments – you have to learn to work with the waves, not fight them, especially when you lever yourself out of the water and onto the glistening rock – but the most fun part is probably the jump into the sea, when you heart pops briefly into your mouth, the water rushes over you, and you come up smiling and breathless.

104 Caving in Bihor

WHERE Oradea, Romania

WHEN June to August

The 2002 discovery of a 35,000-year-old jawbone – the oldest modern human fossil in Europe – has brought a surge of adventure-seekers to explore Romania's *pe tera* (caves). If spending long, dark days climbing, jumping, swimming, and diving through tight passages is your idea of adventure, then cast aside whatever impressions you have about Romania and get there – now.

Due to their delicate ecosystems – stalactites, stalagmites, unique flora and fauna and the cemeteries of prehistoric animals – only a handful of Romania's 12,000 caves are open to tourists. Of these, the most accessible and popular is the *Pe tera Ur ilor*, 82km southeast of Oradea and the site of countless natural sculptures. For the more adventuresome, the staggering *Pe tera Sc ri oara* ice cave is near to Beiuş in the Apuseni mountains; entrance to this cave necessitates a 13-kilometer hike.

Many of Romania's caves are found at the bottom of extinct rivers or karstic lake systems, where limestone erosion has formed sinkholes and tunneled underground streams. You'll need to negotiate a series of complex junctions and caverns leading down the strong currents from mountain springs and siphons to branches, galleries, and submerged underwater passages known as sumps. Once here, you'll don your diving gear and propel your way past steep calcareous walls through pitches, squeezes, slender canyons, and varying depths of water, sand, mud, clay, and silt that can obliterate underwater visibility in seconds when stirred up. Unlike simple spelunking, cave diving is a form of technical penetration diving, meaning that in an emergency divers cannot ascend immediately to the surface.

105 Bagging a Munro

WHERE Mount Keen, Scotland

WHEN May through September

Equipped with a decent mountain bike, your journey starts at Ballater and rolls you through picturesque Royal Deeside along the banks of the River Dee until you point your nose upwards, through the forest of Glen Tanar. The forest does a good job of hiding the mountain just around the corner but by the time you've left the relative comfort of the Mounth Road, the challenge ahead becomes crystal clear – Mount Keen (939m), Scotland's most easterly Munro (or Scottish mountain).

The approach from the northeast is certainly not the easiest ascent – steep, technical, rocky tracks to test your bike skills that eventually give way to a 2km bike-a-hike where the only way up is to push or carry your bike to the summit. The views at the top – a spectacular 360-degree panorama, taking in Lochnagar and the Cairngorms – soon make you forget your shaking legs and burning lungs.

The considerable effort on the way up only serves to make the descent even more enjoyable, as you hurtle down a sinuous strip of well-prepared track that snakes away like a yellow ribbon down over the brow of the mountain. Sure, the scenery around you is amazing, but soon you'll have to concentrate intensely on just one view – the one straight ahead.

Storm channels crossing the path every 100m or so require

hopping your bike in the air keeps you on your toes until you begin your final roll through Glen Esk. Once back on the road, you will constantly turn around to glance up at your conquest as you make your way to some much needed refreshment in Edzell.

106 Kayaking the Ardèche Gorges

WHERE Ardèche, France
WHEN June to August

PHYSICAL ✦ ✦
PSYCH ✦ ✦
SKILL ✦ ✦
WOW! ✦ ✦

Mention the word "Ardèche" to in-the-know kayakers and pulses start racing. Nestled between Provence and the Riviera deep in France's Massif Central, the Ardèche valley is one of Europe's best adventure kayaking spots. Spend just one day paddling through this thrashing river

valley swallowed up into the greatness of a 500m-wide gorge, the sun beating at your back and the limestone crags of the Cévennes soaring above, and you'll understand why.

The gorges of the rugged Ardèche comprise some of the most astounding natural physical geography in Europe. Beginning at the Pont d'Arc, a landmark 60m-wide, 45m-high arch carved by river erosion over several thousands of years, the carved gorge meanders gracefully from bend to bend awash with the warm waters of the Ardèche river. Paddle down the river as it drops 300m to the Plateau Gras, shooting past stalagtite-filled caverns whose walls display millenia-old cave paintings. After cascading over each rapid, reach for your telephoto lens to capture the diverse range of wildlife that makes its home in these mountains and forests: wild boars, goats, foxes, and birds of prey, to say nothing of the numerous species of fish that thrive in the river itself. If you need still more to lure you, the region offers an unrivaled track record of consistently great weather: three hundred sunny days a year, year-round temperatures upwards of 20˚C, blue skies that allow for spectacular day-time views, and the clearest night skies in Europe.

float to paradise

The Isle of Capri, a tiny Italian paradise, has long been considered the exclusive domain of Roman Emperors and the jet set. But the island has a purely natural side that deserves exploration by the adventurous. You can hike one of the many trails that crisscross the island, including one to Arco Naturale, a dramatic natural stone arch with splendid views. You will want to hike down to the opening of the Blue Grotto, where you take a boat through a tiny opening into a secluded and brilliantly blue limestone cavern used by ancient Romans. Most dramatic when the sun is high; safest when the sea is calm. Be sure to catch of glimpse of the Faraglione, three giant eroded monoliths that stand as sentinels guarding the island. Hiking is best in the cooler and less busy months of spring and fall.

He who would travel happily must travel light.

Antoine de Saint-Exupery

NO DESERT HERE

Europe is often described as the only continent with no desert, a claim complicated by the Tabernas Desert, in the parched Spanish province of Almería. It receives 24cm of rain a year (most definitions classify anything received less than 25cm a year as desert), and was used as the setting for Sergio Leone's *For a Few Dollars More*. If that were not enough, many observers point to the drying out of farmland in large swathes of the Russian steppe – notably in the Kalmyk Republic, in the far southwest of Russia – as the early stages of a desertification that could spread far and wide.

volcanology

Active volcanoes are a geologic enigma, following their own set of rules and capturing attention whenever they act up – or threaten to. Named for the Roman God of Fire, Vulcan, theologians, scientists, and philosophers were equally stumped for generations on how to explain the baffling explosive, noxious, and red-hot behavior of some mountains. Difficult to study when erupting and tough to analyze eons later, volcanoes have eluded precise explanation even by modern geologists. The first detailed history of an eruption was written by Pliny the Younger, only 17 at the time, whose uncle, Pliny the Elder, was killed in the eruption of Vesuvius in 79AD. The fumes and rain of ashes asphyxiated the residents of nearby Pompeii and Herculaneum and left eerily preserved communities. Since then, explosive eruptions became known as Plinian eruptions in honor of his valuable observations. Home to 29 volcanoes, including the ever-spewing Mount Etna, Italy claims the title of birthplace of volcanology.

HIGHWAYS OF WATER

Europeans have always depended on large slow-moving and navigable rivers for transportation and boundaries. These historic rivers ferried passengers, moved merchandise, carved the landscape, and decorated the countryside.

- The longest river in Europe, the Volga, begins northwest of Moscow and flows for over 3700km into the Caspian Sea.
- The 2800km Danube begins in Germany and flows through ten countries before it drains into the black sea.
- Tumbling down the Alps in Switzerland, the Rhine flows north through the Netherlands on its 1300 km journey to the North Sea.
- Over 1000km in length, the Loire is the longest river in France, concluding its journey at the Bay of Biscay.
- Only 300km in length, the River Thames begins in the Cotswolds and flows through London and on to the North Sea.

Man cannot discover new oceans unless he has the courage to lose sight of the shore.

André Gide

Hannibal's Alpine adventure

Hailed as the greatest military strategist of ancient times, Hannibal is best known for marching thousands of Carthaginian troops and 37 war elephants over the Alps and Pyrenees during the Second Punic War. In 221 BC, he assumed command of the army on the Iberian Peninsula following the death of his brother-in-law and within two years had taken control of all of Spain. In the fall of 219 BC, Hannibal set out on his famous military advance, suffering heavy casualties of both soldiers and animals due to bad weather and attacks by mountain tribesmen. However, in a little over two weeks he accomplished the historic passage through the Alps, where he won a stunning victory over an unprepared Roman army. The exact details and location of his passage remains a mystery and a source of debate among alpine trekkers.

Tours de France

The first documented bicycle race was held in May 1868 at the Parc de Saint-Cloud, Paris. Englishman Dr. James Moore took first prize, riding a bicycle with solid rubber tires. Today, the Tour de France is the world's largest cycling race, with around 200 athletes competing for over 3 million in prize money – although many make more from their team contracts.

THE VIKINGS

Much of what we know as fact about the Vikings is decidedly dubious – they rarely wore horned helmets, which would have been spectacularly impractical in battle, and many were traders rather than warriors. Yet their travels seem amazing to this day. They ranged south to Sicily, east to Russia and the Middle East, north to Greenland and west to Newfoundland, roaming on graceful longships up the Volga, through the Mediterranean and across the Atlantic. Icelandic sagas claim that the voyage to North America was the result of a merchant getting blown of course – which should serve offer some

perspective to anyone who's misread a compass. Clashes with the skrælingjar (native Americans) and each other, and a lack of support from their homeland, led to the settlement's decline, but elsewhere they proved more resilient, conquering much of Britain, Ireland and Northern France, settling around the Caspian Sea and ruling Sicily until the end of the twelfth century.

An adventure is only an inconvenience rightly considered. An inconvenience is only an adventure wrongly considered.

G.K. Chesterton

SKIING: A BRIEF (AND EUROCENTRIC) HISTORY

3000BC Rock drawings in Scandinavia depict people swathed in furs, their feet clad in planks.
2000BC Iranian tribes experiment with skis made from animal hide.
1600s AD The Norwegian Army formalize their use of skis and begin to hold competitions.
1850 Telemarking, a techique that would dominate skiing for the next sixty years, developed.
1894 German Wilhelm Ritter Von Arlt, known as the father of ski mountaineering, becomes the first man to climb to over 3000m on skis.
1903 The first package ski holiday is organized by the Public Schools Alpine Sports Club, taking keen aristocrats from Britain to Switzerland.
1910s The stem technique, invented in the late nineteenth century, begins to dominate skiing, bringing the much-cursed snowplow turn with it.
1936 Alpine skiing makes its Olympic debut.
1939 Finnish troops, mounted on slim wooden skis, slaughter around 250,000 Soviet infantry.
1951 First ski descent of Mont Blanc

1970s Skiing goes mass market.
1990s Snowboarding encourages the growth of carving skis, off-piste skiing and jumps.
2006 Lyndsey Jacobellis, leading the Snowboard Cross at the Turin Winter Olympics by a large margin, attempts a grab trick towards the end of the race and falls to miss out on gold, proving, if nothing else, that sliding down a hill at speed remains a sport for the bold and the foolish.

Europe's waterfalls

Looking for a long plunge? Head to Norway, home to not just the tallest waterfall in Europe (at 860m, Vinnufossen is ranked sixth in the world, with Venezuela's 979m Angel Falls taking top spot), but the fifteen tallest waterfalls – Slovenia's Levo Savice, at 600m, is the first to break the Norwegian monopoly.

MOUNTAINEERING: FIVE EUROPEAN LANDMARKS

121 AD Roman emperor Hadrian mounts Etna (3350m) to watch the sunrise.
1316 French philosopher and priest Jean Buridan (whose writings were later banned by the Catholic Church) climbs Mont Ventoux, a feat often claimed as the first mountain ascent since the Classical era.
1786 Two Italians, Michel Paccard and Jacques Balmat, make the first ascent of Mont Blanc.
1857 The Alpine Club, generally held to be the world's first mountaineering club, formed in London.
1865 Edward Whymper makes the first ascent of the Matterhorn, signaling the close of the "golden age of alpinism". Four of his party die in the attempt.

To err is human. To loaf is Parisian.

Victor Hugo

AFRICA

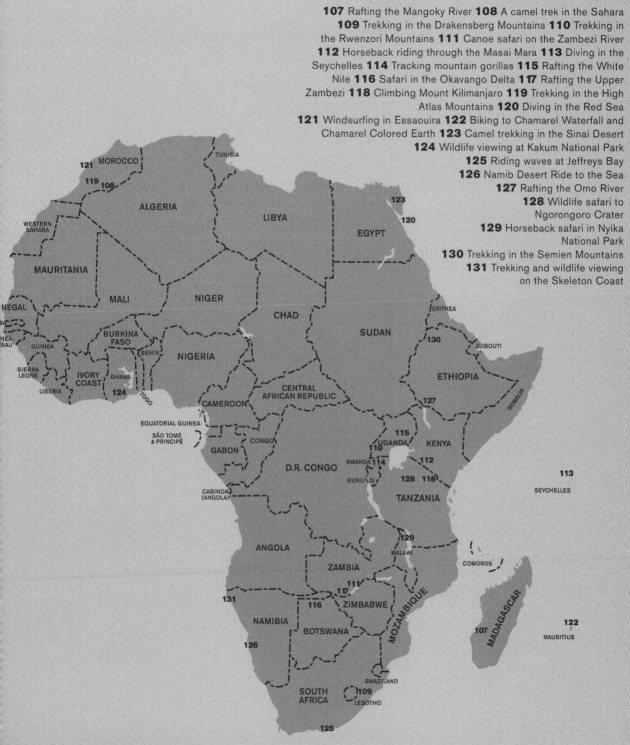

107 Rafting the Mangoky River

>> Float past baobabs

By any measuring stick, this much is clear about Madagascar: it's a peculiar place. Lying in the middle of the Indian Ocean off the southeastern coast of Africa, the island nation teems with oddities that defy easy descriptions, from lemurs – tiny primates with bulging eyes – to fantastical baobab trees that appear to have been uprooted and stood on their heads. Half of the world's chameleons live on the island, while its largest land carnivore, the fossa, looks like a cross between a cat and a dog and will eat just about everything, including chameleons and lemurs.

lemurs and fossas

When humans first arrived on Madagascar approximately two thousand years ago, the island was home to a host of unusual creatures, including lemurs the size of gorillas, a three-meter tall flightless bird and a tiger-sized fossa. While this dreamlike picture of Madagascar's megafauna eventually disappeared through extinction, Madagascar's distinctive animal population still teases the imagination. Perhaps the most well-known animals in Madagascar are lemurs – primates with long tails, large round eyes and opposable thumbs.

Lemurs aren't the only creatures of Madagascar to enchant the imagination, however. All natural environments need a predator to keep the balance, and the largest carnivore in Madagascar's jungle is a tree-climbing, long-tailed, sinewy-muscled mongoose called a fossa. Only in recent years have researchers begun to untangle the legends surrounding this mysterious cat-like predator, which weighs less than 13kg, hunts during both day and night, and is often the last thing a lemur sees alive. Centuries ago, 102-kilogram fossas that would have been strong enough to prey on humans roamed the island, and in some respects this larger fossa is the Loch Ness monster of Madagascar. Local folklore inspires fear and has prompted a few hopeful researchers to search the unexplored regions of Madagascar for signs that the larger species still exists. So far, no search has been fruitful, and it is likely that the animal exists now only in lore.

Madagascar wasn't always so unusual. About 160 million years ago it was pretty much like the rest of the planet, part of the supercontinent known as Gondwanaland. But its early separation from the supercontinent resulted in eons of evolution in isolation. Madagascar's endemism continued unabated with humans only arriving in the past two thousand years. As a result, most of the 200,000 plant and animal species in Madagascar are found nowhere else on earth, making the island a biodiversity hotspot and a dreamland for ecologists.

In this land of the strange, the Mangoky (man-GOOK) River, which flows for 560km down Madgascar's rain-shadowed western highlands into the Mozambique Channel, is decidedly straightforward. No rapids or portages – just days on end of big volume, slow moving, sometimes muddy water. It is a conduit of exploration and a means of transporting you into the remote and hidden reaches of the "Great Red Island" where you can uncover for yourself the wondrous natural phenomena.

There's only one way to run the Mangoky and that's from Beroroha to Bevoay on an eight-day, fully supported, self-contained expedition carried out in six-passenger inflatable rafts. There's a steady current, but navigating the raft downriver will require some paddling, with outboard engines only used as a backup to ensure you arrive at your take-out on time. With a cook staff and coolers to keep you supplied with fresh food and cool drinks, the journey is surprisingly comfortable; still, less than 25 people per year ever travel this 160-kilometer isolated stretch of the river basin on the island's southwest side. Time spent on the river is relaxing, which allows you to enjoy the openness of the landscape that spreads out from both sides of the river. Occasional side-hikes along tributaries and sloping hillsides will bring you in contact with wildlife and allow you to explore the richly diverse vegetation. Throughout the trip birds – and their sounds – provide constant companionship, particularly herons, egrets and white-faced whistling ducks. Evening camps are typically made on broad sandbars, and offer time to venture further into the backcountry.

On the Mangoky you'll spend a few days passing through the world's largest baobab forest. Madagascar has seven species of baobab tree – the entire continent of Africa has just one. These trees, also called "upside-down trees," are instantly identifiable by their immense trunks, often 7m in diameter, with a capacity of storing up to 120,000 liters of water to sustain the tree through the dry season.

In addition to the distinctive baobabs, the river is generally lined by dry deciduous forests along its course. In some of these trees live lemurs, which can only be found naturally on Madagascar and a few adjacent islands where they come in varying in colors and sizes from the 25-gram pygmy mouse lemur to the 10-kilogram indri. On side hikes throughout the trip you'll encounter diurnal lemurs, and at night, shining a light into wooded areas, you'll spot the bulging reflective eyes of the more common nocturnal *lemurs*, and understand why their name is derived from the Latin lemures, or "spirits of the night." While many species have died out, there are approximately 35 known species of lemur alive today and many more subspecies. Many lemur species border on extinction because of deforestation over the past forty years that has greatly reduced habitat. This deforestation has also led to significant soil erosion which is evident in the Mangoky Basin with expanding sandbars in the river and silty ponds and swamps in the delta.

And then there are the people of Madagascar, who are known for being exceptionally gracious, friendly and endearing. On a Mangoky rafting journey you'll likely come into contact with villagers, some of whom have never met a Westerner – not unusual considering how few outsiders ever make it as far as Madagascar, let alone to such a remote region of the island. Their simple lifestyle plays close harmony to the uncommon natural melody of Madagascar and the Mangoky.

need to know

A rafting trip down the Mangoky is almost exclusively offered as part of a more extensive tour which explores various regions and ecosystems, including national parks and reserves, enabling you to more fully capture Madagascar's surprising beauty and charm.

guides and gear Remote River Expeditions (☎ 261 20 95 52 347, ⓦ www.remoterivers.com) offers a broad range of custom and group tours within Madagascar.

when to go The Mangoky is only run in May, once the November to April rainy season comes to an end making access to the put-in possible. Temperatures then range from 18 to 32°C during the day and cool comfortably at night.

getting there Fly into Antananarivo's Ivato Airport. Internal flights and ground services within Madagascar and to the Beroroha put in can be arranged on site or through your tour operator.

suggested reading Hilary Bradt, *Madagascar, The Bradt Travel Guide* (Globe Pequot). Uncovers Madagascar in vivid descriptions of people, wildlife and extraordinary places. Steven M. Goodman & Johnathan P. Benstead, *The Natural History of Madagascar* (University Of Chicago Press). At 1782 pages this weighty volume is an excellent resource in preparing for a trip to Madagascar.

is this for me?

PHYSICAL ✦ ✦ ✦ ✦ ✦
Calm waters

PSYCH ✦ ✦ ✦ ✦ ✦
Relaxing experience in unfamiliar cultural setting

SKILL ✦ ✦ ✦ ✦ ✦
Paddling skills learned on site

WOW! ✦ ✦ ✦ ✦ ✦
Richly satisfying with fascinating wildlife

A camel trek in the Sahara

108

MOROCCO

ERG CHEBBI

>> **Fall under a desert spell**

It seemed like a good idea at the time. It was early in the morning when the camels last had a slurp of brackish water, and after a day of baking in the Saharan sun and crossing nearly eight miles of shadeless sand, a drink from the cameleer's canvas bucket in camp would be a welcome refreshment and reward for the beasts of burden that had performed so admirably. Seeing the filled bucket, one dromedary quickly plunged his hairy nose and rank yellow teeth into the bucket and lapped furiously with his whip-like tongue. The other camels, not about to miss a drop, flung their heads into the bucket. Never mind one camel getting his nose under the tent; four camels were now vying for water from the same bucket. And amazingly, those four enormous tongues all seemed to get their fair share until the bucket was licked dry.

Surprisingly, camels are not indigenous to the Sahara, but arrived around 200 AD from the Arabian Peninsula, where they had been domesticated and used in trade caravans for over a thousand years. They feed on dry grasses and can go for weeks without water, not because their humps are filled with water as commonly believed – the hump is actually a fat repository – but because of several biological adaptations like huge padded feet that help them endure hot desert sand, a coat that reflects sunlight, oval blood cells that both dehydrate and absorb water more easily and a digestive system that produces syrupy urine and feces dry enough to kindle your evening campfire.

Riding a camel is every bit as comfortable as a kidney stone. Unlike a horse, you can't put your foot in the stirrup and swing your leg over the top, since camel saddles don't have stirrups and the top of the hump is about two meters above the ground. Instead, the camel crouches, allowing you to mount a small saddle at the top of the hump. Then the fun begins: the camel lurches from the ground with the grace of a mechanical bull as each of its eight knees unfold, sending you heaving unpredictably back and forth. Once standing, your head is about three meters off the ground. Then the camel starts to move with a gait that's a combination of horse and kangaroo, and you become the bobble-head doll on top. If you have back problems, this isn't the cure. Hold on tight and be ready for unannounced stumbles and sways.

Then somehow, it happens. Magically, you fall under the spell of the Sahara, the romance of the dunes, the allure of a caravan stretched across the sands – and it's off to the casbah. After a day in the saddle you come to realize that this docile animal is more stable than you first thought. All you need now is a generous application of Vaseline to your chafed inner thighs and you're ready for another day.

the Berbers

The Berbers, or *Imazighen* as they sometimes call themselves, are an indigenous group of people who have populated North Africa for as long as records of the region exist. In fact, genetics indicate that most North Africans descend predominantly from this ethnic group alone. These days the Berber people are a minority, concentrated mainly in Morocco and Algeria. They are also the main inhabitants of the Atlas Mountains, a range worshipped by the ancient Berbers, along with rocks, rivers and the sun. Most Berbers make a living through farming, an arduous task in the harsh terrain of the Maghreb. Despite this rough existence, the Berber community is linked by a devotion to hospitality – a fact you'll happily discover firsthand.

In Tataouine, Tunisia another distinctive com-

need to know

Life on a camel trek requires a hardy spirit and being able to walk or ride 12–18km per day, although you may find it easier to walk than to lollop on a camel.

guides and gear Wilderness Travel, in the US, offers a three-day camel trek as part of an extended cultural and adventure-oriented tour of Morocco (☎ 1-800/368-2794 or 510/558-2488, Ⓦ www.wildernesstravel.com).

when to go February to May and October and November are ideal for comfortable temperatures in the high desert. June to September brings severe heat.

getting there International flights service Casablanca Mohammed V Airport and Marrakech-Menara Airport. Ground operators can provide transportation to Erg Chebbi from each.

suggested reading Michael Benanav, *Men of Salt: Crossing the Sahara on the Caravan of White Gold* (Lyons Press). Absorbing account of the author's forty-day journey on the enduring salt caravan route in Mali. William Langewiesche, *Sahara Unveiled: A Journey Across the Desert* (Vintage). A vividly poetic account of encounters and observations from a 1,900-kilometer trans-Saharan journey.

is this for me?

PHYSICAL: ◆ ◆ ◆ ◆ ◆
Mildly aerobic walking and riding

PSYCH ◆ ◆ ◆ ◆ ◆
Exotic culture and a harsh environment

SKILL ◆ ◆ ◆ ◆ ◆
All skills learned on site

WOW! ◆ ◆ ◆ ◆ ◆
Desert and dunes come alive on a camel

> *The scenery is always the same; but if one has the love of great emptinesses, and of the play of light on long stretches of parched earth and rock, the sameness is part of the enchantment.*
>
> **Edith Wharton**

Though camel treks in the Sahara can be arranged for as brief as a day-trip, that's too short a time to begin to know the people and come to terms with the desert's many natural wonders. A trek that lasts at least three days will give you a true sense of the boundless emptiness of the Sahara, provide opportunities to connect with the Berber and Tuareg cultures and allow you to savour the starlit splendour of desert nights. Organized treks include the services of Berber guides and Tuareg cameleers whose knowledge of the landscape is legendary; they can spot a waterhole miles away and follow the most direct route in spite of the ever-shifting sands. Leading and tending to the camels are blue-robed Tuareg cameleers, whose traditional culture still revolves around trade and travel. During the day you'll glimpse the large goat-hair tents used by these nomads of the desert, but when dusk falls you'll make a temporary camp, stay in modern dome tents and perhaps enjoy a meal of meat kebabs and *harira* (a spicy bean soup), with a nightcap of mint tea.

To experience the most spellbinding camel safari head to Fez, from where a classic trek leads to the eastern side of Morocco's Atlas Mountains through a high desert plateau into the Moroccan Sahara near the Algerian border. You can either ride or walk along hard-packed earth dotted with rocky outcroppings and through parched riverbeds bereft of flowing water for thousands of years. The land is as lifeless as the sky is cloudless, but its inherent magic never wanes. Nowhere is the desert more entrancing than at Erg Chebbi, where sand dunes cover an area 8km wide and 20km long, with some individual dunes standing up to 150m high. The flowing, peach-coloured formations contoured against the horizon creates a striking effect, luring you to leave fleeting footprints in the shifting sands.

Trekking in the Drakensberg Mountains

109

DURBAN

SOUTH AFRICA

>> **Seeking solitude in the Barrier of Spears**

Rising from the lowlands of Transkei, the Drakensberg Mountains are the highest in southern Africa, forming a natural border between the South African province of KwaZulu-Natal and the land-locked Kingdom of Lesotho. Among the Zulu, these ancient peaks are known as uKhahlamba – Barrier of Spears. Later Boer settlers, sure they had seen a dragon flying above the cliffs, renamed them Dragon's Mountain, or Drakensberg in Afrikaans. This 600-kilometer bastion is no less visually arresting today, providing trekkers with some of the most inspiring terrain available on the African continent.

the Berg's baboons

Baboons, found throughout the Drakensberg, are among the largest members of the monkey family. Their four-legged gait, close-set eyes, and long, canine muzzle easily distinguish them from other primates. When it comes to finding food, they can be opportunistic and aggressive, and they've earned a reputation for eating farmers' crops and young sheep and goats. In the largely uninhabited Drakensberg, however, they feed on grasses, bark, rodents and birds.

Baboon troops have strong social structures, ruled by dominant males who mediate squabbles between members and protect the group from predators. Individuals reach sexual maturity at around four and a half years, and after a five-month pregnancy give birth to a single baby. The average lifespan for a baboon in the wild is 30 to 35 years.

While baboons are not aggressive toward humans, they are highly intelligent and will tear open an unguarded backpack in search of food. Never leave hiking equipment unattended, and bring all your gear into your tent at night.

The Berg, as the range is colloquially known, is comprised of sheer 1000-meter cliffs, threatening basalt spires, sandstone caves with prehistoric rock paintings, sweeping high plateaus, and a watershed that supplies one third of South Africa's water. Trekking here is, understandably, no light pursuit; the routes are arduous, often rough and remote, and sometimes there's no track at all. But what really catches visitors off-guard in the Drakensberg is the altitude. Hiking for days on end at an average elevation of 3000m can soon take its toll. On extended treks, many hikers accustomed to lower altitudes and carrying twenty-kilogram backpacks find themselves completely drained of energy, and climbing 1300 to 1400m on a day-hike can be excruciating. This is an adventure for the seriously fit.

The whole of the lower Berg is in the uKhahlamba-Drakensberg National Park, a UNESCO World Heritage Site renowned for its dramatic scenery, diverse plant and animal life, and ancient rock paintings. Day-hikes abound, and on overnight trips hikers can sleep in caves or huts. In the heights of the upper Berg, though, the landscape and the demands on trekkers change. The huts disappear, there's nowhere to replenish supplies, and all cooking must be done on gas stoves, as open fire is prohibited. The faint to non-existent trails require good route-finding and map-reading skills, and the weather can change frighteningly fast; you should come prepared with solid outdoor experience, since rescue services are five to seven hours away at any given time.

The classic trek in the Berg is a 75-kilometer, high-level traverse of the northern escarpment, running from the Sentinel, a squared peak in the north, to Cathedral Peak in the south, and taking five to seven days to complete, and starting at a trailhead about 70km south of the town of Harrismith, South Africa. The first test of your resolve comes as you climb one hundred rungs of chain ladders to the top of the Amphitheatre, a magnificent rock face with cliffs over 1000m deep and 4km long, where you'll have spectacular views to the Devil's Tooth, a lone pinnacle, and the Eastern Buttress, a massive flat-top escarpment. Continuing southward, you spot Thukela Falls, the world's second highest waterfall, with a total drop of 947m spread over five tiers, and as you continue up the escarpment you'll soon be right at the top of the falls. Past the falls, the stunning views from Mweni Needles, basalt expose an immense valley below you and dazzling pinnacles above. The Rockeries, with its vulture colony, is a bastion of rock that looks like a giant fort and offers commanding views down into the Cathedral Peak Valley. Throughout the traverse, fantastic views abound, since you're following the range's ridgeline.

What's most singular about this trek is its solitude – it's quite possible to spend four or five days without seeing anyone outside of your group. Alone in this vastness, it's easy to be overcome by the mountains' grandeur or mesmerized by the seemingly endless grasslands. There is, however, much life here: over 1800 varieties of flower, 400 of which are endemic, bloom at all elevations. Giant eland, with their distinctive, twisted horns, graze throughout the region, as do grey rhybuck and oribi, the latter among South Africa's most endangered antelope species, which often startle hikers with a shrill whistle before bouncing away. Baboons, too, populate the Berg's various altitudes, adapting to a spectrum of ecosystems.

After you explore the upper reaches of the Drakensberg, you'll also want to see the fascinating rock art in the park's lower elevations. To protect these antiquities, which evidence one million years of human habitation, access is only permitted with a resident guide employed by the park. Some 600 sites and 35,000 individual images have been catalogued, with the oldest painting, on a rock shelter wall, dating over 4000 years old. At the same time, you may have the chance to meet the modern-day residents of the region, particularly when you cross into the Kingdom of Lesotho. Whether it's the remains of generations past, a smiling local, or simply the towering mountains that inspire you, a trek in the Drakensberg will convince you that this place is eternal.

need to know

KZN Wildlife (☎ 033 845 1000. ⓦ www .kznwildlife.com) manages the uKhahlamba-Drakensberg Park. A wide variety of accommodation, including guesthouses and small inns are available near the park.

guides and gear Bergfree Adventures offers guided day-hikes and multi-day treks (☎ 033 239 5019 or 082 443 4287, ⓦ www. bergfree.co.za).

when to go Depending on the elevation, hiking in the Berg can be a year-round pursuit. The most enjoyable conditions occur in March, April and May, after the rains have stopped, when the mountains are still green and water is abundant. September and October are also pleasant. In the austral summer months of January and February, thunderstorms appear from nowhere and temperatures push 35°C, so get an early start on the day. The summer sun factor and frequently lead to heat exhaustion, dehydration and sunburn.

getting there International flights service Durban International Airport and Johannesburg International Airport. Local transportation is available to the town of Harrismith and key access points 2 to 3hr away.

suggested reading David Bristow, *Drakensberg Walks* (Struik, South Africa). Now in its third edition, this authoritative guide lists 120 graded hikes. R.O. Pearse, *Barrier of Spears: Drama of the Drakensberg* (Timmins or Printpak, South Africa). The best overall work on the range, with stories of the mountains and the men who climb them.

is this for me?

PHYSICAL ✦ ✦ ✦ ✦ ✦
Backpacking 10 to 15km a day in altitude

PSYCH ✦ ✦ ✦ ✦ ✦
No easy exit routes

SKILL ✦ ✦ ✦ ✦ ✦
Route-finding, camping skills essential

WOW! ✦ ✦ ✦ ✦ ✦
Amazing views, natural wonders

Trekking in the Rwenzori Mountains

>> A journey through the mist

110

UGANDA

● KASESE

In 150 AD, when Ptolemy wrote of snow-capped peaks near the equator in Africa, the idea seemed ridiculous. The Greek geographer named them *Lunae Montes*, Mountains of the Moon, and he correctly claimed that they fed the Nile. For centuries after, the mountains remained largely unknown to the Western world. Then, in 1889, Henry Morton Stanley's expedition, which had unwittingly been camping within thirty miles of the mountains for over three months, spotted them through a break in the cloud cover and equatorial haze. In choosing a new name for the watershed mountains, Stanley retained the native moniker, Rwenzori – "the rainmakers."

My eyes were directed by a boy to a mountain, said to be covered with salt, and I saw a peculiar shaped cloud of a most beautiful silver colour, which assumed the proportions and appearance of a vast mountain covered with snow.

Henry Morton Stanley

Unlike most other African ranges, the Rwenzori are not volcanic, but are a remnant of the upheaval that formed the Rift Valley. Along this valley they straddle the border between Uganda and the Democratic Republic of the Congo. Packed into the 128 kilometer range are six massifs, each with summits over 4500m and divided by yawning gorges; the tallest peak, Margherita on Mount Stanley, tops out at 5109m. While the high-altitude climbs alone make the mountains one of Africa's top trekking and mountaineering destinations, their best feature is their approach: misty slopes laced with rivers and ravines, crawling with dense vegetation and bountiful wildlife.

The classic Rwenzori excursion is a seven-day guided circuit, customizable to your skill level and interests. Most trekkers begin at the entrance to Uganda's Rwenzori Mountains National Park, which protects the upper slopes of the range and is open to foot traffic only; the Congo's Parc National des Virunga is less politically stable and has inadequate support services. Most trekkers opt to climb Mount Stanley, typically lengthening their trek by a night – not an unwelcome addition, since they're accompanied by an entourage of porters and cooks and housed in a series of wooden huts.

Over the course of 10km from the national park's Ibanda entrance gate, the route ascends about a thousand vertical meters, from small farm plots into dense forests. By the time you reach the Nyabitaba hut (2650m) for your night's stay, you're enveloped by the range's ever-present mists. The second day takes you through a spectrum of foliage zones on a strenuous course with several river crossings. Days three, four, and five stay between 3500–4400m in a land of bogs, rivers, lakes

Luigi Amedeo, Duke of the Abruzzi

Luigi Amedeo had an unlikely pedigree for a mountain climber – his father was the king of Spain, his grandfather and uncle were both kings of Italy. At the age of six Luigi was enlisted in the Italian navy to commence his education and destiny as a naval officer. But boyhood adventures in the Italian Alps had a powerful pull on the young royal, and in his teens after climbing Mont Blanc, Monte Rosa and the Matterhorn, Luigi vowed to devote his life to mountaineering and exploration. After climbing the Matterhorn's difficult Zmutt Ridge at the age of 21, circumnavigating the globe, making a pioneering first ascent on Mount St Elias, the second highest peak in both the United States and Canada, he led an 1899 expedition to the North Pole. He came to within 381km of the North Pole, closer than any previous attempt.

Luigi Amedeo then turned his attention to Africa's Rwenzori Mountains which had been first viewed by Henry Morton Stanley just seventeen years earlier, but remained unclimbed. Never one to settle for the easy way out, the duke made the first ascent of all sixteen summits in the Rwenzori over 4500m. He named the highest of those summits (5109m) Margherita Peak for Italy's queen mother. But the duke's expedition was more than just peak-bagging – they produced the first modern maps of the range and conducted scientific studies of the area's vegetation, geology and glaciology.

After his naval command in World War I, the Duke of the Abruzzi retreated to an Italian-style villa on a plantation in Somalia where he lived until his death at the age of 60. His restless pursuits of adventure on far-flung mountains, and on the polar icecap made him one of the most wide-ranging explorers of his time or any other.

need to know

A trek into the alpine reaches of the Rwenzori covers some tough terrain and makes for a difficult traverse, and must be supported by guides and porters, but the rewards found in and above the clouds are matchless in Africa.

guides and gear Rwenzori Mountaineering Services in Kasese has the sole concession to operate hikes and treks into Rwenzori National Park. They can also coordinate ground arrangements, accommodation and services in the area before and after your trek (☎0483 444 936 or 0414 237 497, Ⓦ www. rwenzorimountaineeringservices.com). If you have limited time, park guides can also arrange day-hikes or short overnight treks into the higher-elevation forests.

when to go Thanks to their position near the equator, the Rwenzori can be trekked and climbed year-round. July to mid-September and December to February offer slightly drier weather.

getting there From Kampala's Entebbe International Airport, it's about 300km (5–6hr) over paved roads to Kasese, the jumping-off point.

suggested reading Philip Briggs, *Uganda, The Bradt Travel Guide* (Bradt). A well-informed, comprehensive guide to the country.

suggested viewing *Mountains of the Moon* (1990). Based on Burton and Speke's 1857 expedition to discover the source of the Nile, and the subsequent feud between the explorers.

is this for me?

PHYSICAL ◆ ◆ ◆ ◆ ◆
Difficult trekking in high altitude

PSYCH ◆ ◆ ◆ ◆
Challenging altitude and weather

SKILL ◆ ◆
Glacier experience needed for summits

WOW! ◆ ◆ ◆ ◆
Demanding routes, varied wildlife

and even alpine zones; on these days, you have chances to climb mounts Baker, Speke and Stanley. On Mount Stanley, you'll traverse the Elena Glacier as part of a rope team with ice axes and crampons, then cross the Stanley Plateau and continue to the summit. From here, your views will likely consist of the tops of clouds, through which an occasional opening may reveal the green valleys and forests below.

As the circuit turns you back toward the park entrance, you'll ascend Freshfield Pass (4282m), named after Douglas Freshfield, president of the English Alpine Club, who failed in his 1905 attempt to climb Mount Stanley due to bad weather. One kilometer after the pass is Bujongolo Cave, used by the Duke of Abbruzzi on the first ascent of Mount Stanley in 1906 and still serving as an overnight shelter. You very well may use it, too: the Rwenzori trek pushes you through some exceptionally difficult terrain, tougher than Kilimanjaro or Mount Kenya and with consistently wet weather and knee-deep mud.

For all its physical and climatic challenges, the Rwenzori reward visitors with unusual vegetation, layered in several distinct zones. Tropical rainforest dominates the lower elevations, giving way to a forested region above 1800m. At 2500m, bamboo takes over; heather moorlands appear above 3000m, and alpine habitat at 4000m. Thanks to the equatorial climate and substantial rainfall, gigantism is a common feature of each of these plant zones: giant lobelia, rarely taller than a meter elsewhere, here grows in forest-like stands sometimes higher than five meters. Giant heather can reach six meters and is draped with a moss known as "old man's beard," which thrives in the moist climate, as do giant groundsels and bunch grasses.

With changes in vegetation come changes in wildlife. Over seventy species of mammal live within the Rwenzori, all primarily below the alpine zone. A variety of primates populate the forest, among them colobus and blue monkeys and the occasional chimpanzee. Mountain elephants, giant forest hogs, leopards and golden cats also inhabit this zone, but sightings are rare; bounding bushbucks and antelopes, on the other hand, can frequently be spotted near lakes and streams or grazing in meadows.

The range of distinctive and recognizable avian species will, after a few days, turn even the most inexperienced birder into a self-proclaimed ornithologist. Nearly two hundred migratory and endemic varieties live in the forest and lowlands: crested Rwenzori turacos, cinnamon-chested bee-eaters, long-tailed cuckoos and long-eared owls will add color and a fitting soundtrack to your trek.

Canoe safari on the Zambezi River

111

ZAMBIA

LAKE
KARIBA

From its source in a marshy bog in northwest Zambia, the Zambezi quickly gains momentum, a 2700km-long river that crosses six countries on its way to the Indian Ocean. The Zambezi's most popular sight is Victoria Falls, located on the border between Zambia and Zimbabwe. The largest curtain of falling water on earth, Victoria Falls provide what are arguably the best one-day whitewater runs in the world as it funnels through the Batoka Gorge. These show-stopping spectacles, however, shouldn't overshadow one of the river's greatest features: the lesser-developed and relatively inaccessible lower Zambezi, which just happens to course through two massive wildlife sanctuaries, providing an unparalleled opportunity to see wildlife up-close and personal on a classic canoe safari.

what's in the trunk?

The most distinctive and identifiable feature of an elephant, whether Asian or African, is the incredibly large and versatile trunk. A synthesis of nose and upper lip, this prominent and powerful proboscis can be used to spray water, gather forage, create an ear-shattering sound, pick up small objects, swat flies, break branches, and communicate with other elephants. Yet its evolutionary history remains a mystery.

Just how elephants developed their trunks has perplexed paleozoologists for decades. Because the trunk is boneless, it leaves no paleontological traces that could provide a definitive clue. Absent a fossilized history, scientists are left reconstructing a most-likely scenario for an evolutionary process involving the elephant's closest ancestor, the tapir. It is believed by some that as the size of the early tapir increased, the mammal's nose lengthened to accommodate its already established foraging practices. Scientists estimate this lengthening may have taken over fifty million years.

For the elephant, the world's largest land animal and a giant herbivore, the trunk's most important task is to harvest up to three hundred kilograms of plant food each day. Doing so can take as long as twenty hours to accomplish. Watching an elephant in the wild gather and consume a meal can be fascinating as thousands of trunk muscles are dexterously engaged for the time-consuming task – plucking leaves from branches, grazing on grasses, snapping off tree limbs, or shaking fruit from a tree. The meal is them nimbly stuffed in a gaping mouth with tusks on either side. The elephants' strength and agility make it a mesmerizing scene. Of course, elephants also use their trunks to drink, sucking a dozen liters at a time through the animal kingdom's largest natural straw. But if the elephant starts pounding his trunk on the ground, he's not hungry, he's angry, and you'd better get out of the way.

A typical safari lasts three to five days, starting at the Kariba Gorge, between Zambia and Zimbabwe. From here, the lower Zambezi River runs downstream to the Mozambique border with a steady 4km per hour current, making relatively light work out of paddling four to five hours a day. As you head downriver, Zambia's Lower Zambezi National Park opens up to your left, a largely undeveloped wilderness whose northern escarpment forms a physical barrier to most of the park's species. This escarpment concentrates wildlife on the valley floor, pushing their habitat to the river's edge and putting you face to face with enormous herds of elephant, waterbuck, and buffalo. You might also see impalas and zebras – and possibly lions lurking nearby in grassy openings at the edge of scrubby mopane woodlands.

Not all the excitement is on the port side of your canoe, however. On the right bank is Zimbabwe's Mana Pools National Park, defined by seasonal riverine pools and stillwater channels with rich foliage. During the dry season, from May to October, the park attracts an abundance of elephant, zebra and kudu; viewing gets better as the season progresses. The undeniable appeal of Mana Pools – unique in all Zimbabwe – is the ability to walk unaccompanied in a park that has large mammals, including carnivores, although you'll do so at your own risk. Better yet, all of the park's game trails are easily accessible by canoe. Along both banks of the Zambezi, the concentration of birdlife is exceptional, with over three hundred species found in Mana Pools alone. Fish eagles can be seen and heard for miles around, and colorful bee-eaters, lilac breasted rollers, parrots, and trogons all appear seasonally.

For a typical four-day canoe safari, a moderate level of fitness is recommended and no prior canoeing experience is required. While participating in a canoe safari is fairly low-risk, being in the midst of an unfamiliar wilderness requires that you be constantly aware of your surroundings both on and off the water. On very rare occasions safari participants have had fatal encounters with water buffalo on the outskirts of camp.

guides and gear A number of tour operators provide packaged canoe trips down the lower Zambezi, with various camping options. More luxurious options are available in supported canoe safaris where you overnight at comfortable bush camps on the banks of the river. Zambezi Safari and Travel Company offers lodge-based as well as camping canoe safaris (☎ 44/(0)1548-830059 ⓦ www.zambezi.com).

when to go In general, a canoe safari on the Zambezi can be undertaken year-round. With the November rains, the wildlife disperses somewhat, but the birdlife becomes more abundant. Though this green season, from November to April, can be wet, it also offers some stunningly beautiful lighting. While mosquitoes are at their peak from February through May, there is a year-round malaria risk that can be prevented by taking a prescription anti-malarial drug and using insect repellent.

getting there Fly into the Lusaka International Airport in Zambia. From there, a shuttle service is available to Lake Kariba, the starting point for most canoe safaris, about 2hr away.

Still, whatever surprises the riverbanks may hold never eclipse the river itself. Along various inlets and tributaries it's possible to glide along the sunlit blue hues of the Zambezi in total silence, making you an unobtrusive visitor in this abundant natural kingdom. The banks vary from overhanging and overgrown vegetation, to more sparsely vegetated floodplain. You'll have frequent opportunities to see crocodiles and pods of hippopotamus. Guides take you down remote channels between islands, where your chances of getting close to game are very high. Because hippos, especially single males, can be territorial and aggressive, you have to be careful in your approach. Typically, as the guide announces your arrival, hippos will head for deeper water, allowing you to ply your canoe through the safer shallow line. Elephant and buffalo spend much of their time in and around the water, and the waterbuck, though not nearly as aquatic as its name might suggest, is a good swimmer and will quickly retreat to the river to escape its predator, the lion.

Most operators use stable, well-tracking, five-meter-long canoes with padded bucket seats. On a self-supporting safari, all gear is carried in the canoe and camps are set up on islands in the river or on the riverbanks. Participants share in establishing camp and in preparing meals around the glow of an open campfire. With nightfall, the sounds of the Zambezi intensify, as grunting hippos, roaring lions, and cackling hyenas call from the distance.

is this for me?

PHYSICAL ✦ ✦ ✦ ✦ ✦
Relaxed paddling

PSYCH ✦ ✦ ✦ ✦ ✦
Exposure to wild animals

SKILL ✦ ✦ ✦ ✦ ✦
Flatwater canoeing

WOW! ✦ ✦ ✦ ✦ ✦
Close-range wildlife viewing

Horseback riding through the Masai Mara

>> **Gallop alongside wild zebra and wildebeest herds**

KENYA

MASAI MARA GAME RESERVE

A morning ride in the Masai Mara, one of the largest game parks in Kenya, begins just as day breaks; leaving early increases the chances of a wildlife encounter. Whether it's seeing an elephant fling its trunk above its head, trumpeting into the air, or a pride of lions lounging after a kill, a meeting with one of Africa's big game species is so exhilarating as to be worth conquering any initial fear. There's no better place to conquer it than in the Masai Mara, famed for its abundant wildlife and wide-open landscape. On horseback, unshielded by a safari vehicle or the walls of a lodge, you truly become part of this glorious landscape.

Kenya's Masai Mara is actually the northern extension of Tanzania's Serengeti, set in the heart of Africa's Great Rift Valley. Named after the Masai (see box) and the Mara River, the region is fed by a moderate year-round rainfall that sustains the active wildlife populations in all seasons. The Mara, as it's called, is savannah, characterized by rolling hills, grasslands dotted with solitary acacia trees, and occasional woodlands. It's precisely the openness of the landscape that makes wildlife spotting here so frequent and spectacular.

A typical day on a horseback safari begins in the shadowless early morning light, while a support crew breaks camp, loads tents, cots and the kitchen into the support vehicles, heading off to the next camp while doing some scouting along the way. The guides and support crews are usually native Kenyans who are at home in the culture and wildlife. Guides don't carry arms and only use bullwhips when absolutely necessary. You'll spend the day traversing the large ranches that form the greater Masai Mara, and are likely to come upon Masai villages in areas not visited by the caravans of commercial coaches and safari vehicles found within the game park. In these simple encounters, the Masai are gracious and friendly, often inviting travelers into their huts and introducing their families.

As you progress through the savannah, animals you'll see along your ride include wildebeest, the area's most dominant species. In fact, with a population numbering well over a million, you'll often be riding among them, through them and around them. During the Great Migration every July and August, huge numbers of zebra, wildebeest and Thomson's gazelle arrive in the Mara from the Serengeti. At this time, it's possible to get the thrilling chance to gallop alongside herds of hundreds.

Another species you're very likely to see is the lion, though because lions are still hunted by the Masai, they tend to be somewhat apprehensive of humans. The spotting of elephant herds is a common occurrence and always an adrenaline rush. Horses recognize elephants as potentially dangerous and are generally leery approaching a herd, but you'll be able to get close enough to hear them ripping grass with their trunks and even hear their "tummy rumble", a low, often subsonic growl that actually comes from their

the Masai

Robed in red, a stark, slender silhouette on the horizon holds a spear, herding cattle with a fluid power and calm confidence. Living mainly in the Rift Valley that stretches from Kenya through Tanzania, the Masai live close to the land. They rely on cattle for their diet, which consists chiefly of cow's blood, milk and meat. However, the use of blood is declining as the number of cattle decreases; diets are now supplemented with maize-meal, rice and potatoes.

Because of the Masai aversion to eating game (lions are hunted primarily as a test of courage and not for meat), the land on which the Masai live is typically abundant with wildlife. A nomadic people, Masai possess a deep-rooted cultural conscience that respects nature and their place in it. Resisting the strong encouragement of the Kenyan and Tanzanian national governments to develop a more agrarian, sedentary lifestyle, the Masai have worked hard to keep their traditions. Today the Masai constitute only one percent of the population of Kenya.

Many Masai work as guides or wildlife ranch employees, and often act as the support for local safari and touring companies. Travelers can request Masai guides and support staff to lead them in their adventures in the African bush.

need to know

Before joining a horseback safari you should be riding regularly, have a good solid seat and have a fair amount of riding expertise.

guides and gear Equitours offers horseback riding adventures worldwide including ground services, accommodation, horses and guides (☎ 307/455-3363, ⓦ www.ridingtours .com).

when to go Since the Masai Mara is near the equator on a high plain, the temperatures are comfortable year-round. The long rains occur from March through May, and the short rains from October through December, so any other time is ideal.

getting there Fly into Kenya at Nairobi's Jomo Kenyatta International Airport. You can connect to the Mara Serena Airport within the game park or take ground transportation from Nairobi to your safari staging area.

suggested reading Jonathan Scott, Angela Scott and Caroline Taggart, *Mara-Serengeti: A Photographer's Paradise* (Hardcover). A celebration of life on the Mara with photos and text.

suggested viewing *Africa the Serengeti* (1994). A Spectacular IMAX documentary featuring footage of the Great Migration, narrated by James Earl Jones.

is this for me?

PHYSICAL ◆ ◆ ◆ ◇ ◇
Endurance, strength and agility

PSYCH ◆ ◆ ◆ ◇ ◇
Long days riding

SKILL ◆ ◆ ◆ ◆ ◇
Demands strong riding skills

WOW! ◆ ◆ ◆ ◇ ◇
Great animal views and rides

vocal chords. Get too close and an elephant will charge a horse, although they'll typically bluff first.

While these species thrive, other species face a more tenuous and threatened existence, though you'll still have a chance of seeing them. The black rhinoceros, once common, is now severely endangered, with a population of less than fifty. Hippos, normally found in groups near rivers, have also suffered population declines after several drought years. The cheetah has seen declining populations as a result of traditional car-based safari viewing, which disrupts its hunting practices.

Various horseback tours and guides are available, and typical trips last ten days. Expect to be in the saddle for about six hours per day, during which you'll cover 35–40km. One of the best things about a riding safari is that the horses have an intuitive sense as to whether or not it's safe to approach potentially dangerous situations or wild animals. Most of the horses used are thoroughbreds crossed with Somali Arabians, known for their sure-footing and good stamina. Quite a few of these horses play polo in the off-season, and respond well to leg cues.

113 Diving in the Seychelles

>> Take a plunge with whale sharks

There aren't many places in the world where you'll see granite islands rising up from the middle of the ocean – not in Hawaii, Polynesia, the Azores or Bermuda, which are all products of volcanic activity. But one hundred million years does some amazing things to granite once it makes its way to the surface and is accessorized with coral sands, palm trees and other tropical vegetation. No wonder the Seychelles are considered one of the most beautiful places on earth. Pitched as "3000 miles from anywhere," this outcropping of 115 islands in the Indian Ocean is really just 1000km east of Mombasa, Kenya.

the Aldabra tortoise

The lifespan of an Aldabra tortoise, more commonly known as the giant tortoise, can easily exceed 100 years and often reach 150. However, a tortoise's age is often hard to track, since the animals tend to outlive their scientific observers. Not only do these gentle giants live long lives, but they're also the largest tortoises in existence: females often weigh over 135kg, and males average about 250kg.

Aldabra tortoises used to be quite common throughout the islands of the Indian Ocean, but they were heavily hunted during the exploration and colonization of the Seychelles in the 1600s, and now they are the only remaining species of the eighteen tortoises that once roamed these waters. Thanks to scientists Charles Darwin and Lord Walter Rothschild, the last of the Aldabra tortoises were preserved and now reside under the protection of the Nature Protection Trust of Seychelles (NPTS), which has developed breeding programmes. Although some of the world's zoos house giant tortoises, to see them in the wild you'll have to visit the Aldabra Atoll; this small group of coral islands in the Seychelles is the only place the tortoise lives free.

The Aldabra tortoise, existing in the wild only in the Seychelles, is the longest-lived animal on earth

Here you'll be dazzled by the variety of flowering plants and unusual animal species, like the giant tortoise and black parrot. But for all their surface appeal, the Seychelles hold even more to fall in love with underwater. The same granite boulders that dot the beaches have also tumbled to the ocean floor to create a distinctive diving experience. They attract an impressive array of fish to their rocky caverns, swim-throughs and encrusted coral, and give the subaqueous landscape an ambience unrivaled by the reef systems of other islands.

If you're a sucker for adventure-diving and swimming with big fish, then the adrenaline rush you'll get while diving alongside massive whale sharks – the biggest fish in the world – will easily be worth your airfare. Whale sharks in the Seychelles range from 6–8m long, though the species can reach up to 18m elsewhere. To locate them, morning flights from the Marine Conservation Society Seychelles scan the waters and record the sharks' whereabouts. In the afternoon, dive boats visit the reported areas, hoping that the creatures are still nearby. When a boat finds a shark, even skilled divers can have some hesitation about entering the water, but they're invariably won over once they take the plunge. The code of conduct for whale shark encounters prohibits you from swimming in front of a shark, since this will spook it and cause it to dive. Stay 3m from the top of a shark so as not to disturb it, and 4m from the tail to prevent a sudden brush with the enormous fin. Non-divers and young children can have an equally compelling experience on the boat, which affords great views of the gentle giants as they rub their broad snouts against the hull.

Whale sharks aren't the only or even the primary attraction for divers in the Seychelles, though. From Mahé, the main island in the Seychelles, you'll have convenient access to protected areas and dive sites that feature other unusual fish: leaf fish, flat specimens with jaws that look like a stem; Indian walkman, which scuttle along the ocean floor much like a crab; and pipefish, looking like a swimming snake. On the inner islands reside hawksbill and occasionally green turtles, which mate in October and hatch in December along beaches in the south.

Wreck divers will find yet more interesting sea life on a number of sunken ships in the area, well suited to all experience levels. The best wreck is the Ennerdale, a 74,000-ton British tanker that sank on a sandbar in 1970 after hitting an uncharted granite pinnacle. Located

11km from Victoria, Mahé's port and the capital of the Seychelles, its three sections lie 30m deep. The collapsing wreck can no longer be entered, but she's impressive enough from the outside. As you glide about the debris, expect to see whitetip reef sharks and stingrays in the tangled structure. You'll also find batfish nearby, recognizable by their elongated dorsal and anal fins, which make them taller than they are long and give them the appearance of bats with extended wings.

While the Seychelles offer plenty of opportunities for expert divers to test their mettle, they're quite suitable for beginners as well. In the safe and shallow waters of Beau Vallon Bay there are no major currents to overexert you or cause long, difficult swims back to the boat. The sheltered environment is more forgiving than fragile coral for developing essential buoyancy-control skills, and the direct and intense sunlight, thanks to the islands' location just below the equator, provides well-illuminated diving conditions for much of the day.

need to know

The Seychelles offer four marine national parks and amazing diversity, making them a tropical dive destination well worth traveling any distance to discover. Since the most popular dive spots are centered among the easily accessed main granitic islands, liveaboards aren't a particularly worthwhile venture here, though you will find them on offer.

guides and gear Underwater Centre, located at the *Coral Strand Hotel* (☎ 248 247 357), and Dive Seychelles, at the *Berjaya Beau Vallon Bay Hotel* (☎ 248 247 516, Ⓦ www.diveseychelles.com. sc), both on Mahé, offer a full range of dives to suit both novice and experienced divers.

when to go Good diving is possible year-round, with the best times being the end of March through May and the end of September through November. Optimal conditions around the outer and lower coral islands, where extended dive trips will take you, are limited to a six- to eight-week window in the spring and autumn.

getting there Scheduled flights and charters from Europe fly into Seychelles International Airport on Mahé. Dive resorts are located nearby.

suggested reading Sarah Carpin, *Seychelles: Garden of Eden in the Indian Ocean* (Odyssey). An in-depth guide rich with insight into the history, culture and legends of these beautiful islands.

is this for me?

PHYSICAL ✦ ✦ ✦ ✦ ✦
Requires balance and coordination

PSYCH ✦ ✦ ✦ ✦ ✦
Standard diving-associated risk

SKILL ✦ ✦ ✦ ✦ ✦
Certification required or obtainable on site

WOW! ✦ ✦ ✦ ✦ ✦
Exceptional diving in a beautiful setting

Tracking mountain gorillas

● KIGALI

RWANDA

>> Face to face with a silverback

It's one of those moments when time stands still. You've been slogging up muddy mountain trails in a light rain for three hours. Your tracker has just located the resting spot for a family of twelve mountain gorillas. He tugs on your sleeve to pull you closer to where the giant silverback is keeping a relaxed watch on the family. Then it happens – the silverback draws forward, plows through the mist-washed vegetation in your direction, and fixes his gaze directly into your eyes. His piercing glance says more than words ever could. You are looking into the eyes of one of the most endangered animals on the planet.

Today, mountain gorillas number around 720 and are divided between two populations in central Africa. One population of 340 lives in Uganda's Bwindi National Park, while 380 live on the slopes of the Virunga Mountains. Of these, about one hundred live on the politically unstable Congo side, with the remaining 280 located in Rwanda.

In Rwanda your quest to locate the elusive gorillas begins at the entrance to the Volcanoes National Park about 2.5 hours north of Kigali. Groups of eight are accompanied by a guide and two trackers, without whom

you could never hope to find the gorillas. A typical day of tracking gorillas involves hiking 5–6km through steep, dense tropical forest at an elevation between 2000–3000m. You'll often face wet weather, difficult slopes and muddy sections of trail, but you'll be rewarded with stunning scenery, exotic birds and chances of spotting other wildlife, including golden monkeys – all before you encounter the gorillas.

Mountains gorillas typically leave their nesting site at sunrise, browse on thick forest vegetation in the morning, rest during midday, then resume feeding in the afternoon before building their nest for the evening. The trackers have the essential job of locating the previous day's nest, then following a faint trail of gorilla feces, broken twigs, partially-eaten leaves, and footprints to the gorilla's nesting location for the remainder of the day and into the evening. Mountain gorillas don't move as much as western lowland gorillas, and can usually be found within about 1km of their previous night's nest.

mountain gorilla populations

A stout, barrel-chested 180kg silverback mountain gorilla standing 1.7m tall on a Rwandan mountainside and beating his fists against his chest is hardly an image of vulnerability. In truth, however, gorillas are rarely aggressive and are one of the most critically endangered wild populations in the world. Both species of gorilla – western and eastern – have been threatened for years. The eastern gorillas of Rwanda, Uganda, and the Democratic Republic of Congo, including mountain gorillas, are threatened mostly by habitat destruction and as bystanders of civil unrest, while western gorillas are threatened by poaching for bushmeat and the outbreak of diseases like Ebola. Although mountain gorilla populations have somewhat stabilized at around 720, western gorilla populations continue to decrease rapidly.

Gorilla viewing by conservation-minded individuals in a limited and carefully controlled program can be an important factor in preserving the species. Not only do eco-tourists fund preservation efforts by purchasing permits and providing jobs and economically sustainable alternatives to the destruction of gorilla habitat, but the mere presence of tourists, guides, and trackers discourages the incursion of poachers.

need to know

Permits for gorilla viewing are issued by the Rwanda Tourism Board (☎ 250/576 514 or 573 396, ⓦ www.rwandatourism.com). Although individuals can purchase permits directly, almost all participate in a group organized by one of several operators that also arrange guides, trackers, accommodations near the park, and other travel services within Rwanda. During most commercial tours, you will track twice which almost guarantees success on at least one outing.

guides and gear The UK's World Primate Safaris (☎ 0870/850-9092, ⓦ www. worldprimatesafaris.com) specializes in mountain gorilla safaris in both Rwanda and Uganda. You'll want warm, waterproof gear for the cool, wet climate; gaiters are highly recommended.

when to go In this equatorial climate, gorilla tracking is a year round activity with no one season offering increased likelihood of sighting.

getting there Fly into Rwanda's Kigali International Airport. The Volcanoes National Park is located about 2hr 30min north of Kigali.

suggested reading Bill Weber and Amy Vedder, *In the Kingdom of Gorillas: Fragile Species in a Dangerous Land* (Simon & Schuster). The two leading gorilla conservationist in Rwanda lay out political and environmental challenges facing gorilla preservation and propose means of protecting populations with ecotourism programs to benefit the Rwandan people.

suggested viewing *Gorillas in the Mist* (1988). Tells the true-life story of naturalist Dian Fossey and her work with gorillas. *Hotel Rwanda* (2004). Based on the true-life drama of the Rwandan Genocide and the quiet courage of one man in protecting innocent countrymen. *Mountain Gorilla* (1991). Filmed in Rwanda, this IMAX feature gets up close and personal with mountain gorillas.

is this for me?

PHYSICAL ✦ ✦ ✦
Strenuous hiking for 5 to 8 hours per day

PSYCH ✦ ✦
Wet weather; contact with gorillas

SKILL ✦ ✦
Trekking and observation learned on site

WOW! ✦ ✦ ✦ ✦ ✦
An emotional, life-changing experience

The midday rest and play is a time when gorillas – particularly the younger members of the group – bond, learn communication skills, and develop patterns of behavior within the group. Crouching on the periphery of a shaded spot selected by the silverback, you'll see some gorillas sleep while others rest or play. Some gorillas will groom each other's fur, carefully removing debris, dirt and parasites; mothers are particularly gentle groomers with their offspring. The younger gorillas are more likely to be playful, which could include some rambunctious chasing or wrestling, and occasional tree climbing. Reigning over the midday rest is the silverback. He's responsible for protecting the group from outside threats, resolving any conflicts within the group, and even supervising play among the younger gorillas – sometimes he'll join in the fun, too.

Observing the simple similarities in human and gorilla behavior can be fascinating, but you're not the only ones doing the watching; some gorillas can seem to be as curious about you as you are about them. They are habituated to frequent human contact and tend to accept – or at least tolerate – your presence at the group's social hour. Sometimes they'll even approach you, but be sure to keep your distance. Strict regulations require that you stay 7m from the gorillas, and if you encroach too far the silverback may beat down vegetation or make a mock charge to put you in your place and let you know who is in command. If this happens, hold your ground and look submissive. The one thing you don't want to do is run the other way.

Observation time is limited to one hour to avoid excessive contact and to limit the potential for transferring human diseases and infections, since even a common cold could decimate an entire family. You cannot go out tracking if you are sick or carrying an infectious disease, nor are you allowed to eat or drink in the presence of the gorillas. You are not allowed to touch the gorillas, although it is entirely possible that they might touch you.

As you observe the mountain gorillas, you can't help but realize that you are participating in one of the rarest of all wildlife encounters – the opportunity to be a guest in the home of the largest primates. You're not detached and shielded from them or enclosed in the comfort of a safari vehicle; you are approaching them on their terms. In the end, it's a simple meeting, but it's one that's likely to leave a lifelong impression.

115 Rafting the White Nile

>> As big as whitewater gets

When it comes to superlatives, it's hard to match the Nile. At over 6400 kilometers it's the planet's longest river. It's been a lifeline to civilizations since the Stone Age, and many of the world's early explorers spent the better part of their lives in search of its source. In the fifth century BC, Herodotus called Egypt "the gift of the Nile." But for today's outdoor adventurers, incredible whitewater rafting may be the Nile's greatest gift.

John Hanning Speke and the source of the Nile

John Hanning Speke, a British explorer during the mid 1800s, began his career when, on leave from the Indian Army, he explored the Himalayas and ventured into Tibet. Later, he accepted Richard Burton's invitation to join a Somaliland (now Somalia) expedition, beginning Speke's short but abundantly productive campaign exploring East Africa. During their expedition, the pair was attacked by natives, but both managed to escape; Burton was hit in the jaw by a spear that pierced him from cheek to cheek and Speke was repeatedly stabbed with a spear before managing an escape. In 1856, the two returned again to East Africa, this time hoping to find the legendary lakes in the hear of the continent, especially Lake Nyassa, rumored to be the source of the Nile River. Along the way, Speke suffered temporary deafness when he cut a beetle out of his ear with a knife. He later went temporarily blind from an infection, so that when the two became the first white men to reach Lake Taganyika's shores, Speke could barely see the lake. Before the two could discover Lake Nyassa, Burton fell ill and Speke decided to continue without him. Heading north, Speke discovered Lake Victoria and decided it was the true source of the Nile, then quickly returned home to spread the news. When Burton returned, he argued that Speke could not be sure of his findings because he had not adequately explored the lake.

Leaving Burton behind again, Speke returned in 1860 to lead a Royal Geographical Society funded expedition to substantiate his claims. He did so by exploring the north side of Lake Victoria, where he discovered Ripon Falls and followed it up to Khartoum. Here he sent a famously presumptive telegraph claiming, "the Nile is settled." This still did not pacify Burton, who argued that since Speke did not follow the river to its end, he could not be sure that it was the Nile. To resolve this issue, they planned a debate in front of the Royal Geographical Association. Unfortunately, the night before the debate could take place, Speke died, while hunting, from a self-inflicted gunshot wound, and whether the shot was intentional or accidental is still unknown.

Whitewater rafting on the Nile is a relatively recent pursuit, following the first raft descent in 1996. The source of the Nile as is Lake Victoria, the second largest freshwater lake in the world, and it has only one outlet – the White Nile. The whitewater adventure begins just below the Owen Falls Dam, which marks the point where the White Nile flows out of Lake Victoria. The most frequently run section of the river is a 32km day-trip below the dam, although an extended 50km section is offered as part of a highly recommended two- or three-day trip

Before you get into the water, the first thing you notice about the river is its size and flow. In most places the Nile ranges from .5km to 1km in width and is dotted with heavily forested midriver islands. You sense that this is a bold, energetic river, and then you step in the 26°C water and find that it's as inviting as it is exciting. You'll be launching on the Nile's south bank, just below cliffs that overlook the source of the river near the town of Jinja. Since the river flows through a populated agricultural region, the aggressive hippos and crocodiles have long since been hunted out of the sections now used by rafters. Shortly after you put in your five-meter eight-passenger raft, you come to Bujagali Falls, a thunderous series of Class IV and V cascading rapids. Some of the heart-stopping Class V rapids that follow, with names like Big Brother, Total Gunga and Itunda, are as big as whitewater gets. The back-to-back stomach-turning drops of Overtime and Retrospect deliver some of the most technical and sustained rafting found anywhere in the world. Along the river's banks and on islands you'll be surrounded by lush rainforest vegetation with tropical hardwoods and giant fig trees. Red-tailed monkeys and giant monitor lizards up to six feet in length are commonly sighted. You'll pass local fishermen in their dugout canoes working the calmer sections of the river, but still able to paddle smaller rapids with amazing speed and agility.

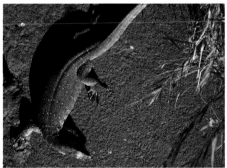

The final spectacle of the one-day trip is an intimidating fifteen-foot drop called The Bad Place, part of the largest vertical drop on the runnable section. This one pushes the limits of a Class V rapid and is regarded the largest commercially-rafted hole in the world. As the guide yells "get down" be prepared to be hit with a solid wall of water and be thrown from the raft. On any given day, most if not all rafters will fall out at The Bad Place, and most rafts will flip. On a typical one-day trip you'll spend about six hours on the river during which you can expect to have your raft flip three or four times, sending terrified (and delighted) participants straight into the washing machine.

The White Nile is a boisterous, exciting river, beautiful and full of life. As a whitewater destination it's still relatively unknown. But some of its towering rapids are currently threatened by the construction of a dam which would submerge Bujagali Falls and a two-mile section of river, forever drowning some of the rapids, however rafting and other whitewater sports will continue on the downriver rapids. Enjoy this fresh adventure on an ancient river while it can still claim to be whitewater rafting at its best.

need to know

In spite of its surging volume and astoundingly large rapids, the White Nile is an exceptionally safe river. Africa is one of the oldest of continents and the Nile flows along ancient bedrock without the fallen slabs and dangerous boulders found in the geology of younger rivers. As a wide multi-channel pool drop river, the Nile enables the guide to choose the precise route, channel, and rapid approach best suited to the skill level and physical capabilities of the raft team.

guides and gear Adrift Adventure Co. (☎0772/237 438 or 0312/237 438, Ⓦwww.surfthesource.com) offers one- and two-day whitewater trips on the White Nile starting near Jinja.

when to go The warm waters of the Nile can be run year-round with minimal seasonal variations in the dam-release flow.

getting there Fly into Entebbe-Kampala International Airport and take local transportation to Jinja, about two hours east of Kampala. Most rafting begins about 10km downriver from the Owen Falls Dam (officially known as the Nalubaale Dam).

suggested reading Christopher Ondaatje, *Journey to the Source of the Nile* (HarperCollins) An outstanding blend of travelogue, history, and photography exploring the Nile.

is this for me?

PHYSICAL ✦ ✦ ✦ ✦ ✦
Upper torso strength and agility required

PSYCH ✦ ✦ ✦ ✦ ✦
Class V rapids

SKILL ✦ ✦ ✦ ✦ ✦
No prior whitewater experience required

WOW! ✦ ✦ ✦ ✦ ✦
Epic rapids that are an exceptional thrill

Safari in the Okavango Delta

116

>> Hear every chirp and rustle

What becomes of a river when it has no place left to go? What happens when there is no sea or lake waiting downstream to swallow its flow? Such a dilemma is faced by the Kavango River, which flows from the highlands of Angola, and it has found a magnificent solution. Known as the "river that never finds the sea," it drains slowly southward, lavishing its minerals and nutrients onto the sands of the Kalahari Desert, a huge basin that covers much of Botswana and parts of Namibia and South Africa. The resulting delta, the Okavango, transforms a 15,000-square-kilometer expanse of the Kalahari into a spectacular maze of channels, lagoons and papyrus-lined islands teeming with wildlife.

Deeper into a realm of absolute tranquillity, your guide poles your *mokoro*, a low-riding dugout canoe. With only the swish of the guide's pole and the gentle lapping of water to contend with, your ears pick up every chirp and rustle of nearby animals, and your quiet approach makes them less suspicious. After the sun sets, the night is just as calm, with virtually no ambient light or pollution to block out what could be the greatest number of stars you've ever gazed upon.

Like the night sky, the clarity of the delta's water surprises most first-time visitors. As the Kavango River travels 250km from Angola, it drops only 62m, resulting in a low sediment load; there aren't any significant grazing, farming or population centers upriver, either. Despite its slight amber color, there's nothing stagnant or brackish about the Okavango, and its lucidity reveals a world of fish and plant roots below the surface. Even in shallow channels and lagoons, the water is fresh and inviting.

On foot, your foray into the habitat of lions, hippos and water buffalo may at first be a bit unsettling, but there's comfort in traveling with an armed guide who knows the terrain and how to act in the presence of wild creatures.

lion and buffalo: sleeping with the enemy

Cape buffalo are dangerous enough to humans, but their sharp, curved horns and solid hooves can even be lethal to lions. Although lions hunt and kill buffalo, a recent two-year study in the Okavango Delta confirmed the delicate balance between hunter and hunted on the Duba Plains, a tract of land on a roughly 200-square-kilometer delta island, where over a thousand Cape buffalo live alongside three prides of lions. Some of the lions depend solely on the buffalo for food, and the herd knows these predators so well that it remains calm even when the pride sleeps in plain sight.

Their close proximity and interrelationship have caused the animals to develop unique behaviors. While lions normally avoid water, the Duba lions are not afraid to wade and even swim while stalking prey. Hunting buffalo has also built their muscles – the Duba prides, with lionesses weighing up to 180kg, are exceptionally powerful. Still, an entire herd of buffalo, each member a hefty 500–900kg, is a formidable foe, and though the lions may kill about 22 buffaloes each month, they are heavily taxed. The buffalo herd often returns aggression to protect a fallen member, and large males will sometimes charge the lions by themselves. A buffalo attack needn't be devastating to be deadly: a horn through a lion's foreleg is enough to cause a fatal infection, and the high number of lions necessary to hunt such daunting prey means that the loss of just one could spell disaster for an entire pride.

need to know

Most lodges are small, intimate outposts that offer both walking and *mokoro* access to wildlife. On a typical four- or five-day safari you'll likely want to experience both approaches, and maybe even include a night or two of camping.

guides and gear
Island-Safari (☎83/960 3391, 🌐 www.island-safari.com) provides packages and custom itineraries at a wide variety of privately owned lodges and camps in the Okavango Delta.

when to go
The peak season of June to October offers the best overall wildlife viewing, as the flooded delta forces animals to higher ground.

getting there
The village of Maun is the hub of the Okavango Delta's well-heeled safari trade. Daily flights from Johannesburg and Botswana's capital of Gaborone arrive at the village's airstrip, then connect via single-engine aircraft (20–30min) to a landing strip near one of the lodges in the Moremi Game Reserve in the eastern delta.

suggested reading
Peter Allison, *Whatever You Do, Don't Run: True Tales of a Botswana Safari Guide* (Lyons Press). A hilarious, highly original collection of essays based on the Botswana truism: "Only food runs!" Dereck Joubert and Beverly Joubert, *Relentless Enemies: Lions and Buffalo* (National Geographic). An examination of the interaction of lions and buffalo living together on an island. Robyn Keene-Young and Adrian Bailey, *Okavango: A Journey* (Struick). An exquisite photographic journey of the delta and its inhabitants by a husband and wife photographer/author team.

---

is this for me?

PHYSICAL ✦
5–6km per day of walking

PSYCH ✦ ✦ ✦
Close contact with wild animals

SKILL ✦
Sitting in a canoe, walking

WOW! ✦ ✦ ✦ ✦
Exceptional setting for wildlife viewing

You'll no doubt marvel at your guide's uncanny ability to approach animals without surprising, threatening or annoying them. Still, expect some heart-stopping seconds as you round a blind bend and come upon a pride of lions at close range. Even though these big cats are typically the most feared animal in the Okavango, water buffalo and hippos present the greater danger. Though these giant herbivores prefer to expend their energy foraging, they can become aggressive and move surprisingly swiftly if they are startled or perceive a threat; you will not want one charging in your direction.

For those who feel safer on the water, *mokoro* excursions are facilitated by most lodges' easy access to delta channels. Made from a single log, the traditional *mokoro* is still used by locals who rely on fishing for their livelihood. Most visitors, though, find the modern fibreglass version more comfortable and stable, and environmentally preferable to felling a 200-year-old Jackalberry tree for a watercraft that may last only five to ten years. The timeless practice of poling, rather than paddling, is still retained, and your guide's standing position allows him to see what looms ahead; better yet, you may be able to convince him to let you try. Finding your balance usually comes quickly, but a more difficult task is steering the *mokoro* without endangering your passengers or yourself.

From June to October, wildlife becomes more visible and concentrated with the gradual rising of the delta's water level, caused by seeping floodwaters from the rains that fell earlier in the year. This annual cycle alters the habitat, diminishing many islands to half their size and bringing renewed life to the region. During this period, you can expect to see lions and spotted hyenas, two species of endemic Lechwe antelope, and the last free-roaming herd of Cape buffalo. Elephants are plentiful as well – in fact, as their already large numbers continue to grow, wildlife authorities are discussing how to deal with the increasing damages they inflict upon the crops of subsistence farmers.

The flatness of the Okavango Delta belies its rich diversity, and the quiescent setting is slow to reveal its wealth of wildlife. Migratory and riparian birds are plentiful throughout the year, with brooding hitting its peak in late March. Wattled cranes, which have meter-long legs and stand at twice that height, are well equipped to feed on land and in the delta's shallow waters. Other frequently sighted birds are Pel's fishing owl, African fish eagles (similar in size and marking to an American bald eagle) and stubby-bodied black herons.

117 Rafting the Upper Zambezi

>> Below the smoke that thunders

In his quest to find a navigable route from the African interior to coastal ports, David Livingstone embarked on a 1500-kilometer journey down the Zambezi River in 1855. But his vision of a "missionary road" to bring Christianity to deepest Africa came to a thunderous end when he arrived at Mosi-oa-Tunya ("the smoke that thunders") waterfall, where he found a solid sheet of water 100m high. Renaming it Victoria Falls, he continued downriver on foot where he could see nothing but impassable rapids for the next 65km. The dejected Livingstone would never have dreamed that a century and a half later, this section of the Zambezi would be the most exhilarating whitewater experience of many adventurers' lives.

just how big is it?

Victoria Falls is generally referred to as the world's largest waterfall. It's certainly not the tallest waterfall. There are easily more than 700 named waterfalls in the world that are taller. Angel Falls in Venezuela, for one, is nine times taller than Victoria Falls. Nor does Victoria Falls have the greatest flow of water. That title could arguably go to Inga Falls on the Congo River, which boasts 42,446 cubic meters per second, nearly forty times the volume of the Zambezi at Victoria Falls, although this 14-kilometer rapid in the Democratic Republic of the Congo stretches the definition of a waterfall. Even then, both Iguaçu and Niagara have more water pouring over their rims than Victoria Falls.

Victoria Falls' claim as the largest waterfall in the world comes from the combined size of its unbroken height and width. At 1.7km wide and with a height of 108m, Victoria Falls forms the largest sheet of falling water in the world – roughly the size of 46 football fields. It's an impressive sight to be sure, and hundreds of thousands of visitors come annually to see it. Relatively few, though, take in the falls from the best vantage point: in the Devil's Swimming Pool on the Zambia side, where you can extend your body out over on the edge of the falls, and see the entire length and height of the falls face-on.

River rats around the world are awed by this deep, large-volume stretch, whose water level determines its ferocity: the shallower it gets, the more turbulent it grows. The southern African rains, which drench the highlands of Angola and Zambia, start in mid-November and fall through April; early January is when the swollen flow first hits Victoria Falls. This means that the wildwater season occurs as things are drying out from June to the end of December, when the water is at its lowest.

Approaching Victoria Falls on foot you'll feel the ground rumbling beneath you – a not-so-subtle warning signal of the monster action just moments away. Along the Upper Zambezi's 24-kilometer low-water section, the river is characterized by short, quick rapids and big, standing waves, followed by sections of strong-current stillwater. From the put-in at the Boiling Pot on the Zambian side, with the falls over your shoulder, you'll encounter the first runnable rapid, Morning Glory, a Class 4/5 wall that forms a cushioning eddy. A torrent of enormous waves and holes, Stairway to Heaven delivers an eight-meter drop in a stretch of just 10m; pray that your guide is experienced enough to avoid the huge pit to the left, known as the Catcher's Mitt. Stairway to Heaven feeds, appropriately enough, into Devil's Toilet Bowl, where powerful surges land you in vicious whirlpools and boils. Water temperatures below the falls are typically 23°C, warming to nearly 30°C by the time you reach Lake Kariba, so there's little discomfort in getting soaked.

The longest and most technical of the rapids is Gulliver's Travels, a 700-

need to know

You can put in on either the Zambia or Zimbabwe side of the river. The Zambian side starts at rapid #1, while the Zimbabwe side begins at rapid #4. After a one-day run, you're faced with a hot, grueling climb out of Batoka Gorge up a 350-meter incline of loose scree, so save some energy for the end of the day.

guides and gear The Zambezi Safari & Travel Company specializes in safaris, tour packages, and adventure travel in the Victoria Falls area (☎ 1548/831-351; ⓦ www.zambezi.com).

when to go The low water of June to December delivers the most punch, but even the milder high water runs of January through May are unforgettable. The perfect time for a one-day trip is in November or December: November has smaller crowds, awesome wildlife viewing in area game parks and better prices, though a December run will definitely flip your raft.

getting there Fly to Livingstone for a Zambia-based trip or into Victoria Falls for travel and a river trip on the Zimbabwe side.

suggested reading Andrew C. Ross, *David Livingstone: Mission And Empire* (Hambledon & London). An evocative account of the diligent missionary and explorer.

meter, Class V behemoth with multiple channels and smaller rapids within it. The gold prize for infamy goes to the Class V/VI Commercial Suicide, normally portaged by all but the craziest of kayakers, and, on the Class IV tumble called Gnashing Jaws of Death, your stomach will barely have a chance to settle before lunch.

In low-water season, Overland Truck Eater is a mammoth Class V barrel, while during the high-water season it's taken as the first rapid on a slightly shorter run of the river. Next comes a lightning-fast Class IV/V wave train called the Mother, followed by an S-curve in the river at Rapid #14, with its dicey center chute. Oblivion is the quintessential boat-flipper, supposedly responsible for overturning more rafts than any other rapid in the world – fewer than one in four make it out upright. This marks the end of the stretch tackled in the low-water season, said to be the wildest one-day run anywhere.

You can do the rapids below Oblivion as part of a multi-day trip, including two Class VI giants that require long portages, and Asleep at the Wheel, where the left channel leads to a survivable rapid and the right to a widow-maker waterfall. In high-water rapids 11–23 form a one-day run and in low-water season you'll be shooting 1–18. Multi-day trips launch from the Zambian side of the river, run the first 25 rapids, and spend the nights on beaches. From this point on, the river widens and becomes gentler – a pity Livingstone didn't make it this far.

is this for me?

PHYSICAL ✦ ✦ ✦ ✦ ✦
Demands torso strength and agility

PSYCH ✦ ✦ ✦ ✦ ✦
Class V rapids

SKILL ✦ ✦ ✦ ✦ ✦
No prior whitewater experience required

WOW! ✦ ✦ ✦ ✦ ✦
World's wildest one-day whitewater trip

Climbing Mount Kilimanjaro

118

>> Where the snow falls in Africa

KILIMANJARO

TANZANIA

"*Pole-pole*," ("gently, slowly") cautions the guide in Swahili, as the summit of Kilimanjaro is still days away. The trail is not particularly steep or tortuous as mountain trails go, but with each step you slowly leave behind the oxygen-rich farmlands and rainforests below toward a high arctic desert. Here each hard-earned breath contains only half the oxygen you took for granted at sea level, and you get winded just bending over to tie your shoes. Few people would imagine that simply walking could be so difficult. But only when you've climbed Kilimanjaro will you understand why it's regarded as the most underestimated mountain in the world.

Kilimanjaro exudes its undeniable siren song far beyond the Serengeti and Sahara, luring over 20,000 climbers per year to ascend to the Roof of Africa. Rising in northeast Tanzania on the border with Kenya, and known affectionately as "Kili", the mountain is the tallest in Africa, its highest peak, Kibo, topping out at 5895m. The climb up is termed a "walk-up", and as the least technical of the popular "seven summits" – the highest peaks on each of the seven continents – Kilimanjaro is the world's highest mountain accessible to hikers; an ascent requires no mountaineering equipment or climbing experience. The allure of climbing a beautiful snow-capped peak surrounded by the world's most famous game parks leads some Kili aspirants, who rarely have climbing experience at similar altitudes, to shortcut acclimatization. As a result, many do not make it to the summit, not because of objective hazards or perilous weather conditions, as is often the case on Mount McKinley or Mont Blanc, but for lack of the physical and mental preparedness that a mountain of this size demands.

There are a number of route options on Kilimanjaro, all of which ascend through a giant staircase of climate zones before merging at the crater to form a single route to the summit. A journey to the mountain typically begins in Arusha, a nearby city in northern Tanzania. Leaving Arusha and cultivated farmland behind, you'll enter Kilimanjaro National Park and the rainforest, the first of the five distinct climatic zones you'll pass through on your journey to the top. Although the rainforest vegetation is dense and makes for enjoyable trekking, you'll have better chances of seeing wildlife in a post-climb safari on the nearby game parks. At lower elevations it's easy to forget that you're on an immense stratovolcano; Kilimanjaro's three peaks – Kibo, Mawenzi and Shira – are actually volcanic cones. As you ascend, the rainforest gives way to an open heath, where giant heather grows up to 3m tall, followed by moorland. Next are the tundra and bearded lichens of the arctic desert zone, where the various routes unite before entering the crater and leading on to the summit.

While most final ascents start from either the Kibo Hut (4730m) or the Barafu Camp (4600m) and make a long moonlit push to the summit, you

take your pick

There are at least half a dozen routes to the top, all of which converge on the crater before uniting below the summit. Here's a quick rundown of the top choices:

Marangu: Dubbed the "Coca-Cola Route" since beverages and snacks are sold at every camp. This popular tourist route offers the questionable luxury of huts with beds and mattresses each night. The route can be done as a five- or six-day climb, and is typically the least expensive option.

Machame: This scenic six-day route is the one most frequently used by Western guide services. It's more physically challenging than the Marangu route, with longer and steeper daily treks.

Umbwe: This shorter, steeper route with spectacular scenery is climbed in six days. The route is known for its caves, and you'll face less traffic here than on the Marangu and Machame routes.

Western Approach: Also known as the Shira Route, this remote and picturesque route offers a gradual ascent over nine days, allowing ample time for acclimatization and an excellent summit success rate. The route also features a daylight summit push, rather than the midnight start used on other routes.

Mweka: A beeline back to oxygen, this is the primary descent line for most routes.

A beautiful snow-capped peak surrounded by the world's most famous game parks

need to know

As a rule, the longer the trip, and the more time given for altitude acclimatization, the better a hiker's chances of reaching Kilimanjaro's summit. Every step of the climb will be more enjoyable if you are in great physical condition. Independent climbing of Kilimanjaro is not permitted. You'll need transportation, permits, at least one guide, and a porter, all of which you could conceivably obtain on your own in Arusha. However, working with a reputable safari company experienced with Kilimanjaro trekking and focused on your safety and well-being eliminates the logistical headaches and risks. Kilimanjaro National Park (Ⓦ www.tanzaniaparks. com/kili.htm) manages conservation on the mountain and administers regulations and permits.

guides and gear Outfitters supply some equipment, but expect to bring the essentials, including a sleeping bag with a 0°F rating, a headlamp, and a method for purifying water. Among the most reputable outfitters are Thomson Safaris, who also run trekking operations in Arusha, with reservation offices in the US (☎ 617/923-0426 or 1-800/235-0289, Ⓦ www.thomsontreks.com).

when to go The best months to go are January, February, August, and September, when the weather is most favorable, though Kilimanjaro can be climbed year-round.

getting there International flights service Tanzania's Kilimanjaro International Airport. Safari operators provide ground transportation to local accommodation and entrance to Kilimanjaro National Park.

suggested reading Henry Steadman, *Kilimanjaro: The Trekking Guide to Africa's Highest Mountain* (Trailblazer Publications). Practical advice on selecting a route and getting to the top.

suggested viewing *Kilimanjaro: To the Roof of Africa* (2002). An IMAX documentary that follows five climbers on their climb up the mountain's Western Breech.

may want to consider a climb that spends the final night at the Crater Camp (5790m), allows you to sleep high on the mountain, enjoy the sunrise cast over the Great Rift Valley, and then make a one-hour strike at the summit. Staying at Crater Camp also gives you time to make a side-trip to the perfectly-formed ash pit nearby – an extraordinary experience and well worth the two-hour round-trip trek, if you have an ounce of energy left. Whether you're starting fresh in the morning from Crater Camp, or as the final push on a longer overnight ascent, the last 100 vertical meters will lead you past Kilimanjaro's steadily shrinking glacier, where every step is slow and exhausting but ultimately puts you on the summit. It's during this final hour when you'll realize most clearly why less than half of the 20,000 climbers who attempt Kilimanjaro each year ever make it to the summit. As most days are clear on Kilimanjaro's summit, you'll likely have sweeping views, with the Shira Plateau to the west and Meru and Mwenzi rising to the east.

is this for me?

PHYSICAL ◆ ◆ ◆ ◆ ◆
Great endurance and conditioning

PSYCH ◆ ◆ ◆ ◆ ◆
Long days, high altitude

SKILL ◆ ◆ ◆ ◆ ◆
Basic hiking

WOW! ◆ ◆ ◆ ◆ ◆
Tremendous accomplishment open to all

Trekking in the High Atlas Mountains

MOROCCO
● JEBEL TOUBKAL

>> **A palette of red, orange and brown**

Just a short flight from several European gateways, the High Atlas Mountains of Morocco are at once nearby and remote, convenient and exotic. Much like in the Alps, heavily trodden trails link peaks throughout the range, however they are used primarily by locals traveling between villages. In these rugged mountains there are no waymarked circuits or cozy refuges, no mobile phone service on every summit. Here you'll be far from the familiar as you hike from one Berber village to the next, passing herds of sheep small enough to be kept in the shepherd's house. During winter snowstorms, the animals' body heat helps to warm the abode – these are the creature comforts to be found in North Africa's highest mountains.

of Berbers, trees and goats

The argan tree (*Argania spinosa*), also known as Morocco ironwood, is a survivor in a harsh environment, much like the Berbers who have discovered how to use its peculiar "fruit." Endemic to the country, the gnarled, spiny evergreen is found throughout the Sous Valley between the High Atlas and Anti-Atlas Mountains.

Each year an argan tree produces a crop of fleshy pods similar to olives, except bitter and inedible by humans. Goats, however, love them, and will even climb into the trees in search of the best ones. After the fruit is gobbled down and processed through the goat's intestinal tract, human harvesters gather the remaining nuts and crack them open. Hidden within are seeds that can be pressed to extract an orange-tinted oil, a manual process taking as much as twenty hours per liter of oil produced. Argan oil has culinary, medicinal and cosmetic uses, making it a vital commodity for the area. Likewise, the residue from the extraction process is blended with honey to make *amlou*, a local delicacy.

Although argan trees can survive bleak climatic conditions and live for over two hundred years, requiring only ten to twenty centimeters of rain per year, the forests have declined dramatically, and various local and international agencies are working to protect them. Still, an estimated 21 million trees remain in this small region of southwestern Morocco, providing sustenance and entertainment for Berbers, trekkers and goats alike.

capturing a liver in the High Atlas

As the summer herding season comes to an end in the High Atlas Mountains, young singles converge on the village of Imilchil for the annual Wedding Fair. Djellaba-draped young men, armed with silver daggers proclaiming their wealth and virility, weave their way through clusters of young women adorned with silver jewelry and handmade lace. When a couple establishes interest in each other, they clasp hands and strike up a conversation, asking specific questions to help them determine if the pairing has potential. If it doesn't, either may let go and look for someone else. But if there's chemistry, the woman will utter "You have captured my liver" since in Berber culture, the liver, not the heart, is the wellspring of love. Once both parties are in agreement, it's off to the wedding tent, where the scribes seal the deal, often performing 150 or more ceremonies during the three-day festival.

Rising from Mediterranean coastal plains through Tunisia, Algeria and Morocco, the Atlas Mountains shield North Africa's coastal populations from the scorching Sahara. All of Morocco's mountains are considered part of the Atlas range, which contains four distinct sub-ranges: the Anti-Atlas in the south, appealing more to rock climbers than trekkers; the High Atlas, with the loftiest elevations, including North Africa's highest peak, Jebel Toubkal (4167m); the Mid-Atlas, consisting of the mountains between Fez and Marrakech; and the Rif Mountains in Morocco's far north, which hide Roman ruins. Throughout the Atlas' cedar forest, juniper steppe and dry alpine meadows are tiny communities where herding and small-scale crop production are the sole economy and sustenance, and where the Berber dialect may differ drastically from the one spoken just over the next ridge.

Excellent trekking routes of varying difficulty and duration wind through the mountains, but the classic adventure, which includes a summit day on Jebel Toubkal, is a five-day, mule-assisted loop through several little-visited valleys. After an early-morning departure from Marrakech, you'll meet your Berber muleteers at a trailhead in the high western foothills. A series of switchbacks lead to the Tizi n'Tacht pass (2000m), with its commanding views beyond the boulders and bluffs. Hamlets of flat-roofed homes, tiered into the hillside near groves of almond trees, mark the Assif n'Ouissedene Valley. By the third day you're on mule track with one lofty pass, Tizi Aguelzim, sitting at 3104m as the track leads on to the Toubkal Refuge (3207m), where you spend the night in anticipation of your summit bid. A 5am start and a steep, steady ascent up respectable trails and non-technical scree lands you atop the peak within three hours. Descending, you'll drop nearly 2500m, passing cirques, waterfalls, streams, terraced farms and

diminutive villages, before holing up in a local guesthouse for the night. An easy jaunt to the trailhead and your return to Marrakech rounds out day five.

On most treks in the High Atlas, mules carry the larger bags, leaving trekkers with just a daypack. A typical day averages three hours of trekking before lunch and three hours after, a comfortable pace for the terrain and elevation. Lunches are leisurely but elaborate Moroccan-style picnics served on mats; in the evenings, your muleteers will set up camp and assist with cooking slow-simmered tagines – the traditional and very filling Moroccan stew, served over couscous.

need to know

Well-used huts are available along well-trodden trails, but the trails are used primarily by locals traveling from one village to another and not by throngs of Western trekkers.

guides and gear Maps of the area are nearly impossible to obtain outside of Morocco and even though the routes are known by the locals, very few waymarkings exist, so the services of guides familiar with the area and who are able to organize muleteers and cooks for the trek is money well spent. UK-based Rediscover the World (☎ 08707/406 306, ⓦ www. rediscover.co.uk) offers a variety of guided treks in the Atlas Mountains and other adventure travel programs throughout Morocco.

when to go During the main season from April to Nov you can travel without full raingear and expect warm days and pleasantly cool nights. If your trek includes climbing the summit of Jebel Toubkal, mid-April through November offers the best conditions. Toubkal can be climbed year-round, but be prepared for snow and ice at higher elevations beyond the village of Sidi Chamharouch and plan on bringing an ice axe and crampons.

getting there Fly to Morocco's Marrakech-Menara Airport with ground service by van available to High Atlas trailheads about 1hr 30min to 2hr away.

suggested reading Michael Brett and Elizabeth Fentress *The Berbers* (Blackwell). An overview of the history and culture of the Berbers. Edith Wharton, *In Morocco* (Ecco). A classic account of the author's travels in Morocco in 1917.

suggested viewing Morocco is a popular location for motion picture producers who want to film iconic desert scenes in a safe, affordable setting. Some of the classics shot on location in Morocco include *The Man Who Knew Too Much*, *Lawrence of Arabia* and *Gladiator*.

is this for me?

PHYSICAL ✦ ✦ ✦
Walking at moderately high altitudes

PSYCH ✦ ✦
Exotic culture, but comfortable surroundings

SKILL ✦ ✦
Trekking on some steep slopes

WOW! ✦ ✦ ✦
Remote but accessible mountains

Diving in the Red Sea

120

>> A corridor of marvels

EGYPT

SHARM EL SHEIKH

In 1952, undersea explorer Jacques-Yves Cousteau took the *Calypso*, a refurbished wooden-hulled minesweeper, to the Red Sea and shot the first color footage ever filmed at a depth of 50m. When it came to dive sites, Cousteau chose well. If you were to pick one place in the world to make a movie exploring the exquisite color, beauty and variety of an undersea world – a world that can only be explored by divers – that place would have to be the Red Sea.

The Red Sea is a corridor of marvels – the happiest hours of my diving experience have been spent there."

Jacques Cousteau

As the tropical sea closest to Europe, the Red Sea has long been a favorite among European divers. Following the 1982 return of the Sinai to Egypt and the development of dive-oriented resorts, both on the Sinai Peninsula and down Egypt's coast, the popularity and worldwide reputation of Red Sea diving has spread quickly. Once-sleepy fishing villages are now sophisticated resorts catering to passionate divers of all experience levels from around the world.

Base your tour of the Red Sea's fabled dive sites at Sharm el-Sheikh, a thriving dive resort on the southern tip of the Sinai Peninsula Its sweeping beaches are set against the backdrop of brown desert mountains, but there are colors to be found offshore underwater. Sharm offers an immense variety of diving experiences, with wall diving, drop offs, coral gardens and convenient access to Ras Mohamed National Park. With its location at the southern tip of the Sinai Peninsula, Ras Mohamed lies at the convergence of three bodies of water, the Gulf of Suez, the Gulf of Aqaba, and the main body of the Red Sea. The nutrient-rich waters and currents funneling through the Straits of Tiran attract an abundance of marine life, including hammerhead sharks that move in schools of 20–30 and are typically quite shy. Reef sharks and schools of barracuda also ply area waters. Anemone City, a favorite dive site within Ras Mohamed, is home to an intense cluster of huge anemones and attendant brilliantly-colored clownfish.

To the north of Sharm el-Sheikh, about halfway up the Gulf of Aqaba, is the Bedouin city of Nuweiba, one of the most photogenic dive sites in the Red Sea. Divers are drawn to Nuweiba for the strange and unusual variety of coral fish and the more protected waters within the Gulf of Aqaba. Rays up to 2m long, sea turtles, green and orange parrot fish, and spotted unicorn fish can all be found here.

wreck diving

There are two ways to find treasure in the ocean: on purpose or by accident. Of course, the first requires researching ship logs, history books, newspapers, court-martial records, and even insurance records; the second just requires luck. Still, with 10% of the world's wealth lying at the bottom of the ocean, you may have a chance of finding something worthwhile. The top places in the world to wreck dive are Bermuda, Florida, the Bahamas, and anywhere along the Spanish Main, the mainland Caribbean coastline of the old Spanish empire.

Sometimes you can spot a wreck from on board a boat by looking for any straight lines of marine growth in the water; this often indicates something manmade below. You should drop a buoy to mark the sight of a wreck (one can be made out of a plastic bottle or carton, some strong twine, and a five pound weight). When you dive, descend on the boat's anchor line to gain a point of reference. Be aware of the underwater currents because they can easily force a diver against a wreck. Bring a canvas or mesh bag and a ping-pong paddle to salvage. Teddy Tucker, a famous diver, developed the technique of fanning a ping-pong paddle over areas of loose silt to reveal objects lying hidden. If you are doing heavy, thorough excavation, a high-pressure water jet and other tools may be needed. Make sure you record everything you find. A sheet of acetate plastic and just an ordinary graphite pencil can be used for mapping and making notes underwater. Identify the wreck if you can. Coins are very useful for identifying when a wreck occurred because they have dates. Be aware of the legal claims and issues of the area you dive in so you know what you may keep. And finally, remember no wreck is completely picked over, there just may be something hidden lying in wait for you.

need to know

Plan on three days to a week at one of the resorts such as Sharm El Sheik or Hurghada, or on a liveaboard, to satisfy your diving ambitions.

guides and gear Emperor Divers (☎ 012 234 0995; ⓦ www.emperordivers.com) has PADI 5-Star dive centers in five Red Sea locations: Nuweiba, Sharm El Sheik, Hurghada, Safaga, and Marsa Alam. They also run live-aboards in varying price ranges. Throughout the Red Sea you'll find warm, inviting water which at 29°C in summer requires little more than a Lycra suit. In winter the northern water temperatures drop to an acceptable 23°C, so with a 5mm wetsuit and hood you won't be underdressed.

when to go The warm water of May to October is ideal and is the peak season for Red Sea diving, but resorts are open and great diving is possible year round.

getting there Scheduled and charter flights serve both Sharm el-Sheikh Ophira and Hurgadah.

suggested reading Alessandro Carlette and Andrea Ghisotti, *The Red Sea Dive Guide* (Abbeville Press). Full-color large-format guide to top sites with diagrams and a guide to the fish of the Red Sea.

is this for me?

PHYSICAL ◆ ◆ ◆ ◆ ◆
Good balance and coordination

PSYCH ◆ ◆ ◆ ◆ ◆
Normal risks associated with diving

SKILL ◆ ◆ ◆ ◆ ◆
Diving certification required

WOW! ◆ ◆ ◆ ◆ ◆
Among the world's most exceptional diving

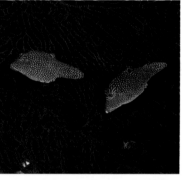

If wreck diving is your delight, the *SS Thistlegorm*, a British supply ship sunk by German bombers in 1941, will be on your wish list. She was bound for the Suez Canal with a load that included trucks, motorcycles, rail cars and an armored Rolls Royce. First discovered by Cousteau in 1956, natural rusting and inevitable plundering have taken their toll. Her cargo is still intact, however, offering an eerie visit into the past. She rests in the Straits of Gobal at the southern end of the Gulf of Suez, and is accessible from Sharm and Hurghada to the west.

As an alternative to land-based dive resorts, the availability of live-aboard dive trips in the Red Sea offers some distinct advantages for dedicated divers. On a live-aboard you'll minimize transit time and maximize dive time. You'll be able to satisfy various interests by choosing an itinerary that captures your attention and allows you to awake every morning at a new dive site. Live-aboards are generally well-equipped and designed to divers' needs. Most have comfortable air-conditioned cabins, and are staffed with skilled professionals.

The increase in resorts and tourist services, along with the availability of live-aboards has introduced some risks to the delicate reefs of the Red Sea. Fortunately, protective efforts such as the creation of underwater parks like Ras Mohammad at the southern tip of the Sinai have had a positive affect in preserving and protecting the Red Sea's wonders.

121 Windsurfing in Essaouira

WHERE Essaouira, Morocco

WHEN Year-round

PHYSICAL	✦ ✦ ✦
PSYCH	✦ ✦
SKILL	✦ ✦ ✦ ✦
WOW!	✦ ✦ ✦

The winds that drove Phoenician sailors to Morocco almost three thousand years ago still blow from the north and west into the bays and beaches of Essaouira. The Portuguese cannons and battlements which once guarded Essaouira now add historic charm to the UNESCO World Heritage Site where most of today's seaborne arrivals are windsurfers. With predictable winds and sandy beaches free of rocks and strong currents, Essaouira is a "something for everybody" windsurfing destination supported with expert instruction and on-site equipment rental.

The crescent-shaped beach of Essaouira Bay offers shallow flatwater near the town, a good chop in the mid-bay, and downwind wave action that appeals to beginners and intermediate windsurfers. Moulay Bouzerktoune, where the North East trade winds hit the Atlantic, is known for its gusty side-shore winds and as one of the best wavesailing destinations in the Atlantic. In winter you'll find 2–4m waves that attract self-assured wave sailors from around the world. To the south, Sidi Kaouki is a five-kilometer-long beach with a cross-shore wind that delivers good winter waves and a launch setting that appeals to beginners and those with intermediate skills. Indeed, across the bay wavefreaks and beginners coexist comfortably on the water and in the evening can share a table over an aromatic tagine at a

122 Biking to Chamarel Waterfall and Chamarel Colored Earth

WHERE Mauritius

WHEN Year-round

PHYSICAL	✦	✦	✦	✦	✦
PSYCH	✦	✦	✦	✦	✦
SKILL	✦	✦	✦	✦	✦
WOW!	✦	✦	✦	✦	✦

It's been over two hundred years since the dodo, a flightless bird found only on Mauritius, became extinct, but it certainly didn't leave the tropical islands bereft of unusual and surprising sights. On a day-trip of easy riding, combining off-road tracks and paved roads, you make your way through coffee, banana, sugar cane, and pineapple plantations to Chamarel Colored Earth, also known as Seven Colored Earth. Here the island's volcanic origins are exposed in dunes with glorious hues of red, yellow, blue, and green, created by the erosion of volcanic ash. The undulating terrain is like a giant artist's palate made up of seven different colored strata, or sheet-like masses of sedimentary rock and earth. The exposed dunes of Chamarel Colored Earth rise from the surrounding landscape, blanketed in lush green native vegetation, to create a striking contrast of colors.

Another fifteen minutes of easy pedaling and you arrive at an accessible overlook to Chamarel Waterfall, a breathtaking plunge of 100m set against a backdrop of thick tropical vegetation. As two rivers, the St Denis and the Viande Salie, flow from the Black River Mountains, they come to an abrupt drop over the vertical cliffs that create the falls. From the falls, its mostly downhill with great views along the way to the island's wild southwest coast where you can cap off the day by sea kayaking in the clear, light-blue water of the coastal lagoons, or by enjoying the sunset on one of Mauritius' famous white sand beaches.

123 Camel trekking in the Sinai Desert

WHERE Sinai Peninsula, Egypt

WHEN April to September in mountainous regions, October to March in the lower eastern region

PHYSICAL	✦	✦	✦	✦	✦
PSYCH	✦	✦	✦	✦	✦
SKILL	✦	✦	✦	✦	✦
WOW!	✦	✦	✦	✦	✦

The Sinai Peninsula has long been an inhospitable doormat, traversed for millennia by prophets, traders, and armies. Moses, Ramses II, Alexander the Great, Napoleon, and more recently, Israeli and Egyptian armies, all had their encounters with this rugged wilderness. Bedouin have roamed the Sinai for ages, but only in the last generation have reliable trekking routes made mountain regions of the southern and eastern peninsula accessible to adventure travelers.

Starting from the Gulf of Aqaba you'll ascend sinuous canyons fed by perennial springs to find pockets of life in this otherwise barren landscape. As you hike from one camp to the next, you'll carry only what is needed for the day; other gear and the camp setup will be packed by camels. Along the way you will encounter local Bedouin who subsist with micro-scale agriculture and by herding a few goats. It's not uncommon to spend the night sharing an encampment in with them and sleeping in their gardens. Most Sinai treks include a climb of 2286m Mount Sinai and a visit to the sixth century St Catherine's Monastery, which houses the word's largest collection of early codices and manuscripts outside of the Vatican Library. Craggy mountains, rocky canyons, granite cliffs, colored sandstone, dunes, and oases are all part of the Sinai experience, as is the occasional spotting of a fox, hyrax, or ibex. Pick your Sinai trek carefully and seek a private guide or operator whose expertise is the desert and natural environment of the mountainous desert, rather than an entrepreneurial cameleer anxious to sell you a ride on his camel; this is no place to test your luck.

124 Wildlife viewing at Kakum National Park

WHERE Ghana
WHEN Year-round

When commercial deforestation threatened the once continuous belt of rainforest from Guinea to Ghana, it became apparent that this primeval canopy would disappear unless it was protected in a way that provided local people alternative benefits and livelihood. Thus the Kakum National Park was founded in Ghana. Situated approximately one hour from Cape Coast, Kakum packs quite a punch in a relatively small amount of wilderness: six endangered species call it home, including Diana monkeys, elegantly striped bongo antelopes, and forest elephants, and an estimated 550 species of butterflies, 269 species of birds, and 100 species of reptiles and amphibians also live in the park.

It's most famous for its canopy walkway, the only one of its kind in Africa, a swinging bridge made of steel cables, wooden planks, and netting that rises 30m high and stretches over 330m. The view from the walkway puts you in the midst of the birds, butterflies, bats, monkeys, and even an occasional tree-climbing python. From your elevated perch it is often difficult to see Kakum's land mammals, such as the mongoose-like merkat and pygmy elephants, through the thick foliage of the rainforest. Local guides on the ground provide walking tours of the Kuntan Trail, where you'll learn about medicinal plants and how to spot signs of animal life.

You can also visit Mesomagor village, adjacent to the park, to catch a glimpse of Ghana's vibrant and colorful rural life and listen to the Bamboo Orchestra. For an adventurous night, bring your own tent, mosquito net, and sleeping bag, and sleep at the park's Afafranto campsite just a few minutes' walk from the visitor center. A day at Kakum is best begun early in the morning, and camping at Afafranto will give you early access to the canopy walkway and help you avoid tourists, which will increase your chances of seeing wildlife.

125 Riding waves at Jeffreys Bay

WHERE Jeffreys Bay, South Africa
WHEN June to August

With perfect placement at the southern tip of Africa, Jeffreys Bay waits with open arms to receive waves that have traveled over 1500km across the Southern Sea. When those waves finally arrive, they deliver rides up to 1.6km. Of the several breaks that form Jeffreys Bay, the pro circuit concentrates on Supertube – widely known as South Africa's best wave and site of the Billabong Pro in July, part of the World Championship Tour. The prototypical Supertube wave is in the two to three meter range and comes back by a southwesterly wind.

It was a break known as the Point that gave birth to the J-bay surf scene in the 1960s, and it still draws crowds today with a bowl that delivers fast take-offs before easing into a bottom turn. These devotees know the breaks intimately, so pay attention as they surf to save yourself a lot of paddling. Just be brave and ask around for a break that matches your abilities. Located fifty kilometers west of Port Elizabeth, Jeffreys Bay is in its prime in the austral winter, and a 3mm wetsuit will keep you surfing year-round.

126 Namib Desert ride to the sea

WHERE Namib Desert, Namibia

WHEN April to October

PHYSICAL	✦	✦	✦	✦
PSYCH	✦	✦	✦	✦
SKILL	✦	✦	✦	✦
WOW!	✦	✦	✦	

Following a classic route pioneered by Namibia's colonial German cavalry, you can ride from the highlands near Windhoek to the summer capital of Swakopmund on the coast, crossing a land that's still wild and remote. The austere landscape and harsh conditions of the Namib, the world's oldest desert, favor tough, seasoned riders who can handle 400km and nine days hard riding, minimalist camping, plus responsibility for tacking and untacking their own horse. Along the way you'll test your physical and riding abilities and gain an immense respect for the stamina of the locally bred horses.

The Namib Desert is quite varied and includes the tallest sand dunes in the world and dry washes ideal for riding. Thorny acacias and tall grasses growing on immense ranches mark the highlands; river drainages that can be easily crossed most of the year might swell with a torrent requiring horse and rider to wait until it subsides. You'll descend narrow canyons, where the steep trail, washed out from spring rains, forces you to dismount and lead your horse up through a rugged boulder field. As you descend to the lowlands you enter cobbled plains and dry drainages before arriving at the Atlantic, where you'll be met by massive coral-colored dunes. Although wildlife isn't the main draw of this adventure, oryx, springbok, zebra and ostrich can always make a cameo appearance.

127 Rafting the Omo River

WHERE Shewan highlands, Ethiopia

WHEN October to early June

PHYSICAL	✦	✦		
PSYCH	✦	✦	✦	✦
SKILL	✦	✦		
WOW!	✦	✦	✦	

Dropping from the highlands of Ethiopia, the Omo River crashes through some of the most exotic and remote landscapes on the African continent. Descending 1800m over its 800-kilometer course, this river holds class III and IV rapids that allow rafters to gather themselves between the chaotic dynamos. Gaining volume from five large tributaries along its path, the Omo builds its energy not only in hydraulic power, but in animal magnetism and cultural flare.

The Omo flows through deep, forested gorges that ascend 1525m to the height of the volcanic Ethiopian Plateau, housing not only exotic plant life, but some of the world's most dramatic landscapes. The remoteness of the Omo has lead to an unspoiled terrain, one absent of modern industry. While the river's banks are carpeted with dense shrubs and climbing vines, and frequently fed by small tributaries, in the water there are often yawping hippos.

The people of the Omo are much like the river: dramatic, passionate, mysterious, and just as isolated. Essentially unknown by the modern world, the various tribes of this region still live in small villages, practice a pastoral and hunter-gatherer lifestyle, and hunt wild animals for meat. A descent of the Omo will invariably offer opportunities to meet the Karo tribe whose women scar their chests as a sign of beauty, while further downriver the women of the Mursi tribe known for their lip dishes, some over 10cm in diameter. Colorful body painting, ritual scarring, draping beadwork, and lively evening dancing can be seen among many of the tribes in the region. Hidden in the environs of the Omo, lounging crocodiles, spry waterbuck, barking baboons and howling colombus monkeys thrive. Even lions can be spotted along the journey. To see as much as you can, you'll need to spend some time on land hiking. Take time for composing photos, hiking, and swimming in the Omo's tributaries. An epic fourteen-day adventure can also be put together in smaller segments on a custom basis. Various guiding companies provide ample camping comfort and expert knowledge of the river: its geography, geology, zoology and anthropology.

View elephants and other wildlife at close range near the Ngorongo Crater

128 Wildlife safari to the Ngorongoro Crater

WHERE Ngorongoro Conservation Area, Tanzania

WHEN Year-round

PHYSICAL	◆ ◆ ◆ ◇ ◇	
PSYCH	◆ ◆ ◆ ◇ ◇	
SKILL	◆ ◆ ◇ ◇ ◇	
WOW!	◆ ◆ ◆ ◇ ◇	

About three million years ago in Tanzania, Mount Ngorongoro rivaled Mount Kilimanjaro in height and majesty. This formidable mountain transformed into a different sort of world wonder when its volcanic top erupted, leaving a 20km-wide, 2km-deep crater in the heart of the Serengeti Plain. Today, you can explore this fantastic crater and its resident wildlife on a safari within the Ngorongoro Conservation Area.

The crater floor is dense with vegetation and has a permanent water supply, providing a habitat for the abundant wildlife that roams the flat, grassy plain. Because the animals are accustomed to safari vehicles, you can view dozens of species like lions, wildebeests, rhinos, and water buffaloes unobstructed and at close range. A popular destination in the crater is Lake Magadi, a shallow soda lake dotted pink by the presence of numerous flamingoes.

While the big game wildlife viewing on the crater floor is best accomplished in a safari vehicle, a camping and walking safari on the forested slopes of the crater rim offers an excellent way to combine the efficient with the primitive. As you slowly ascend the gargantuan outer rim of the crater, the air thins and cools down; eventually you reach the lip of the crater, with a lush bowl beneath you. In the forested crater highlands you can make use of numerous established or wilderness campsites, and with 5 to 7 hours of trekking per day over a three- to five-day day period encounter the indigenous people of the area, the Masai, who herd livestock near the crater floor, right alongside the wildlife. It is not uncommon to see the Masai's livestock grazing meters away from a lion or a rhino. A highlight of the crater highlands is the Empakaai Crater where a small lake fills the crater floor and where thousands of flamingoes find a peaceful home, only occasionally disturbed by hyenas looking for a quick chase and an easy meal.

129 Horseback safari in Nyika National Park

WHERE Malawi

WHEN October to May

PHYSICAL	✦ ✦ ✦ ✦ ✦
PSYCH	✦ ✦ ✦ ✦ ✦
SKILL	✦ ✦ ✦ ✦ ✦
WOW!	✦ ✦ ✦ ✦ ✦

Take more than a thousand square miles of African plains and plateau largely inaccessible to vehicles, carpet it with wildflowers and windswept grasses, fill it with antelope, zebra and leopards, and you have a range-rider's dream come true. Nyika, which means "where the water comes from," is Malawi's largest national park, a gigantic dome of high-elevation rolling grasslands, swept by crystalline air and sprinkled with evergreen forests, 200 species of orchids, and miombo woodlands on the lower slopes.

While it's ideal for trekking and mountain biking, the best way to take in the expanse is on horseback, where your elevated position will enhance the game-viewing, expand your already sweeping vistas and enable you to cover more of the park's far-flung terrain.

Antelopes roam Nyika's plains in large herds – the species here range from the tiny duiker to the giant eland, which can weigh some 308kg, with twisted horns up to a meter long. Zebras are common and tend to scatter as you ride among them. Nyika also has the highest populations of leopards in central Africa, plus you'll find abundant populations of elephant and buffalo. Lion live in the park, but tend to remain at the lower elevations. Finally, the plateau has 300 species of nirds, best see from October through December.

The 2500m plateau elevation means you'll escape the tropical heat melting most of central Africa, travel in a malaria-free region, and even find accessible viewing during the January and February main rains.

130 Trekking in the Semien Mountains

WHERE Semien Mountains National Park, Ethiopia

WHEN October to April

PHYSICAL	✦ ✦ ✦
PSYCH	✦ ✦ ✦
SKILL	✦ ✦
WOW!	✦ ✦ ✦

Ehtiopia may not spring to mind when you think of lush, verdant hiking destinations, but its Semien Mountains more than fit the bill. The peaks rise up from a huge green, moss-covered plateau split by spectacular gorges and the Great Rift Valley, which slices the country in two and is one of the few geologic features that can be seen from the moon.

Treks of a few days or up to a week can be arranged that will take you into a rugged mountainous region, the highest in Ethiopia, with peaks over 4000m. It's possible to hike through deep cut gorges in view of escarpments, with spectacular sharp cliffs and waterfalls that cascade over the edge. In this beautiful tropical range you can encounter a good variety of wildlife, such as the red-chested gelada baboon, and the elusive Ethiopian wolf with its striking chestnut and white markings. There's no better place to find the endangered walia ibex, with its immense backflung scimitar-shaped horns, than in the Semien Mountains.

On your return to Addis Ababa, after several days of guided trekking within the park, plan on a side-trip and a day-hike to spectacular Blue Nile Falls a 400m-long curtain of water that plunges 45m from a sharp cliff into a large pool. These falls, fed by the Blue Nile, go on to join the White Nile before flowing into Egypt.

Outside the national park, within the Semien Mountains region you will also enter the seat of the Queen of Sheba's kingdom, the ancient city Axum, which lies high up in the plateaus. At Axum you will see incredible rock structures or "stelae" that weigh hundreds of tons and are engraved with different cryptic symbols. How such huge masses of stone were brought up into the Semien Mountains still remains a mystery.

During your explorations, you will also pass numerous ancient monasteries carved right into the face of a single rock cliff. Debre Mariam Korkor is one of the largest rock-hewn churches and is beautifully decorated inside with arches and intricate murals. Debre Damos is another interesting monastery not far from Axum. It lies at the top of a plateau surrounded by steep cliffs on all sides so the only way to reach the actual monastery is by climbing a rope lowered by priests at the top. Still, there is another even more limiting restriction to reaching the monastery – you must be male. Even the animals atop the plateau at the monastery conform to this restriction: no females can be found among the chickens or sheep.

131 Trekking and wildlife viewing on the Skeleton Coast

WHERE Namibia

WHEN Year-round on the coast, May to August for inland travel

PHYSICAL	◆ ◆ ◆	◆ ◆
PSYCH	◆ ◆	◆ ◆ ◆
SKILL	◆ ◆	◆ ◆ ◆
WOW!	◆ ◆ ◆	◆ ◆

A wasteland of sand dunes, barren expanses of coarse gravel, and ranges of jagged hills stand in distinct contrast to wave upon wave of sapphire blue undulations capped with white sea-froth. It's a stark and dramatic landscape accentuated by the white brittle ribs of animal carcasses and shipwrecks. Here along the Skeleton Coast, it's up to the thick nightly mists blowing in from the ocean to provide the desert with some kind of relief.

Although access to the sparsely populated region is limited and best accomplished by air or safari vehicle, you'll want to be on foot to discover the isolation and austere beauty of the coast. Walking to the truly remote areas might gain you a

vision of an ostrich, giraffe, Damara tern, jackal, hyena, lion, or Namib porcupine, while by the sea watch for seals and rare Heaviside's dolphin. In the northern reaches of the Namib desert endangered African elephants plod along stoically. Shipwreck sites, prehistoric villages, water seeps, and dramatic bones create a distinct landscape. In a traditional walking safari the deadly beauty of the Skeleton Coast will surely give an experience not easily forgotten. The evenings get quite cool and the one thing that never seems to change is the constant wind.

falling water

▶ **Boyoma Falls**, Democratic Republic of the Congo. Formerly known as Stanley Falls, this is the largest volume waterfall in the world with 17,000 cubic meters cascading per second, about three times that of Niagara Falls.

▶ **Murchison Falls**, northern Uganda. Also known as Kabarega Falls, it squeezes the Nile River through a narrow gap and tumbles 43m.

▶ **Tugela Falls**, South Africa. The second highest waterfall in the world, it plunges almost 1000m in five dramatic cascades.

▶ **Victoria Falls**, border of Zambia and Zimbabwe. A steep drop: more than five hundred liters of water crash every minute from heights up to 450m. Locals call it Mosi-oa-Tunya, or "the smoke that thunders."

I never knew of a morning in Africa when I woke that I was not happy.

Ernest Hemingway

ONE BIG BEETLE

Watch your step in African jungles. The enormous Goliath beetle, found in equatorial African jungles, grows up to 12cm long and is one of the biggest insects in the world. About the size of the human hand, it is the largest of the scarab beetles. You will definitely notice when the beetle becomes airborne, as the pounding of its hard wings creates a sound like a small aircraft taking off.

survival of the fastest

Some of the fastest animals of the world come from the African savannah. In many cases, speed is the key to survival. The vulnerability of the wide open savannah rewards those who do not become someone else's lunch. Some of the fastest are:

▶ **African lion** Can tear across the bush at 60kph.

▶ **Cheetah** Can burst into hyperspeed at 120kph to attack an animal it has chosen for prey.

▶ **Elephant** Can stir up dust to the tune of 40kph.

▶ **Giraffe** Can escape most predators with a gangly gallop over 55kph.

▶ **Thomson's gazelle** Can reach speeds in excess of 70kph.

▶ **Wildebeest** Can run upwards of 55kph, especially when in a stampede.

▶ **Zebra** Can move faster than a lion at 65kph and can sustain the speed longer.

BLACK DEATH

Slithering up to 20kph, the black mamba, is a speed demon among poisonous African reptiles. Found primarily in southern and eastern Africa, this venomous viper typically reaches 2–3m in length, and can exceed 4m. Considered one of the world's most deadly snakes, the black mamba is not named for the color of its skin, which is a bland grey, but for the black color of the inside of its mouth which it flaunts as it prepares to strike. It has received a lot of bad publicity due to the toxicity of its venom; a bite from a black mamba can be fatal in less than twenty minutes as neurotoxins paralyze the diaphragm. In spite of stories to the contrary, the snake is not normally aggressive to humans and primarily uses his deadly bite to subdue a rodent for lunch. However, care should be taken in any area where the Black Mamba is prevalent as the snake will certainly strike if disturbed, threatened or stepped on and anti-venom may be unavailable.

superlatives

Everyone could guess, even if they didn't already know, that the Sahara was the largest desert in Africa; probably too that Kilimanjaro, in Tanzania, is its tallest mountain. Lake Victoria, bordering Kenya, Uganda and Tanzania, is the continent's biggest lake, and the world's second-largest freshwater lake. Tanzania scores again with the Selous Game Reserve, Africa's largest wildlife sanctuary and home to hundreds of thousands of mammals and nearly 450 different species of birds.

LUNCH ON THE LIMB

Found throughout regions of Africa that are seasonally affected by drought is the distinctive baobab tree. Also known as monkey bread tree, it produces edible leaves that are added to soups and stews, as well as velvety fruit pods known as sour gourds. Reaching upwards of 25m in height, the baobab tree stands out on a parched savannah. When in full leaf, it provides much-needed shade as well as nourishment. To survive dry periods, the baobab tree can hold up to one thousand liters of water in its trunk. The elephant has discovered this little-known resource and when thirsty will chip away at the bark to get to the water inside.

The most dangerous animal in Africa

The mosquito. Specifically, it is the female *anopheles* mosquito and her blood-sucking habits that can pass along the malarial parasite that causes the greatest number of deaths. Malaria is a significant problem throughout much of sub-Saharan Africa, especially for children under five. The male mosquito, although part of the equation, does none of the actual biting. The female begins as an egg, floating on the surface of standing water, and once mature flies in search of blood, which is required to develop her eggs. She prefers to feed at night, making mosquito nets and repellent important while asleep.

AFRICAN PROVERBS TO SAVE YOUR LIFE

No one tests the depth of a river with both feet. **Ghana**

Restless feet may walk into a snake pit. **Ethiopia**

Do not call the forest that shelters you a jungle. **Ghana**

You do not teach the paths of the forest

to an old gorilla. **Congo**

It is the calm and silent water that drowns a man **Ghana**

Only food runs **Botswana**

The gladdest moment in human life is the departure upon a distant journey into unknown lands.

Sir Richard Francis Burton

Egyptian inventions

The greatest minds in Egypt were determined to find solutions to problems that perplexed them. Some of these solutions are still being used today. Just a few that might come in particularly handy to travelers include:

3500 BC Sail-powered boats

3000 BC Sundial

3000 BC Candles

1500 BC Shoes

1500 BC Water tap

1150 BC Topographic map

400 AD Hydrometer for weather prediction

953 AD Fountain pen (good for writing about your exploits)

Where all this water goes is a mystery.

Dr Aurel Shultz (on viewing the Okavango Delta)

THIS FOOD MAY BUG YOU

Every traveler needs some nourishment to keep up his or her stamina and energy; in Africa, what's in those snacks may sometimes surprise you. The practice of eating bugs, known as entomophagy, isn't particularly prevalent in most of the world, but consuming fried termites and toasted crickets, for a start, is not uncommon here. In Nigeria, the sago grub – 10cm in length and

3cm wide – is considered a delicious, nutty-tasting, high-calorie treat. Another larva, known as kanni, is boiled and dried before it's eaten. that was not the case just a few generations ago. Though many may cringe at this habit and find it unappetizing, current research actually supports insect consumption as a highly sustainable and cost-effective way of absorbing certain nutrients, especially protein. So don't be surprised if ants, worms, caterpillars, honeybees, moths, lakeflies or locusts show up on the menu, and remember, they're good for you.

Fish River Canyon

Situated at the southern tip of Namibia, the dramatic depth and exposed layers of Fish River Canyon are a secret for devoted canyoneers who ache to see terrain that the casual hiker will never view except on a postcard. Carved by the Fish River and deepened by movement along a geologic fault, the canyon rivals the Grand Canyon is size. The 90-kilometre adventure is only possible from May to September when temperatures are bearable and the Fish River still has water. With no marked trails, you flow with the trickle in the canyon and camp whenever you've had enough. Plan on spending three to six days to see unblemished and uninhabited canyon landscape.

LOOK BUT DON'T DARE TOUCH

If your only knowledge of the hippopotamus is the local zoo, greeting cards or animated movies, you may assume that hippos are docile, friendly, and playful. The truth is they are strongly territorial and potentially dangerous in the wild. They have no natural enemies except humans. Semi-aquatic, they live much of the day in the river to keep cool, with all but their eyes, nose and ears submerged. They seem to have a feisty temper and can use their bulky bodies of over 1500kg to flip a boat or chomp a passenger.

ASIA

RUSSIA

KAZAKHSTAN

UZBEKISTAN

TURKMENISTAN

KYRGYZSTAN

TAJIKSTAN **159**

MONGOLIA **158** **138**

NORTH KOREA

SOUTH KOREA

JAPAN

152

CHINA

142 **137**

TAIWAN

SYRIA

LEBANON

ISREAL & THE PALASTINIAN TERRITORIES

IRAQ

JORDAN

KUWAIT

IRAN **155**

AFGHANISTAN

147 **141** **160** **148** **156**

QATAR

UAE

SAUDI ARABIA

OMAN

PAKISTAN

150 **146** **136** **145** **151** **132** BHUTAN **134**

NEPAL

BANGLADESH **143** **153**

INDIA

BURMA (MYANMAR)

LAOS **157**

THAILAND

VIETNAM **135**

PHILIPPINES

YEMEN

149

SRI LANKA

CAMBODIA

139

SINGAPORE

MALAYSIA

154 **133** **140**

INDONESIA

144

EAST TIMOR

PAPUA NEW GUINEA

132 The Chomolhari trek

>> In the land of the Thunder Dragon

The notion of an isolated earthly paradise, a land where people live in harmony with each other and with nature, is an enduring and endearing myth. Reports by seventeenth-century missionaries returning from the East led to the modern concept of Shangri-La, an idyllic land set beneath snow-capped peaks, surrounded by dense forests, flowing with water and able to produce every food imaginable. It was a repository of cultural wisdom, where violence and materialism had no place. Of the ancient mountain kingdoms that adorn the southern slopes of the Himalaya – Kashmir, Nepal, Ladakh, Sikkim – only Bhutan has retained such a pristine national heritage in a mountain setting worthy of consideration as a modern-day Shangri-La.

Taktshang – the Tiger's Nest

Twelve centuries ago, Padma Sambhava (Guru Rinpoche), a Buddhist saint, soared from Tibet to Bhutan on the back of a flying tiger. Landing on a granite cliff near Paro, Bhutan, the monk spent three years meditating in a cliffside cave before descending into the verdant valley to preach his tantric Mahayana Buddhism. In doing so, he became the patron saint of Bhutan, and the location of his arrival became the site of Bhutan's most famous monastery, Taktshang Goemba (The Tiger's Nest Monastery).

Today, Taktshang is one of the most venerated pilgrim sites in the Himalaya. It hangs on a cliff at an elevation of 3100m, nearly 800m above the valley floor. After suffering destruction by fire in 1998, reconstruction of the monastery commenced in 2000 and was meticulously restored using old photographs and diaries that described the interior features. It was rededicated in the presence of Bhutan's king in 2005. Today by prior arrangement, invited guests, normally practicing Buddhists on a religious retreat, may climb to the monastery on foot or by mule. Mere mortals can view and photograph Taktshang from an observation point.

Tourism in this remote kingdom is limited and independent travel is not permitted. As a result, you won't find armies of budget backpackers, cluttered campgrounds, and teahouse-lined villages where trekking is the lifeblood of the local economy. Trekking in Bhutan is decidedly not adventure on a shoestring; but it is an exquisite foray into a diverse natural environment and a captivating culture. While there are numerous great trekking possibilities throughout Bhutan, the classic experience is the eight-day Chomolhari trek that takes you into northwestern Bhutan to Chomolhari (Mountain of the Goddess), the divine mountain of Bhutan, a 7314m shining summit sacred to Bhutanese and Tibetans alike. Throughout the trek you're supported by packhorses, your camps are pitched by dependable Bhutanese staff, and flavorful carb-laden meals are served in a dining tent.

The route begins at a lofty 2800m elevation near the town of Paro, just 20km west of the capital of Thimphu in western Bhutan, passing plots of potatoes and millet and ascending along the Paro River through rich deciduous forests giving way to conifer, pine, fir and spruce. Forests of rhododendron with bright red blossoms blanket the hillsides, and in the fall apple orchards glisten with fragrant fruit.

After two days of dedicated trekking along a gentle ascent with several bridge crossings, you emerge from the forest cover into high alpine pastures under the watch of glorious peaks. On the third day of trekking, deep valleys soon open to views of Chomolhari and other peaks that play with clouds and

need to know

Travel in Bhutan is restricted in order to protect both the land and the traditional culture. All travel arrangements must be made in advance through an authorized tour company.

guides and gear Bhutan Men-Lha Adventures & Travelers (☎ 975 2 321555, Ⓦ www.trekkingbhutan.com) with offices in Thimphu specializes in treks and adventure travel. Trekking is an inclusive offering in Bhutan and includes all accommodation, guide and camp staff, meals, pack animals, and all other activities and services within the country.

when to go The spring months of March to May and the autumn months of September to November are the ideal seasons for trekking; conversely, avoid the monsoon months of June to mid-September.

getting there There are only two ways into Bhutan: the Paro airport where the only airline is Bhutan's flagship carrier, Druk Air, or by land on a single road crossing the border with India. You must have a visa secured in advance to enter Bhutan.

suggested reading Bart Jordans, *Bhutan: a Trekker's Guide* (Cicerone). A pragmatic guide to different treks in Bhutan with color photos and detailed maps. John Berthold, *Bhutan: Land of the Thunder Dragon* (Wisdom Publications). Photographs guide the reader to rarely seen ancient fortresses and temples, colorful festivals, and religious ceremonies. Russ Carpenter and Blyth Carpenter, *The Blessings of Bhutan* (University of Hawaii Press). Essays explore a nation on the cusp of change while holding onto tradition.

sky, as you ascend the Nyelela pass and reach an altitude of 4700m before arriving at the commanding hilltop monastery fortress of Lingshi Dzong and descend to a camp at 4000m. On these high slopes you may find ibex and horned bharal, or Himalayan blue sheep, but you're unlikely to see their sole predator, the snow leopard; not only are these graceful alpine cats elusive, but there are only about two thousand remaining in the world, most of which live in Bhutan.

Chomolhari forms the centerpiece of this part of the range with the slightly smaller, but similarly impressive peaks of Khangphu to the right and the icy pyramid of TseringmaGang within view. The second major pass, Yali, tops out at 4820m and then the undulating return descent begins. Yaks, guarded by seminomadic herders, graze at surprisingly high elevations and you share the slopes with them for your days above treeline.

Once again dropping below the treeline on the seventh day of the trek you return to forests of rhododendron, and this time juniper, as you follow a downward track along the Thimphu River, before returning to Thimphu valley and Thimphu – possibly the only capital city in the world with no traffic lights. Wandering among the epic Himalayan peaks would normally be adventure enough, but in Bhutan the treat is twofold as you take in its colorful and distinctive architecture, and visit museums and seventh-century monasteries where you'll come to appreciate the heritage of this beautiful mountain kingdom.

is this for me?

PHYSICAL ✦ ✦ ✦ ✦ ✦
Stamina, aerobic fitness for altitude

PSYCH ✦ ✦ ✦ ✦ ✦
Exotic culture, long distances

SKILL ✦ ✦ ✦ ✦ ✦
Supported trekking, some glacier travel

WOW! ✦ ✦ ✦ ✦ ✦
Pristine landscapes, Himalayan peaks

Exploring the Mulu Caves

>> Get wet and dirty in the dark

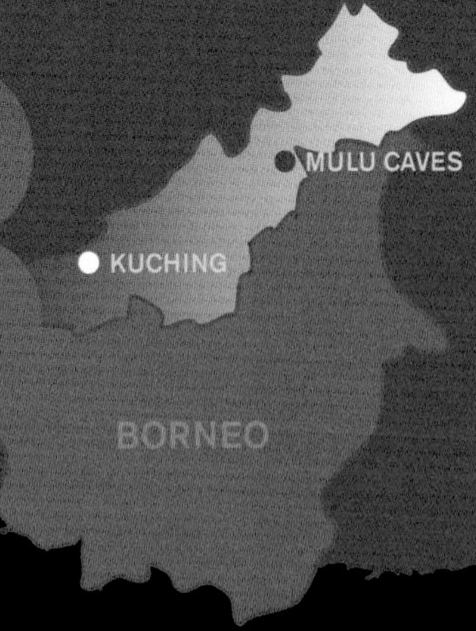

MULU CAVES

KUCHING

BORNEO

Just when you think you've seen it all – when you imagine that every corner of the earth has been purchased, pumped, plowed or paved – someone uncovers something so unfathomably immense and exceptionally fascinating that the most obvious question is how it could have possibly remained hidden for so long. Such is the case of Borneo's Mulu Caves.

While the region's aboriginal inhabitants, the Penan and Berewan people, were aware of some of the cave entrances, it was only relatively recently that the extent of the caves' interiors was realized. In 1977 the Royal Geographical Society mounted one of its largest expeditions ever when they sent 115 scientists to Sarawak in northeastern Borneo to study the flora and fauna of the newly established Gunung Mulu National Park in collaboration with the Malaysian government. Near the end of the fifteen-month survey a small group of cavers were invited to come and explore some of the area caves to determine what existed. What's subsequently been found in this honeycomb of mountainous, jungle-covered limestone is over 290km of cave passages – perhaps just a fraction of the total – including the world's largest cave passage, the world's largest natural chamber and the longest cave in Asia.

Four of Mulu's most spectacular caves have been developed as show caves, so called because they are accessible to all park visitors by plankwalks and well-lit concrete paths. The most visited of these is Deer Cave, the largest cave passage in the world at over 2km in length and never less than 90m high and wide. So capacious is its gaping entrance that rays of sunlight reach deep into the main chamber, which is 174m wide and 122m high. It's an immense space and it's hard not to feel both physically and emotionally dwarfed when first setting foot inside – the acrid smell of bat guano piled to the side of the walkway and the abundance of feasting earwigs and beetles is likely to provide little comfort. Initial feelings of unease quickly turn to amazement as you make your way further in, walking past columns of water gushing down from the cave's roof into a twisting river passage 30m below. Once beyond the splashing of the falling water, listen for the squeaking sounds of three million bats, as they ready themselves for their nightly sojourn (see box). Just one hundred meters from Deer Cave is Lang's Cave, a more narrow and intimate space, with well-lit intricate formations and long shawls adorning the walls. Look closely into its many clear rimmed pools and you might see small white cave prawns swimming ethereally in the water.

Two other show caves, Clearwater Cave and Wind Cave, are about 4km up the Melinau River and can be accessed by boat or by hiking; both approaches allow you to absorb the smells and sounds of the jungle, from the sweet fragrance of flowering tropical plants to the birds that command the canopy. Clearwater Cave, at 151km, is the longest cave in Asia and gets its name from a strikingly crystal clear river that flows for 5km near the opening. Downriver is Wind Cave, home to a wonderful variety of stalactites, stalagmites, flowstones, rock corals and gravity-defying helictites and blessed with cool breezes that seem to gather speed as they're funneled through narrow channels. Both can be visited as a day-trip from the park headquarters or as part of a longer trek into the park's northern forests and caves.

the bats of Mulu

Each night, shortly before dusk – barring a downpour – visitors at Gunung Mulu National Park gather in an observation shelter near the mouth of Deer Cave to watch between one and two million bats make a mass exodus from the cave's gaping mouth. The first groups emerge looking like puffs of smoke in the sky, then quickly swell into a waving black column that darkens the sky as they begin their nightlong pursuit of insects. Each bat weighs about 18g, yet they consume two-thirds of their weight each feeding night; in total, the bats in Deer Cave eat about 15,000kg of insects every evening. This keeps the resident insect population in balance, which has the added effect of allowing most humans to enjoy exploring and camping in the park without the need for mosquito netting and heavy doses of repellant – a refreshing rarity in a jungle environment.

need to know

Plan on a minimum of two full days in the park to see the show caves, and a longer stay for adventure caving. Reservations for accommodation, booking of guided tours or general enquiries may be made to Gunung Mulu National Park (☎ 85 792 300 or 85 792 301, ⓦ www.mulupark.com).

guides and gear A number of tour operators in Miri provide packaged tours to Gunung Mulu National Park, including the show caves and the pinnacles, but only park-employed guides are permitted to lead adventure caving trips. For adventure caving, plan on contacting the park a month in advance to arrange for a guide and accommodation. Technical caving equipment and ropes are generally not required for adventure caving in Mulu Caves.

when to go You can visit the park and the caves year-round, although March through October is the dry season and may make your trekking more enjoyable.

getting there From Miri in northeast Sarawak there are daily flights to Mulu, adjacent to the national park. Once only accessible by a two-day riverboat trip and trekking through primary rainforest, you can now fly into Mulu airport adjacent to the national park and find comfortable accommodation around the airport, and hostel-style dormitories and camping in the national park.

suggested reading Wendy Hutton, *East Malaysia and Brunei: Periplus Adventure Guides* (Periplus). Detailed, insider's-type guide to Sarawak, Saba, and Brunei.

is this for me?

PHYSICAL ✦ ✦ ✦
Some steep ascents and scrambling

PSYCH ✦ ✦ ✦
Dark caves, underground running water, and bats

SKILL ✦ ✦
Prior caving or climbing experience helpful

WOW! ✦ ✦ ✦ ✦
Immense caves and captivating setting

After you've visited the show caves you might experience the urge to try something a bit more adventurous, leaving the planked and lit chambers for less visited reaches. Toss aside any hang-ups you have about getting wet and dirty in the dark and accompany one of the park guides on a program crafted to your particular interests and capabilities. Unless you have prior caving experience, you'll want to start with a beginner cave before attempting a more challenging one – the latter requires more scrambling, wading through waist-deep water and covering a greater distance. Either way, you'll explore, walk, climb, swim, and occasionally crawl to depths few others have seen.

A good choice for basic adventure caving is Racer Cave where you'll explore not only the formations but the fauna, specifically the namesake cave racer, a snake adapted to living its entire life in complete darkness. If the thought of descending by fixed ropes and crawling into a somewhat stuffy dark cave filled with snakes gives you the willies, rest assured that the 1.5 meter-long cave racer is non-poisonous and generally not a threat to humans, though it has the ability to strike out nearly a meter and snatch a bat in flight – a stunning sight if you happen to catch it. Racer Cave is also a good place to find cave crickets and other denizens of dark places like swiftlets, a bird species that relies on echolocation to find its way in the blackness. As in all of the caves, you'll be instructed to speak in hushed tones so as to not disturb the animal life – and in the quiet you'll also be able to hear underground waterfalls and rivers.

For a more strenuous and lengthy adventure (but still possible to accomplish in a day), go deep into Wind Cave, past the show cave section into the unlit wild chambers, to the point where it connects with Clearwater Cave. Your route will take you over boulders, as you inch your way down muddy slopes with some assistance from fixed ropes. The most fantastic part of the trip lies further on, when you wade through cool water that flows in a beautifully sculpted kilometer-long passage.

Though Mulu is unparalleled for its embrassment of underground riches, leave time for some of the park's topside spectacles. A visit to the Pinnacles, a collection of 45m silver-gray limestone needles that spring from the side of Gunung Api (Fire Mountain), is the ultimate destination on a challenging 6–8 hour day hike starting from the Camp 5 forest lodge. The toughest part is the steep scramble where you climb 1200m in just 2.4km to a commanding overview of the intriguing spires wrapped in dense vegetation.

134 Bicycling in Yangshou

>> Pedal deep into rural China

CHINA

YANGSHOU

When you arrive in Yangshuo, a bustling town in southern China's Guangxi province, you will instantly realize that to do the gorgeous landscape justice, a car is simply too fast and walking, too slow. Here along the Li River, where craggy limestone ("karst") pinnacles rise from the enveloping mist and the surrounding rice paddy fields, a bicycle is the perfect conveyance. Not only is cycling the ideal way to experience the extraordinary beauty of the Li River valley, but it puts you on par with the locals, transporting you into a way of life that has persisted for nearly a century.

cormorant fishing

A remarkable traditional practice, cormorant fishing was first employed in Japan, finding its way to China over a thousand years ago. Cormorants are seabirds with excellent fishing skills and, happily for fisherman, can be trained to fish on command. A fisherman, normally working from a bamboo raft, will have one or more cormorants, each tethered by a ring around the base of their necks. The fisherman first holds a lantern over the water to attract the fish. On command, the cormorants dive for fish and return to the boat, while the ring around their necks prevents them from swallowing any large fish. The fisherman then removes the catch from the birds' gullets and readies for the next dive. At the end of the day the fisherman takes the rings off and gives the birds a good feeding. While a dedicated fisherman and a well-trained cormorant can feed a family, and two or more birds can help provide an income, cormorant fishing is slowly giving way to more efficient methods.

Most westerners have seen this otherworldly topography in photos and only know that it's someplace in China, while others may even know the area as Guilin. Guilin is in fact a major city in northeastern Guangxi, a province about the size of the UK that borders Vietnam to the south. While you will find some wonderful scenery in Guilin, most follow the ethereal landscape southward to the Li River valley, where the town of Yangshuo puts you in the heart of the karst towers. Exposed limestone is responsible for these striking formations: the world's largest concentration of it is found in southern China, with much of it occurring here in Guangxi. Besides pinnacles, this limestone manifests itself in unusual and dramatic caves (some of the world's largest are in China), sinkholes, underground rivers, and hillocks. Around Yangshuo, you can experience the topography in a rural, traditional setting – all it takes is a bicycle for you to make this serene countryside your own.

From the bustling center of Yangshuo you can take off in any number of directions and enjoy meandering rides for hours. Ten minutes of pedaling quickly transports you into a rural China where the industrial revolution might not seem like it's hit, and cars seem oddly out of place. One recommended day outing is to the town of Xingping, 25km to the north. Begin by crossing over the Li to the east of Yangshuo, where you can ride on dirt paths under a horizon gracefully dotted with jade-colored towers in every direction and engulfed in a constant haze. At Fuli, a small village where local farmers sell chilies from their carts, turn north on a path that leaves Yangshuo, and the rest of China, far behind. You are now biking in an area where even native Mandarin speakers are left confused by the local dialect, a world made up of paddy fields and persimmon groves.

It's particularly lovely here in the spring, well before the early harvest, when the fields are soaked and glistening and the rice shoots are green or turning golden. But for a cultural experience, visit during the late harvest in October, when scores of people come out to pull the crop. With the help of water buffalo, adults and children all busily engage in the pulling, drying, flooding, plowing, and replanting of the rice. Amid the bustle, the karst towers, most rising over 200m high and decorated with lush shrubbery, offer a peaceful and relaxing backdrop.

Arriving along this route in Xingping, you return to the river at a point where the Dayuan, a tributary from the northeast, flows into the Li. Enjoy lunch or a snack at a simple local restaurant and take in the town's scenic setting on the river, the pinnacles perfectly reflected in the placid waters. You may have already taken a hundred photos on your way up from Yangshuo, but with the river as your route home, you can easily take a hundred more. It's possible to return to Yangshou by retracing your route by bike, but you'll likely find the new scenery and activity on the river far more appealing and opt to take a passenger boat downriver. From Xingping back to Yangshuo, the Li flows steadily through seven giant bends, where fishermen on small boats work their nets and some remaining traditionalists practice cormorant fishing. Beyond Yangshuo, the Li flows into the Pearl River or Zhu Jiang, China's third largest river, before finding it's way to into the South China Sea.

need to know

Although getting around rural China is not always easy for Westerners, Yangshuo can be more accommodating than many other areas. Guesthouses used by foreign backpackers for over twenty years are still available, but now larger hotels and some upscale lodges and inns are being built to serve the needs of a growing number of Chinese and international tourists.

guides and gear A leading active travel company, Backroads (℡510/527-1555, or 1-800/462-2848, Ⓦ www.backroads.com) offers a variety of guided cycling programs including Yangshuo and other areas of China. They use titanium-frame mountain bikes with front shocks that provide good stability and ease of handling on both dirt paths and paved roads.

when to go Spring and fall, especially April & May, Sept–Nov, are ideal in Yangshuo. Summer in subtropical Yangshuo brings hot muggy weather and monsoons.

getting there From Hong Kong there are numerous flights and trains to Guilin, where you can take a local shuttle or bus to Yangshuo, about one hour and thirty minutes south. Passenger service on the Li River is also available.

suggested reading Peter Hessler, *Oracle Bones: A Journey Through Time in China* (Harper Perennial). Exploration into a country undergoing momentous change before our eyes. Cao Lei, *Guilin* (Foreign Language Press). Photographic album of scenic, cultural, and historic sites from Guilin to Yangshuo. Text in Chinese and English.

suggested viewing An adaptation of the W. Somerset Maugham novel, *The Painted Veil* (2006) was set in China and filmed mainly in Guilin and on the Li River.

is this for me?

PHYSICAL ✦ ✦
Mild aerobic activity and ascents

PSYCH ✦ ✦ ✦
Unfamiliar culture, basic facilities

SKILL ✦ ✦
Basic cycling skills

WOW! ✦ ✦ ✦
Stunning scenery

Diving in Palawan
135
>> Watching dugongs dine

THE PHILIPPINES

CALAMAIN ISLANDS

Dotted with countless islands that were once lorded over by the infamous Moro pirates, the Sulu Sea today is a haven for divers and snorkelers. Some dive to impossible depths for a glimpse of life rarely seen at the surface, while others revel in the vibrant coral reefs that teem with perennial pelagic favorites like sharks, rays, turtles, and iridescent schools of fish. No matter where you go in the Sulu Sea, there are underwater riches to be found.

In the remote Maricaban Bay in northern Palwan's Calamian Islands, live some of the area's greatest treasures: dugongs. Here it's possible to swim in the shallow waters alongside the gentle giants that inspired the lore of the mermaids and are the world's only herbivorous sea mammal. As you dive or snorkel among them, they'll continue doing what they always do: devouring grass like a vacuum in long, deliberate sweeps, almost oblivious of your presence and fascination. Guided by one of the local dive masters who closely tracks the 20 or so dugongs in the bay, the chance of finding a dugong to swim with is high.

Aside from dugongs, the bay – which has two resorts and a small fishermen's village – has a string of uninhabited isles that are fringed by pristine coral reefs. Snorkeling just 50m off the beaches of the isles, you'll find a bewildering array of marine life living in a world of dense coral gardens that are riotous with colors. Sharks dart to and fro in search of prey, green turtles flap languidly, thick shoals of jackfish block the sun, octopuses morph into different shapes and colors, barracudas loiter on the surface, giant clams twitch their one-meter-wide mouths, and scorpion fishes and lion fishes float past looking like weightless rocks.

More diversity still can be found at Apo Reef, about 60km away in the middle of the Mindoro Strait, where there's a lot to explore in the two v-shaped reefs that are separated by an abyssal depth. On the reeftops, the coral is in impeccable condition and species such as turtles, whitetip sharks, barracudas, and rays are common; more species lurk in the yonder world where the coral plateaus drop sharply towards a deep darkness that will send a shiver down your spine. The visibility is great, and this is a boon for snorkelers, who can see almost everything that scuba divers can. But divers have the luxury of exploring the deeper reaches of the cliff-face where there is a greater chance of finding big tuna, marlins, mantas, and, if you're lucky, dolphins as well as hammerhead sharks. Just take your time and plan on an extended stay – chances are one dive here will only whet your appetite for many more.

gentle giants

Dugongs grow to a weight of 400–500kg, and spend much of their time devouring 25–30kg of sea-grass daily at a depth of 3–9m; their voracious feeding is interrupted only by their need to surface every four or five minutes for gulps of air. Reproduction rate is slow: females bear their first young at around the age of eight years, and then have about one offspring every decade, or a maximum of six offspring in a lifetime. This, coupled with their docility, makes them easy prey: impoverished fishermen are tempted by the considerable income from the sale of dugong's meat and valued tusk. Hunting is one of reason accounting for the decimation of dugong populations – other threats include accidental ensnarement and suffocation in fishing nets, as well as coastal pollution and sedimentation that degrades sea-grass meadows – and it's estimated that the population of dugongs in Southeast Asia has plunged by ninety percent since the seventies. Although dugongs retain strongholds in northern Australia and some Gulf countries, they are now classed as an endangered species. There are only a few safe herds in Southeast Asia. In the Philippines – where populations are down to critical numbers – the herd in Maricaban Bay may be the largest extant community in the Philippines.

need to know

There are two places to stay in Maricaban Bay: at the upscale *Club Paradise* (Ⓦ www. clubparadisepalawan.com) set in a private isle, or at the fan rooms of *Vicky's Guesthouse* in the fishermen's village (the guesthouse is run by the Dugong Dive Center). The best reef in the bay is at *Club Paradise*'s private isle, and if you're not staying at the resort you can visit by day to go snorkeling for a nominal fee.

guides and gear The Dugong Dive Center (Ⓦ www.dugongdivecenter.com) offers diving courses, as well as various diving or snorkeling tours which include dugong-watching and trips to Apo Reef.

when to go You can have great diving year-round with March April, May, September, October, and November offering the best weather and visibility..

getting there Basuanga, the largest island of the Calamian group is served by scheduled flights from Manila, 300km to the northeast. From the airstrip at Basuanga, Maricaban Bay is to get to the bay from the airstrip entails a 30-minute drive and short boat ride down the river – these can only be privately arranged through Club Paradise or Vicky's Guesthouse.

is this for me?

PHYSICAL ✦ ✦ ✦ ✦ ✦
Easy snorkeling or diving

PSYCH ✦ ✦ ✦ ✦ ✦
Overcoming instinctive fear of sharks

SKILL ✦ ✦ ✦ ✦ ✦
Prior certification makes the trip more rewarding

WOW! ✦ ✦ ✦ ✦ ✦
Impressive marine habitat with exceptional variety

Trekking in the Annapurna Himal

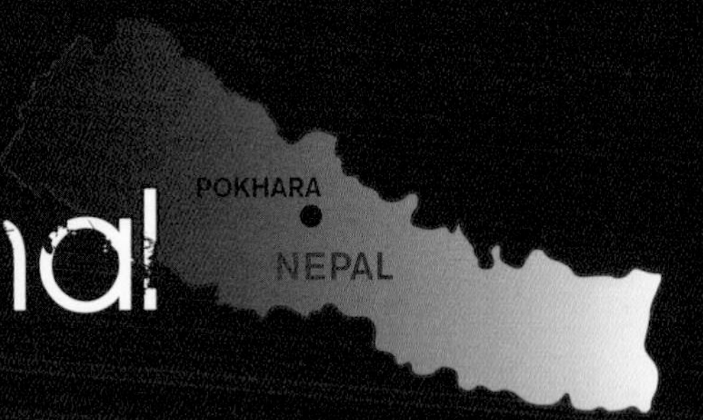

>> The lure of legendary massifs

POKHARA

NEPAL

Names can be deceiving. Take Annapurna for example – no mountain on earth has a more caressing, soothing name. The name comes from the Sanskrit meaning "Goddess of the Harvest," denoting the nourishing rivers that flow from its slopes. But don't be fooled. Annapurna is far and away the most deadly mountain in the world. It's also the most rarely climbed of the world's fourteen 8000m peaks. Since the first ascent in 1950 by Maurice Herzog, it's been climbed 142 times, and at last count it has taken 58 lives – a horrific fatality rate of 40 percent. With this kind of risk and reputation, it's easy to see why just trekking in the shadows of Annapurna is adventure enough for most people.

"For the first time Annapurna was revealing its secrets. The huge north face, with its great rivers of ice, shone and sparkled in the sunlight. Never had I seen so impressive a mountain. It was a world both dazzling and menacing, and the eye was lost on its immensities."
Maurice Herzog, on first ascent of Annapurna, 1950

Within the vast Himalaya Range which arcs across Asia for 2400km, there are numerous subranges, massifs or *himal*, including eleven *himal* within Nepal alone. The Annapurna Himal set in north central Nepal is one of the most dominating shields of rock and ice on the planet, with an elevation in excess of 6000m for over 35km along its spine. At the west end of that spine is Annapurna, the kingpin of the *himal*, and the tenth highest peak in the world at 8091m.

Since 1950 the *himal* has quickly become a legendary destination for trekkers, and today most who come to hike in Nepal do so in the Annapurna region. The area offers exquisite scenery, a variety of elevations and route options, and accessibility from Pokhara, the second largest city in Nepal. If you can commit the three or more weeks to the complete Annapurna Circuit, then the trek of a lifetime awaits, but if you have less time, there are some shorter, but still impressive treks for Annapurna-bound trekkers which mustn't be overlooked.

The three hundred-kilometer circumnavigation of the Annapurna Himal, known as the Annapurna Circuit, is one of the great treks of the world as it rises from subtropical rice fields to a pass at 5416m where you skirt the Tibetan plateau. Throughout the 16- to 25-day trek you remain within 40km of the *himal*'s icy spine. On the backside you'll cross over the Thorung La, which at 5416m is the highest regularly traveled mountain pass in the world. Successfully completing the clockwise loop returns you to the village of Dumre, about 40km to the southwest of Pokhara.

In recent years a route known as the Royal Trek – so named because Prince Charles made the trip in 1981 – has become a popular option for budget-minded trekkers in search of a guided trek. It follows an easy course around the beautiful Pokhara Valley along a one-way semi-circular track to the east and

the first to summit an 8000-meter peak

When the French Himalayan Club mounted an expedition to climb Annapurna in 1950 they were working with only the sketchiest of information. Club president Lucien Devies recalled: "...other expeditions have picked mountains in regions already known and explored. But we have absolutely no information...We know nothing about the approach routes. The maps at our disposal are practically useless..." The French found Annapurna and climbed it, becoming the first to scale a summit over 8000m. In doing so, they opened approach routes to the range and were the first Europeans to cross Thorong La, the highest pass on the Annapurna Circuit.

super Sherpas

Apa Sherpa has successfully climbed Mount Everest a record eighteen times as of May 2008, while Lhakpa Gelu Sherpa climbed from base camp to the summit in less than 11hr – also a record. Both men are ethnic Sherpas – the unsung heroes of Everest expeditions. Sherpas have long been recognized for their toughness in carrying heavy loads and performing much of the expedition's legwork at high altitudes, and their guiding prowess at Everest has led to a new way for these Nepalese mountain-dwelling agriculturists to make a living. Indeed, the word "sherpa" is often used simply to mean any Himalayan mountaineering guide, although the two terms don't necessarily always overlap.

Sherpas have been part of Mount Everest expeditions from the beginning, with Sherpa guide Tenzing Norgay being one of two men to first reach the summit. Now, scientists are trying to figure out what makes Sherpas so resilient. Both Apa and Lhakpa Gelu are involved in a study being conducted by researchers at the University of Utah Orthopedic Specialty Hospital, and preliminary results of the study indicate that five thousand years of high-altitude genetic adaptation may be partly responsible for Sherpas' remarkable ability to cope with extreme elevations. Previous studies have shown that Sherpas have naturally higher pulmonary ventilation rates than lowlanders, which allow them to conserve oxygen, and Sherpa metabolism does not rise quite as high, allowing them to conserve energy. Of course, this is no reason to underestimate the effects of hard work and training. Not only are Sherpas able to adapt physiologically to low oxygen levels as they grow up in hypoxic environments, but the sturdy Sherpas have also had plenty of experience carrying heavy loads at high altitudes. Without such training, genetics would not climb the summit alone.

need to know

Independent trekking with accommodation at lodges and teahouses is available throughout the Annapurna *himal*, where the higher you go, the more simple the accommodation becomes. At higher elevations, and especially in the Annapurna region, avalanche danger can linger into spring.

guides and gear Mountain Travel-Sobek (℡ 510/594-6000 or 1-888/687-6235, Ⓦ www.mtsobek.com) offers guided trekking to the Annapurna Sanctuary in spring and fall. Trips include accommodation, expert leadership, meals and all trekking arrangements. World Records Expeditions and Treks (℡ 01/4413458, Ⓦ www.worldrecordsexpedition.com) based in Kathmandu organizes custom treks throughout Nepal and provides logistical support and guiding on mountaineering expeditions in the Himalaya.

when to go March to April, with blooming rhododendrons, and October to November in the green post-monsoon season, are the best months for treks in the Annapurna Himal. From June to September you'll face monsoons, when views are typically poor and trails can be slippery.

getting there A flight of less than an hour takes you from Nepal's capital of Kathmandu to Pokhara where in fair weather you'll have Everest views from the aircraft. The Annapurna Circuit route begins about an hour northwest of Pokhara by car.

suggested reading Bryn Thomas, *Trekking in the Annapurna Region* (Trailblazer Publications). A dependable trekking guide with excellent detail and illustrations. David Roberts, *True Summit: What Really Happened on the Legendary Ascent on Annapurna* (Simon and Schuster). A surprising revision of the first ascent showing an expedition torn by dissent.

is this for me?

PHYSICAL ✦✦✦✦✧
Strenuous high altitude hiking

PSYCH ✦✦✦✧✧
Extended trek with high altitude

SKILL ✦✦✧✧✧
High altitude trekking and camping

WOW! ✦✦✦✦✧
Fantastic mountains, fascinating cultures

south – actually taking you in the opposite direction of Annapurna. The trail follows a ridge through villages with small cultivated plots and orchards, where the highest point is just 1830m at the village of Kalikathan, the starting point for the four-day, 39km trek. Given the lower elevation and warmer climate you can trek comfortably from October to May and the terrain is suitable for even young children or the not-so-fit. What initially was intended to be an off-the-beaten-path trek into some remote rural villages has since become a rather over-beaten and often crowded circuit. Still, the villages are charming, especially the thatched-roof homes of Syaklung, and the people are particularly gracious. As for mountain scenery, it's not in your face, but you will have views of the Annapurna Range, the unclimbed fish-tail summit of Machhupuchhare (6997m) and Dhaulagiri (8167m).

With more time and a passion for high elevations and fantastic mountain views, a trek to the Annapurna Sanctuary takes you into the heart of the Annapurna Himal. It's a vigorous ten-day trek with some steady ascents and a maximum elevation of 4100m, but at that relatively modest elevation you find yourself in the enviable position of standing in the base camp of Annapurna looking up at the near-vertical south face. As with the Annapurna Circuit, you start about one hour by road northwest of Pokhara in the village of Nayapul. The Garung villages set in terraced fields on your ascending route are festooned with rhododendron and giant poinsettia shrubs that grow to 6m in height. Well-worn footpaths, stone steps and an occasional suspension bridge link one village to the next. By the third day, views of both Dhaulagiri and Annapurna appear from a vantage point on Poon Hill at 3193m, but you'll drop again into rhododendron and bamboo forests before making a steep ascent to the Machhupuchhare base camp (3720m). On the following day a morning hike leads to the dramatic glacial amphitheatre, the Annapurna Sanctuary, base camp for epic climbs of Annapurna's summit. Here you are ringed by six glistening peaks in a deep bowl of moraine and snow. Departing the sanctuary, a speedier three-day descent brings you to rural villages set in dense clusters of fern and bamboo before you return to Nayapul and onward by road to Pokhara.

137 Climbing Mount Fuji

>> Join a thousand-year-old procession

You might hear it a dozen times before you've even left Tokyo: "If you never climb Mount Fuji once you are a fool, if you climb it more than once you are twice the fool." No doubt a chestnut coined by the Japan National Tourist Office, and not some ancient Shinto saying. However, the climb is actually not technical: it's a brisk walk and can be a horrendously crowded one at that. After about forty minutes from Tokyo, as the *Shinkansen* bullet train sweeps past cities and power lines at 240km per hour, there is a break in the urban congestion: the perfectly formed volcanic cone suddenly overtakes the horizon.

your own private Fuji

Although Fuji's height at 3776m puts it well below the major peaks of the world, including most of the major summits in the Alps and Rockies, Fuji-san has one characteristic that sets it apart from any other major mountain peak: it's privately owned. In fact, it may be the world's most prominent privately owned natural feature. In 1609, the land above the Eighth Station (at about 3000m) was granted in perpetuity to Fujisan Hongu Sengentaisha, a Shinto shrine, by samurai warlord Tokugawa Ieyasu. In 1957, the shrine's owners sued for possession of the land, citing a 1947 law providing for the return of state-owned lands to traditionally held Shinto shrines. The claim was upheld by Japan's Supreme Court in 1974, with the stipulation that the transfer of property rights would take place in 2004, and that some facilities, such as the observatory and various roads, would remain under government jurisdiction.

Now that Fuji is privately owned, is anything likely to change? Probably not. A Shinto priest at the Sengentaisha shrine, Norihiko Nakamura, has declared that the shrine would never keep anyone from climbing Fuji's sacred slopes: "Mount Fuji is a mountain of the world, not an asset for individuals."

Fuji is the ultimate Japanese icon, its image more ubiquitous than that of Hello Kitty and all the Pokémon creatures combined. The mountain has been the leading subject of Japanese art for hundreds of years – murals of Fuji commonly adorn bathhouses to create a soothing ambiance, and it's a fixture on postage stamps and currency. The mountain is regarded as sacred by Japan's two major religions, Shinto and Buddhism, and adherents see mountain climbing as a metaphor for spiritual growth and enlightenment. Worship of Fuji has its roots in Shugendo, a Buddhist sect that developed in the fourteenth century. Shugendo advocated mountain climbing as an inherently sacred pursuit, an opportunity to commune with deities on mountaintops. The sect's devotees developed Fuji's first climbing routes, resulting in a steady stream of faithful pilgrims to its summit. By the eighteenth century, thousands of worshipers climbed the mountain as part of an annual pilgrimage.

Fuji-ko pilgrims still climb the mountain today, to pray at summit altars and worship at the Konohana Sakuya Hime shrine. But now, most of the 240,000 people who climb the mountain each year do so as part of a deeply ingrained cultural tradition, rather than for religious purposes; many others are eager to immerse themselves in this cultural experience, and about thirty percent of those who climb the mountain are foreigners. Japanese typically refer to the mountain by the honorific name *Fuji-san*, and since the *san* suffix implies "mountain", calling it Mount Fuji-san is redundant.

May our five senses be pure, and may the weather on the honorable mountain be fine.
Japanese pilgrim's motto

One common way to approach the mountain is from the Shin-Fuji train station (accessible via the speed train from Tokyo). From Shin-Fuji, buses take climbers on a 2hr 15min ride up a winding, narrow, two-lane road through deep cedar forests to the Fifth Station. Mount Fuji is divided into ten stations or levels, with the base of the mountain being the first station and the summit the tenth. There are four separate Fifth Stations (*Shingogome*) on different sides of the mountain; all are accessible by paved roads. From each of these Fifth Stations, four separate trails lead up the mountain, converging near the summit. The most widely used trail, due to its proximity to Tokyo, is Yoshidaguchi, located on the north side, with a Fifth Station elevation of 2305m. However, one of the better ways to climb is the Fujinomiya trail. Apart from its being slightly less crowded, its spot on the south side of the mountain is the highest starting elevation (2400m), putting you on the summit in the shortest time (4–6hr) with what is still a reasonably convenient bullet train access point from Tokyo, Nagoya, and Osaka. Although it's possible to ascend Fuji from any of the First Stations at the base of the mountain, climbing up forested slopes and passing dozens of shrines toward the Fifth Stations, almost no one does.

Within minutes of the ascent on the Fujinomiya trail, you'll break out above the tree line; here the mountain becomes a lifeless slope of volcanic scree, ash, and larger volcanic rocks. You can make the climb at any time of day or night, though most Japanese climb at night so that they arrive on the summit in time to see the rising sun. There are five successive stations on the climb leading to the summit, each of them offering a limited selection of food and drinks, as well as sleeping arrangements – huts filled with bunks, futons, blankets, and traditional buckwheat hull pillows. In these crowded and noisy dormitories there's no guarantee of a decent night's rest, so a night climb by headlamp, with stops for resting or even napping along the trail, is no great sacrifice.

Along the trail, hikers come from all walks of life – young children, grandparents, and an even mix of men and women. While most seem generally up for the challenge, there are always varied paces: some stop every few minutes, others literally run up the mountain. Because the mountain is featureless and the trailside barren, people watching becomes as much a part of the scenic appeal as the beauty of the light, clouds, and changing weather. Being a part of this thousand-year-old procession of humanity, which during climbing season can consist of up to three thousand people a day (and more on weekends), is an essential element of the Fuji-san experience.

Beyond *Hachigome* (Eighth Station) the pitch steepens and the pace naturally slows with the thinning air. At the approach to the summit you'll pass though a large *torii*, or Shinto gate, heralding the entrance into the highest realm of Fuji-san. From here it's a short walk to the true summit, next to the old weather station – at 3776m, the highest point in Japan. At the rim, standing above the clouds, you may have a view of an expansive cloudbank, though on clear days it's possible to see to the ocean, to Tokyo, or beyond. Starting at the summit, many people often make a loop of the crater rim, which takes about an hour, while the descent back to the Fujinomiya Fifth Station takes a speedy 2–4hr.

need to know

Even in summer, night temperatures on Fuji often drop to 0°C, while during the day you'll be exposed to the sun on a shadeless slope, so bring warm clothing, sunscreen, and a hat. During the main climbing season, no special skills are necessary to reach the summit.

guides and gear Mount Fuji Mountaineering School GoRiki (☎0555-24-1032, ⓦ www.fujitozan.jp/english) conducts guided mountaineering ascents of Fuji outside of the main summer climbing season.

when to go The best time to climb is from July through August, when the weather is mild and trails are free of snow. The first two weeks in July have generally lighter traffic. Peak crowds appear during school vacations, from around July 20 to the end of August, with mid-August being exceptionally busy. If you really want to avoid the crowds, June and September are possible, but the huts will be closed. Only experienced and prepared mountaineers should attempt the climb from October through May.

getting there From Tokyo, a popular option is to take the Tokaido Shinkansen train to Fujinomiya and connect to a bus that takes you to the Fujinomiya Fifth Station on the mountain. You can also take direct bus or train from Tokyo to nearby points with bus access to all of the Fifth Stations.

suggested reading Cathy Davidson, *36 Views of Mount Fuji: On Finding Myself in Japan* (Duke University Press). An American teacher writes of her travels in Japan in the 1980s, and her struggle to understand Japanese culture.

is this for me?

PHYSICAL ✦ ✦
Aerobic hiking, moderate altitude

PSYCH ✦ ✦
Crowded conditions

SKILL ✦ ✦
No special skills required

WOW! ✦ ✦
Age-old cultural experience

Horseback riding in the Darhat Valley

>> Escaping the hordes

HATGAL

MONGOLIA

Pounding across steppeland on horseback, Genghis Khan and his Mongol hordes united scattered herders to forge a far-flung nomadic confederation in the thirteenth century. Between 1206 and 1227 he conquered an area four times the size of the Roman Empire and left behind a legacy of military strategy, global trade, religious tolerance and administrative genius. He is revered as the founding father of Mongolia and is credited with the first widespread use of paper money and creating a writing system still in use today. Yet, it's doubtful you would have ever heard his name were it not for the Mongolian horse – a durable, robust and responsive breed – and the expert horsemanship of the Mongols.

For Mongols, life has always been portable – homes, families and livelihoods are all carried on horseback. There's simply no better conveyance for this rolling grassy terrain than their well-trained steeds, and there's certainly no better way to immerse yourself in this last great nomadic culture. Nowhere is the essence of the Mongolian nomadic lifestyle and devotion to the horse more vibrantly maintained and displayed than in Mongolia's Darhat Valley.

A horse trek into the Darhat Valley begins 650km from Mongolia's lone metropolis of Ulan Bator. From a tented camp near the shores of Lake Khovsgol, a 160km-long glacially carved alpine lake in northeastern Mongolia, you'll saddle up and ascend Jigleg Pass, where a narrow notch in the mountains offers a gradual ascent through forests of Siberian larch trees laced with magenta fireweed, before descending into the Darhat Valley by way of a rocky river drainage. Beyond the small town of Renchinlumbe at the head of the valley, isolated encampments, or *ail*, dot the grassy expanse, each with several *gers*, the traditional lattice-framed, felt-covered home of nomadic herders. Throughout the Darhat Valley, horsemen and herders seek prime summer pastures and you'll find expansive skies and wide open plains where you can get your fill of trotting, loping and galloping.

In the saddle for six to seven hours and covering 48–56km per day, you'll be riding with the Mongols and like the Mongols. Riding abreast with local wranglers – only defeated soldiers ride single-file – you'll find the preferred gait for these spirited, short-legged horses is a fast trot. At first, you might feel silly on a small, rough-looking Mongolian horse – like a grown man sitting on Great Dane – but you'll soon fall in love with these horses and their battle-tested endurance.

Bring your love of riding and a sense of balance and follow the Mongols' lead – they are still superb horsemen. Wielding a pole-lasso, a seven-meter willow rod with a rawhide noose, a Mongol horseman is able to capture a horse or gather a herd of sheep, goats, yaks, and camels with ease. At a full gallop, Mongol horsemen have a purposeful, erect posture that comes from a life in the saddle.

the Mongolian horse

Don't let the small stature of the Mongolian horse cause you to underestimate it. Though tiny and shaggy looking, the horse, or *moori* (pronounced "moord") in Mongolian, played a large role in the victories of Genghis Khan. In fact, these horses are still preferred for transportation today by many families in the countryside of Mongolia. Mongols don't shoe their horses – the horses have developed iron-hard hooves. You can tell a horse that's just fast enough by the crescent-shaped scar on the hindquarter – the result of a wolf bite. Horses that aren't fast enough will fall prey to the wolves in the winter.

Since the horses are stout with short limbs, they lose less heat through their extremities than bigger horses and their organs stay warm. Their shaggy coats protect against fierce winters, but they can also withstand a high degree of heat, shedding much of their hair in the summer. Such traits are invaluable in the widely varied Mongolian climate, where temperatures can range from −40°C in the winter to 38°C or more in the summer.

Mongul hun morindeeree baihad alzahgui.

"As long as a Mongolian is on his horse, he'll be just fine."

Genghis Khan

need to know

A horse trek through the Darhat Valley involves about nine days in the saddle, no matter the weather – and snow is not uncommon in July. Evenings will be spent in comfortable *ger* camps and in tents with all the accoutrements of catered camping, though don't count on a shower.

guides and gear
Boojum Expeditions (☎ 239/695-3299, 1-877/567-0679, Ⓦ www .boojum.com) offers scheduled and custom horsetrekking and *ger* camping in the Darhat Valley.

when to go
In Mongolia's cool climate, a horse trek in late June to mid-September is ideal. July has the added attraction of Naadam festivities, which include horse racing..

getting there
From the Mongolian capital of Ulan Bator take scheduled air service to Muren. Hatgal, the staging point for trips into the Darhat Valley, is two hours to the north of Muren by private vehicle.

suggested reading
Jack Weatherford, *Genghis Kahn and the Making of the Modern World* (Three Rivers Press) A lively history of the world's greatest conqueror, showing his kinder, gentler side and his amazing legacy.

is this for me?

PHYSICAL ✦ ✦ ✦
Endurance for long days in saddle

PSYCH ✦ ✦ ✦
Remote outdoor setting and exotic culture

SKILL ✦ ✦ ✦
Previous riding experience highly recommended

WOW! ✦ ✦ ✦ ✦
Beautiful environment and riding culture

With their famous hospitality, Mongols have managed to shake Genghis Khan's bad-boy image of plundering and butchering. They are quick to invite you inside for a cup of tea or perhaps even a bowl of *airag*, a fermented horse milk beverage – think fizzy sour milk with a kick. It's an acquired taste, but it quenches thirst and a swig will help wash down that morsel of roasted marmot you've been gnawing. You may even witness the Mongols' shamanistic rituals as they call for rain or predict the future from the shoulder bone of a sheep. As you approach the southern skirt of the valley you might also encounter the Tsaatan, a tribe of reindeer people who both ride and herd reindeer. They're not always easy to find, as their small community is fighting an uphill battle to maintain their traditional nomadic lifestyle. The Darhat Valley is their favored home for summer grazing before they retreat to the more protective forest highlands in the winter.

With fresh horses, you'll leave the Darhat Valley through mountainous birch woods, bringing you back to Lake Khovsgol. What you'll experience through mountain meadow and sculpted steppe is more than just a horseback ride – it's a passage into a proud and vigorous way of life.

THAILAND

PHUKET

139
Sea kayaking in Phang Nga Bay

>> Like entering a lost world

It's called "kiss the oyster," an acrobatic move unfamiliar to most sea kayakers outside Thailand's Phang Nga Bay. As you inch your kayak through the entrance to a giant sea cave, you flatten your body as tightly as possible into the base of the inflatable kayak, arms close to your chest, knees down and head pushed back. If the water is calm and the tide just right you glide through the low hanging entrance of the chamber without scraping your head on the sharp rocks and oysters that line the ceiling of the passageway. The rising and falling water forms a secret door that often conceals these caves, except at low tide, and even then only to a small low-lying craft like a sea kayak or inflatable canoe.

James Bond

Bond films always have their exotic locations, but Phang Nga Bay actually has a place commonly known as "James Bond Island" (Khao Tapu), for the role it played as a hideaway in *The Man with the Golden Gun* (1974). A few other movies have used this vivid setting as a backdrop, including another Bond flick, *Tomorrow Never Dies* (1997), and *The Beach* (2000), which imagined the kind of remote idyllic island that travelers often dream of – and try to find off the coast of Thailand.

Tsunamis

In December 2004, nearly a quarter million people, including 10,000 in Thailand, perished in a single day from a devastating tsunami wave that surged ashore in various coastal cities in Southeast Asia. The Andaman coast was hit as hard as anywhere, and Phuket was the first place to be affected by the wave hitting land.

Although there was detection of an undersea earthquake in the Indian Ocean, scientists were unable to accurately predict the timing, size and landfall of the subsequent wave, which reached a height of 30m on some beaches. Tsunamis do not accompany every earthquake and are most frequently generated by a sudden rise in the sea bed along a fault. The wave then ripples across the ocean at speeds up to 1000km/hr. In deep ocean water, the change at the surface is almost imperceptible. The destructive tsunami only grows to its monstrous size when reaching the shallow coastline; in this case, it made landfall between 15 minutes and seven hours after the quake, depending on the coastal city's distance from the epicenter.

Following the disaster, there was a movement to establish a tsunami detection system, especially in areas vulnerable to significant seismic activity. A combination of measuring, recording and transmitting devices have since been placed on the ocean floor and strategically placed buoys to measure changes that would indicate the imminent danger of an approaching tsunami, though the processes required to maximize accuracy and communicate rapidly are still very much in development.

The caves are one of the defining elements of shallow Phang Nga Bay, which ranges in width between 50 and 100km and encompasses the protected waters between the Malay Peninsula on the east and the island of Phuket on the west. Forty or so limestone karst islands rise up from the waters; these distinctive formations give an other-worldly look and feel to the place, though even that pales in comparison to the experience of trolling into the *hongs* (Thai for "room"), or collapsed cave systems, that you can reach via the caves. The *hongs* closest to Phuket are well known and regularly visited on day-trips, but on some of the more remote islands, you might be one of a few to explore the *hong* that year. At least you'll certainly feel that way.

As you quietly paddle through the caves, tucked out of view beneath the heavily forested limestone cliffs, you really have no idea what's on the other side, the inland side. Some open to huge, echoing, cavernous chambers with stalactites plunging down to the waters' surface; others are claustrophobic little passageways that require you to repeatedly flatten yourself into your kayak. Some let in only enough light to illuminate the first thirty meters or so, that is if they are thirty meters – the cave might be just a few meters long or it might be up to a kilometer. Then, paddling in the dark you see a flicker of light in front of you that brightens as you get nearer. Emerging into the bright light of the island's interior, you've suddenly entered the *hong* and are surrounded 360 degrees by lush green walls rising up hundreds of meters and blue sky above. The floor is a tidal lagoon often consisting of mud flats, mangrove swamp, and channels. Some small *hongs*, with a floor area about half the size of a football field, can be circumnavigated in a matter of minutes, while others extend three to five kilometers and take hours to explore.

It's like a lost world, a Jurassic playground decorated with prehistoric cycads and ferns. The animal life adds to the Mesozoic ambiance, with crab-eating macaques, omnivores that will eat about anything they can find, roaming freely in the mangrove canopy. Also present is the banded water monitor, a semi-aquatic lizard that can stay underwater for up to

thirty minutes before making a lightning speed strike on other reptiles and mammals. On land it feeds on carrion and the eggs of other reptiles, but its size – up to 3m long – and its menacing forked tongue make it a frightening sight for many humans, too.

About 200km south of Phang Nga Bay, but well worth adding into a week of sea kayaking, is Tarutao Islands National Marine Park, Thailand's most pristine national park. While the geology of Tarutao is also karstic, you'll see a different family of limestone – more flowing, not quite as rugged as Phang Nga Bay, and lacking the red, orange, and yellow

oxide staining, but striking nonetheless. On land, hikes lead though dense rainforest where you'll find mouse deer, the smallest of all ungulates, and wild pigs that sometimes make their way down to the beach to see what's for dinner. In the open waters of the Andaman Sea you may have more challenging paddling, but you'll also be rewarded by a vibrant coral reef, sand coves with idyllic beaches, and some spectacular hongs.

need to know

Paddling an inflatable kayak in Phang Nga Bay and the Tarutao Islands is most efficiently done with the support of an escort boat – usually a long tail or a small launch – to cover some of the longer distances between islands. Extended trips from three to seven days give you ample time to explore some of the less frequented islands, caves, and hongs. Most of the islands are uninhabited, so you can camp on the beach or in bungalows provided by the park. Access to sea caves and *hongs* is dependent on tides and is best accomplished on a guided paddle trip.

guides and gear From their base in Phuket, John Gray's Sea Canoe (℡66 76 254505 ⓦwww.johngray-seacanoe.com) offers custom excursions into Phang Nga Bay and Tarutao.

when to go The protected waters of Phang Nga make sea kayaking possible year round. The open waters to the south, and particularly around Tarutao, get rough outside the January to April prime season and should be avoided in a sea kayak, with especially rough water in September and October.

getting there Phuket is located in southern Thailand and is served by regular flights from Bangkok. Single and multiday trips to Phang Nga Bay including its caves and *hongs* are available from Phuket.

suggested reading: Belinda Stewart-Cox and John Hoskins; Gerald Cubbit, photographer, *Wild Thailand* (MIT Press). Organized by area of the country with over 400 photographs of Thailand's wildlife.

is this for me?

PHYSICAL ✦ ✦ ✦
Strength for sustained paddling

PSYCH ✦ ✦ ✦
Caves and unusual wildlife

SKILL ✦ ✦ ✦
Basic paddling skills

WOW! ✦ ✦ ✦ ✦
Top caliber eco-adventure

Wildlife viewing in Borneo

>> Pygmy elephants and two-horned rhinos

In recent years Borneo's long-standing reputation as one of the most biodiverse places on the planet has begun to take a back seat to its logging prospects. The island currently produces half of the world's tropical timber; widespread and rapid deforestation has eliminated half of the island's forest cover since the 1980s. With fewer and fewer forests to call home, several of the island's animal species – including the orang-utan and pygmy elephant – are endangered. Fortunately, viewing Borneo's wildlife remains a seminal experience – perhaps more now than ever. Not only is this an increasingly rare opportunity to see these animals in the wild, but viewing the island's wildlife may be the only way to save it.

Borneo, the third largest island in the world, is divided up among three countries: Malaysia, Indonesia, and the small independent nation of Brunei Darussalam. One of the best access points for wildlife viewing is in the Malaysian state of Sabah, located in northeastern Borneo along the Kinabatangan River (Sungai Kinabatangan). The Kinabatangan is Sabah's longest river, dropping from mountainous headwaters and swelling with seasonal monsoons as it flows northwards 560km into the Sulu Sea. The main city where eco-tours of this remarkable river can be arranged is Sandakan or nearby Sukau. From there it's a short trip to the Kinabatangan, where, gliding silently along the riverbanks on one of the many awning-covered flat-bottom boats, you'll have incredible opportunities for viewing much of Borneo's wildlife as unobtrusively as possible, at close range. You can see everything from the famous Proboscis monkey, found only in Borneo, to spotted civet cats, spindly macacques and, of course, the highly intelligent, tree-dwelling orang-utan, literally "man of the forest".

Along the river you'll also discover a rich eco-system comprising limestone caves, lowland freshwater forests and saltwater mangrove forests, all home to an incredible biodiversity. There are seven hundred native tree species in Borneo, for example (as a point of comparison, there are only three hundred in North America). These trees blanket the island throughout its dense rainforests, swamp forests and lowland jungles, though it's precisely the island's hardwood largesse that has made it a lumberjack's dream. While the upper Kinabatangan River has been hardest hit by logging, the lowland forests have survived surprisingly well, considering how little official protection they've received. Traveling along the river, it's in these lowland forests and oxbow lakes where you'll find the most interesting variety of wildlife – though not always immediately apparent, with some patience, and willingness to get out of the boat and go looking, you're sure to find it.

The most easily spotted and prevalent animals on the Kinabatangan floodplain are birds. Here alone there are six species of vibrantly colored hornbills, all with long, downcurving bills. The most unusual of the lot, the rhinoceros hornbill, has a large, reddish, rhino-like horn that protrudes from its forehead and rests on top of its bill, an evolutionary marvel. The snake-bird or oriental darter is a large web-footed bird that feeds on fish and looks like a cormorant.

Larger inhabitants of the Kinabatangan jungles can also be seen from the river. As you quietly cruise up the Kinabatangan's lower still waters, you're likely to see otters and crocodiles. Continue upriver though a network of

Borneo's one-of-a-kind diversity

Deep in the murky lowland Borneo swamp is a venomous snake with an extremely unusual skill: it can change the color of its skin. Scientists have only encountered the creature in the Kapuas River drainage system and have appropriately named it the Kapuas mud snake. Rare and bizarre animal species like this one are abundant in the rich, unparalleled biodiversity of Borneo. Highly diverse rainforest eco-systems like the dipterocarp forest, peat swamp forest, and heath forest are where the island's large array of plant and animal species thrive. In Borneo there are about 15,000 species of flowering plants, 3000 species of trees, and over 220 land mammals. In one recent 18-month survey, over 50 new species were discovered. Included in these discoveries is the world's largest flower, the Rafflesia, an amazing red bloom that grows three feet across and weighs up to 7kg. The plant has no leaves, no stem and no roots, with a fragrance akin to rotting meat. Other oddities include flying frogs, bearded pigs, and bats that fly with night vision rather than by echolocation. Many animal species here, such as elephants and rhinos, exhibit insular dwarfism, in which large animals are reduced in size when a small environment (like the island of Borneo) restricts their gene pool. Sadly, increasing deforestation on the island threatens to isolate and eventually destroy some of the world's most rare and endangered habitats. Actions to preserve these areas will hopefully save at least some part of the island's one-of-a-kind biodiversity.

need to know

The best place to access the Kinabatangan floodplain by riverboat and jungle walks is from the town of Sukau located about 90km by road from Sandakan. Here you'll find accommodation, including some lodges that cater to a growing ecotourism market, and a variety of packaged tours for wildlife viewing.

guides and gear Programmes in Borneo's Kinabatangan floodplain and other wildlife viewing areas in Sabah are offered through Adventure Center (☎510/654-1879, ⓦwww.adventurecenter .com). On any jungle walk, it's necessary to wear leech socks to protect your feet.

when to go Sabah is subject to monsoons during the rainy season, from October to March. While the animals are there year-round, you'll find viewing easier and more comfortable from April to September.

getting there From Kuala Lumpur take a nonstop flight to Kota Kinabalu, capital of the Malaysian state of Sabah in Borneo, and continue on to Sandakan on Sabah's northeastern coast. The best place to access the Kinabatangan floodplain by riverboat and jungle walks is from the town of Sukau, about 90km by road from Sandakan. Here you'll find accommodation, including some lodges that cater to a growing ecotourism market, and a variety of packaged tours for wildlife viewing.

suggested reading Nick Garbutt and Cede Prudente, *Wild Borneo: The Wildlife and Scenery of Sabah, Sarawak, Brunei, and Kalimantan* (MIT Press). Covers Borneo's wildlife and conservation efforts, plus the people, culture and sights, with over 200 full-color images.

is this for me?

PHYSICAL ✦ ✦ ✦ ✦ ✦
Walking in hot jungle

PSYCH ✦ ✦ ✦ ✦ ✦
Animals in the wild

SKILL ✦ ✦ ✦ ✦ ✦
Remaining alert

WOW! ✦ ✦ ✦ ✦ ✦
Diverse wildlife viewing

lagoons and tributaries, where spotting monkeys in the trees that hug the shores is easy. But the jungle does an excellent job of hiding its denizens, and for every animal you see from the river, there are hundreds more within the forest canopy. Guides will lead groups off the boat to find them, and walks of several hours are possible. It's at this point that the chances are highest of seeing Borneo's famed orang-utans, although for a guaranteed sighting many pay an additional visit to the Sepilok Orang Utan Rehabilitation Centre, just outside Sandakan.

Another of the jungle's highlights is the Proboscis monkey, a large potbellied species endemic to Borneo's lowland forests, and best spotted in the late afternoon. The male has a huge bulbous nose, up to seven inches long, that is both cartoonish and disarmingly human. This protrusion has both a sexual and a protective function. Female Proboscis monkeys find the large nose particularly attractive, and it also forms a resonating chamber that amplifies the males' warning calls. As the male becomes alarmed, its nose swells and its calls become louder.

Borneo clouded leopards, recently certified as a distinct species, are elusive, as are the smaller marbled cats. Boars, nocturnal mongoose-like civets and macaques fill the jungle. But of all the jungle's varied inhabitants, two of the largest are also some of its rarest, so keep your eyes peeled: they are the pygmy elephant and the Sumatran rhinoceros. The Borneo pygmy elephant is an unusually docile elephant, possibly because it is a descendant of domestic stock. Though its origin is uncertain, it is considered a smaller subspecies of the Asian elephant. The dual-horned Borneo Sumatran rhinoceros is the smallest of the five existing rhino species, and found almost exclusively in Sabah – another reason to focus your attention on this rich, diverse and relatively accessible corner of Borneo.

Trekking in the Karakoram

>> No huts, no roads – just mountains

"Blank on the map." That's how famed English mountaineer Eric Shipton described the Karakoram prior to his pioneering 1930s expeditions of the mountain range, located west of the Himalaya. At that time the range formed a virtually unexplored boundary between cultures, nations and religions, with China on the east, India on the south, Afghanistan to the north, and an emerging Pakistan to the west. But the range dwarfs mere countries – it has the earth's highest concentration of glaciers, some of which are the longest outside the Polar regions, and the largest concentration of tall peaks in the world, with more than sixty peaks over 7000m. Among these is K2, which at 8611m is the second highest mountain in the world.

Though few will ever climb K2 – its ascent is considered the world's most difficult climb, more challenging than Mt. Everest's – many can still experience the Karakoram's awesome beauty by trekking to an area known as Concordia. Located at the confluence of the Baltoro and Godwin-Austen glaciers, Concordia is nestled between K2 and three more of the world's tallest peaks. Dubbed "the throne room of the gods", reaching this spot is a mountain lover's holy grail.

A trek to Concordia begins in Skardu, set in a valley on the Indus River in the Kashmir region of northern Pakistan. In most other parts of the world, an elevation of 2290m would place you halfway up a mountain, but in this high-elevation region, where mountains below 7000m don't even merit names, Skardu is merely a low-elevation meeting place, a traditional jumping-off point for expeditions and treks into the Karakoram.

Made remote by its altitude, inaccessible by its jagged peaks, and uninhabitable by its streaming glaciers, you won't find the villages, populations, and mountain cultures in the Karakoram that exist in the Himalaya to the east. The range is a mantle of absolute wilderness, where you can walk for weeks without ever seeing any sign of civilization. European explorers first encountered the Karakoram in the early nineteenth century, and by 1856 British explorers had made a few forays into the area as part of the Great Trigonometric Survey of India. Exploration of the region was slow-going, though, further hampered by China's attempts to restrict outside travel to the Karakoram in the twentieth century. It was nearly a hundred years after the first survey of the Karakoram that the summit of K2 was finally reached, by an Italian team, in 1954.

a mountain by any other name

Most everyone agrees that "K2" is an odd name for a mountain, especially the second tallest mountain on earth. Straddling the border of Pakistan and China, it has also been known as Mount Godwin-Austen, Dapsang, Qogir (Chinese for "big mountain"), and Lamba Pahar (Urdu for "tall mountain"). However, in spite of these other names, the name K2 has persisted as the most commonly used. Why is difficult to explain, but its origin is simple.

In 1856 a British team led by Thomas Montgomerie explored and surveyed the massive peaks of the remote Karakoram. The first peak the expedition came across was named K1, the second K2, and so on, through K5. Later, many of the mountains were given more appealing names. Because Henry Haversham Godwin-Austen, a member of Montgomerie's team, was the first to explore and survey the sides of K2 and the glaciers at its base, it was suggested the mountain be named after him. However, many believed personal names to be unsuitable for Himalaya and Karakoram peaks (though not glaciers), and K2 has remained the only Karakoram mountain designated by just a letter and a number.

Trekking in this remote place, and even just reaching the point where you can see any of the Karakoram's giant summits, requires time, preparation, and organization. Porters must be hired, provisions gathered, and permits obtained – all best done in the company of a local trekking operator in Skardu. From Skardu it's still another eight hours on a pocked and rock-strewn four-wheel-drive road to Askole (3050m), the village from which a trek to Concordia really begins. For the residents of Askole, life depends on subsistence farming and portering expeditions. Once you pass through the wooden arch that marks the town's boundary, there are no supplies, no huts, no roads – just you and the mountains.

From Askole the trek continues for two days on a pleasant ascent to Paiju, a campsite where you'll see your last tree before climbing onto the 56km-long Baltoro Glacier. The Baltoro, along with other connected glaciers, acts as a kind of highway through the Karakoram. For the next week the trek proceeds up the length of the glacier, crossing from one side to the other in order to skirt crevasses. Camps are set up on the glacier's three-kilometer-wide surface or on the nearby lateral moraine.

Though the objective is Concordia, the journey passes dozens of beautiful spire-like peaks and snow-capped massifs, including Trango Towers, a cluster of dramatic angular shafts which form some of the world's tallest vertical cliffs and one of the world's premier climbing challenges. Trango's three highest towers soar over 6000m and contain more polished granite than is found in all of Yosemite National Park.

Finally, after a week or more of being immersed in the shadows of these spectacular mountains, you reach Concordia. There are only fourteen 8000m peaks in the world; Concordia is located below four

of them. During the trekking season, the camp, with an elevation of 4500m, is host to scores of tents and hundreds of trekkers. Its popularity is attributable both to the stunning views it affords as well as its hub-like access to other base camps and sights in the area. The K2 base camp, for example, is located directly up the Godwin-Austen Glacier from here and can be visited on a long day-excursion, while the base camp of Broad Peak, the 8047m mountain originally dubbed "K3", can be reached on a shorter excursion. The base camps for Gasherbrum I (8080m) and Gasherbrum II (8035m) are also short day-trips, but at this elevation, nothing is easy. From Concordia many trekkers opt to make the return back down the Baltoro Glacier, but consider booking a trek that takes a return route via Gondogoro La. The trip across this 5450m pass requires a 13–14 hour day at high elevation that will test your mettle; however, trekkers are rewarded with spectacular panoramic views in a kind of mountain amphitheater before heading to a descent route.

need to know

Although physically challenging, a trek in the Karakoram is aided by porters and includes all meals. Trekkers typically cover about 10km per day and carry daypacks weighing less than 10kg. For the trek to Concordia it is necessary to be comfortable with glacier travel and familiar with the use of an ice ax and crampons. Although Pakistan has experienced political instability, traveling in the north and particularly in the Karakoram is generally worry-free, especially in the company of a local guide.

guides and gear Guide services are expert in securing local porters and all provisions at reasonable rates. Karakurum Treks and Tours (☏333/5376366 or 0788/430 5742 in the UK, ⓦwww.karakurum.com.pk) in Islamabad, Pakistan, has been guiding treks and mountaineering expeditions in both the Karakoram and Hindu Kush ranges since 1978.

when to go June through August is ideal, as high passes remain snowbound until May and cold weather descends in early September. Since there is no monsoon season in the Karakoram, summer offers better weather than what you might find in the Himalaya during the same period.

getting there Fly into Islamabad International Airport, then take a one-hour flight to Skardu in northern Pakistan, the most logical starting point for trekking and climbing in the Karakoram.

suggested reading Shiro Shirahata, *The Karakoram: Mountains of Pakistan* (Cloudcap). Exquisite mountaineering photography, much of it aerial, of the Karakoram's great peaks.

is this for me?

PHYSICAL ✦ ✦ ✦ ✦
Demanding even for the fit

PSYCH ✦ ✦ ✦ ✦
Remote setting, disrupted sleep

SKILL ✦ ✦
Glacier travel with crampons

WOW! ✦ ✦ ✦ ✦ ✦
Superb mountain experience

Walking the Nakasendo

>> The "way" of the samurai

142

JAPAN

KYOTO   TOKYO

During Japan's Edo period (1603–1867), only feudal lords and their loyal class of aristocratic warriors, the samurai, were allowed to travel along the country's roadways. The most famous of these was the Nakasendo, which led from Kyoto to Edo (modern-day Tokyo). Today, though most of the Nakasendo has fallen victim to urban sprawl, paved or buried beneath industrialized Japan, portions of the road survive. Unlike in the past, anyone can make the gentle walk along these stretches – which amount to about 100km – through rural Japan, and in the process gain an unspoiled and scenic glimpse into a vanished time and place that few visitors ever experience.

In the Edo period, when feudal lords (called "daimyo") traveled along the Nakasendo to visit the emperor in Edo, they brought with them retinues of samurai numbering in the thousands. As samurai passed along the highway, peasant farmers were required to bow down; failure to bow resulted in a swift beheading. Eventually, travel on the Nakasendo was opened to artisans and merchants who traveled to Edo to provide housing, furnishings and supplies to the daimyo and samurai. By 1720, Edo was the largest city in the world, with more than one million inhabitants.

The road itself, which dates back to the eighth century, was typical of the imperial Chinese style of road building adopted by the Japanese – about 3m wide, lined with trees, carefully maintained, and regularly interspersed with post-towns, resting points along the route intended to serve a traveler's needs. At its peak, the Nakasendo, literally "road through the mountains", stretched 531km from Kyoto to Edo as Japan's main artery. Ultimately, Japan's feudal era came to an end, and its samurai class was abolished, in 1868; this, along with the completion of railway lines, made the ancient throughways increasingly obsolete. The Nakasendo is now the only remaining strand of the five highways that once knit the country together.

The best place to begin a walk along the Nakasendo is in Kyoto, an ancient capital and the cultural epicenter of Japan. From here, travel by train to a starting point in Hikone, a town whose former geisha quarter and vibrant merchant district are still visible; this is where samurai were entertained and provisioned. Most remarkably, the daimyo's moated castle is also still preserved, with its pointed roofs casting a forceful presence on the hillside.

As you walk, you will be led into ancient post-towns with traditional inns where Westerners are virtually unseen. In Okute you'll see a 1200-year-old cedar on the grounds of a landmark shrine. In the beautifully preserved village of Tsumago, most of the buildings date from the Edo period, when they served as lodgings and restaurants for travelers. Along the Nakasendo, other picturesque old post-towns feature Zen temples and Shinto shrines,

the way of the warrior

While English knights were cultivating a code of conduct based on chivalry, the samurai were adhering to *Bushido* ("the way of the warrior"), a strict, almost Spartan-like code of ethics. Focusing on fealty to the lord, honor at the cost of death (if required, by one's own hand – "seppuku"), and prowess in combat, the samurai was expected to be a kind of a Renaissance man, a cultured and literate warrior. The single biggest requirement of a samurai was that he be prepared to die, and to die a good, honorable death became one of Bushido's key principles.

Today, Bushido still has adherents, who refer to their belief as Modern Bushido, incorporating many of the basic principles derived from the combative culture of the samurai. Many martial arts also continue in the tradition of Bushido, and Judo, originating in Japan in the nineteenth century, represents a further evolution of Bushido's precepts. Although Judo means "the way of gentleness", it is characterized by formalism and an exacting code of conduct. The originator of Judo, Kano Jigoro, advocated the theory of "maximum efficiency", relying on movements that would redirect opponents' movements, taking advantage of leverage and balance. Kano taught his students to push Judo beyond the practice arena or the combative situation, and urged its use as a way of life.

Because of its trade route origins, many of Japan's major rail lines, including the Takasaki Line and the Shinetsu Main Line, follow the Nakasendo

need to know

You can leave your heavy hiking boots behind, but do bring your raingear. As far as adventures go, the Nakasendo is an illuminating walk, averaging about 11km per day over a twelve-day period – not a vigorous hike or a strenuous trek.

guides and gear The Nakasendo can be walked independently, but if you're not fluent in Japanese and want a deeper appreciation of the route's cultural and historical significance, consider going as part of a guided tour. Walk Japan offers guided walks on the Nakasendo and other routes (☎090/5026-3638,ⓦwww.walkjapan.com).

when to go To avoid the summer heat and the cool winters, a spring walk from late March to early June is ideal. September to October also provides comfortable temperatures and beautiful fall colors, though shorter days.

getting there Fly into Osaka's Kansai International Airport and take Japan Rail's service to Kyoto station for an overnight stay, prior to starting the walk.

suggested reading Alan Booth, *Looking for the Lost: Journeys Through a Vanishing Japan* (Kodansha Globe). A warm first-person narrative of three walking trips through Japan.

is this for me?

PHYSICAL ✦ ✦ ✦ ✦ ✦
Easy walking, gentle terrain

PSYCH ✦ ✦ ✦ ✦ ✦
Peaceful setting, foreign culture

SKILL ✦ ✦ ✦ ✦ ✦
No technical skills required

WOW! ✦ ✦ ✦ ✦ ✦
A historical and cultural adventure

and many charming, traditional inns have somehow survived into the modern world, providing comfortable lodging and exquisite food.

Pressing forward, some of the best preserved parts of the old flagstone road lead deep into the mountains. Along the route you'll climb several mountain passes through fragrant cedar forests. These passes have gentle inclines and can be taken at a comfortable pace. Traditional farmsteads and lotus ponds are visible as you walk, and during the spring season it's possible to see blossoming cherry trees and paddy fields being flooded and farmed as they have been for centuries. Autumn brings crisp air and vibrant colors to the deciduous slope. Wildlife sightings are rare, but occasionally deer and raccoons can be spotted.

Sadly, the Nakasendo is unknown to most Japanese today, despite the fact that long stretches of the highway remain much the same now as two hundred years ago. The most well-known preserved stretches are in the Kiso Valley, between Tsumago-juku in Nagano Prefecture and Magome-juku in Gifu Prefecture. Even where modern roads have been laid on top of the original Nakasendo, they are often quiet one- or two-lane country roads that see little traffic.

143 Tiger tracking in the Sundarbans

WHERE Sundarbans, Southwest Bangladesh
WHEN November to March

PHYSICAL	◆ ◆ ◇ ◇ ◇
PSYCH	◆ ◆ ◆ ◆ ◇
SKILL	◆ ◆ ◆ ◇ ◇
WOW!	◆ ◆ ◆ ◆ ◇

You've been lying prone, waiting in your cramped jungle hide for an entire sweltering week. You've braved waist-deep mud, tropical humidity and impenetrable mangrove forest to get here. Finally, a striped tiger slinks into view, aware of your presence but driven by the scent of the fresh bait just beyond. You ready the gun: if your aim isn't true the drug won't take hold and you could have one irate, half-tranquilized tiger on your hands. You fire, the tiger bolts off, and away you spring after it, hoping to fit a tiny radio collar around this mysterious beast's neck in the name of science.

Tiger tracking is not for the faint of heart. In one of the most densely populated nations on Earth, Bangladesh's Sundarbans remains a remote wilderness with zero road access and transport by boat hire only. The jungle is ruled by deadly predatory Royal Bengal Tigers, whose feline beauty masks the fact that they frequently stalk humans as their prey. Inside this thick jungle, you'll join researchers from the Sundarbans Tiger Project (STP) on their hunt to learn more about this mysterious and fascinating animal. STP researchers estimate that well over one hundred people are killed here every year by hungry tigers who seize unsuspecting victims by the neck and drag them off into the jungle for piecemeal consumption. After a successful collaring, know that you'll be saving lives by preventing future violent encounters between

144 Surfing in G-Land

WHERE Eastern Java, Indonesia

WHEN March to November

PHYSICAL	✦ ✦ ✦ ✦ ✦	
PSYCH	✦ ✦ ✦ ✦ ✦	
SKILL	✦ ✦ ✦ ✦ ✦	
WOW!	✦ ✦ ✦ ✦ ✦	

For surfing aficionados dreaming of riding the warm waters of the Indian Ocean, G-land hits the spot. G-land, or Grajagan as it is properly known outside the surfing world, is an idyllic place to catch waves in a jungle setting, and you'll find some of the longest barrel rides in the world here. Perhaps most important, it's secluded and uncrowded, unlike surf sites like Superbank, Jeffrey's Bay or one of the rush hour traffic breaks that you find all over California and Hawaii.

Thanks to the consistency of the sets, your mission is simple: wake up, surf, eat, nap, surf, eat, surf, relax by a fire comparing stories about best waves, sleep through the night, then start the cycle all over again. Multiple breaks in the area provide all sorts of waves for different skill levels, from double overhead barrels to playful one-meters.

If you manage to drag yourself away from the swells, you can do some wildlife viewing – panthers, leopards, monkeys, and exotic birds can be found in the tropical greenery beyond the beach.

145 Jungle safari in Royal Chitwan National Park

WHERE Terai lowlands, Nepal

WHEN September to June

PHYSICAL	✦ ✦ ✦	
PSYCH	✦ ✦ ✦	
SKILL	✦ ✦	
WOW!	✦ ✦ ✦	

Located in the subtropical inner Terai lowlands, Royal Chitwan is one of Asia's premier wildlife sanctuaries and Nepal's oldest national park.

Once the private hunting grounds of Nepal's royalty, it was established largely to preserve the rhinoceros population

and is now home to some of the continent's rarest and most exciting wildlife. Multi-activity safaris bring you face-to-face with the park's forty-plus species of mammals, 450-some-odd species of birds, and numerous amphibians and reptiles. Guided walks take it slow and easy, giving you the most time to examine the action around you, and they're especially conducive to birding: woodpeckers and kingfishers are among the most common types spotted. Gliding down the Rapti river in a dugout canoe is the best way to catch crocodiles resting on the riverbanks as well as wading birds like herons. But nothing quite compares to the thrill of getting on the back of an elephant and seeing the world from a little higher up; you'll get to see plenty of the local animals in their habitat from your perch.

146 Whitewater rafting on the Karnali River

WHERE Nepal
WHEN September to June

For a weeklong escape from the comforts of the modern world, the violent waters of Nepal's longest and widest river may just be the ticket. Frequently cited as one of the world's top ten rivers for rafting and kayaking, the Karnali is wild, remote and virgin. Commercially run but rarely visited by the throng of foreign travelers to Nepal, this adventure is a test in logistical preparedness. With an absence of western influences, small mountain villages on the banks of the river give a genuine experience in cultural exchange.

A Class V river during the low and mid-flow seasons, the Karnali is at its runnable peak during the June to August monsoon season, but the uncomfortable weather and unpredictable rapids make it a less favorable time to go. The first half of the trip is full of intense whitewater runs, while the second half is much calmer and allows you to rest up those tight muscles and simply enjoy the jungle-clad walls of the canyon. The river comes to an end in the Royal Bardia National Park, where you might get the chance to catch a glimpse of a Bengal tiger. That's just the tip of the iceberg in terms of resident wildlife: the verdant jungle is full of leopards, bears, jackals, crocodiles, snakes, and mongoose as well.

147 Trekking at Snow Lake

WHERE Northern Pakistan
WHEN July and August

Nestled in northwestern Pakistan where the Hindukush, Karakoram and Himalaya mountain ranges collide, and where the Silk Road trade route passes, Snow Lake (also Lupke Lawo) provides one of the worlds great glacial vistas. Not an actual lake, but a 16km-long glacial basin, Snow Lake sits at an astonishing altitude of 4877m and takes 22 to 28 days to trek. The trek starts from the small alpine village of Askole that lies a week of hiking away from your glacial destination. Because of the challenge of the trek and the short season for hiking it – July and August – only around twp hundred people complete the adventure each year. Having competent guides and traveling in a group is essential as is proper gear for combating cold, high altitude, and hiking on ice.

The first leg of the trek leads along a winding and scenic pathway with huge glacial pinnacles that loom ahead of you like turrets on a fortress. Further along, you'll cross onto Bafio glacier and travel along a giant road of ice turned brown by rocks and dirt. You will camp in beautiful grassy meadows ablaze with colorful wildflowers and, when you reach Snow Lake, you'll camp on the ice itself.

There, peaks such as the Latoks and the Ogre jut through the ice and tower over you, interspersed with wide, deep crevasses. In summer, streams of water flow across the surface forming pools along the top of the basin and waterfalls in deep, dark glacial folds. If you get a clear sky at night, a good-sized moon reflects off the ice and illuminates the landscape with its magical, ethereal glow.

148 Horse trekking in Songpan

WHERE Sichuan, China
WHEN April to September

Sichuan, China, on the massive Tibetan Plateau, has long been one of the most inaccessible regions of China. Though these days visitors by the busload manage to make their way to the beautiful valleys of Jiuzhaigou and Huanglong Nature Reserves, seeing a more nuanced version of the province remains rare. One option for doing so, allowing you to experience firsthand the culture and weather-beaten elements, is to set out on a horse trek from Songpan.

Songpan can be reached via an eight-hour bus ride from Chengdu or a flight to the Jiuzhaigou airport located in Zhuanzhusi, a short car ride away. A number of horse trekking outfitters in the area offer day-long or week-long adventures, or anywhere in between. You can choose different itineraries, some of which might include time in less-disturbed Tibetan villages, where you'll encounter traditional clothing, music, and traditional yak herding. You can also go for a day at the Huanglong Nature Reserve: you'll have to get off your horse and walk several hours up the well-maintained path, but the terraced limestone pools of clear water, the unique plant life at this intersection of floral regions, the glimmering waterfalls, Buddhist temple and chance to see giant pandas are well worth the effort.

Much of the trek will not be easy galloping, more like slow walking through dense foliage. The ground is hard and your butt will bear the brunt of it – making you appreciate the rewards all the more.

149 Trekking in the Coorg

WHERE Karnataka, India
WHEN October to February

The lush forests of the Coorg, in the Western Ghat mountains, look as if they come from a Kipling story. Small shrines and shimmering waterfalls dot the greenery; the odors from the jungle flora mix with those of coffee and tobacco plantations shaded by rosewood and oak, interspersed with wisps of wild cardamom.

Trekking through the highest peaks takes you over passes at elevations above 3000m – small, perhaps, in comparison to the epic heights of the Himalaya, but it more than compensates with colorful festivals, tantalizing (non-vegetarian) local dishes and some lush mountain scenery. There is no shortage of highlights: bonnet macaques and elephants in Nagarahole National Park, Madikeri's old fort and its orange groves, cascading Irupu Falls.

You can travel independently or in the company of experienced local guides, the better choice if you're worried about what to do in the face of charging elephants or preying tigers.

150 Trekking in Rajasthan

WHERE Western India
WHEN October to March

Enchanted palaces and ancient forts, intricately adorned temples and gigantic sculpted reservoirs, vast stretches of dry desert and one of the oldest mountain ranges anywhere – Rajasthan has got pretty much every base covered. Most visitors will likely be taking the train to navigate around the state, but that would bypass much of the magnificent countryside and tiny villages that give the place its character.

The hills of the Aravallis cut right through the region, starting around Mount Abu in the southwest, the tallest mountain in the chain at 1220 meters. Kumbalagarh, northeast of there, is perfect for trekking round, a fort perched on the edge of an eponymous wildlife sanctuary and nestled in the mountains above Udaipur. In the northwest portion of Rajasthan, the Thar Desert takes over, and the dusty sands make the ideal setting for a camel trek, typically organized in Jaisalmer or Bikaner on either side of the desert. Go for a couple of days or a couple of weeks, if you want to make it all the way from Jaisalmer to Bikaner.

Guides are nearly a necessity no matter what kind of trek you're on; detailed maps of the hikes that you intend to do are a must.

151 Rafting the Sun Kosi

WHERE Nepal
WHEN October to December and March to May

Putting in on the Sun Kosi, or "River of Gold," in Dolalghat, about three hours east of Kathmandu, affords an isolation not frequently felt by the trekkers who pack Nepal's famed walking paths. The first major commercially run river in Nepal represents the watershed for the eastern part of the country as it makes its way south into the Ganges. With run-off from the largest mountains in the world draining into the Sun Kosi's canyons and gorges, a compounding hydraulic forms in one of the most remote areas of the world as holes and waves increase in power as you descend. The rapids, generally Class II–V,

increase in difficulty as the 275-kilometer trip progresses, allowing rafters to improve their teamwork before the real work starts. A trip along the commercially run 275km stretch normally takes six to ten days depending on flows and the number of hours per day spent on the river. And with powerful pool-drop rapids, followed by flatwater stretches, the water gives you just time to enjoy the scenery before bracing for the next raft-eating waves.

152 Exploring the Mogao Caves

WHERE Gansu, China
WHEN May to October

PHYSICAL	✦ ✦ ✦ ✦ ✦
PSYCH	✦ ✦ ✦ ✦ ✦
SKILL	✦ ✦ ✦ ✦ ✦
WOW!	✦ ✦ ✦ ✦ ✦

Visiting the Mogao Caves may sound like one of the tamer adventures going – indeed, a ticket and tour guide are required and the experience is far more culturally and religiously significant than anything else – but that doesn't mean they lack for drama. Carved into sandstone cliffs along a stretch of China's Silk Road some 25km southeast of Dunhuang, the caves sit high up in the desert (indeed, Mogao translates to "high up in the desert") on the eastern slope of Mingsha Shan. A 1600-meter-long road takes you to the cave's openings, which tower to a height of five stories. There are 750 caves in all, including a system of 492 Buddhist temples, construction and work on which spanned ten dynasties. Mogao sculptors decorated the caves lavishly inside and out: in front of the cave walls stand numerous clay statues, the tallest at 34m, while improvised paintings and carvings cover the rock surfaces of the side walls and ceilings with carved relief murals explode with color. Only a small percentage of the caves can actually be explored, but it's a full day's work to make your way through the development of Buddhist art over the centuries.

153 Trekking in Xishuangbanna

WHERE Yunnan, China

WHEN Year-round, but the weather is best from November through March

PHYSICAL	◆ ◆ ◆ ◇ ◇
PSYCH	◆ ◆ ◇ ◇ ◇
SKILL	◆ ◆ ◇ ◇ ◇
WOW!	◆ ◆ ◆ ◇ ◇

The earth is rich red, the air is sultry, and the foliage seems to be on growth drugs. A poinsettia bush the size of a house protrudes from the side of the path; in a pond to your left, a bright pink water lily looms large and lush. You're hiking through the jungle near Jinghong, in China's Xishuangbanna; the Burmese border is a mere five kilometers away. It's not a difficult walk. The path is well-trodden and the undulations are slight, leaving you relaxed and able to enjoy the extraordinary scenery.

After only a couple of hours, you arrive in a village of the Akha tribe where you'll spend the night. Its three hundred inhabitants live in stilted houses with slate pitches that line narrow mud lanes. You go to the headman's house. "Are they expecting us?" you ask. "No," your guide laughs. "There aren't any telephones in the jungle." You're not the only guests. Two men from a neighboring Dai village have come to buy some cows. The Dai word for cow is "moo" they explain as your guide interprets. This is because Dai cows say moo. English cows say moo, too, you tell them. It is heartening to think that your cows could communicate, even if you can't.

Stewed dog is the only dish on the dinner menu. It's old, tough and stringy. You eat with the headman's son. "These people are very poor," your guide says. "Sometimes they even eat rats." A bony cat enters the hut and slinks around the table looking for scraps. "Do they eat cats as well?" you ask, trying to make conversation. The headman's son looks horrified. "Cats?" he exclaims. "No way!"

154 Hiking up Mount Kinabalu

WHERE Saba, Malaysia

WHEN Year-round

PHYSICAL	◆ ◆ ◆ ◇ ◇
PSYCH	◆ ◆ ◇ ◇ ◇
SKILL	◆ ◆ ◇ ◇ ◇
WOW!	◆ ◆ ◆ ◆ ◇

It's not often you can easily ascend a mountain over 4000m, but given its proximity to the equator, the barren granite summit of Borneo's Mount Kinabalu has no ice or snow to slow you down. What it does have is mist – lots of it – and, at its lower elevations, a bewildering collection of orchids, ferns, butterflies, birds, frogs, lizards, oversized earthworms, giant red leeches, and carnivorous plants that can eat small mammals. A climb up Mount Kinabalu is, therefore, as much about reveling in its flora and fauna as it is about reaching its summit.

The starting point for the three-day/two-night climb is Timpohan Gate, thirty minutes inside Kinabalu National Park. The base of the mountain, drenched in over 250cm of rain a year, is considered one of the most biologically diverse areas on earth. The climb requires professional guides supported by porters, but can be completed by any who are in reasonably good shape. It's not without its hazards, however; heavy rain and dense fog can create a slippery surface on the exposed treeless granite. A combination of hand-carved stone steps, steep wooden stairs and fixed ropes assist in the ascent. You'll be starting your final ascent to Low's Peak in the dark hours of early morning so you'll need a headlamp to light the path and keep your footing steady. You should summit near dawn allowing for a sweeping view of the jungle below. The air is thin and frosty at 4095m and may cause altitude sickness – make a quick turnaround if you feel its effects. Be aware that the steep descent can be hard on feet, knees and ankles. Conclude your trek with a stroll to refreshing Kipungit Waterfall or a soothing soak in the Poring Hot Springs.

155 Snowboarding in Iran

WHERE Alborz, Iran

WHEN December to March

So you've tamed the moguls of the Alps, skied the bowls of the Rockies and off-pisted your way through northern BC. How about shredding the Axis of Evil?

Two of the world's best places to freeride are set smack in the middle of Alborz mountain range that stretches from the Caspian Sea to the salt flats of Iran. A decade ago, these mountains had strictly segregated slopes for men and women. These days they're filled with Iranian teens and twenty-somethings, though they remain much less crowded than most Western resorts, with nary a lift line in sight.

Just over an hour's drive north of Tehran and lying at the foothills of the Mount Damavand volcano is Dizin, Iran's largest ski resort. For over six months a year the gorgeous slopes here – which reside a full 350m higher than Europe's highest ski mountain – receive an average of seven meters of fresh powder. Once a fresh snowfall has blanketed the range, the powdery off-piste skiing here is outstanding – though it's highly recommended you go with a guide. A 12km descent from Dizin is Shemshak, a resort particularly well-known for its warm breezes, moguls, steep trails and night skiing. Both centers are known for their après-ski scenes, though as this is an Islamic republic, don't expect shots of Jäger or bottles of Becks at the hotel bars. But make friends with some locals on the slopes and you might just find yourself invited to an Iranian underground after-hours fête.

156 Rafting the Brahmaputra River

WHERE Brahmaputra River, Tibet

WHEN May to October

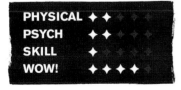

When you first set your eyes on the Tibetan *gowa*, a traditional boat made of yak's skin, you wonder how a boat that looks so flimsy (it's light enough to be hauled by one man) is going to carry ten people downriver for several days. But then the river journey begins, the *gowa* drifting with the flow of the Brahmaputra River, and you become mesmerized by the view. The empty parched land undulates in every direction, with distant snow-dusted peaks dramatically piercing the luridly blue sky, views that are ever shifting from your perspective in the boat, each bend revealing a different vista.

The river trip, which starts near Lhasa, helps you understand why the Brahmaputra is considered the holy lifeline of Tibet. Its waters sustain the Tibetan hamlets – clusters of stone houses – sparsely scattered along its banks, and its waters nourish the stands of poplar trees and barley fields set along its banks. The river also carries you on metaphysically: multi-day commercial descents include hikes to villages and monasteries and nights spent in camps on the riverbank; the river takes something of an intimate, reassuring presence. And it's that quality that perhaps inspired the spiritual profundity you will see during the course of your journey, especially at the holy caves of Drak Yangdzong. Perched high up a white cliff, the caves hold holy petroglyphs and equally evocative vistas of the landscapes. Fittingly, then, the journey ends at the Samye Monastery, one of Tibet's oldest, with a circular design modeled on a Mandala – a monastery that symbolizes the cosmos.

157 Kiteboarding in Hainan

WHERE Yalong Bay, Sanya, China

WHEN June to February

Yalong Bay in Hainan's southern tip is graced by a seven-

kilometer-wide tropical beach and wind conditions – the monsoonal winds are complemented by thermal winds triggered by the location of coastal mountains – that have made it a prime kiteboarding playground. It draws seasoned kiteboarders, and one look at them dashing across the bay and nimbly flinging themselves into the air is enough to whet your appetite for the sport.

But if you're a beginner, don't imagine you can do the same; and in any case the local centers won't rent you out any equipment unless you can prove your proficiency. So your best bet, as a beginner, is to enroll on a beginner's two-day course. And when you first get on the board, and the winds starts tugging you, you'll be gripped with adrenaline and shakiness, but confidence quickly builds up. After two days, you can start testing the winds, pushing your skills further and further, and that's when the wind becomes a liberating force. Then you can start attempting doing flings or jumps; these are an addictive challenge, and it takes patient practice before you can land on your board and continue surging ahead in one graceful move. It also takes many gulps of seawater, but that's part of the fun:

at the end of the day, despite your exhaustion, you'll share tales of folly and adventure with other kiteboarders, and the first thing you'll do the next morning is go out to check the conditions of the wind.

158 Trekking at Lake Baikal

WHERE Lake Baikal, Russia

WHEN June to September

PHYSICAL	◆ ◆ ◆ ◆ ◆
PSYCH	◆ ◆ ◆ ◆ ◆
SKILL	◆ ◆ ◆ ◆ ◆
WOW!	◆ ◆ ◆ ◆ ◆

Among the network of about 500km of trails that can be trekked along the shores of Lake Baikal, one of the most rewarding is the most accessible. It starts at Litsvyanka, which is within an hour's drive of the regional city of Irkutsk, and extends for some 47km, weaving among slopes of taiga forest, passing small villages (where homestays are possible), skirting pebbly beaches, and offering great vistas over the southern portion of lake. It then joins another trail, which is 30km long, and the most remote in this area – many caves can be explored along this part – and then finishes in Sandy Bay, an alluring beach that beckons for a swim.

More remote trails can be found in the northern tip of the lake, all of them emanating from the town of Severobaikalsk.

In the north there is a network of nature reserves, and landscapes are more pristine: wetlands reverberating with the thrills of birds, two lakes set among pine forests, many glorious sandy beaches, invitingly deep-blue and calm water, and dense pine forests that are the haunt of rare animals (including black bears, an animal you can dream about, but not one you would want to encounter). Yet it's not all solitude and wilderness either; if you set up base camp at the Echo Tour Camp, run by the Great Baikal Trail organization (which is building trails, running tours, and promoting eco-tourism, you'll share the camaraderie and evening get-togethers with other travellers and environmental volunteers.

159 Mountain climbing in Eastern Tajikistan

WHERE Gorno-Badakhshan, Tajikistan

WHEN July to September

PHYSICAL	◆ ◆ ◆ ◆ ◆
PSYCH	◆ ◆ ◆ ◆ ◆
SKILL	◆ ◆ ◆ ◆ ◆
WOW!	◆ ◆ ◆ ◆ ◆

With clear skies, turquoise-blue rivers and blooming orchards, the alpine pastures and irrigated village fields of eastern Tajikistan are home to bands of shepherds who tend their sheep, goat, cattle and yak in the shadow of the majestic Pamir mountain range. Known to Tajiks as the Bam-i-Dunya (Roof of the World), these mountains stand at the junction of the Himalaya, Karakorum, Hindu Kush and Tien Shan ranges and dominate the eastern half of Tajikistan. They remain some of the most unexplored places on the planet, boasting magnificent landscapes and exhilarating trekking and mountaineering opportunities.

Most of the country's hundred-odd mountains have never been scaled, but the highest peak, Ismoil Somoni Peak (known as Communism Peak in Soviet times), is accessible to climbers, with a network of high and wide valleys offering pass access to the peak. After several days of prep and acclimatization at the 4000m glaciered moraine base camp, you begin your nine-day group climb

to the 7495m summit across a range of terrain, including wide and steep snow-covered spurs and crevassed icy slopes. Above you, barren shards of rock shoot off impossibly sheer into the sky. But with sudden blizzards, flash floods, avalanches, and mudslides, these mountains are not without their dangers. If this peak poses too much risk for your palate, trekking from village to village in the region's lower altitudes is a sublime experience and an ideal opportunity to witness the region's wildlife, including rare snow leopards, Marco Polo sheep, ibex and wild boar.

160 Panda viewing in Wolong Nature Reserve

WHERE Sichuan, China

WHEN March to November

PHYSICAL	✦ ✦ ✦ ✦ ✦
PSYCH	✦ ✦ ✦ ✦ ✦
SKILL	✦ ✦ ✦ ✦ ✦
WOW!	✦ ✦ ✦ ✦ ✦

Sometimes the best wildlife can be seen in black and white – in this case, the color of giant pandas. Located three hours from Chengdu, the renowned Wolong Nature Reserve was originally established to preserve the dwindling panda population and is now the largest panda reserve and research center in China. The animal is native to central and southern China, with only 1600 of them living in the wild and a fraction of that number in captivity, most (around one hundred) in Wolong; other reserves exist in Sichuan and a couple of southern provinces. You can observe these pandas in something resembling their natural habitat from wildlife observation areas around the research center. You might also take a leisurely walk through the Wuyipeng panda observation station to see other rare creatures, like golden monkeys, white-lipped deer, and red pandas or, for something a little more active, hike into the nearby Balang Mountains.

monotonous mealtime

The giant panda, with its charming, large black eye patches and round shape, is classified as a bear and has teeth designed for a carnivore. Strangely, though, it lives on an almost exclusively bamboo diet, using sharp teeth and strong jaws to tear through the tough and fibrous stalks. Because bamboo provides little protein and the panda's stomach must remain full, as much as 36kg of bamboo needs to be consumed daily. When available, pandas will eat other food such as eggs, honey, meat or fish.

CHINA'S MAGNETIC PERSONALITY

Historical records indicated that as early as the second century BC China may have developed a rudimentary compass, formed with magnetic material, shaped like a spoon and placed on a metal plate with mystical designs. However, it was used for prognostication rather than navigation. By the seventh century AD, the Chinese had learned how to magnetize an iron needle and by the eleventh century had found a way to suspend that needle in water. Despite an inward-looking political climate that hardly encouraged exploration, Chinese sailors were able to navigate over great distances, reaching east Africa by the fifteenth century.

We don't fly into clouds, because in Nepal the clouds have rocks in them.

Royal Nepal Airlines pilots' maxim

remnants of the Silk Road

Trade routes over land and sea, which linked much of Asia and Europe, became known as the Silk Road. One of the highest and most dangerous sections became the foundation for the Karakoram Highway, the highest paved highway in the world. Having taken over twenty years to complete, it connects China to Pakistan through the Khunjerab Pass at 4877m. During construction, almost 900 workers lost their lives from landslides or falling. Also known as the Friendship Highway, it provides access to some of the world's tallest mountains, including K2.

SHERPAS

A Sherpa is not always a Sherpa. The term is generally used to describe mountain guides and porters in Nepal, but these may not be ethnic Sherpas, a people who migrated from eastern Tibet to Nepal four or fives centuries ago: their name translates as "people from the east". They settled higher than anyone else, and their ability to cope with high altitude made them highly valued members of mountaineering expeditions from the early twentieth century onwards.

project tiger

Mystified and terrified by the ferocious yet beautiful Bengal tiger, humans were nearly successful in eliminating its natural habitat and driving the animal into extinction. Project Tiger, a conservation project initiated in India in 1973, has resulted in the creation of forty animal reserves, allowing the natural population to triple to nearly 4000 according to official figures. However, lack of resources and poor land use planning may threaten the tiger once again. Currently, there are more tigers in zoos than there are in the wild.

IT'S A BIRD...IT'S A PLANE...IT'S A LIZARD

The birds of Borneo are beautiful, but it's the other species that have taken to the air that will take your breath away.

▶ **Black-bearded gliding lizard** Swoops from tree to tree with thin webbing on the sides of its green spindly body.

▶ **Flying gecko** This brown, speckled lizard glides through the air on large flaps of skin.

▶ **Flying lemur** Nocturnal glider (also known as colugo) that's neither a lemur nor can really fly. Can still soar in excess of 100m between trees in search of fruits and leaves.

▶ **Paradise flying snake** Mildly venomous serpent that can suddenly (and unnervingly) flatten itself and fly like an unfurled ribbon. These animals are hard to catch in midair, but if you do it's a prize-winning photograph.

▶ **Wallace's flying frog** This green and yellow frog, about 10cm in length, uses webbing between its toes to parachute from tree to tree, gliding as far as 15m.

"If you reject the food, ignore the customs, fear the religions and avoid the people you might better stay home."

James Michener

animal madness

Animals have been eaten, used as transport and adopted as companions across the world, and Asia, with its wide range of fauna and landscapes, is no exception. One of the most unusual activities on the continent is yak skiing, an extreme sport so niche that it has only one regular practitioner. Peter Dorje runs the activity from the Indian resort of Manali. He leads a roped-up yak up a hill, attaches the rope to a pulley and asks the ski-toting participants to hold the other end of the rope, then shake and deposit a basket of nuts on the ground. The yak hares down the hill in search of nuts, pulling the skier at great speed in the opposite direction.

By comparison, Elephant polo seems positively everyday. Essentially a joke by and for expats, the sport – played on a three-quarter-size pitch, with a mahout and player sat on each beast – was invented at the start of the twentieth century and still has an enthusiastic

following, particularly in Nepal and Thailand. The world championships, held each December on the edge of the Chitwan National Park in Nepal, make for a surprisingly competitive and entertaining spectacle, although animal rights groups point to the often brutal training undergone by almost all "tame" elephants.

BIG BANG THEORY

The loudest noise ever known was produced by a volcanic eruption at Krakatoa, near Java, in 1883. The sound was heard as far away as Mauritius, off the cost of east Africa, almost 5000km away. The explosion was13,000 times more powerful than the bomb that fell on Hiroshima.

highest unclimbed mountains

According to most reckoning, the highest unclimbed mountain in the world is Gangkar Puensum, on the border between Tibet and Bhutan, at 7570m. Several attempts have been made to climb it, including a 1998 ascent which reached a subsidiary peak just below the main summit, via the Chinese-Tibetan side. Efforts have been held back by official Bhutanese policy, which bans access to peaks of over 6000m out of respect for their spiritual importance, and places severe restrictions on mountaineering of any kind. Gangkar Puensum may keep its title for some time to come.

NEVERENDING STORIES

If physical adventure has tired your legs, you might want to take on a mental marathon. In the South Indian state of Kerala, *kathakali* plays are the definitive art form, highly stylized performances that focus on the struggles of gods and demons and run from dusk until

dawn. For similar themes and even more epic treatment, *kudiyattam* is one of the oldest theatre forms in the world. A single act can last ten nights and a play forty, while an actor might take a half an hour of mime and symbolism to describe a leaf falling to the ground. The towns of Thrissur and Guruvayur and the regional capital of Thiruvananthapuram are good places to catch a performance.

ups and downs

Everest (Chomolungma), on the Nepal–Tibet border, lies at an altitude of 8848m, but its bulk is dwarfed by the deepest place on earth. The Mariana Trench lies between Japan and New Guinea, and Challenger Deep, its deepest point, is around 11,000m below sea level. Here pressure is one thousand times surface levels, but some animals survive – mostly tiny, soft-shelled organisms.

MOUNT TAMBORA

The eruption of Indonesia's Mount Tambora volcano in 1815 sent a column of sulphur and volcanic dust into the stratosphere that created a worldwide climate anomaly for the next year. A dry fog covered much of the northeastern US resulting in May frost, June snowstorms, and massive crop failures in what came to be known as "The Year Without a Summer." In London, visible sunspots and a red fog persisted throughout much of the year. The eruption of Mount Tambora spewed out nine times as much dust and rock as the 1883 eruption of Krakatoa.

As the sun dries the morning dew, so are the sins of man dissipated at the sight of the Himalaya."

from the Puranas

AUSTRALIA AND OCEANIA

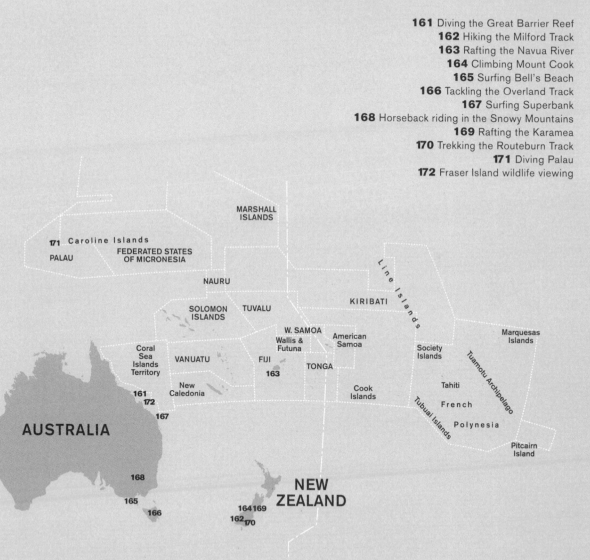

161 Diving the Great Barrier Reef

>> **Swim with creatures great and small**

Let's put this niggling question to rest right now: is the Great Barrier Reef the largest living thing in the world? While it *is* immense, stretching for 2300km off the coast of northeastern Australia, the Great Barrier Reef is not *a* living thing; it's actually a collection of many living things and can be described as a superorganism. It can also be accurately described as the world's largest structure made by living organisms. But just what are these living organisms? They're polyps, invertebrates the size of a pinhead that secrete a limestone skeletal shell as they grow. When one dies, it leaves its shell behind and new polyps build on top of the old shells. It's a slow process to be sure, and a vibrant coral reef may only grow a centimeter in a year. In fact, it's taken the Great Barrier Reef about 8000 years to reach its present size.

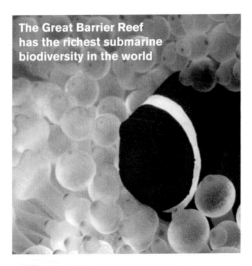

The Great Barrier Reef has the richest submarine biodiversity in the world

coral bleaching

In Shakespeare's day the color "coral" actually meant white because most people only saw coral out of the water; at this point the coral had experienced such drastic changes in atmosphere and temperature that it had bleached and died leaving it the false color of white. Similar bleaching, though not as extreme, has been occurring in reefs all over the world because of an increase in ocean temperature. Higher temperatures caused two major bleaching events on the Great Barrier Reef in 1998 and 2002, and a rise in temperature, although slight, is still greatly affecting coral. Coral needs a very specific environment to live, requiring very salty, clear water that sunlight can penetrate, no harsh wave movement, water temperatures above 20°C and lots of limestone.

Also vital for most coral is symbiotic algae called zooxanthellae, which transmits needed organic elements to coral through photosynthesis as well as providing oxygen and helping remove coral waste. If the water temperature around coral remains too warm for too long, the coral becomes physically stressed and starts to expel the zooxanthellae it needs to survive. As this occurs, the coral begins to starve and its white skeleton becomes more visible through the coral's transparent outer tissues. If the process continues the coral will die, leaving behind just a white skeleton, the "coral" in Shakespeare's time.

As the world's largest coral reef system, the Great Barrier Reef is a network or open maze of turquoise lagoons and 3400 individual reefs. Interspersed among the reefs are over 600 islands, some with mature rainforest and freshwater streams, plus over 300 coral cays ranging from barren stretches of sand to wooded mangrove systems. It's both a landform and an underwater realm, covering 345,000 square kilometers, and extending from near Fraser Island in the south to Papua New Guinea in the north. Not only does it contain one third of the world's soft coral species, but also 1500 species of fish, 4000 species of mollusks and many species of endangered marine turtles, sharks and breeding whales. It has the richest submarine biodiversity in the world, not to mention warm clear waters that are easily accessible from the coast of Queensland. All of this makes the Reef a peerless dive destination.

With moderate depths maxing out at about 20m and calm waters, the Great Barrier Reef offers exceptional diving for both novice and experienced divers alike. With over 1500 vessels and 700 dive operators serving the Great Barrier Reef, there is no shortage of options for exploring the undersea world, though most fall under three broad categories: day boats, dive island resorts, and liveaboards. Day dive boats depart from the mainland and cater to divers and snorkelers of all abilities who want to spend about 4–5hr on the Reef and make up to two dives. If you're not already a certified diver and want to discover the Great Barrier Reef in a few days, this is a great option. Dive island resorts such as Green, Heron, and Lady Elliott give you wonderful diving right from the beach and just steps from your room, plus short boat rides to some of the Reef's best dive sites. These resorts also offer plenty to enjoy while you're not diving,

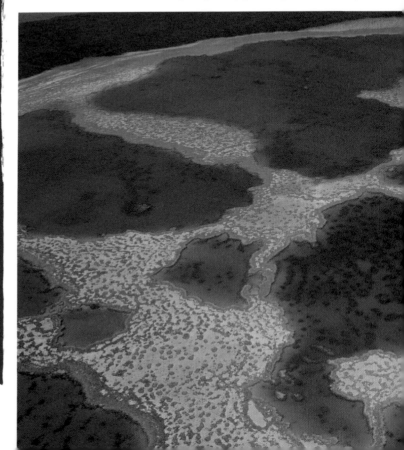

including a wide range of activities for non-divers. Finally, liveaboard dive boats may be the best way for dedicated and experienced divers to discover the most remote and outstanding dive sites, take many dives per day and spend several days exploring the Great Barrier Reef. Most liveaboards cater to the three-day market and centre operations around shallow sandpit, no-current sites and while it's unmistakably great diving, it doesn't reveal the extraordinary diversity of the Great Barrier Reef. There are bigger fish, better sites and fewer people to be found in some of the more remote locations accessible on the longer-duration liveaboards, where at uncrowded sites you'll capture a sense of wilderness and experience a more diverse ecosystem.

On an extended dive trip to the more remote locations you're likely to encounter hammerhead sharks, manta rays, thresher sharks, grey reef sharks and the most commonly sighted shark in the Great Barrier Reef, the whitetip reef shark. But if there is a singular eye-popping dive experience it would be an encounter with Minke whales. Swimming eye to eye with an 8–10m mammal that weighs six to seven tons, and doing so on its terms, is an experience that will long remain with you. From the platform of your drifting vessel, you enter the warm water and soon see their massive forms approach. Before long, it's clear that word of you and your boat's arrival has gotten out, and you may very well see several Minke whales who are as curious about you as you are about them. With increasingly closer passes they become more confident as they display their grey ballet. As the sun sets and the boat departs, the whales follow in your wake and you can only wonder if the experience was as powerful for them as it was for you.

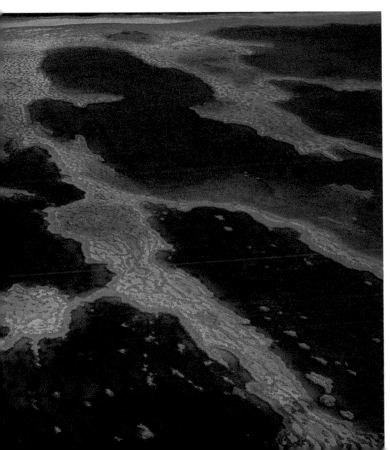

need to know

The majority of the Reef falls under the management and care of the Great Barrier Reef Marine Park (Ⓦ www.gbrmpa.gov.au).

guides and gear Hundreds of dive operations and liveaboards provide access to dive sites on the Great Barrier Reef. Undersea Explorer is a liveaboard scuba diving operation, which combines adventure diving with marine research and education and has particular expertise in the study of Minke whales (Ⓣ 07/4099 5911, Ⓦ www. undersea.com.au).

when to go There is no bad time to dive on the Great Barrier Reef; it's more a matter of picking the season based on the marine life you want to see. The wet season is December to March, when you'll still find great diving. June to August spells rougher waters; it's also the best time to find migrating Minke whales. Local divers particularly enjoy Sept to December, with water temperatures around 29°C and visibility up to 50m.

getting there International flights serve Cairns in the heart of the North Queensland Coast with easy access to dive resorts on the mainland and islands on the Reef that can be reached by charter cruise or air service.

suggested reading Neville Coleman and Nigel Marsh, *Diving Australia: A Guide to the Best Diving Down Under* (Periplus Action Guides). The best diving down under, with a focus on the Great Barrier Reef.

is this for me?

PHYSICAL ◆ ◆ ◇ ◇ ◇
Mildly aerobic, non-strenuous swimming

PSYCH ◆ ◆ ◆ ◇ ◇
Underwater encounters with large marine animals

SKILL ◆ ◆ ◆ ◆ ◇
Solid diving skills a big asset

WOW! ◆ ◆ ◆ ◆ ◇
Stunningly beautiful and varied wildlife

Hiking the Milford Track

NEW ZEALAND

MILFORD SOUND

>> **The finest walk in the world**

It was probably inevitable that a trail be built to connect New Zealand's largest glacial lake with its highest waterfall and its most famous fjord – and that's essentially how the Milford Track came about. When it was completed in the early twentieth century, word of its beauty quickly spread, luring nature lovers from afar, including English poet Blanche Baughan. After completing the Milford Track she declared it to be "the finest walk in the world," – a claim that no one has successfully refuted in the hundred years since.

The Milford Track traverses the heart of Fjordland National Park from Lake Te Anau, over the Mackinnon Pass and down into Milford Sound. It can only be hiked in one direction – from south to north – and you are only allowed to stay in a hut or lodge for one night, since the next day's trampers are hot on your tail and already booked to fill the limited space in huts and lodges. Still, the pace is comfortable, the track is well groomed, and it's virtually impossible to get lost. You'll find a closely knit, highly sociable group of

walkers on the trail – a fascinating and instantly emulsified mix of nationalities – yet you never feel part of a throng; the trail is not crowded and you can walk for long stretches in relative solitude.

A seventy-five-minute boat ride from Te Anau Downs, located about halfway up Lake Te Anau, brings you to the head of the lake at Glade Wharf. With your pack in place, your hip-belt cinched, and your raingear at the ready, you embark on a wide flat trail along the Clinton River. You'll cross the river on the first of the track's nine suspension footbridges – strong and safe, but with enough swing to make them fun. Day one is no more than a few kilometers, but enough to get you into the wilderness with a little time left over for a side hike on a wetland walkway. Although daily walking distances vary depending on whether you're a guided walker staying at lodges or an independent walker staying in the huts, the track and the scenery are splendid throughout.

Day two is about 16km of fairly flat terrain where a luxuriant moss-padded beech forest opens to meadows that reveal the dramatic depth of the waterfall-speckled Clinton Valley and its glacial origins. In your gradual ascent up the valley you'll cross many avalanche runouts in the early season and several swollen streams that require fording. Keep your eyes peeled for – and items safeguarded from – native Kea, an alpine parrot species with a powerful beak and talons, which have a reputation as brazen vandals that will steal food from under your nose, pick apart your pack and boots, and carry off any clothing you've left unattended.

Day three is the most testing as you switchback your way over the 1073m Mackinnon Pass, the highest point along the track, where in fair weather you'll have exceptional views of surrounding lakes

wet weather hiking

The best weather advice for the Milford Track is to plan on rain. In southern New Zealand's typically cool, wet weather, staying dry is not only the key to comfortable hiking, it's the best way to prevent the onset of deadly hypothermia. Ideally, you've had some experience in wet weather hiking before you go tramping in New Zealand, so you'll know what works best at keeping you dry, what type of fabrics are most comfortable, and what dries fastest. If you've never hiked in a downpour or a full day of rain, here's a quick tiplist to get you started on the right track:

Poncho or raincoat: It's a matter of personal preference, but you may enjoy the flexibility and loose drape of a one-size-fits-all poncho that can also double as a pack cover. One downside of a poncho is that it doesn't provide the wind protection of a form-fitting jacket, and can even go flying in a good gust. A raincoat (with a hood) should be waterproof, and many fabrics billed as "breathable," "water-resistant," or "water-repellant" simply won't cut it in a rainstorm lasting several hours or more.

Over trousers: Again, make sure they are waterproof.

Gaiters: These waterproof leggings prevent water from dripping into your shoes and keep your lower pants dry as you kick up puddle water or walk through grasses.

Backpack: Many packs come with a stowable elastic-rimmed raincover that can be quickly pulled over your pack at the first sign of rain. If your pack doesn't have one, an inexpensive separate raincover will do the trick. The last thing you want to discover at the end of a long wet day on the trail is that your change of clothes is also sopping wet, because your pack wasn't waterproof.

With an average annual rainfall of nearly 7m, Milford Sound is the wettest place in New Zealand, and one of the wettest places on the planet.

need to know

You can walk the track independently or as part of a guided group, and either option requires that you make reservations well in advance. Trail access is limited to forty independent walkers per day, and you must complete the track in four days and three nights. For an independent walk, contact the Department of Conservation (☏03/249-8514, Ⓦwww.doc.govt.nz) for bookings.

guides and gear Ultimate Hikes (☏03/450-1940, Ⓦwww.ultimatehikes.co.nz) is the only DOC approved operator for overnight guided walks on the Milford Track. Guided walks (up to fifty walkers per day) are staged from Queenstown as a five-day/four-night adventure, offered from November through April.

when to go The peak walking season is mid-October to April, with mid-November to mid-April delivering the best weather, though always expect some rain. The track can be hiked year round independently, and no reservations are required from May to mid-October.

getting there The track starts at the head of Lake Te Anau and finishes at Milford Sound. Te Anau is located about two hours by road southwest of Queenstown on New Zealand's South Island. In addition to boat transportation at both ends of the track, you'll also need bus or private transport at the end of the track from Milford Sound back to Te Anau, about two hours by road.

suggested reading *Milford Track Independent Tramping* (Department of Conservation). A complete guide for independent walkers, with regulations, planning tips, maps, detailed itinerary, and a guide to the history, flora and fauna. Available as a free download from the DOC.

and peaks. A steep rocky descent from the pass leads on to a wooded boardwalk and staircase beside the narrow Roaring Burn with numerous waterfalls. But the granddaddy waterfall of the track, Sutherland Falls, is reached by a hardly optional ninety-minute side trip to the base of the falls, where if the thundering roar and the surge of mist-filled wind generated by the pounding water isn't enough excitement, you can even go behind the falls for a heart-pounding cold soaking.

The final day on the track is a gentle descent along the Arthur River where the greater rainfall and milder coastal temperatures yield a more diverse beach forest carpeted with ferns, mosses and lichens. Waterfalls and swinging bridges continue to festoon the route before arriving at aptly-named Sandfly Point and the end of track. A short boat crossing takes you from Sandfly Point to the head of Milford Sound for the return; but don't miss the opportunity to reward yourself with an extended day cruise on Milford Sound, where waterfalls plunging down cliffs into deep blue waters, home to dolphins and fur seals, provide the grand finale to a scenic symphony on the Milford Track.

is this for me?

PHYSICAL ◆ ◆ ◆ ◇ ◇
Generally easy hiking with some steep sections

PSYCH ◆ ◆ ◇ ◇ ◇
Beautiful, wet setting with minimal risk

SKILL ◆ ◆ ◇ ◇ ◇
Walking on a safe, well-groomed trail

WOW! ◆ ◆ ◆ ◆ ◇
One of the world's must-do hikes

Rafting the Navua River

>> Waterfalls of every imaginable size and shape

FIJI

SUVA

The quintessential South Pacific river – warm, idyllic and inviting – the Navua is one of Fiji's most entrancing waterways. Despite that, its relative remoteness on Vita Levu has placed it well off the track of most – islanders and visitors alike – and it's only recently that rafting guides have begun to lead a lucky few down this hidden marvel of imposing canyon walls, rare wildlife, lush vegetation and crashing waterfalls. And while the rapids are unlikely to lead you to pray to the island's gods for safe passage, they will provide plenty of thrills just the same.

Captain James Cook

Adventuring to the far end of the world, Captain James Cook's courageous navigation led to knowledge, fame and death. Concurrent with the century "Age of Reason," Cook brought order to the mass of chaotic information regarding the great Pacific Ocean. Indeed, the voyages he led brought back a wealth of scientific information regarding plants, animals, and astronomy, but Cook's major contribution lay in his navigation and cartography skills. Just a few of his accomplishments include mapping the eastern coast of Australia, circumnavigating and mapping New Zealand, disproving the myths of the southern continent and the northwest passage, and being the first European to land on Hawaii. While Cook never landed on Fiji's islands, he met Fijians in Tonga whom he described as formidable warriors, ferocious cannibals, and builders of the finest vessels in the Pacific. Cook was aware of the islands' location and passed nearby.

The circumstances surrounding Cook's death are still a source of contention. While it is certain that he was killed by Hawaiians after returning to the islands to repair his ship, it is less clear why he was attacked. Western lore maintains that native Hawaiians regarded him as a deity when he first arrived during the festival of peace and plenty for the God Lono, but that he was less welcome when he returned. By this account, Cook was killed because of tensions that arose after he violated sacred customs. However, others claim that this account of Cook's deification is a product of Western imperialism, and that Cook was really killed because of a temper tantrum.

The commercially rafted upper half of the Navua River runs for about 21km, most of it through the Upper Navua Gorge and protected area where logging, mining, and road building are restricted. The gorge and surrounding Upper Navua Conservation Area are home to many rare and endemic plant, bird, and amphibian species, including the world's rarest conifer – only two trees remain – the giant blue earthworm, and the flying fox (a bat). This captivating section of the river is offered as a day-trip from the many of the resort areas on the coast. A total of 40km of the Navua are raftable and can be guided as longer trips on request.

The trip starts at Savuitini Creek, from where the black lava which forms the walls of the gorge constrict the river to a continuous chasm ranging between five and twelve meters in width. Looming large alongside you, the walls tower 30 to 46 meters. Immediately the rapids swell to Class III as drops create a hydraulic force capable of sucking unsuspecting novices out of the raft and flushing them down the river. The gorge continues with intermittent Class II and III rapids for the next nineteen kilometers. The rapids are broken up by languid stretches that require paddling and you'll no doubt be tempted by the first of many dips in the tropical waters.

While the rapids and smooth stretches make for a varied run, the lure of

need to know

Rafting the Navua is easily achieved as a day-trip from Suva, with pickups at many hotels on Viti Levu's southern coast. Trips can be arranged prior to arrival or on site in Fiji.

guides and gear O.A.R.S. (☎209/736-4677 or 800/346-6277, ⓦwww.oars.com), a worldwide whitewater outfitter, offers day-trips throughout the year on the Navua through Rivers Fiji, their operation in Suva.

when to go While the Navua can be rafted year round, the greatest adventure will be found during the rainy season from mid-December to May. You may even find that the best rafting experience on the Navua is during a rainstorm, when water levels in the gorge can rise 6m in less than two hours.

getting there Fly into Suva Nausori International Airport on the island of Viti Levu. Shuttle service to the river is available from Suva and the surrounding area.

suggested viewing Both the original 1948 film *Blue Lagoon* and its 1979 remake with Brooke Shields were filmed in Fiji. *Contact* (1997) with Jodie Foster and *Cast Away* (2000) with Tom Hanks were filmed in Fiji's Yasava Islands.

the Navua River has at least as much to do with the profusion of waterfalls springing, spraying, plunging and cascading from the lip of the canyon. In this opulent gorge, water trickles down everywhere, punctuating the canyon's black volcanic lava and hanging gardens of vines and ferns and hidden grottoes and side canyons. You'll pass scores of waterfalls of every imaginable size and shape; during the rainy season the number of waterfalls and cascades can easily exceed two hundred.

Side canyons lead to primary growth hardwood forests that are the habitat for dozens of bird species, such as the common yellow-breasted musk parrots with their bright yellow front, green back and black mask. Many rafters hear a barking sound on the river and assume they are approaching a village with dogs, only to discover the sound is coming from a barking pigeon, a species endemic to Fiji.

As you exit the Upper Navua Gorge, you begin to see signs of human development. The fragrant ginger flowers and ferns of the gorge give way to palms, plantations, cattle grazing, and small villages. As you complete your voyage through Fiji's verdant volcanic heartland you'll understand why the Navua is often referred to as the "River of Eden."

is this for me?

PHYSICAL ✦ ✦ ✦ ✦ ✦
Relaxing paddling and some swimming

PSYCH ✦ ✦ ✦ ✦ ✦
Class III rapids in warm tropical waters

SKILL ✦ ✦ ✦ ✦ ✦
No prior whitewater experience required

WOW! ✦ ✦ ✦ ✦ ✦
Lush and inviting with exceptional scenic beauty

Climbing Mount Cook

164

>> All the trappings of the world's biggest peaks

In the shadow of Mount Cook, a lanky young man discovered his destiny. "It all started with the Sealy Range. I scrambled upwards to the summit of my first mountain, Mount Ollivier," Sir Edmund Hillary later recalled, "It was the happiest day I had ever spent." As he gazed across the valley, the South Ridge of Mount Cook, scraping the sky to the north, must have left him spellbound. How could he have not longed to climb it? And he did. In 1949 Hillary made a first ascent of Mount Cook's challenging South Ridge, a feat that led him to Himalayan peaks and his historic conquest of Everest.

The thirty highest peaks in New Zealand are all within the glistening Southern Alps, a 600km-long range that forms the spine of the South Island. Mount Cook, the highest of these snowclad summits, is the most imposing mountain in New Zealand with an impressive bulk that dominates Aoraki/Mount Cook National Park and soars 3000m from the Tasman Valley floor. Even though it's not an exceptionally high mountain – just 3754m – it has all the trappings of much larger peaks in the Himalaya – glaciers, crevasses, steep slopes, and ice walls. Together this makes Mount Cook a significant mountaineering challenge that demands respect, solid technical skills, and physical stamina to reach the summit. It's a complicated mountain with a variety of faces, ridges, and ice cliffs, where summit success favors the well-rounded mountaineer.

In big mountain style, your climb begins with a flight to the Plateau Hut on the Grand Plateau, the base for most of the routes on the eastern side of Mount Cook. From here there are just 1500m of vertical ascent between you and the summit. Still, you'll want to allow some time on the mountain, since weather can be unpredictable. In a seven-day period, you may have only three days with decent weather. By taking more time and using the Plateau Hut as your base you increase your chances of success.

The Linda Glacier, which flows into the Grand Plateau, is the most straightforward way up a mountain with no easy routes. Roped up and on the glacier you'll thread a maze though gaping crevasses and over delicate ice bridges where you're under the threat of avalanche-prone ice cliffs on either side. Under the glow of headlamps, there's a fair amount of anxiety on the route as you zigzag your way up the glacier for about four hours.

Sir Edmund Hillary

Born in Auckland, New Zealand in 1919, and a beekeeper by profession, Hillary got his start on local peaks and increased his skill by summitting multiple mountains in the Southern Alps before making his way to the Himalaya where he topped out on eleven different peaks all with heights over 6000m. Two reconnaissance missions to Everest in 1951 and 1952 put Hillary in contact with John Hunt, the leader of the one expedition allowed to make a summit attempt in 1953 by the Nepalese government. Hunt paired Hillary with Tenzing Norgay, a Nepalese porter and experienced climber who had accompanied five previous expeditions up Everest. Another team of Charles Evans and Tom Bourdillon was also selected by Hunt to make the push to the top.

Using a team strategy, these expeditions applied individual strengths to get past the many obstacles the mountain presented. Setting up base camp in March of 1953, the group made progress up the icy monolith at a slow pace until May 26 when Bourdillon and Hunt made an effort to reach the top but turned back within 100m of the summit due to Hunt's oxygen tank running out. Hillary and Tenzing continued on. A storm forced them to pitch a tent and wait it out. Tenzing slept with his boots on, while Hillary awoke on the morning of May 29 with frozen boots that he thawed over a stove before making the last stab at the peak. Laden with heavy packs and feeling the fatigue of spending so much time at such an extreme altitude, the pair ascended the twelve-meter rock face now called the Hillary Step. "I looked upwards to see a narrow snow ridge running up to a snowy summit. A few more whacks of the ice-axe in the firm snow, and we stood on the top." After five hours of continuous climbing, the two hugged and smiled as they looked out over the expanse of Himalayan peaks. In their fifteen minutes on the summit, Tenzing dug holes for gifts to the gods; Tenzing left chocolate and Hillary left a small cross. Hillary took a photograph of Tenzing, but no summit photo was taken of Hillary. He later said, "As far as I knew, he (Tenzing) had never taken a photograph before, and the summit of Everest was hardly the place to show him how."

need to know

Within the scenic and accessible confines of Aoraki/Mount Cook National Park you'll find nineteen peaks over 3000m. The park provides seventeen huts positioned to provide accommodation for mountaineers, and you need climbing skills to reach them. Mount Cook can be climbed independently by experienced climbers or as a guided ascent.

guides and gear Located in Mount Cook Village, Alpine Guides (Aoraki) Ltd (☏ 03/435 1834, Ⓦ www.alpineguides.co.nz) offers guided climbs of Mount Cook including air access, food, accommodation, technical equipment, and a strict 1:1 guiding ratio.

when to go November into late January is the recommended season, after which the route deteriorates; warm weather and rain at high levels melt ice bridges and open crevasses, making the mountain unclimbable by the Linda Glacier route.

getting there Located on the west side of New Zealand's South Island, Mount Cook Village, the logical staging point for an ascent on the peak, is a five-hour drive from Christchurch.

suggested reading Hugh Logan, *Classic Peaks of New Zealand* (Craig Potton Publishing). Each chapter is a photographic tribute to seventeen of New Zealand's great peaks.

is this for me?

PHYSICAL ◆ ◆ ◆ ◆ ◆
Requires aerobic conditioning and endurance

PSYCH ◆ ◆ ◆ ◆
Icefall, avalanche, crevasses, and steep slopes

SKILL ◆ ◆ ◆ ◆
Solid mountaineering skills are essential

WOW! ◆ ◆ ◆ ◆
Great climb on a classic glaciated peak

Nearing the top of the glacier and to your left you arrive at the Linda Shelf, an icy bulwark, which although not that difficult, does require caution as you make an ascending traverse on a 45-degree slope. Once again you're faced with an intimidating gauntlet. Below the traverse the slope terminates in 200m ice cliffs, while above you another face of ice cliffs drain down into a couloir dubbed the "Gun Barrel," so you'll need to move steadily but quickly. At the top of the Linda Shelf in the warming glow of dawn, you'll find yourself at the base of the Summit Rocks – perhaps the most pleasant part of the climb because the icefall and avalanche hazards are behind you, and five pitches of enjoyable mixed climbing with secure belay stations lie ahead. Take a moment to look down from the Summit Rocks base to a dramatic view of radiating semicircle of crevasses on the Linda Glacier.

The route up Summit Rocks varies considerably from year to year and depending on the season; it could be mostly rock or mostly ice. Topping out on the Summit Rocks puts you on the ice cap, where some steep slopes of sustrugi – windswept hardened snow – requires surefooted crampon placement before arriving at Mount Cook's summit. Here views capture not just the surrounding glacial systems below, but a string of Southern Alps peaks to the north and south, the Tasman Sea to the west and bright green touches of New Zealand's gorgeous countryside in between.

165 Surfing Bell's Beach

WHERE Victoria, Australia

WHEN Year-round

PHYSICAL ✦ ✦ ✦ ✦ ✦
PSYCH ✦ ✦ ✦ ✦ ✦
SKILL ✦ ✦ ✦ ✦ ✦
WOW ✦ ✦ ✦ ✦ ✦

If you were to pinpoint the heart of Australia's legendary Surf Coast, it lies 5km southwest of the little town of Torquay, Victoria, just an hour and a half drive from Melbourne. Bell's Beach is the focal point of Australian surfing for a number of reasons, all of which could be distilled to one single factor – consistently great waves. The broad sediment-rock reef break of the beach is subject to many different swells coming in from huge southern ocean storms that occur roughly every couple of days. The leftovers from these ocean storms cause the surf to break over numerous sections of reef with waves between one to three meters high, and often much larger. The main break is Bells Bowl, which often benefits from northwest wind.

The appeal of Bell's Beach remains strong with the pros, and the Rip Curl Pro, the oldest professional surfing contest in the world, is hosted here annually. That said, it's by no means exclusive territory. A wide range of surfers flock here, from the fifty-year-old just looking for a good time in the sun and sea or the aspiring teen out to polish up his skills; on a good day, there may be as many as fifty surfers hoping to catch some of the legendary waves Bell's Beach has to offer. If you're looking to test your skills on the Surf Coast, look no further.

166 Tackling the Overland Track

WHERE Tasmania, Australia
WHEN November to April

PHYSICAL	◆	◆		
PSYCH	◆	◆		
SKILL	◆	◆		
WOW	◆	◆	◆	◆

Almost as feisty as a real Tasmanian Devil is the rugged island's 65km wilderness hike known as the Overland Track. The adventure takes you from majestic and moist Cradle Mountain to shimmering Lake St Clair through the only dolerite mountains in the world. Traveling from Ronny Creek in the north to Cynthia Bay in the south is the traditional route, beginning in the rainiest region and concluding where the sun may actually shine.

The verdant landscape that forms the backdrop to the trek depends on generous rainfall – and usually reliable. Some of the muddiest sections of the track have been made more manageable with boardwalks, but you can be certain your boots will slog through a fair bit of mud along the way. Schedule at least five days for the track, though tempting side spurs could entice you to extend your hike to eight or nine days. A favorite side track gives you the opportunity to summit Tasmania's highest peak, Mount Ossa (1617m). There are huts conveniently stationed all along the track, but they often fill quickly during high season (December to March) so you must carry a tent. You will also need a fuel stove to cook your meals

and be prepared to pack out your rubbish. To ensure minimal impact, groups are limited to be six or less. Plan your trip carefully; nighttime temperatures can be surprising chilly and sif you go high enough or late enough you may be hit with a snowstorm.

Colorful toadstools, bright green cushion plant, tree ferns and pencil pines line the trail, while gurgling streams, oddly shaped peaks, and tumbling waterfalls provide a backdrop. As you walk, comical wallabies, snub-nosed wombats, or the little Tasmanian devil – an animal not to be trifled with – may cross your path. If you are lucky, you may even catch a glimpse of the platypus paddling in one of the deep glacial lakes. After a week of such stunning scenery you might understandably feel the urge at the end of the track to just keep walking along Lake St Clair, but most choose a leisurely ride on the ferry that returns you to the north end of lake.

167 Surfing Superbank

WHERE Queensland, Australia
WHEN Year-round

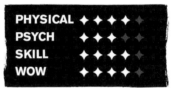

PHYSICAL	◆	◆	◆	◆
PSYCH	◆	◆	◆	
SKILL	◆	◆	◆	◆
WOW	◆	◆	◆	◆

A local project to ensure shipping lanes of a nearby tributary stay clear for imports and exports, Superbank originally consisted of several amazing breaks spread apart by mediocre surfing. Located on the Gold Goast in Queensland, Australia, Superbank did not exist until 2001. A human enhanced sandbar break that can generate 2km-long leg-cramping rides, Superbank is a loner's worst nightmare, where you can often have over five hundred in the lineup. The crowds are worse than Hawaii's most popular breaks, but Superbank still hosts a stop on the Quicksilver Pro circuit every year.

Superbank is the ultimate right hander, with reliable ten- to fifteen-second barrel rides. The epic curls are startlingly picture-perfect and you can be forgiven for thinking less of your home break upon first sight of a wave – let along after riding one. Although it's a year-round spot, it's best during the austral summer season at low tide with an east facing swell and south facing winds. The atmosphere is cut-throat, so good luck trying anything snazzy; as you work a cutback you might just get cut off as someone else drops in on the wave. Keep in mind that if you are looking for a good longboard wave, then Superbank is definitely not for you; bring your shorty and pray that you get a run in before it is overrun.

168 Horseback riding in the Snowy Mountains

WHERE New South Wales, Australia

WHEN November to May

PHYSICAL	✦ ✦ ✦ ✦ ✦
PSYCH	✦ ✦ ✦ ✦ ✦
SKILL	✦ ✦ ✦ ✦ ✦
WOW	✦ ✦ ✦ ✦ ✦

When you think of outdoor pursuits like skiing, fishing in high alpine streams, and horseback riding in the mountains, Australia isn't the first destination that comes to mind. But for well over one hundred years those have been traditional pastimes in the Snowy Mountains of Australia's Great Dividing Range, located on the eastern coast between Sydney and Melbourne. The Snowies showcase sparkling streams set in a backdrop of rugged but inviting mountains. When the snowmelt gives way and the June to October ski season comes to an end, hikers and mountain bikers descend on the mountains, but the best way to see them is on horseback.

On an Australian Stock Horse and Clydesdale cross you put in 30km per day through forests of mountain ash and snow gum that open to ridgelines and high country hillsides. Your horse won't be surprised by the wildlife, but you may be, as you encounter kangaroos, wombats, and emus. You'll follow in the boot tracks and haunts of gold rush miners and bushranger outlaw Ned Kelly. By day you're on bush trails and stock routes, crossing streams, and ascending canyons to overlooks of valleys, lakes, and distant ridgelines. By night your choice of accommodation could be a bedroll in a rustic mountain hut or a more luxurious option by riding inn-to-inn or basing your rides from a single mountain lodge.

169 Rafting the Karamea

WHERE South Island, New Zealand

WHEN September to May

PHYSICAL	✦ ✦ ✦ ✦ ✦
PSYCH	✦ ✦ ✦ ✦ ✦
SKILL	✦ ✦ ✦ ✦ ✦
WOW	✦ ✦ ✦ ✦ ✦

Anytime a whitewater rafting trip requires a helicopter ride up a granite gorge to reach the put in, you know you're in for a great descent on a wild river. A one- or two-day whitewater rafting trip on the Karamea River will not disappoint, with Class V rapids set in exceptional canyon scenery. Starting from the town of Karamea on the northern end of New Zealand's West Coast (South Island) your helicopter with raft in tow will swoop up into the Karamea Gorge wilderness. Once you're on the river, you're not likely to see anyone who's not in a raft or kayak, since there is limited access and no track along the banks which often rise to steep gorge cliffs.

Kiwis aren't shy or prudish about naming their whitewater rapids. Among the named Class III–V rapids are Ass-Kicker, Growler, Scare Case, and the legendary Holy Shit, a 400-meter-long Class IV that deserves to be scouted. The Roaring Lion, a chute barely as wide as your raft, will torpedo you as swiftly as any runnable rapid in the world. The Karamea is a big volume river with rapids clad in granite and set in a deep canyon, so it's wetsuit and helmet all the way.

170 Trekking the Routeburn Track

WHERE South Island, New Zealand

WHEN November to April

PHYSICAL	◆ ◆ ◆ ◇ ◇
PSYCH	◆ ◆ ◇ ◇ ◇
SKILL	◆ ◆ ◇ ◇ ◇
WOW	◆ ◆ ◆ ◇ ◇

Straddling two national parks – Fiordland and Mount Aspiring National Parks – New Zealand's Routeburn Track rambles through the valleys of the snow-topped Humboldt Mountains, taking you on a three-day journey into a glacially carved wilderness. Although the Routeburn Track receives less rain than neighboring Milford Track, the 3–5m of rain per year assure you a lush and verdant environment for your tramp through the base of the Southern Alps on the southwest corner of South Island. Downpours can quickly push streams from sinuous to surging and may even alter availability of some portions of the trail. Always have raingear with you and don't be surprised by a dusting of snow in the higher elevations.

The north–south orientation of the 45km Routeburn Track can be traveled successfully from either direction with huts and campsites located along its length. Both huts and camping permits must be secured in advance. Depending on your needs and budget, guided huts provide comfy beds, hot showers and meals; independent huts have gas stoves and flush toilets.

Beginning in the south, you tramp through beech forests draped in moss, ferns, epiphytes and orchids. Waterfalls, from drizzling to dramatic, appear at the edge of the well-maintained track and spray you with a cool mist. A one-hour side track to Key Summit, where three separate rivers begin their journey to the sea, gives a marvelous 360-degree view of the region. Watch for bladderworts and sundews, two carnivourous plants you may see along your walk. Lake MacKenzie, dramatically cradled in a glacial valley, demands your attention as it reflects Emily Peak. Harris Saddle, the highest point on the track takes you to an elevation of 1280 meters and signals the beginning of your descent. Routeburn Falls, adjacent to Routeburn hut, is a splendid multi-tiered cascade waterfall where you are most likely to see the olive-green alpine parrot, the Kea. The final day takes you through grassy Routeburn Flats along the Routeburn River, with swing bridges to help you make multiple crossings to arrive at Dart River Trailhead.

171 Diving Palau

WHERE Palau

WHEN Year-round

PHYSICAL	✦ ✦ ✦ ✦ ✦
PSYCH	✦ ✦ ✦ ✦ ✦
SKILL	✦ ✦ ✦ ✦ ✦
WOW	✦ ✦ ✦ ✦ ✦

A thousand kilometers east of the Philippines, the 200-island archipelago of Palau dots the blue Pacific with only eight inhabited islands. Divers, lured by the coastal waters of the uninhabited and unspoiled islands, would have it no other way. The islands were formed by a series of powerful geologic and natural forces creating a remarkable variety of underwater environments, which provide amazing dives in both shallow and deep water. Shipwrecks enhance the diversity and give the area an eerie feel.

Palau's Rock Islands, also known as the Floating Garden Islands, are coral reefs and atolls that have been uplifted and then eroded from beneath creating mushroom-shaped islands with arches, caves and tunnels to explore. Some of the vine-draped tiny islets poke above sea level just enough to make their presence known.

Once beneath the surface, there is a dazzling array of marine life visible at each of the dive sites. A giant clam over a meter across gaped open near a bright red spiny sea cucumber as big as a baseball bat. Brilliant blue, red, and burgundy starfish stretch out over multihued coral reefs. Clown fish poke out from the swaying tentacles of the anemone. Schools of sparkling blackfin barracuda swish past as you study the moral eel below you. Azure openings, yawning caverns, and steep drop-offs demand multiple visits to experience it all.

Just a few degrees north of the equator, the temperature of both air and water are warm year-round. Visibility can be up to 60m in November and April, but during the rainy months July to October water clarity may be affected by runoff. As diving and tourism are the major industries of Palau, there are suppliers and outfitters to meet every budget, schedule, ability, and requirement.

One stop that must be made is a visit to Jellyfish Lake. Though no scuba gear is allowed, no trip to Palau would be complete without this firsthand experience in adaptation and evolution. Jellyfish, cut off from the rest of the ocean, continued to thrive in a large salt water lake and over numerous generations lost potency in their sting making it possible for divers to safely swim among creatures that resemble pulsing pale pink balloons.

172 Fraser Island wildlife viewing

WHERE Queensland, Australia

WHEN Year-round

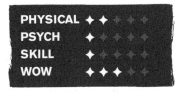

PHYSICAL	✦ ✦ ✦ ✦ ✦
PSYCH	✦ ✦ ✦ ✦ ✦
SKILL	✦ ✦ ✦ ✦ ✦
WOW	✦ ✦ ✦ ✦ ✦

Jutting out from the northeastern Australian coast is Fraser Island, the largest sand island in the world. Named for Emily Fraser who survived a shipwreck there in 1836, it's known by the Aboriginal people as K'gari, meaning "paradise." Much of the island is reserved for hiking and exploring, and its protected areas in particular hold a surprisingly diverse and thriving collection of flora and fauna. Still more unexpected are the turquoise-colored fresh water lakes rimmed with pure white sand that are found throughout the island.

When you visit Fraser Island bring plenty of sunscreen and plan on walking the 12-kilometer track between Lake McKenzie and Lake Wabby that takes you through tall forests to sand dunes to the island's deepest lake. Don't forget your binoculars – the island is home to over 350 species of birds. As you walk about you may see the colorful rainbow bee-eater that eats flying insects, the azure kingfisher with bright blue wings, brilliant orange breast and a high-pitched shrill, the Australian pelican, and even the smallest penguin in the world, the aptly named little penguin. Monitoring the skies above the island is the white-breasted sea eagle, the largest bird of prey on Fraser Island. Seeing one soaring in search of its next meal is an impressive sight to be sure, though perhaps one matched by the spectacle of a jabiru, or black-necked stork, unfurling its three-meter-long wingspan. And if you are very observant you may catch a glimpse of the perfectly camouflaged and endangered ground parrot.

There are many more animals that thrive on the island than just birds, however. With a guide who can assist with spotting you might see the echidna, or spiny anteater, an egg-laying mammal that burrows into the sand. Dingoes, a native wild dog, are becoming rare but are still found on the island. Monitor lizards, or goannas, with sharp teeth and claws can look quite threatening but they normally will flee when disturbed. You may also see swamp wallabies, sugar gliders and flying foxes. The action's not just limited to the land. Whale watching is popular in July and August, while the dugong, a relative of the manatee, lives near the coastline year round. Should you be tempted to cool off in the ocean, be aware that currents on the east make the water too rough to swim in.

Miscellany

willing and Abel

In 1642, Abel Tasman, a Dutch mariner and explorer staked his claim to an island off the southeastern coast of Australia and named it Van Diemen's Land after the Governor of the Dutch West Indies. Due to the difficulty of getting there, it would be 61 years before a European colony was established, and even then it would be a penal colony. Now known as Tasmania, it is a natural treasure that is surprisingly untouched. Over one third of the island is protected as national park, reserve, or UN World Heritage Site.

MAORI

Emigrants from Polynesia in the thirteenth century, the Maori people planted themselves in New Zealand and developed a distinct culture in their new homeland. They called themselves "*maori*", meaning "ordinary", to differentiate themselves from deity. The Maori thrived until the arrival of Europeans in the late 1700s when diseases were introduced to which they had no immunity. Populations began to rebuild in the late 19th century and Maori culture began to resurge in the 1960s.

I have no fear of losing my life - if I have to save a koala or a crocodile or a kangaroo or a snake, mate, I will save it.
Steve Irwin

coast to coast

The coast to coast multisport event, held each February in Greymouth, New Zealand, involves cycling, mountain running and kayaking some 243km. It can take anywhere from half a day to nearly a day to complete.

hills to climb

Australia is an extremely flat country, its tallest mountain woefully small in comparison to the extremes of other continents. According to the Australian government, the top five by height (all in New South Wales) are:
Mount Kosciuszko (2228m)
Mount Townsend (2209m)
Mount Twynam (2196m)
Ramshead (2190m)
Unnamed peak, Etheridge Ridge (2180m)

THREE IS BETTER THAN TWO

Kangaroos do not walk, they hop. In fact, they are the only large mammals to do so. But do they use two feet or three? Their tail muscles are very strong and can help the kangaroo balance or propel itself forward when moving slowly. That makes the kangaroo tripedal instead of bipedal. However, when they decide to pick up speed they can hop faster than a human can run, hitting speeds up to 70kph.

Australia is an outdoor country. People only go inside to use the toilet. And that's only a recent development.

Barry Humphries, Australian comedian

EXPLOSIVE SWIMSUIT

The two-piece bikini swimsuit takes its name from the Bikini Atoll, a nuclear test site in the Marshall Islands. The swimsuit designer believed his design would have a similar explosive impact on swimwear fashion.

get out the sunscreen

What do pigs, humans, hippos, and hammerhead sharks have in common? They are the only species known to get sunburn after prolonged sun exposure. Hippos, who normally spend most of the day submerged, create their own sunscreen by excreting a thick pink substance to protect exposed areas when on land.

ADVENTURE CENTRAL

New Zealand may well be the capital of the world in terms of adventure sports – certainly the ones geared toward fast thrills. Past all the great walking, rafting and diving, it was the first place to introduce commercial bungy jumping. It is also the home of zorbing, in which you are fastened inside a giant plastic sphere, then sent down a hill to roll and bounce along.

not a lizard

If you ran into a tuatara on a trail in New Zealand, you would immediately assume that you had a come across a lizard. But you would be wrong. This green leathery-skinned reptile with a spiny ridge down its back claims an ancient genealogy that connects it to dinosaurs more closely than to the lizards of today. Scientists are trying to distribute these endangered zoological oddities to small, less inhabited islands near New Zealand.

ENDANGERED SPECIES

The tuatara are not the only threatened species in New Zealand. Just a small sampling of others include:
Hamilton's frog A competitor for the rarest frog in the world.
Kakapo Indigenous parrot, of which fewer than one hundred are left.
Kiwi The national bird, small, brown, flightless and fuzzy.

"In some ways I believe I epitomize the average New Zealander. I have modest abilities, I combine these with a good deal of determination and I rather like to succeed."

Sir Edmund Hillary

Uluru...who knew?

Uluru, also known as Ayers Rock, is a large red sandstone formation almost dead center in the continent of Australia. At 348m high, it stands as a visual icon in the midst of a vast desert. Through a slow erosion process, it is believed to be the last remnant of an entire mountain range. Considered sacred to the aboriginal people, the word *uluru* has no known meaning.

DEADLY ENCOUNTERS

Australia harbors some of the world's deadliest creatures, including the estuarine crocodile, which constitutes an active threat to humans. Three-quarters of the world's most venomous snakes are found in Australia, though few ever enter humans' prime habitats. The venomous box jellyfish hits tropical coastal waters in summer months and its poison can cause rapid unconsciousness or paralysis of the heart muscles. And of course Australian television star Steve Irwin was fatally felled by the barb of a stingray off the country's northeast coast.

The fact that few people go there is one of the most persuasive reasons for traveling to a place.

Paul Theroux, *The Happy Isles of Oceania*

hole in the bottom of the sea

Where is the deepest part of the ocean? On the western edge of Micronesia in the Mariana Trench, the Pacific Plate is subducted under the Philippine Plate and the ocean floor dips to almost 11,000m below sea level. That is deeper below sea level than Mt Everest towers above. First surveyed in 1951, it was explored by bathyscaphe by the US Navy in 1961.

AUSTRALIAN DIVE SITES

The Great Barrier Reef gets most of the attention, but the following offer excellent diving as well.

▶ **Bourgainville Reed, Queensland** Clear water and 1000-meter coral walls attract fish and divers from miles around.

▶ **Cod Hole, Queensland** Pose with a huge maori wrasse or feed a fat-lipped giant potato cod; both weigh in at up to 100kg.

▶ **Coral Bay, Ningaloo Reef, Western Australia** Walk right off the beach and paddle out over the reef.

▶ **Princess Royal Harbour, Albany, Western Australia** A choice of shallow-water wreck dives in a huge, sheltered natural harbor.

▶ **Port Lincoln, South Australia** Your chance to see the great white shark's toothy smile – from the safety of a cage, naturally.

your local volcano

New Zealands's only active marine volcano, White Island, rises 321m above sea level in the Bay of Plenty. The dramatic caldera has to push layers of lava through 1600m of ocean to reach the surface. The Maori name, Te Puia o Whakaari, means "dramatic volcano". British explorer Captain James Cook named it White Island when he spied it 1769 because it was shrouded it white steam. Apparently he never got close enough to notice it was a volcano.

THE RIVER WILD

Once in a blue moon the Finke River actually flows from its source just west of Alice Springs for 700km all the way to Lake Eyre in South Australia. But the fact that it's been doing it for 400 million years makes many scientists claim it to be the world's oldest river. On the odd occasion a tropical cyclone reaches far enough south to soak the Central Deserts and get the Finke flowing, keen kayakers get twitchy. Leaping into the thick orange current with a few days' supplies, they aim to get as far downriver as possible before the flash flood peters out.

THE POLAR REGIONS

173 Skiing to the South Pole

>> **A monumental challenge**

It's a relatively simple proposition when you think about it: crossing an ice sheet from the coast to the center of the continent. There are no mountains to climb, no rivers to cross, and no boundaries – manmade or otherwise – to impede your progress. It's just one foot in front of the other. But Antarctica is a continent of extremes, the most inconvenient place on the planet, and nothing there is quite that simple. It's the coldest, windiest, driest, loneliest, most inhospitable place on earth. Just getting here requires extraordinary logistical considerations and surviving in this harsh environment takes careful planning, preparation, and immense determination – let alone trying to reach its heart.

the driest place on earth

Cold as a cryogenics lab, it's not your typical desert; but the driest place on earth – and the biggest desert – lies within the interior region of Antarctica. In general, Antarctica receives about the same amount of precipitation as the Sahara does – less than two inches a year. The interior region of Antarctica is called the Dry Valleys, and it hasn't received a single drop of rainfall for over two million years. The culprit behind this never-ending dry spell is the 160km/h katabatic down winds that evaporate any potential moisture. Antarctica's freezing temperatures don't help the situation. The frigid environment helps eliminate the possibility of any water, plant life, or animal life. To say it's an otherworldly land is no tired cliché – the continent is being used as a training ground for future expeditions on Mars.

The ice sheet that covers Antarctica is the largest body of fresh water on earth, containing about 91 percent of the world's ice and 70 percent of the fresh water. If it were divided up, every person on Earth could have a chunk of ice larger than the Great Pyramid.

We took risks. We knew we took them. Things have come out against us. We have no cause for complaint.
Robert Falcon Scott, found in his diary after the party froze in Antarctica

What motivates a person to embark on this quest no doubt varies from one adventurer to the next, but Ernest Shackleton, who probably knew more about Antarctic endurance than any man who ever lived, said "Men go out into the void spaces of the world for various reasons. Some have the keen thirst for knowledge, and others are drawn away from the trodden path by the 'lure of little voices,' the mysterious fascination of the unknown." While capturing the legacy of great polar explorers is part of the experience – and you'll certainly gain a renewed respect for these legendary explorers – you'll commit to the expedition for the challenge, for the opportunity to have a monumental life experience, and for very personal reasons that you may never fully understand.

Preparation for a trip to the South Pole typically begins several months in advance. If you've never skied before don't fret – most expedition members have never done a long distance trek or expedition and are not high performance athletes or marathon runners. They are often small and slight and will undertake a regimen that has them adding weight, and most importantly, building endurance. One proven pre-expedition workout involves putting on a waist harness and towing car tires around a track for a couple hours a day, several days a week. This type of conditioning builds endurance and the kind of strength in the quadriceps and adductors needed to pull a 60–70kg sled for over 1000km. Beyond the physical conditioning, you need to come equipped with incredible determination and the resolve to undertake a monumental challenge with an unpredictable outcome.

In early November you'll arrive in Punta Arenas, Chile, with your boots, skis and personal gear, where you'll meet your guide and other expedition members to begin a several days of training in the details of the expedition, use of equipment, and the responsibilities and duties in which all expedition members will be required to share. You then board a workhorse Ilyushin 76TD aircraft, which lands on wheels on a naturally occurring ice runway at your Patriot Hills base camp, latitude 80° south.

With your feet firmly planted on Antarctica, you'll have a day or two to acclimatize, test your equipment and clothing onsite in Patriot Hills, practice doing tasks in the cold and wind with gloves on, and make any last minute repairs or corrections before boarding a ski-equipped Twin Otter DHC-6 for a fifteen-minute flight to your "coastal" starting point at Hercules Inlet, where the floating Ronne Ice Shelf meets the ice sheet overlaying the Antarctic continent.

In the first three days you'll cover 50km and return back to Patriot Hills in what amounts to a shakedown trek as you ascend 800m of elevation from sea level and grow accustomed to the rigors of sled-hauling. Based on these

first few days you may decide to leave any unnecessary items behind before continuing in earnest on your southward journey to the pole. Pointing your skis to the south and setting your back to the Patriot Hills camp may be the most committing event of your life as you cross over a saddle at Windy Pass and leave the coastal Ellsworth Mountains behind.

For the next 45 to 60 days you'll walk southbound on sustrugi, a rippled and ridged windswept surface of hardened snow and ice. Ahead of you is a flat terrain with imperceptible rolls. Here you can stand and watch someone walk away for hours until they become a dot that vanishes below the horizon. In a journey with almost no landmarks, the sight of just about any landform takes on a special significance, particularly the Thiel Mountains, a small escarpment on the horizon off to the west, and other nunatuks, exposed peaks of mountains whose mass is submerged below thousands of feet of ice. Once past the Thiel Mountains there is no distinguishing feature on the horizon for over six hundred miles. In this stark land devoid of life there is a sense of wonder in shadows, clouds, and the changing directions of light. The ceaseless wind coming down from the South Pole, generally blowing at 10–20 knots, is always in your face. You'll wear a full face covering of ski goggles with a fleece flap sewn to the bottom. Use it, and you'll generally come out unmarred; without it you're risking touches of frostbite on your cheeks and nose. As well, you need to constantly guard against deeper frostbite – a polar souvenir that no one wants to bring home – that can result in the loss of fingers and toes. Typical temperatures at the start of the trek are around 15°C and by the time you arrive at the higher elevations at the South Pole in January they will hover around –25°C, though on the journey they rarely drop below –30°C. You'll even be surprised on occasion by how warm it can be inside your tent as the sun's 24-hour radiance can create a toasty 15°C "greenhouse."

As you step continually southward, you find yourself getting deep into your own head and thinking through your past and future. You learn quickly, that if you're going to survive this expedition you need to work as a team. Your success in the expedition depends on teamwork, and you discover that getting along with other people is not up to them, it's up to you. Everyone is involved in the daily routine of setting up camp, melting snow, and preparing meals. Then you see a dot on the horizon which for the next two days becomes larger and more distinguishable as the Amundsen-Scott South Pole Station and your long awaited destination where a plane will return you to Patriot Hills. It's likely your journey to the South Pole will influence where you go from there.

need to know

In such a pristine environment, all travel should be planned and conducted with both environmental protection and safety in mind. The International Association of Antarctica Tour Operators (℡ 970/704-1047, Ⓦ www.iaato.org) is a trade organization that manages Antarctic tourism and establishes guidelines for private-sector travel to the Antarctic. Their members are respected and experienced operators committed to high standards and responsible practices.

guides and gear Antarctic Logistics & Expeditions (℡ 801/266 4876, Ⓦ www.antarctic-logistics.com) provides air services, logistic support, and safety backup for a wide range of land-based adventure and scientific expeditions to Antarctica including programs offered through their tour operator Adventure Network International (℡ 801/266-4876, Ⓦ www.adventure-network.com) which features climbs of the Vinson Massif and guided expeditions to the South Pole from their base camp at Patriot Hills.

when to go Expeditions to the South Pole take place in the austral summer from November to January.

suggested reading Richard Bird, *Alone: The Classic Polar Adventure* (Island Press). A remarkable story of physical and psychic survival during a five-month solo gig on the Ross Ice Shelf. Clint Willis, *Ice: Stories of Survival from Polar Exploration* (Adrenaline Books). A compilations of historical (Scott, Shackleton, Byrd) and current (Jon Krakauer and Bill Bryson) account of what humans are capable of when faced with the challenges of surviving in the polar world.

suggested viewing *The Endurance: Shackleton's Legendary Antarctic Expedition* (2000). Retelling of Sir Ernest Shackleton's ill-fated Antarctica expedition.

is this for me?

PHYSICAL ✦ ✦ ✦ ✦
Demands incredible endurance

PSYCH ✦ ✦ ✦ ✦
Determination in extreme cold and wind

SKILL ✦ ✦ ✦
Solid winter survival skills required

WOW! ✦ ✦ ✦ ✦
An exceptional polar triumph

Expedition to the North Pole

>> On top of the world

Along with the South Pole, the North Pole has always been the planet's final frontier. In the early twentieth century, men like Roald Amundsen and Robert Peary risked fortunes and lives to simply go to the literal end of the earth, to experience what no one ever had before. The fact that all the Arctic's grand polar prizes have long since been claimed, that no real firsts are left to be had there, matters little – an expedition to the North Pole is as epic as adventures come.

These days most polar adventurers travel on skis with skins, which are preferred for their superior ability to displace weight and prevent falls through thin ice. You'll tow your gear behind you on a sled attached to a hip harness. That configuration works well on smooth ice or packed snow, but when you hit large pressure ridges, plan on taking off your skis, removing your harness, and maneuvering or carrying your sled across the rough spots. You'll need to be in top physical condition, have proven ability to endure harsh conditions and carry with you a reservoir of emotional strength and mental toughness. Bragging rights for this one come at a high price.

the first to the North Pole

The Robert E. Peary and Matthew Henson expedition was the first ever to reach the North Pole of Alaska on April 7, 1909. Peary had begun his attempts to reach the North Pole as a young naval engineer. For years, Peary struck out toward the pole, but each time was forced to turn back because of impossible conditions. Peary, however, used each previous attempt to prepare for his next journey. In 1908, Peary sailed on the *Roosevelt* from New York to San Francisco, then all the way up Alaska to Cape Sheridan, as far north as the boat could possibly go. Matthew Henson, an accomplished seaman, had taken employment with Peary years earlier and was also on the expedition. Bundled in fur clothing used by the Eskimos, Peary, Henson, and their group set out with dog teams into the −50ºC weather. Two other groups went ahead of Peary's group and built shelters, brought food, and traded sledges. Conditions were extreme, and often the men had to cross leads where ice shifted and floated in open gaps of water. A sledge was commonly used to bridge a lead or a piece of ice was cut using pickaxes to create a ferry to pull across the gap of water by rope. When Peary's tiny group of six men finally reached the Pole, they were exhausted, but knew they had achieved what was once considered impossible.

My life work is accomplished... I have got the North Pole out of my system. After 23 years of effort, hard work, disappointments, hardships, privations, more or less suffering, and some risks, I have won the last great geographical prize.

Robert E. Peary

need to know

An expedition to the North Pole starts months in advance with physical training and polar skills training for a trip of about two weeks in mid-April of each year.

guides and gear Polar Explorers, a division of The Northwest Passage (☎ 1-800/732-7328, Ⓦ www.polarexplorers.com), is the premier polar guiding company and offers dogsled, ski and flight expeditions to the North Pole.

when to go Expeditions to the North Pole are only attempted in April when longer days and warming weather still permit access and travel on a melting icecap.

getting there Most commercial expeditions start from Longyearbyen, on the Norwegian island of Svalbard.

suggested reading Bruce Henderson, *True North: Peary, Cook, And The Race To The Pole* (W.W. Norton). A saga of jealousy and competitive zeal in the race to the North Pole. Matthew A. Henson, with commentary by Robert E. Peary and introduction by Booker T. Washington. *A Negro Explorer at the North Pole* (Dodo Press). Although Admiral Peary received many honors, his seaman and expedition companion Henson was largely ignored. This is Henson's account of the expedition.

is this for me?

PHYSICAL ✦ ✦ ✦ ✦ ✦
Takes exceptional strength and endurance

PSYCH ✦ ✦ ✦ ✦ ✦
Extreme cold, high winds, and barren surroundings

SKILL ✦ ✦ ✦ ✦
Cold weather survival experience essential

WOW! ✦ ✦ ✦ ✦ ✦
An accomplishment unlike any other

From the Arctic outpost of Longyearbyen, Norway, you'll board a 26-passenger aircraft for a flight to the Barneo Station, a Russian base set up during April of each year to provide logistical support for polar research and expeditions. The station is located near the 89th parallel on the drifting ice near the Pole.

Once on the ice, your northward journey will take place under the light of a sun that never sets, but that is the only certainty you're likely to experience. Weather can range from sunny clear days, to overcast or foggy, to zero visibility snowstorms. Winds can be calm and to your back, or howling and piercing, forcing you to wait it out in your tent. The constant sunlight gives you the option of traveling when weather conditions are most favorable and sleeping during the more severe weather, regardless of the hour.

Traveling on the polar ice sheet can be like walking on a giant treadmill. You can make good distance during the day, only to have your gains eroded while you sleep as the ice pan on which you camp drifts south three kilometers or more. With clear weather and good ice conditions you might travel 12–16km per day. But be prepared for days with foul weather and a route strewn with rubble, pressure ridges, and other jumbled blocks of ice that slow travel to just a few kilometers per day.

As you make your way north you can expect to encounter leads, or channels of open water which separate one ice sheet from another. Leads can be a few meters wide or hundreds of meters wide. They can freeze overnight, creating a useable route or crossing, or they can remain as open water, creating a barrier that may force you hours or even days away from your target. Either way, they present a constant navigational challenge and an element of uncertainty and risk. The line of travel is rarely straight, even though your elevation is relatively flat. Throughout the journey you need to remain aware of changing weather conditions and the thickness of the ice sheet, since frostbite and falling through the ice are real risks.

Arctic ice can reveal itself in starkly beautiful ways, from blue chunks the size of a bus to a blanket of diamond-like crystals. As you journey onward you'll hear the cracks and groan of the moving ice sheet and the grinding of ice pans colliding. There are few life forms in this harsh environment, but occasional sightings of seals and polar bears, while rare, can occur along the way.

In the end, though, there is nothing to "see" at the North Pole, no markers man-made or otherwise to tell you that you've joined an elite group of less than fifty per year who persevere to reach this point. In fact, this point is not even fixed – the geographic North Pole is an ever-changing position on the ice sheet identified only by a GPS. But for those who have endured the extreme temperatures and grueling physical demands – often traversing 160km across an unpredictable surface – the sense of accomplishment for making it to the very top of the world is immeasurable. From here there is only one way to go: south.

175 Sea kayaking Greenland's fjords

PHYSICAL	✦ ✦ ✦ ✦ ✦	
PSYCH	✦ ✦ ✦ ✦ ✦	
SKILL	✦ ✦ ✦ ✦ ✦	
WOW!	✦ ✦ ✦ ✦ ✦	

WHERE Eastern Greenland

WHEN JUNE to mid-September

In the Arctic waters of East Greenland's Ammassalik Island, the endless days of summer offer a spectacular passage through normally ice-bound fjords and channels. As glaciers calve and icebergs drift through the fjords you can discover the beauty and riches of a land the Inuit have known for ages. It's fitting then that there is no better way to explore this icescape than in a kayak, the watercraft invented by the Inuit.

The stunning scenery conceals many hidden dangers and the logistical demands of entering this realm are high – you'll need an experienced guide and full support. You and your fellow kayakers will paddle though placid protected waters littered with chunks of ice, some smaller than your kayak and other hotel-size icebergs so large that you don't dare draw too near; a single calving chunk off one of these icebergs would be enough to take out an entire expedition. Still, the eerie blue glow cast from these bergs has a powerful allure, and the popping and cracking of the expanding ice is locally known as the Greenland coastal artillery. Camping both on land and on the glaciers, exploratory day-hikes take you where you can forage for wild blueberries and mushrooms or traipse through fields of resilient Arctic wildflowers. In your paddling you may discover the remnants of long abandoned Inuit settlements. Arctic land mammals are sparse, but in the frigid waters you can expect to be entertained by seals, walruses, and a variety of whales.

176 Walking in the footsteps of Shackleton

WHERE South Georgia Island

WHEN March to November

PHYSICAL	✦ ✦ ✦ ✦
PSYCH	✦ ✦
SKILL	✦ ✦ ✦
WOW!	✦ ✦ ✦ ✦

In 1916 massive ice flows trapped the *Endurance*, the ship of the explorer Ernest Shackleton and his 27-member expedition crew, leaving the men stranded on Elephant Island off the coast of Antarctica. Faced with the prospect of starvation, Shackleton and five of his men sailed 1300km in a lifeboat to South Georgia Island. There they made a grueling trek across the island's treacherous mountains and glaciers in order to reach a small whaling outpost on the other side. It was a feat never previously attempted – indeed, no one had ever risked ventured inland, much less across the island. Today, with the benefit of the latest and warmest cold weather gear, it is possible to retrace Shackleton's footsteps and traverse the entire 39-kilomtere original route across this remote island and its rugged alpine slopes.

The weather is brutal and the crossing is rough. Roping up on the freezing slopes, you'll be carrying a pack and pulling a sled loaded with supplies. A bleak panorama of icy peaks, glaciers slowly plowing into the roaring ice-cold sea, and a deeply indented coastline mark your journey north. Since you probably won't attempt to make the traverse in a 36-hour non-stop life-or-death marathon as did Shackleton and his crew, plan on about five days – plenty of time to appreciate how fortunate you are to not be shipwrecked in Antarctica.

177 South Georgia Island wildlife viewing

WHERE South Georgia Island

WHEN November to January

PHYSICAL	✦ ✦ ✦
PSYCH	✦ ✦
SKILL	✦ ✦
WOW!	✦ ✦ ✦

It wouldn't be a stretch to say that South Georgia Island is among the most visited islands in the world – that is, if penguins can be counted in the mix. Its forbidding, rocky, and cliff-flanked coastline has never welcomed more than a few human outposts, however. Its prospects for mass tourism were noted by Captain James Cook who first landed on the island in 1775 and declared that it was "not worth the discovery." Still, the pristine coastline teems with wildlife every bit worth traveling to the bottom of the earth to see. Aided by relatively warm converging currents that deliver an abundant food supply, the island's deep-cut inlets and glacial bays are favored breeding grounds for elephant seals and Antarctic birds including albatrosses and penguins.

Standing nearly a meter tall, king penguins, with their distinctive white bellies, black backs, and iridescent golden necks are the island's star attractions. Luckily, they're not hard to find – hundreds of thousands nest in beach rookeries. Though not the most graceful of animals on land, they are an altogether different sight underwater. They can dive to depths of over 300m, swim at speeds of 10km per hour, and stay submerged for nearly nine minutes, while foraging for krill and small fish throughout the dive. Wildlife viewing expeditions are typically based from cruise ships, often departing from Ushuaia, Argentina and include stops at other sub-Antarctic islands, where shore excursions are a field-day for wide-eyed wildlife photographers.

alone at the top

Naomi Uemura of Japan became the first person to reach the North Pole alone. He traveled by dogsled on a 57-day, 1000km trek, arriving at the pole on April 30, 1978. Uemura was also the first ever to raft the Amazon solo and the first to climb Mount McKinley solo.

Nothing easier. One step beyond the pole, you see, and the north wind becomes a south one."

Robert Peary, explaining how he knew he had reached the North Pole.

self-rescue in an icefall

If you fall through ice into freezing water, try to remember these potentially life-saving steps:

1. **Face the direction from which you came**. This is likely the area with the thickest ice.
2. **Place both elbows, and as much of your upper arms as possible, onto the edge of the ice**. Relax and let excess water drain from your clothes.
3. **Dig into the ice**. You might use a ski pole, keys, knife or anything that can minimize your slipping on the ice surface.
4. **Kick your feet**, as if you were swimming, to propel yourself back up onto the ice.
5. **Once on the ice, do not stand up**. Distribute your weight as evenly as possible across the ice and steadily move back to the shore or to thicker ice.

WHAT KEEPS ANTARCTIC FISH ALIVE?

Antarctic waters comprise about ten percent of the earth's oceans, yet have only one percent of the fish species. The temperature of Antarctic waters is below the freezing point of most fish blood, but Antarctic species have special protein which acts as an antifreeze. Also, the metabolism of many Antarctic species is particularly low, with some having a heart that beats only once every six seconds.

"Adventure is just bad planning."

Roald Amundsen

polar ice sheets

The glacial ice sheet covering Greenland is about 1.5km thick, but the ice covering Antarctica is three times thicker, up to 4.8km thick. Beneath the Antarctic ice sheet are over 140 subglacial lakes, of which the largest is Lake Vostok, the world's seventh largest freshwater lake, similar in size to Lake Ontario. Vostok has an average depth of 344m and an island in the center of the lake.

SILVER LININGS

In both Polar regions the frigid winter sky may display a rare and visually stunning event – nacreous clouds. Also known as polar stratospheric clouds, these high-flying wispy clouds produce an eerie multi-coloured glow as they swirl across the dark sky from a height of up to 16km. This peculiar light show can only be seen in the two hours preceding sunrise or after sunset as the height of the clouds causes them to reflect sunlight from below the horizon.

If there really is a pole at the North Pole, I bet there's some dead explorer-guy with his tongue stuck to it."

Bob Van Voris

first women at the South Pole

On January 17, 1989, Victoria Murden and Shirley Metz became both the first women and the first Americans to reach the South Pole overland when they arrived with nine others at the conclusion of a 1200km, 51-day trek on skis.

SNAKE-FREE

Antarctica is the only continent with no reptiles.

fire on ice

Mount Erebus on Antarctica's Ross Island is an active volcano, the southernmost on earth. It was in a state of eruption when it was first sighted in 1841 and has been active throughout its recorded history, erupting regularly in 2008 and showing no signs of slowing down.

End matter

#	USA and Canada	Jan	Feb	Mar	Apr	May	Jun	Jul	Aug	Sept	Oct	Nov	Dec
1	Heliskiing in British Columbia	■	■	■	■								■
2	Surfing Oahu's North Shore	■	■	■								■	■
3	Paddling the Everglades	■	■	■								■	■
4	Hiking the Grand Canyon rim to rim				■	■				■	■		
5	Canoeing the Missinaibi River					■	■	■	■	■			
6	Climbing El Capitan					■	■			■	■		
7	Exploring Gros Morne						■	■	■	■			
8	Kayaking the Kern River				■	■	■	■					
9	Mountain biking the Slickrock Trail			■	■	■				■	■	■	
10	Climbing Denali					■	■	■					
11	Hiking the Zion Narrows						■	■	■	■			
12	Rafting the Middle Fork of the Salmon River						■	■	■				
13	Climbing Mauna Loa					■	■	■	■	■	■		
14	Canoeing in the Boundary Waters					■	■	■	■	■			
15	Skiing hut to hut in the Rockies	■	■	■	■							■	■
16	Hiking the Pacific Crest Trail				■	■	■	■	■	■			
17	Sea kayaking the Kenai Fjords						■	■	■				
18	Canoeing the Bonaventure River						■	■	■	■			
19	Rock climbing in Joshua Tree	■	■	■							■	■	■
20	Hiking the Appalachian Trail					■	■	■	■	■			
21	Rafting Cherry Creek						■	■					
22	Climbing the Grand Teton						■	■	■	■			
23	Exploring Isle Royale						■	■	■	■			
24	Windsurfing in the Columbia River Gorge						■	■	■	■			
25	Hiking the John Muir Trail							■	■	■			
26	Dogsledding in the Yukon	■	■	■									■
27	Climbing Colorado's Fourteeners						■	■	■	■			
28	Sea kayaking in the San Juan Islands						■	■	■	■			
29	Hiking the Na Pali Coast					■	■	■	■	■			
30	Climbing Mount Rainier						■	■	■				
31	Paddling the Atchafalaya Basin		■	■	■			■	■				
32	Exploring the Escalante Canyons				■	■				■	■		
33	Running the Grand Canyon in a dory			■	■	■	■	■	■	■			
34	Hiking Half Dome					■	■	■	■	■			

#	Activity	Jan	Feb	Mar	Apr	May	Jun	Jul	Aug	Sept	Oct	Nov	Dec
	USA and Canada Best of the rest												
35	Climbing Devils Tower					●	●	●	●	●	●		
36	Hiking the Continental Divide Trail				●	●	●	●	●	●	●	●	
37	Tracking polar bears in the tundra				●	●	●	●	●	●	●	●	
38	Hiking in Glacier National Park						●	●	●	●	●		
39	Canyoneering in Paria River and Buckskin Gulch			●	●	●	●	●	●	●			
40	Rafting the Klinaklini River						●	●	●	●			
41	Ice-climbing in Québec	●	●	●								●	●
42	Diving with manta rays in Kona	●	●	●	●	●	●	●	●	●	●	●	●
43	Mountain biking on the Kokopelli Trail			●	●	●	●	●	●	●	●	●	
44	Bodysurfing Steamer Lane	●	●	●	●	●	●	●	●	●	●	●	●
45	Paddling Tatshenshini-Alsek Park						●	●	●	●			
46	Hiking the West Coast Trail					●	●	●	●	●			
47	Magpie river rafting						●	●	●	●			
48	Hiking the Hoh Rainforest				●	●	●	●	●	●	●		
	Latin America and the Caribbean												
49	Kayaking in the Sea of Cortez	●	●	●	●	●						●	●
50	Trekking the Paine Circuit	●	●	●							●	●	●
51	Diving in Belize	●	●	●	●	●	●	●	●	●	●	●	●
52	Rafting the Futaleufú					●	●	●	●	●			
53	Exploring the Amazon Basin	●	●	●	●	●	●	●	●	●	●	●	●
54	Trekking the Inca Highlands	●				●	●	●	●	●	●		●
55	Exploring Cockpit Country	●	●	●	●	●	●	●	●	●	●	●	●
56	Kiteboarding at Preá		●	●	●	●	●	●	●	●			
57	Exploring Copper Canyon	●				●	●	●	●	●	●	●	●
58	Wildlife viewing in Costa Rica	●	●	●	●							●	●
59	Trekking in the Cordillera Huayhuash	●				●	●	●	●	●			
60	Rafting the Pacuare	●	●	●	●	●	●	●	●	●	●	●	●
61	Wildlife viewing in the Galápagos	●	●	●	●	●	●	●	●	●	●	●	●
62	Climbing the Cordillera Blanca					●	●	●	●	●	●		
63	Windsurfing in Bonaire	●	●	●	●					●	●	●	●
	Latin America and the Caribbean Best of the rest												
64	Trekking to Angel Falls	●			●	●	●	●	●	●	●		●
65	Caving in Camuy	●	●	●	●	●	●	●	●	●	●	●	●
66	Seeing the jungle in Manu Biosphere Reserve	●	●	●	●	●	●	●	●	●	●	●	●
67	Climbing the Masaya and Maderas volcanoes	●	●	●	●	●	●	●	●	●	●	●	●
68	Trekking to Panama's Caribbean Coast	●				●	●	●	●	●	●	●	●
69	Horseriding with gauchos in the Pampas	●	●	●	●	●	●	●	●	●	●	●	●
70	Hiking in the Serra do Mar	●	●	●	●	●	●	●	●	●	●	●	●
71	Wildlife viewing on Peninsula Valdés	●	●	●	●	●	●	●	●	●	●	●	●
72	Birdwatching on the Pipeline Road	●	●	●	●	●	●	●	●	●	●	●	●
73	Biking down the World's Most Dangerous Road	●				●	●	●	●	●	●	●	
74	Sea kayaking to the San Rafael Glacier	●	●	●			●	●	●	●	●		●

		Jan	Feb	Mar	Apr	May	Jun	Jul	Aug	Sept	Oct	Nov	Dec
	Europe												
75	Climbing the Matterhorn							X	X	X			
76	Walking England from coast to coast					X	X	X	X	X			
77	Via ferrata climbing in the Dolomites						X	X	X	X			
78	Sea kayaking in Iceland						X	X	X				
79	Trekking the GR20						X	X	X	X			
80	Mountain biking in Cappadocia					X	X			X	X		
81	Climbing Ben Nevis						X	X	X	X			
82	Hiking the Haute Route							X	X	X			
83	Cross-country ski touring in Norway			X	X								
84	Climbing Mont Blanc							X	X	X			
85	Hiking Hadrian's Wall				X	X	X	X	X	X			
86	Hiking Kungsleden							X	X	X			
	Europe Best of the Rest												
87	Hiking the North Devon Coast	X	X	X	X	X	X	X	X	X	X	X	X
88	Diving the Zenobia	X	X	X	X		X	X	X	X		X	X
89	Cross-country ski touring in Lapland	X	X	X	X							X	X
90	Walking in the Cévennes	X	X	X	X	X	X			X	X	X	X
91	Cycling in the Southern Piedmont	X	X	X	X	X	X		X	X	X	X	X
92	Hiking in the Pindos Mountains	X	X	X	X	X	X			X	X	X	X
93	Mountain biking King's Trail				X	X	X		X	X	X		
94	Walking the Kerry Way	X	X	X	X	X	X	X	X	X	X	X	X
95	Hiking in the Carpathians	X	X	X	X	X	X	X	X	X	X	X	X
96	Walking the West Highland Way	X	X	X	X	X	X	X	X	X	X	X	X
97	Kayaking in the Ionian Sea				X	X	X	X	X	X	X		
98	Horseback riding in Andalucia			X	X	X	X			X	X	X	
99	Hiking the Snowdon Horseshoe	X	X	X	X	X	X	X	X	X	X	X	X
100	Walking the Camino de Santiago				X	X	X		X	X	X		
101	Walking across the Llyn	X	X	X	X	X	X	X	X	X	X	X	X
102	Ice diving in the White Sea		X	X	X								
103	Coasteering in Anglesey	X	X	X	X	X	X	X	X	X	X	X	X
104	Caving in Bihor	X	X	X	X	X	X	X	X	X	X	X	X
105	Bagging a Munro	X	X	X	X	X	X	X	X	X	X	X	X
106	Kayaking the Ardèche gorges	X	X	X	X	X	X	X	X	X	X	X	X
	Africa												
107	Rafting the Mangoky River					X							
108	A camel trek in the Sahara		X	X	X					X	X	X	
109	Trekking in the Drakensberg Mountains	X	X	X	X	X	X	X	X	X	X	X	X
110	Trekking in the Rwenzori Mountains	X	X	X	X	X	X	X	X	X	X	X	X
111	Canoe safari on the Zambezi River	X	X	X	X	X	X	X	X	X	X	X	X
112	Riding horseback through the Masai Mara	X	X	X	X	X	X	X	X	X	X	X	X
113	Diving in the Seychelles	X	X	X	X	X	X	X	X	X	X	X	X
114	Tracking mountain gorillas	X	X	X	X	X	X	X	X	X	X	X	X
115	Rafting the White Nile	X	X	X	X	X	X	X	X	X	X	X	X

		Jan	Feb	Mar	Apr	May	Jun	Jul	Aug	Sept	Oct	Nov	Dec
116	Safari in the Okavango Delta						■	■	■	■	■		
117	Rafting the Upper Zambezi						■	■	■	■	■	■	■
118	Climbing Mount Kilimanjaro	■	■	■					■	■	■	■	■
119	Trekking in the High Atlas Mountains				■	■	■	■	■	■	■		
120	Diving in the Red Sea					■	■	■	■	■	■	■	■
	Africa Best of the rest												
121	Windsurfing in Essaouira	■	■	■	■	■	■	■	■	■	■	■	■
122	Biking to Chamarel Waterfall and Chamarel Colored Earth	■	■	■	■	■	■	■	■	■	■	■	■
123	Camel trekking in the Sinai Desert	■	■	■	■	■				■	■	■	■
124	Wildlife viewing at Kakum National Park	■	■	■	■	■	■	■	■	■	■	■	■
125	Riding waves at Jeffreys Bay						■	■	■	■	■		
126	Namib Desert ride to the Sea					■	■	■	■	■	■		
127	Rafting the Omo River	■	■	■	■	■		■	■	■	■	■	■
128	Wildlife safari to Ngorongoro Crater	■	■	■	■	■	■	■	■	■	■	■	■
129	Horseback safari in Nyika National Park	■	■	■	■			■	■	■	■	■	■
130	Trekking in the Semien Mountains	■	■	■	■				■	■	■	■	■
131	Trekking and wildlife viewing on the Skeleton Coast	■	■	■	■	■	■	■	■	■	■	■	■
	Asia												
132	The Chomolhari trek				■	■				■	■	■	
133	Exploring the Mulu Caves	■	■	■	■	■	■	■	■	■	■	■	■
134	Bicycling in Yangshou	■	■	■	■	■	■	■	■	■	■	■	■
135	Diving at Palawan	■	■	■	■	■	■	■	■	■	■	■	■
136	Trekking in the Annapurna Himal			■	■					■	■	■	
137	Climbing Mount Fuji							■	■				
138	Horseback riding in the Darhat Valley						■	■	■	■	■		
139	Sea kayaking in Phang Nga Bay	■	■	■	■							■	■
140	Wildlife viewing in Borneo	■	■	■	■	■	■	■	■	■	■	■	■
141	Trekking in the Karakoram						■	■	■	■			
142	Walking the Nakasendo				■	■	■			■	■	■	
	Asia Best of the rest												
143	Tiger tracking in the Sundarbans	■	■	■							■	■	■
144	Surfing in G-Land			■	■	■	■	■	■	■	■		
145	Jungle safari in Royal Chitwan National Park	■	■	■					■	■	■	■	■
146	Whitewater rafting on the Karnali River	■	■	■						■	■	■	■
147	Trekking at Snow Lake						■	■	■	■			
148	Horse trekking in Songpan					■	■	■	■	■	■		
149	Trekking in the Coorg	■	■								■	■	■
150	Trekking in Rajasthan	■	■	■						■	■	■	■
151	Rafting the Sun Kosi									■	■	■	
152	Exploring the Mogao Caves	■	■	■	■	■	■	■	■	■	■	■	■
153	Trekking in Xishuangbanna	■	■	■						■	■	■	■
154	Hiking up Mount Kinabalu	■	■	■	■	■	■	■	■	■	■	■	■
155	Snowboarding in Iran	■	■	■									■

		Jan	Feb	Mar	Apr	May	Jun	Jul	Aug	Sept	Oct	Nov	Dec
156	Rafting the Brahmaputra River					■	■	■	■	■	■		
157	Kiteboarding in Hainan	■					■	■	■	■	■	■	■
158	Trekking at Lake Baikal						■	■	■	■			
159	Mountain climbing in Eastern Tajikistan						■	■	■	■			
160	Panda viewing in Wolong Nature Reserve			■	■	■	■	■	■	■	■	■	
	Australia and Oceania												
161	Diving the Great Barrier Reef	■	■	■	■	■	■	■	■	■	■	■	■
162	Hiking the Milford Track	■	■	■	■							■	■
163	Rafting the Navua River	■	■	■	■	■	■	■	■	■	■	■	■
164	Climbing Mount Cook	■											
	Australia and Oceania Best of the Rest												
165	Surfing Bell's Beach	■	■	■	■	■	■	■	■	■	■	■	■
166	Tackling the Overland Track	■	■	■			■	■	■		■	■	■
167	Surfing Superbank	■	■	■	■	■	■	■	■	■	■	■	■
168	Horseback riding in the Snowy Mountains	■	■	■	■	■						■	■
169	Rafting the Karamea	■	■	■	■	■					■	■	■
170	Trekking the Routeburn Track	■	■	■	■							■	■
171	Diving Palau	■	■	■	■	■	■	■	■	■	■	■	■
172	Fraser Island wildlife viewing	■	■	■	■	■	■	■	■	■	■	■	■
	The Polar Regions												
173	Skiing to the South Pole	■										■	■
174	Expedition to the North Pole				■								
	The Polar Regions Best of the Rest												
175	Sea Kayaking Greenland's fjords								■	■			
176	Walking in the Footsteps of Shackleton	■										■	■
177	South Georgia Island Wildlife Viewing	■										■	■

IMAGE CREDITS

Cover
Front cover Whitewater rafting, view from raft, Idaho © Getty/Karl Weatherly
Back cover strip (from left to right) Via ferrata © iStock/Alessandro Contadini
Salmon River © Zachary Collier/ECHO
Camel safari in Sahara © iStock/Jonatha Borzicchi
Trekking the Drakensberg Mountains © iStock/Gordon Laurens
Slickrock trail © iStock/Geir-Olav Lyngfjell

Introduction
p.4 Climber, Yosemite © Kevin Steele/Getty
p.6 top: Parque Nacional Torres del Paine © Minden/Getty
p.6 bottom: Marine Iguana, Galápagos Islands ©Todd Gustafson/drr.net
p.7 top: Okavango © photolibrary
p.7 middle: Punta Aracale, Corsica © Bowater/Mira.com/drr.net
p.7 bottom: Expedition to the North Pole © PolarExplorers

The adventures
01 Heliskiing in British Columbia © randylincks.com
02 Surfer at North Shore © James Davis Photography/Alamy; Backdoor Pipeline © Marc Prefontaine/iStock; Surfing at Sunset Beach, North Shore © Greg Ward/Rough Guides
03 Alligator © Paul Tessier/iStock ; Everglades in summer © John Anderson/iStock; Turner River © Gene Barryman
04 Sunset at Hopi Point, the South Rim © Greg Ward/Rough Guides; Cairn © Paige Falk/iStock; Lonely hiker © Alessandro Contadini /iStock
05 Canoeing the Missinaibi River © David Morin/Missinaibi Headwaters Outfitters; Group canoeing the Missinaibi River © David Morin/Missinaibi Headwaters Outfitters; Canoeing Missinaibi Rriver © Janusz Wrobel/Alamy
06 Climbing El Capitan © Paul Whitfield/Rough Guides
07 Tour boat beside the cliffs of Western Brook Pond, Gros Morne National Park © All Canada Photos/Alamy; Norris Point and Gros Morne mountain from the Woody Point Lighthouse © Jim Parkin/istock; Moose © All Canada Photos/Alamy; Traversing Gros Morne © Gros Morne Adventures
08 Kayaking the Kern River © Peter Grigsby/ Catapult Stock/drr.net; Kayaker on the Kern River © Sierra South; Kayakers on the Kern River © Phil Berry/iStock
09 Mountain biking on Slickrock © Ben Blankenburg/iStock; Slickrock panorama © Sarah Neal/iStock; Slickrock texture © Ashok Rodrigues/iStock
10 Mount McKinley above the clouds © Beverley Vycital/iStock; Alaska license plate © Paul Whitfield/Rough Guides; Climbers on Denali © okonek@mtaonline.net
11 Hiking Zion Narrows © Geir-Olav Lyngfjel/iStock; Seasonal Falls Sinewava © Nancy Zizza/iStock; Upper Narrows © Eldon Griffin/iStock
12 Boaters on the Middle Fork Salmon River © Scott Smith/Corbis
13 Hiking Mauna Loa, Big Island © Photo Resource HI/Danita Delimont Agency/drr.net; Mauna Loa eruption © Photolibrary; Sign, Mauna Loa © Anne Walker; Mauna Loa © Anne Walker
14 Sunset at Boundary Waters © Gary Bistram/drr.net; Remote campsite in the Boundary Waters © George Peters/iStock
15 Skiing hut to hut © Paragon Guides
16 The Pacific Crest Trail © Mike Tittel/Photolibrary; Evening Primrose © George H H Huey/Corbis; Crater Lake hikers © Ashok Rodrigues/iStock
17 Beloit glacier © Paul Whitfield/Rough Guides; Sea kayaking © Max FX Photography/iStock; Ice © Sandra vom Stein/iStock; Eagle in flight © Dave Walsh/iStock
18 Canoeing the Bonaventure River © Dylan Page/Cime Adventure
19 Rock climbing in Joshua Tree © Paul Whitfield/Rough Guides
20 Hiking the Appalachian Trail © Jerry and Marcy Monkman/Danita Delimont Agency/drr.net
21 Clavey Falls © Galen Rowell/Corbis; Rafting Cherry Creek © Sierra Mac River Trips
22 Teton Reflection © Aimin Tang/iStock;Grand Teton Summit © Geir-Olav Lyngfjell/iStock
23 Sunrise, Isle Royale National Park © Michael Thompson/iStock; Seaplane taking off © M. Timothy O'Keefe/Alamy; Oyster Mushroom © Michael Westhoff/iStock; Fox © Michael Westhoff/iStock
24 Windsurfing the Columbia River © David R. Frazier/Danita Delimont Agency/drr.net; Windsurfing the Columbia River © Norman Eder/iStock; Windsurfer © Kativ/iStock
25 Hiking the John Muir Trail © Paige Falk/iStock; Hiking the John Muir Trail © Paul Whitfield/Rough Guides; Bear in Yosemite © Ian Leonard/Alamy
26 Dogsledding in the Yukon © imagebroker/Alamy; Trapper tent © iStock/Roman Krochuk; Dogsledding in the Yukon © WorldFoto/Alamy
27 Hikers on the trail © Natasha Japp/iStock; Snow covered mountains © Ken Canning/iStock; Hiking in the Rocky Mountains © scottcramerphotography.com
28 Orca © Discovery Sea Kayaks; Sea lions © Richard Fitzer/iStock; Orca breaching © Tammy Wolfe/iStock; Kayak, San Juan Islands © Jim Mercure/iStock
29 Coastline from helicopter © Michelle Malven/iStock; Kalalau Valley © iStock; Island tropicali © Brian Acord/iStock
30 Climbing Mount Rainier © Matt Farner; Wildflowers © Nathan Fabro/iStock; Climber on rocks © Danny Warren/iStock
31 Kayak exploring the swamp © drr.net; Kayaking © John Williams; Alligator © Chad Purser/iStock; Cypress tree © iStock
32 Exploring Escalante Canyons © Excursions of Escalante; Sunset Arch © Ron Adcock/istock
33 Dory on Colorado River © Chad Ehlers/Alamy; Rafting the Colorado River © David Smith/Alamy; Lava Falls Rapid © Greg Ward/Rough Guides
34 Half Dome from Glacier Point © Paul Whitfield/Rough Guides; Climbing Half Dome © Scott Cramer/iStock; Cables © Tim Pleasant/iStock
35 Devils Tower National Monument © Mike Norton/iStock
37 Polar Bear Safari © floridastock/iStock
39 Paria River/Buckskin Gulch © Lange Photography/iStock
43 Mountain Biking the Kokopelli Trail © media colors/Alamy
46 West Coast Trail, BC © Marisol O'Brien/iStock
48 Hiking Hoh Rainforest, Olympic National Park, WA © Natalia Bratslavsky/iStock
49 Sea Kayaking in the Sea of Cortez © David Schrader/iStock; Seals © Tammy Perluso/iStock; Pelicans © Marvin Sperlin/iStock
50 Cuernos del Paine © Marco Simoni/Photolibrary; Cuernos del Paine © David Mathies/iStock
51 Diver jumping in © Juan-Carlos Cuellar/drr.net; Blue Hole © Greg Johnston/Danita Delimont Agency/drr.net; Nurse sharks in Belize © Craig Chiasson/iStock
52 Cataraft © Photolibrary; Rafting the Futaleufú River © James Rodger
53 Aerial view, Amazon © Johnny Lee/iStock; Huaorani Indians © Pete Oxford/Danita Delimont/drr.net; Giant tree frogs © iStock
54 Walking the Inca Trail © Oscar Schnell/ iStock; Machu Picchu at sunrise © Gregory Witt; Trekking the Inca Trail © Suzanne Porter/Rough Guides
55 Jamican Boa © Katie Rothert/iStock; Jamaican Tody © Rolf Nussbaumer/Naturepl.com; Dromily Cave © Alex Schroeder; Exploring Jamaica's Cockpit Country © Robert McCarthy
56 Kiteboarding, Brazil © Franck Camhi/iStock; Kiteboarding Brazil © Karen Beber
57 Hiking Copper Canyon © Phil Schermeister/Corbis; Copper Canyon © Macduff Everton/Corbis; Woman making pine-needle baskets © Alan Tobey/iStock
58 Blue Morpho © Greg Roden/Rough Guides; Arenal Volcano © Daniel DeSlover/iStock; Tree frog © Mark Kostich/iStock; Leatherback turtle © Andrea Gingerich/iStock; Toucan © iStock
59 Trekking in the Cordillera Huayhuash © Tom Dempsey /photoseek.com
60 Rafting the Pacuare River © Greg Roden/Rough Guides
61 Galápagos marine iguana, Ecuador © Sebastien Cote/iStock; Wildlife viewing in the Galápagos © Colin Ochel/iStock; Blue-footed booby © iStock; Galápagos Islands © Alexander Deursen/iStock; Giant turtle © iStock; Land iguana © Rebecca Picard/iStock

62 Climbing in the Cordillera Blanca © Galen Rowell/Alamy; Cliimbing in the Cordillera Blanca © Gregory Witt

63 Windsurfing in Bonaire © Walter Bibikow/Danita Delimont Agency/drr.net; Windsurfing in Bonaire © Nlls Patrick Geisselbrecht

64 Trekking to Angel Falls © Janne Hämäläinen/iStock

71 Whale watching © Warwick Lister-Kaye/iStock

73 Mountain biking, Bolivia © Aurora Creative/Getty

74 Kayaking to the San Rafael Glacier © Photographer's Choice/Getty

75 Trail to Hornlihutte © Marko Heuver/iStock Matterhorn Summit © Gregory Witt

76 Lakeland Valley © Andrew Martin/iStock; Walking coast to coast © Helena Smith/Rough Guides; Hellvellyn, Lake District © Alan Crawford/iStock

77 Via ferrata in the Dolomite © Alessandro Contadini/iStock; Mount Soripis © Hadleigh Thompson/iStock

78 Sea kayaking in Icelandic Fjords © David Leffman/Rough Guides Paddlers on glacier © Martin Kawalski/iStock

79 Trekking Corsica's GR20 © TourAventure; Trekking Corsica's GR20 © David Abram/Rough Guides

80 Fairy Chimneys, Cappadocia © Robert Harding/drr.net; Mountain biking in Cappadocia © Mehmet Nuri Ozden/Argeus Tourism and Travel

81 Hiking Ben Nevis © TNT Magazine/Alamy; Climbing Ben Nevis © Alan Kimber/West Coast Mountain Guides

82 Hiking the Haute Route © PatitucciPhoto/Photolibrary; Argentiere glacier © NeigeLib/Alamy; Glacier de Moiry © Pictorial Press Ltd/Alamy

83 Cross-country Ski Touring © Ewen Martin; Nupsfonn glacier © Tom Hermansson Snickars/iStock

84 Climbers on Mt Blanc © Tomasz Cieply/iStock; Glacier Valle Blanc © Roberto Caucino; Mountaineer 4800m © iStock; Mount Blanc © Nicole Newman

85 Hiking Hadrian's Wall © Robert Holmes/drr.net; Roman granary © John Miller/iStock; Hiking Hadrian's Wall © Martyn Unsworth/iStock

86 Skiing the Kungsleden Trail © Henrick Trygg/Corbis; Lake Laoudojare © Stefan Larsson/iStock

87 Hiking the North Devon Coast © Michelle Bhatia

89 Cross Country Ski Touring in Lapland © Carole Gomez /iStock

95 Hiking in the Carpathians © Falk Kienas/iStock

96 West Highland Way © Helena Smith/Rough Guides

98 Riding in Andalucia © Timo McIntosh/iStock

99 Hiking the Snowdon Horseshoe © Matt Wales/iStock

106 Kayaking the Ardéche Gorge © Tom De Bruyne/iStock

107 Chameleon © Pete Oxford/NPL; Baobab Trees © William Wang/iStock; Ring-tailed Lemurs © Pauline Mills/iStock; River rafting © www.remoterivers.com

108 Camel and guide, Morocco © Jonatha Borzicchi/iStock; Caravan in Morocco © Oleg Seleznev/iStock; Camel safari in Morocco © Suzanne Porter/Rough Guides

109 Hikers on the Drakensberg Mountains © Gorden Laurens/iStock; Rock art © Henk Badenhorst/iStock; Baboon eating grass © Johan Swanepoel/iStock; Amphitheatre foothills © Jacynth Roode/iStock

110 Rwenzor © Cam McLeay/www.adrift.ug; Crossing the Lower Bigo Bog © Ulf Amundsen/iStock

111 Canoeing the Zambezi River © Craig Lovell/drr.Net; Grazing hippo © Zambezi Safari & Travel Company

112 People under an acacia tree © Galen Rowell/Corbis; Baby giraffe © Frank Parker/ iStock; Mara horseback riding © Equitours; Lion © Graeme Purdy/iStock; Jumping Masai © Equitours; Wildebeest grazing in the Masai Mara © Graeme Purdy/iStock; Zebras in the grass © Lucie Caizlova /iStock

113 Moyenne Island, Coral Cove © Sergio Pitamitz/drr.net; Seychelles © Dreamstime /Radovan; Aldabran tortoise © Holger Ehlers/iStock; Whale shark © Alexey Stiop/iStock; Emperor angelfish © Pete Oxford/drr.net

114 Silverback gorilla © Christine Eichin/iStock; Baby gorilla © Andy Diamond/iStock; Dominant male gorilla © Guenter Guni/iStock

115 Rafting the White Nile © Marcus Wilson-Smith/Rex Features; Rafting the White Nile, Uganda © Cam McLeay/www.adrift.ug; Monitor lizard © Cat London/iStock

116 Traveling along Okavango Delta © Torsten Karok/iStock; Okavango Delta safari © Peter Malsbury/iStock

117 Zambian falls © Lance Bellers/iStock; Rafting © Zambezi Safari & Travel Company; Falls at sunset © rotofrank/iStock

118 Climbing Mount Kilimanjaro © Alex Ekins/drr.net; Climbing Mount Kilimanjaro © Torleif Svensson/Photolibrary; Campsite © Ulf Amundsen/iStock

119 Hikers in High Atlas Mountains © David Samuel Robbins/Corbis; Young Berber girl during wedding © Photolibrary; Goats in a tree © Tom Fakler/iStock; Campsite © Andy Scase/Rediscover the World

120 Shark © Sergey Popov/iStock; Coral fish, Red Sea © Joshua Haviv/iStock; Pufferfish on Red Sea Fan © Tammy Peluso/iStock; Wreck © Miguel Angelo Silva/iStock

121 Windsurfer at sunset, Essaouira © Diana Jarvis

123 Camel and tourist © Urmas Ääro/iStock

125 Kelly Slater at Jeffrey's Bay © JOLI/drr.net

126 Namib Desert © Equitours

128 Elephant in Ngorongoro Crater © Paul A. Souders/Photolibrary

130 Trekking in the Semien Mountains © Robert Bremec/iStock

131 The Atlantic coast, Namibia © Alexander Hafemann/iStock

132 Tamchhog Lhakhang © Dave G. Houser/Corbis; Paro Valley © Jon Larson/iStock; Tiger's nest, Bhutan © narvikk/iStock

133 Daylight portal in Clearwater Cave © Robbie Shone/Alamy; Exploring the Mulu Caves © Reinhard Dirscherl/Alamy

134 Crossing a river in Yangshuo © Tibor Bognar/Photolibrary; Fisher on Li River © Christian Frieß/iStock; Peak reflections on Lijiang River © Zubin Li/iStock

135 Dugong © Dejan Sarman/iStock; Diving in the Philippines © Simon Gurney/iStock

136 Annapurna © Worldwide Picture Library/Alamy; Ascending a Himalayan peak, Annapurna © Martin Kawalski/iStock; Thorong-La Pass © Wojciech Zwierzynski/iStock

137 Sunrise on Mount Fuji © Selden Allan/Photolibrary; Lakeside view of Mount Fuji © Craig Hansen/iStock

138 Horseback riding in Darhat Valley © Robert Churchill/iStock; Mongolian ger camp © Chris Ronneseth/iStock; Horseback riding in Darhat Valley © Francesco Fiondella/iStock

139 Sea kayaking Ang Thong Marine National Park © Karen Trist/Rough Guides

140 Orang-utan © Norma Cornes/iStock; Black hornbill bird © Elijah Low/iStock; Elephant, Kinabatangan © Jollence Lee/Alamy; Orang-utan © Omar Ariff/iStock

141 Skiers pull sleds, Baltoro Glacier © Colin Monteath/Photolibrary; Trekking and climbing in the Karakorams © Grazyna Niedzieska/iStock

142 Hikone Castle © JTB/drr.net; Karuizawa © JTB/Photolibrary; Stone lanterns at a Shinto shrine © Don Werthmann/drr.net; Cherry blossoms © JTB/drr.net

143 Tiger tracking in Bandhavgarh NP © Richard Packwood/Photolibrary

145 Jungle safari, Royal Chitwan National Park © Jez Gunnell/iStock

152 Exploring the Mogao Caves, Xinjiang Province © Alan Tobey/iStock

154 Hiking up Mount Kinabalu © Wei Yee Koay/iStock

159 Mountain climbing in Eastern Tajikistan © Rob Broek/iStock

160 Pandas, Wolong Nature Reserve © Frank van den Bergh/iStock

161 Sea fan and diver © Tammy Peluso/iStock; The Great Barrier Reef © JTB/drr.net; Spinecheek Anemonefish © Stuart Westmorland/drr.net

162 Hiking the Milford Track © Bill Bachman/Alamy; Mitre Peak near Milford Track © Tom Till/drr.net

163 Rafting the Navua River © Rivers Fiji

164 Mount Cook and Lake Pukaki © David Wall/Danita Delimont Agency/drr.net; Ice hiking, Mount Cook © Julian Apse/drr.net; Lake Matheson with Mount Tasman and Mount Cook © Linda & Colin McKie/iStock

165 Surfers at Bells Beach © David Wall/Alamy

166 Tasmania's Cradle Mountain © Linda & Colin McKie/iStock

169 Rafting at Shotover River © Paul Whitfield/Rough Guides

170 Trekking the Routeburn Track © Paul Whitfield/Rough Guides

173 Antarctica exploration © Bryan and Cherry Alexander

174 Expedition to the North Pole © Nordicphotos/Alamy; Expedition to the North Pole © Polar Explorers

175 Kayaking in Nuuk, Greenland © Robert Landau/drr.net

177 South Georgia Island © Alexander Hafemann